CW00719612

CLASSICAL
MUSIC ON
CD
1995

Julian Haylock &
Alexander Waugh

MITCHELL BEAZLEY

Classical Music on CD 1995
A Mitchell Beazley Pocket Guide

First published in Great Britain in 1994
by Mitchell Beazley,
an imprint of Reed Consumer Books Limited
Michelin House, 81 Fulham Road
London SW3 6RB
and Auckland, Melbourne, Singapore and Toronto

Coordinating Editor Kirsty Seymour-Ure
Editor Christopher Atkinson
Art Editor John Grain
Production Controller Michelle Thomas

Executive Editor Sarah Polden
Art Director Jacqui Small

A CIP catalogue record for this book is available from the British
Library
ISBN 1 85732 446 3

Set in Linotype Caslon 540 and M Gill Sans
Produced by Mandarin Offset
Printed in Malaysia

Contents

4

Introduction

Since the appearance of the highly successful first edition of this pocket guide, the market has continued to expand at an alarming rate. As a result, this fully revised 1995 edition features over 400 new entries in addition to a further 200 recommendations which have been changed due to deletions or changes in price category. Although the past year has witnessed a significant number of fine premiere recordings, it is also encouraging to note that the central repertoire (as witness the new set of Beethoven piano concertos from Pollini, for example) has also enjoyed a large number of distinguished new releases. Companies are now beginning to take the lower price ranges more seriously; even as we go to press we learn of a significant new budget series from Deutsche Grammophon entitled Classikon, and that BMG have just obtained the rights to issue the Russian Melodiya catalogue at mid-price. These will no doubt both be reflected in the 1996 edition of the guide!

In addition to expanding our coverage of the best available versions of the classics on CD, we have taken the opportunity to include two entirely new sections. Firstly, a list of one hundred of the most popular works ever composed, intended as a basic guide for those readers who are making their first tentative forays into the world of classical music. Secondly, a list of fifty essential historical recordings dating from the pre-stereo era and which therefore normally lie outside the the the main body of the guide, but which are of such extraordinary artistic excellence that we felt a special mention was clearly merited.

The compact disc was officially launched in 1983 and its success now, little more than a decade later, is so complete that many shops no longer stock black vinyl records, while the majority of recording companies have stopped making them altogether. The stylus and groove medium that dominated commercial recording since its teething days in the early part of this century has been spectacularly usurped. Cassette sales, too, have fallen during recent years with the introduction of portable CD players and in-car CD.

For those still unconverted to the compact disc medium, i might be as well to rehearse here some of its important advantages. The materials used in its manufacture and the fact that it is a non contact medium (since the music is read by a laser beam instead o by a stylus or cassette head) make for a much more reliable and longer-lasting product than either the record or magnetic tape cassette. No more groove debris or erosion. No more crackle, hiss, wear and tear. The collector can now reap the rewards of state-of-the-art technology unspoilt by warped pressings, end-of-side distortion, misplaced central holes, mistracking and scratches.

In theory the compact disc should provide distortion-free sound enhanced by unrivalled clarity, pitch stability and wide dynamic range. In practice, unfortunately, this is not always the case. Nor i it unusual for a technically distinguished recording to be let down by disappointing musicianship. This guide is designed to point the collector towards CDs that are both technically well recorded and musically satisfying. Operas and Operettas are excluded from this volume, but a companion guide, *Opera on CD*, is available for the benefit of those who want a complete classical music collection.

AW & JH

Key to Abbreviations

AAM	Academy of Ancient Music	alt	alto
ASMF	Academy of St. Martin-in-the-Fields	arr.	arranged
BPO	Berlin Philharmonic Orchestra	bar	baritone
CBSO	City of Birmingham Symphony Orchestra	bs	bass
		bsn	bassoon
COE	Chamber Orchestra of Europe	Ch	choir/chorus
CSO	Chicago Symphony Orchestra	cl	clarinet
DG	Deutsche Grammophon	cont	contralto
DHM	Deutsche Harmonia Mundi	cor ang	cor anglais
EBS	English Baroque Soloists	cvd	clavichord
ECO	English Chamber Orchestra	db	double bass
FNO	French National Orchestra	dir	director
FRNO	French Radio National Orchestra	fl	flute
HM	Harmonia Mundi	fpno	fortepiano
LAPO	Los Angeles Philharmonic Orchestra	gmba	viola da gamba
LCP	London Classical Players	gtr	guitar
LGO	Leipzig Gewandhaus Orchestra	hn	horn
LPO	London Philharmonic Orchestra	hp	harp
LSO	London Symphony Orchestra	hpd	harpsichord
NPO	New Philharmonia Orchestra	kbd	keyboard
NRO	National Radio Orchestra	lte	lute
NYPO	New York Philharmonic Orchestra	mez	mezzo-soprano
ORTF	Orchestre Radiofusion et Télévision Français	min.	minor
		narr	narrator
OSR	Orchestre de la Suisse Romande	ob	oboe
PJWE	Philip Jones Wind Ensemble	orch.	orchestrated
RLPO	Royal Liverpool Philharmonic Orchestra	org	organ
		perc	percussion
ROHO	Royal Opera House Orchestra (Covent Garden)	pno	piano
		rec	recorder
RPO	Royal Philharmonic Orchestra	sax	saxophone
SFSO	San Francisco Symphony Orchestra	sop	soprano
SNO	Scottish National Orchestra	synth	synthesiser
VCM	Vienna Concentus Musicus	tbn	trombone
VPO	Vienna Philharmonic Orchestra	ten	tenor
		tpt	trumpet
CO	chamber orchestra	trb	treble
O	orchestra	vcl	cello
PO	philharmonic orchestra	vib	vibraphone
RSO	radio symphony orchestra	vla	viola
SO	symphony orchestra	vln	violin
YO	youth orchestra		

Key to Symbols

O	Orchestral (including concertos)
C	Chamber
S	Solo instrument
V	Vocal (including choral/orchestral works)
◇	Authentic (recording made on original instruments)
*****	Links corresponding pieces with performers
[A]	Analogue
[D]	Digital
F	Full price (over £10)
M	Mid-price (£6–£10)
B	Budget price (under £6)

How to use this book

This guide is not a catalogue: every CD listed is a recommendation. In order to find out which is the best recording of any given piece of classical music, simply look up the work under its composer, and the CD listed will be the one to buy. Occasionally, more than one outstanding recommendation is given, leaving the collector free to choose according to the suitability of the couplings. If the works/couplings are identical, then the first version listed should be considered the guide's first choice. Look out for the ◇ (authentic) sign: sometimes two recommendations have been given so as to offer a choice to those who prefer authentic performances on period instruments to modern instruments in certain repertoire (see below).

Composers are listed in alphabetical order. On the same line as the composer's name are the composer's dates and country of birth followed (in rare cases) by the composer's adopted country: eg HANDEL, George Frideric (1685–1759) Germany/England.

Under each composer the CDs are divided and listed according to the following categories in the following order: Orchestral (including concertos), Chamber, Solo instrumental, and Vocal (including choral/orchestral works). (See Key to Symbols on page 5.) Where there is more than one type of music on a disc, the disc will be listed under the category that includes the first-named work. Where a particular performer appears on only one particular work on a disc, asterisks (*) have been used to link the performer with the corresponding piece.

Each CD entry is listed as follows:

1. the name of the piece(s) with, where helpful, the type of piece in brackets: eg (tone poem), (cantata), etc.;
2. the names of soloists, chorus, orchestra/conductor. After the soloists' or singers' names their instrument or vocal range is given in brackets;
3. where there are also pieces on the CD by one or more additional composer(s) these are listed in brackets: eg (+ Reich: *Variations for Wind*);
4. the record company, the CD reference number (see below), the number of CDs (if more than one), whether the recording was originally digital or analogue (see below), and the price range.

Period instrument recordings As music written before c.1600 (Medieval and Renaissance) is nowadays almost inevitably recorded using period instruments (certainly the bulk of the recommendations in this guide), we have limited the authentic sign (◇) to music of the Baroque, Classical and mainstream Romantic periods (c.1600–1760, c.1760–1830 and c.1830–1915 respectively). However, with keyboard instruments the whole question of authenticity is so complex and hotly debated that in the case of solo instrumental music the authentic sign has been used only with regard to the Classical and early Romantic fortepiano.

If a required piece cannot be found It should be noted that the contents of each CD are listed with its most prominent, important or popular piece first. Other works thereafter are listed alphabetically. Certain works may be found tucked away under one of his more famous or important compositions. Malcolm Arnold's *Tam O'Shanter* overture, for instance, can be found under his Symphony No. 1. With more than 10,000 pieces recommended in this guide it is worth browsing as the required work is sure to be listed somewhere! If you are unsure as to the composer try the Index of Selected Works on pages 251–5.

[A] & [D] analogue and digital recordings Analogue [A] means that the recording was made on magnetic tape. Digital [D] means that the music was recorded onto some form of computer tape, usually Digital Audio Tape (DAT) or video tape. The advantage of a digital recording is that, in theory, there should be no deterioration in sound quality between the music when it is recorded in the studio and when it is played on a CD at home, whereas analogue recordings are prone to tape noise, pre- and post-echo known as 'print through', harmonic distortion and tape wear.

All CDs have a three-letter digital/analogue symbol on them which is usually found on the back cover. These symbols have led to a great deal of misunderstanding, which is why this guide employs the simple one-letter symbols [A] and [D]. The standard explanation for the three-letter coding is as follows:

DDD: digital tape recorder used during session recording, mixing and/or editing, and mastering (transcription);

ADD: analogue tape recorder used during session recording, digital tape recorder used during subsequent mixing and/or editing and during mastering (transcription);

AAD: Analogue tape recorder used during session recording and subsequent mixing and/or editing; digital tape recorder used during mastering (transcription).

Since the CD is itself a digital format, the final letter must always be a D and can therefore be ignored. Similarly, the second letter (the editing) is not necessary since, if the original recording was analogue, a digital edit does not improve its analogue shortcomings any more than the final digital transfer onto CD. The only letter of interest is therefore the first one, which denotes whether the original studio recording was made onto digital or analogue tape.

CD reference numbers These are invaluable when buying or ordering a CD. Many shops order and replace their stock using computerized systems which are entirely reliant on the numbers supplied by the record companies and can find a disc more quickly and easily using a number than a disc title. During the age of the LP disc numbers could vary markedly from one country to another, but the arrival of the CD has led to greater standardization. U.S. numbers sometimes, though infrequently, differ from those printed in this guide. For EMI/Angel in the U.S. drop the 7 prefix and 2 affix so that, for example, the European CDM7 54321-2 simply becomes CDM 54321. All U.S. Vanguard, Sony/CBS and Deutsche Harmonia Mundi/BMG disc numbers can be double-checked using the latest Schwann catalogue, available through most record stores.

About the recommendations The recommendations in this guide have been chosen for technical and artistic merit, for faithfulness to the composer's score and, of course, for truth and clarity in sound engineering. Because the CD is a state-of-the-art digital sound medium, this guide recommends, where possible, only recordings that have used stereo recording technology. For this reason, mono recordings (despite often spellbinding artistic interpretations) have been largely excluded except where an excellent stereo alternative could not be found. By buying only those CDs recommended in this guide, the classical music enthusiast will be able to build a collection which not only avoids any unnecessary and expensive duplication of works, but will provide a lifetime's listening pleasure.

100 Essential Works

With such a bewildering variety of classical music to choose from, it is difficult for the beginner to know quite where to begin; it is hoped that the following highly selective list will help get things off to a flying start. Whilst the works listed below are by no means all amongst the greatest of their kind ever composed, they are certainly amongst the most popular, and once sampled it is hoped they will encourage further listening, leading to a lifetime of rewarding investigation and revelation.

ALBINONI
Adagio in G minor

ALLEGRI
Miserere mei

J.S. BACH
Brandenburg Concerto No. 2
Orchestral Suite No. 3
Toccata and Fugue in D minor, BWV565
Mass in B minor

BARBER
Adagio for Strings

BARTÓK
Concerto for Orchestra

BEETHOVEN
Piano Concerto No. 5 (Emperor)
Violin Concerto
Symphony No. 5
Piano Sonata No. 14 (Moonlight)

BERLIOZ
Symphonie fantastique

BIZET
Carmen: Suites

BORODIN
Prince Igor: Polovtsian Dances

BRAHMS
Piano Concerto No. 1
Violin Concerto
Symphony No. 2

BRITTEN
Young Person's Guide to the Orchestra

BRUCH
Violin Concerto No. 1

BRUCKNER
Symphony No. 4 (Romantic)

SCHUBERT
Symphony No. 5
Piano Quintet (Trout)
Die schöne Müllerin

SCHUMANN
Piano Concerto
Kinderszenen

SHOSTAKOVICH
Symphony No. 5

SIBELIUS
Violin Concerto
Finlandia

JOHANN STRAUSS II
Blue Danube

RICHARD STRAUSS
Also sprach Zarathustra
Don Juan

STRAVINSKY
Firebird
Petrushka
Rite of Spring

TCHAIKOVSKY
Piano Concerto No. 1
Violin Concerto
Nutcracker
Romeo and Juliet Overture
Sleeping Beauty
Swan Lake
Symphony No. 5

VAUGHAN WILLIAMS
Fantasia on Greensleeves
Fantasia on a Theme of Thomas Tallis

VERDI
Overtures

VIVALDI
The Four Seasons, Op. 8/1-4

WAGNER
Operatic excerpts

WEBER
Overtures

Editors' Choice

THE BEST OF RECENT CLASSICAL MUSIC RELEASES ON CD

BEST OVERALL RECORDING

Schubert: *Die Winterreise, D911*
Peter Schreier (tenor), András Schiff (piano)
Decca 436 122-2 [D] F

This uniquely absorbing account of Schubert's epic song cycle finds Schreier, alongside his distinguished Hungarian colleague, at the very height of his powers, singing with a command and authority to silence criticism. From the almost dignified isolationism of *Gute Nacht*, to the desperate resignation of *Der Leiermann* (The Organ Grinder), we are spared nothing throughout this most poignant of musical journeys. A deeply disturbing experience, just as it should be.

BEST MEDIEVAL RECORDING

Cantus selecti: Gregorian Chant
Choralschola of the Niederaltaicher Scholaren,
Konrad Ruhland
Sony CD 53372 [D] F

Sony's early music Vivarte series continues to maintain the very highest standards, both in terms of performance and recorded sound. Here, Ruhland's choral scholars intone with a phrasal sensitivity, and absolute security of intonation and ensemble that are uniquely compelling. Rarely can these pearls of musical purity have been delivered with such rapt selfless devotion, enhanced by sound of alluring transparency.

BEST RENAISSANCE RECORDING

Ludford: *Missa Christi Virgo Dilectissima; Domina Ihesu Christe*
The Cardinall's Musick, Andrew Carwood
ASV CDGAU 133 [D] F

ASV's pioneering Gaudeamus label picks up its second award following on from last year's trailblazing Carver series. A contemporary of Robert Fayrfax and William Cornysh at the court of Henry VIII, very little is actually known about Nicholas Ludford beyond his very considerable significance as a composer, as is triumphantly borne out by these deeply moving performances from Andrew Carwood's Cardinall's Musick. Excellent recording.

BEST BAROQUE RECORDING

J.S. Bach: *Cantatas Nos. 39, 93 & 107*
Agnès Mellon (soprano), Charles Brett (alto), Howard Crook (tenor), Peter Kooy (bass), Collegium Vocale Chorus & Orchestra, Philippe Herreweghe
✧ **Virgin VC7 59320 2 [D] F**

Right from the opening bars of *Brich dem Hungringen dein Bro* (Cantata No. 39), this remarkable recording casts a magic spell over Bach's matchless inspirations to have one listening to these remarkable scores as if for the very first time. All four soloists are inspired to give of their considerable best, and receive tinglingly sensitive support from the Collegium Vocale under an inspired Philippe Herreweghe.

BEST CLASSICAL RECORDING

Beethoven: *Piano Sonatas: No. 21 in C (Waldstein), Op. 53; No. 22 in F, Op. 54; No. 28 in A, Op. 101; Andante in F (Andante favori), WoO57*
Alfred Brendel (piano)
Philips 438 472-2 [D] **F**

The finest release so far in Brendel's latest Beethoven sonata cycle, one that ideally tempers the youthful vigour and intensity familiar from his celebrated old Vox recordings with an accumulated wisdom and understanding in this repertoire matched by few artists of any age. Whether in terms of the music's structural implications, tonal coherence, spiritual intensity or sheer physical exuberance, Brendel is all-embracing. Unimpeachable recording quality.

BEST ROMANTIC RECORDING

Elgar: *Violin Concerto in B minor, Op. 61; Introduction and Allegro for Strings, Op. 47*
Kyoko Takezawa (violin), Bavarian Radio Symphony Orchestra, Colin Davis
RCA 09026 61612-2 [D] **F**

Elgar's great B-minor Violin Concerto has proved surprisingly elusive on records, often inspiring more in the way of admiration than affection. At a stroke, the highly gifted Kyoko Takezawa establishes herself as an Elgarian of the first rank and proves triumphantly that this still underrated work deserves an honoured place alongside the likes of the Brahms, Sibelius and Tchaikovsky concertos. Superb accompaniment from Davis, and a refreshingly uncluttered reading of the great string work which grows in stature with each hearing.

BEST 20TH CENTURY RECORDING

Henze: *Symphony No. 7; Barcorola per grande orchestra*
City of Birmingham Symphony Orchestra, Simon Rattle
EMI CDC7 54762-2 [D] **F**

As a vital supplement to Deutsche Grammophon's excellent survey of Symphonies Nos. 1–6, comes this magnificently played and stunningly recorded performance of the four-movement Seventh (1983–4), coupled to the ear-tingling textural diversity of the *Barcorola*, composed in memory of Paul Dessau. No more triumphant affirmation that the future of the symphony is assured has emerged in recent years. A remarkable success all round.

BEST CONTEMPORARY RECORDING

Feldman: *Piano and String Quartet* (1985)
Aki Takahashi (piano), Kronos Quartet
Elektra-Nonesuch 7559 79320-2 [D] **F**

The Kronos Quartet's unceasing devotion to the contemporary scene has resulted in some of the most challenging and rewarding recordings of recent years. Here, over a continuous period of nearly an hour and twenty minutes, they sustain the greatest possible intensity and frisson throughout a work that is essentially slow moving, harmonically narrowly obsessive and confined to a relatively narrow dynamic range. Hypnotically engrossing nonetheless.

BEST CONCERTO RECORDING

Mendelssohn: *Piano Concertos Nos. 1 & 2; Capriccio brillant*
Howard Shelley (piano/director), London Mozart Players
Chandos CHAN 9215 [D] **F**

At last a modern recording to equal the classic Katin performances of the late fifties. Shelley is as masterly when the note-rate increases alarmingly as he is movingly sensitive throughout two of the most sheerly beautiful slow movements in the concerto repertoire. On this sort of form Shelley really has very few equals, and the London Mozart Players (as well they might) follow him every inch of the way.

BEST SYMPHONY RECORDING

Arnold: *Symphony No. 6; *Fantasy on a Theme of John Field; Sweeney Todd Suite; Tam O'Shanter Overture*
*Lill (piano), RPO, Handley
Conifer CDCF 224 [D] **F**

Arnold's importance as a symphonic composer has never been more comprehensively demonstrated than via this definitive performance of the Sixth (like Sibelius's, inexplicably neglected, but considered by many to be his finest). The *John Field Fantasy* also finds the most persuasive advocacy via the work's dedicatee, John Lill, and in the remaining works the RPO continue in a similarly virtuoso vein, captured in a demonstration recording.

BEST ORCHESTRAL RECORDING

Delibes: *Coppélia* (complete)
Lyon Opera Orchestra, Kent Nagano
Erato 4509 91730-2, 2 CDs [D] **F**

Kent Nagano's virtually uninterrupted string of recorded successes continues here with a compelling new performance of Delibes's outrageously tuneful ballet score *Coppélia*, fully worthy to stand beside the classic Dorati recording of the sixties. Those listeners already familiar with the three great Tchaikovsky ballets should waste no time in adding this masterly recording to their collection, captured in sound that ideally combines depth of perspective and internal clarity.

BEST CHAMBER RECORDING

Janáček: *String Quartets Nos. 1 & 2*: Dvořák: *String Quartet No. 10 in E♭*
Vanburgh Quartet
Collins 13812 [D] **F**

There have been several fine recordings coupling the two Janáček quartets over the years, none finer than the Vanburgh's here, which uncovers a whole new spiritual dimension, whilst lacking nothing in forward momentum and physical presence. Given the excellence of both playing and recording, and a generous and highly attractive 'makeweight', this remarkable new issue now leads the field.

BEST PIANO RECORDING

J.S. Bach: *Goldberg Variations*
Andrei Gavrilov (piano)
DG 435 436-2 [D] **F**

As if further proof were needed, Andrei Gavrilov confirms with this stunning new recording his status as one of the world's greatest pianists. Complimented by Deutsche Grammophon's extraordinarily lucid '4D' sonics, Gavrilov is our spellbinding guide throughout one of the most sublime sets of variations ever penned. A stunning achievement.

BEST ORGAN RECORDING

Dupré: *Symphonie-Passion, Op. 23; Evocation, Op. 37*
Yves Castagnet (organ)
Sony CD 57485 [D] F

Brilliantly recorded, the Grand Orgue de l'Abbatiale Saint-Ouen de Rouen emerges, in Yves Castagnet's highly capable hands, as a truly formidable instrument. From the opening ear-catching timbres of the *Symphonie's* Allegro agitato, to the monumental, rolling textures of the *Evocation's* Allegro deciso, one can hardly help but be overwhelmed by the sheer audacity and breadth of Dupré's imagination.

BEST CHORAL RECORDING

Bruckner: *Mass No. 1 in D min.; Te Deum*
Joan Rodgers (soprano), Catherine Wyn-Rogers (contralto),
Keith Lewis (tenor), Alistair Miles (bass), James O'Donnell
(organ), Corydon Singers & Orchestra, Best
Hyperion CDA 66650 [D] F

Not since Jochum's celebrated Deutsche Grammophon recordings has Bruckner's First Mass and *Te Deum* blazed forth with such incandescence and spiritual intensity. Matthew Best inspires his soloists and combined choral and orchestral forces to give of their very best, achieving a sense of rolling forward momentum which captures the very essence of these underrated scores with unfailing accuracy. Highly atmospheric recording to match.

BEST STEREO REISSUE

The Bernard Haitink Symphony Edition: Beethoven, Brahms,
Bruckner, Mahler, Schumann, Tchaikovsky
Royal Concertgebouw Orchestra, Bernard Haitink
Philips 442 355-2, 35 CDs [D/A] M

There are very few living conductors who could sustain this degree of consistency throughout some of the most challenging and searching works in the symphonic repertoire. Whatever one's occasional reservations (in perhaps the Beethoven and Schumann cycles), the scale of the overall achievement here, blessed throughout with orchestral playing and engineering of unusual sophistication, is simply astonishing.

BEST MONO REISSUE

The Jascha Heifetz Complete Edition
Jascha Heifetz (violin), Various orchestras, conductors and
accompanists
RCA 09026 61778-2, 65 CDs [A] Mono/Stereo M

As a stunning successor to their integral Rachmaninov cycle which received this award last year, RCA have gone one better by collecting together every single commercial recording, whatever the original source, made by arguably the greatest violinist this century, Jascha Heifetz. This is playing at an altogether exalted level to leave one lost in admiration. Even bearing in mind the other distinguished mammoth collected editions to have appeared in recent years, this one is quite literally indispensable.

Stop Press

The following CDs were issued too late for inclusion in the main text.

BACH, Johann Sebastian (1685–1750) GERMANY

Organ Works: Vol. 5
Bowyer (org)
Nimbus NI 5400 [D] **F**

BEETHOVEN, Ludwig van (1770–1827) GERMANY

Diabelli Variations, Op. 120; Piano Sonata No. 28 in A, Op. 101
Donohoe (pno)
EMI CDC7 54792-2 [D] **F**

BLOMDAHL, Karl-Birger (1916–1968) SWEDEN

Symphonies Nos. 1–3
Swedish RSO, Segerstam
BIS CD 611 [D] **F**

DUKAS, Paul (1865–1935) FRANCE

Symphony in C; Polyeucte Overture
BBC PO, Tortelier
Chandos CHAN 9225 [D] **F**

DUSSEK, Johann (1760–1812) BOHEMIA

Piano Sonatas, Op. 35/1–3; Op. 31/2 in D
Staier (fpno)
◇ DHM 05472 77286-2 [D] **F**

HAYDN, Franz Joseph (1732–1809) AUSTRIA

Symphonies Nos. 50, 64 & 65
Tafelmusik, Weil
◇ Sony CD 53985 [D] **F**

POULENC, Francis (1899–1963) FRANCE

Mass in G; Quatre Motets I & II; Litanies; Quatre Petites Prières; Exultate Deo; Salve Regina
Westminster Cathedral Ch, O'Donnell
Hyperion CDA 66664 [D] **F**

SCHUBERT, Franz (1798–1828) AUSTRIA

Piano Sonatas: No. 5 in A♭, D557; No. 9 in B, D575; No. 18 in G, D894
Schiff (pno)
Decca 440 307-2 [D] **F**

SCHUMAN, William (1910–1992) USA

String Quartets Nos. 2, 3 & 5
Lydian Quartet
HM HMU 907114 [D] **F**

TCHAIKOVSKY, Pyotr (1840–1893) RUSSIA

*String Quartet No. 3 in E♭, Op. 30; *Souvenir de Florence, Op. 70*
Keller Quartet; *Kashkashian (vla), Perenyi (vcl)
Erato 4509-94819-2 [D] **F**

COLLECTIONS

American Orchestral Works Babbitt, Cage, Carter, etc.
Chicago SO, Levine
DG 431 698-2 [D] **F**

Recommended Recordings

ADAM, Adolphe (1803–1856) FRANCE

O   *Le Corsaire* (ballet) ECO, Bonynge
Decca 430 286-2, 2CDs [D] **F**

Giselle (ballet) ROHO, Bonynge
Decca 433 007-2, 2CDs [D] **M**

ADAMS, John (born 1947) USA

O   *The Chairman Dances* (foxtrot); *Christian Zeal and Activity;
Common Tones in Simple Time; 2 Fanfares: Tromba Lontana;
Short Ride in a Fast Machine* SFSO, de Waart
Elektra-Nonesuch 7559-79144-2 [D] **F**

*Fearful Symmetries; *The Wound-dresser* *Sylvan (bar), St.
Luke's O, Adams
Elektra-Nonesuch 7559-79218-2 [D] **F**

Shaker Loops SFSO, de Waart
(+ Reich: *Variations*)
Philips 412 214-2 [A] **F**

*Bump; Cerulean; Coast; Disappointment Lake; Hoodoo Zephyr;
Tourist Song; Tundra* Adams (synth)
Elektra-Nonesuch 7559 79311-2 [D] **F**

Harmonium SFSO & Ch, de Waart
ECM 821 465-2 [A] **F**

ADDINSELL, Richard (1904–1977) ENGLAND

Warsaw Concerto Ortiz (pno), RPO, Atzmon
(+ Gershwin: *Rhapsody in Blue;* Gottschalk: *Grande fantaisie;*
Liszt: *Fantasia on Hungarian Themes;* Litolff: *Concerto
symphonique No. 4*)
Decca 430 726-2 [D] **M**

ALAIN, Jehan (1911–1940) FRANCE

Complete Organ works M-C Alain (org)
Volume 1
Erato 2292 45402-2 [D] **F**
Volume 2
Erato 2292 45508-2 [D] **F**

ALBÉNIZ, Isaac (1860–1909) SPAIN

*Cantos de España, Op. 232: Córdoba; Mallorca, Op. 202; Suite
española, Op. 47: Cádiz; Cataluña; Granada; Sevilla* Bream (gtr)
(+ Granados: *Guitar works*)
RCA 09026–61608–2 [D] **F**

*Cantos de España, Op. 232; Azulejos; Malagueña; Mallorca; La
Vega; Zambra granadina; Zaragoza* de Larrocha (pno)
EMI CDM7 64523-2 [A] **M**

Iberia (complete); *Navarra; Suite española, Op. 47*
de Larrocha (pno)
Decca 417 887-2, 2CDs [D] **F**

ALBINONI, Tomaso (1671–1751) ITALY

Adagio in G min. (arr. Giazotto) Orpheus CO
DG 429 390-2 [D] **F** (see collections – *Popular Baroque*)

O *12 Concerti a cinque, Op. 5* Carmirelli (vln), I Musici
Philips 422 251-2 [D] **M**

*12 Concerti a cinque, Op. 7; Sinfonie e concerti a cinque, Op. 2: Nos.
5 & 6* Holliger (ob), Bourgue (ob), I Musici
Philips 432 115-2, 2CDs [D] **F**

12 Concerti a cinque, Op. 7: Nos. 2, 3, 5, 6, 8, 9, 11 & 12 Holliger
(ob/dir), Elhorst (ob), Berne Camerata
DG Archiv 427 111-2 [A] **M**

12 Concerti a cinque, Op. 9: Nos. 1, 4, 6, 7, 10 & 12 Ayo (vln),
Holliger (ob), Bourgue (ob), Garatti (hpd), I Musici
Philips 426 080-2 [A] **M**

12 Concerti a cinque, Op. 9: Nos. 2, 3, 5, 8, 9 & 11 Holliger (ob),
Bourgue (ob), Garatti (hpd), I Musici
Philips 434 157-2 [A] **M**

Trumpet Concerto in C Wilbraham (tpt), ASMF, Marriner
(+ Haydn: *Trumpet Concerto;* Hummel: *Trumpet Concerto;* L.
Mozart: *Trumpet Concerto;* Telemann: *2 Oboe and Trumpet
Concerto No. 1*)
Decca 417 761-2 [A] **M**

C *Sonate de camera, Op. 4; Trattenimenti Armonici per camera, Op. 6*
Wallfisch (vln), Locatelli Trio
✧ Hyperion CDA 66831/2, 2 CDs [D] **F**

ALFVÉN, Hugo (1872–1960) SWEDEN

O *Symphony No. 1 in F min., Op. 7; Drapa, Op. 27; Revelation
Cantata, Op. 31: Andante Religioso; Swedish Rhapsody No. 2
(Upsala-rapsodi), Op. 24* Stockholm PO, Järvi
BIS BIS-CD 395 [D] **F**

*Symphony No. 2 in D, Op. 11; Swedish Rhapsody No. 1
(Midsummer Vigil), Op. 19* Stockholm PO, Järvi
BIS BIS-CD 385 [D] **F**

*Symphony No. 3 in E, Op. 23; Swedish Rhapsody No. 3
(Dalarapsodi), Op. 47; The Prodigal Son (ballet): Suite*
Stockholm PO, Järvi
BIS BIS-CD 455 [D] **F**

*Symphony No. 4 in C min., Op. 39; En Skärgårdssägen, Op. 20
*Högman (sop), *Ahnsjö (ten), Stockholm PO, Järvi
BIS BIS-CD 505 [D] **F**

Symphony No. 5; Bergakungen: Suite; Gustav II Adolf: Elegy
Royal Stockholm PO, Järvi
BIS CD-585 [D] **F**

ALKAN, Valentin (1813–1888) FRANCE

S *12 Études, Op. 35: Allegro barbaro; 12 Études dans les tons
mineurs, Op. 39: Comme le vent; En rhythme molossique; Scherzo
diabolico; Le festin d'Esope; Grande sonate: Les quatre âges, Op. 33;
25 Preludes, Op. 31: La chanson de la folle au bord de la mer*
Smith (pno)
EMI CDM7 64280-2 [A] **M**

*12 Études dans les tons mineurs, Op. 39: Scherzo diabolico; Gigue e
air de ballet dans le style ancien, Op. 24; 3 Marches, Op. 37/1; 2
Nocturnes, Op. 57/1; Quatrième recueil de chants, Op. 67:
Barcarolle; Saltarelle, Op. 23; Sonatine, Op. 61; Zorcico (danse
ibérienne)* Ringeissen (pno)
HM HMA 190 927 [A] **M**

S *25 Préludes dans les tons majeurs et mineurs, Op. 31*
Mustonen (pno)
(+ Shostakovich: *24 Preludes*)
Decca 433 055-2 [D] **F**

13 Prières, Op. 64; Petits préludes; Impromptu, Op. 69
Bowyer (org)
Nimbus NI 5089 [D] **F**

ALLEGRI, Gregorio (1582–1652) ITALY

V *Miserere mei* Stamp (sop), Tallis Scholars, Phillips
(+ Mundy: *Vox patris caelestis;* Palestrina: *Missa Papae Marcelli*)
Gimell CDGIM 339 [A] **F**

ALWYN, William (1905–1985) ENGLAND

O *Autumn Legend; Lyra Angelica; Pastoral Fantasia; Tragic Interlude*
Masters (hp), Daniel (cor ang), Tees (vla), City of London
Sinfonia, Hickox
Chandos CHAN 9065 [D] **F**

Concerti Grossi Nos. 1–3; Oboe & Harp Concerto Daniel (ob),
City of London Sinfonia, Hickox
Chandos CHAN 8866 [D] **F**

*Film Music: The Fallen Idol: Suite; The History of Mr. Polly; Odd
Man Out: Suite; The Rake's Progress: Calypso* LSO, Hickox
Chandos CHAN 9243 [D] **F**

*Symphony No. 1; *Piano Concerto* *Shelley (pno), LSO, Hickox
Chandos CHAN 9155 [D] **F**

*Symphony No. 2; Derby Day; Fanfare for a Joyful Occasion; The
Magic Island; Overture to a Masque* LSO, Hickox
Chandos CHAN 9093 [D] **F**

*Symphony No. 3; *Violin Concerto* *Mordkovitch (vln),
LSO, Hickox
Chandos CHAN 9187 [D] **F**

Symphony No. 4; Elizabethan Dances; Festival March
LSO, Hickox
Chandos CHAN 8902 [D] **F**

*Symphony No. 5; *Piano Concerto No. 2; Sinfonietta* *Shelley (pno),
LSO, Hickox
Chandos CHAN 9196 [D] **F**

C *String Quartets Nos. 1 & 2* Quartet of London
Chandos CHAN 9219 [D] **F**

*String Quartet No. 3; String Trio; *Rhapsody for Piano Quartet*
*Willison (pno), Quartet of London
Chandos CHAN 8440 [D] **F**

S *12 Preludes; Fantasy-Waltzes* Ogdon (pno)
Chandos CHAN 8399 [D] **F**

V *Song Cycles: Invocations; *A Leave-Taking* Gomez (sop),
Constable (pno); *Rolfe Johnson (ten), Johnson (pno)
Chandos CHAN 9220 [D] **F**

ALYABYEV, Alexander (1787–1851) RUSSIA

O *Introduction and Theme with Variations in D min.; 2 Russian Pieces
with Variations, Op. 6; Piano Trio in A min.; 12 Romances*
Various artists
Olympia OCD 181 [A] **F**

C   *Violin Sonata in E min.* Ambarpumyan (vln), Voskresensky (pno)
     (+ Glinka: *Divertissement brillant; String Quartet; Valse-fantaisie*)
     Olympia OCD 184 [A] **F**

ANDERSON, Leroy (1908–1975) USA

O   *23 Orchestral Miniatures* Eastman-Rochester Pops O, Fennell
     Philips Mercury 432 013-2 [A] **M**

APOSTEL, Hans (1901–1972) AUSTRIA

C   *String Quartet No. 1, Op. 7* LaSalle Quartet
     (+ Zemlinsky: *String Quartets Nos. 1–4*)
     DG 427 421-2, 2CDs [A] **M**

ARENSKY, Anton (1861–1906) RUSSIA

O   *Piano Concerto in F min., Op. 2; Fantasia on Russian Folksongs,
     Op. 48* Coombs (pno), BBC Scottish SO, Maksymiuk
     (+ Bortkiewicz: *Piano Concerto No. 1*)
     Hyperion CDA 66624 [D] **F**

     Violin Concerto in A min., Op. 54 Stadler (vln), Leningrad PO,
     Chernushenko
     (+ Tchaikovsky: *Suite No. 3 in G*)
     Olympia OCD 106 [A] **F**

     5 Silhouettes, Op. 23 Danish National RSO, Järvi
     (+ Scriabin: *Symphony No. 3*)
     Chandos CHAN 8898 [D] **F**

     *Symphonies: No. 1 in B min., Op. 4; No. 2 in A, Op. 22; A Dream
     on the Volga* (opera), *Op. 16: Overture* USSR State Academy
     SO, Svetlanov
     Olympia OCD 167 [A] **F**

C   *Quartet in A min. for violin, viola & 2 cellos, Op. 35*
     Raphael Ensemble
     (+ Tchaikovsky: *Souvenir de Florence*)
     Hyperion CDA 66648 [D] **F**

     Piano Trio No. 1 in D min., Op. 32 Borodin Trio
     (+ Glinka: *Trio pathétique*)
     Chandos CHAN 8477 [D] **F**

     Piano Trio No. 2 in F min., Op. 73 Borodin Trio
     (+ Prokofiev: *Overture on Hebrew Themes, Op. 34;* Shostakovich:
     7 Romances on Verses by Alexander Blok)
     Chandos CHAN 8924 [D] **F**

ARNE, Thomas (1710–1778) ENGLAND

O   *6 Favourite Concertos* Nicholson (kbds), Parley of Instruments,
     Holman
     ◇ Hyperion CDA 66509 [D] **F**

     8 Overtures AAM, Hogwood
     ◇ L'Oiseau-Lyre 436 859-2 [A] **F**

     Symphonies Nos. 1–4 Cantilena, Shepherd
     Chandos CHAN 8403 [D] **F**

V   *Cymon and Iphegenia* (cantata); *The Desert Island* (stage play):
     What tho' his guilt; Frolick and free (cantata); *The Morning*
     (cantata); *Jenny; Much Ado about Nothing* (stage play): *Sigh no
     more, ladies; Thou soft flowing Avon* (ode); *The winter's amusement;
     The lover's recantation* Kirkby (sop), Morton (ten), Parley of
     Instruments, Goodman
     ◇ Hyperion CDA 66237 [D] **F**

ARNOLD, Malcolm (born 1921) ENGLAND

○ *Clarinet Concerto No. 1, Op. 20; Flute Concerto No. 1, Op. 45; Horn Concerto No. 2, Op. 58; Double Violin Concerto, Op. 77* Collins (cl), Jones (fl), Watkins (hn), Sillito (vln), Fletcher (vln), London Musici, Stephenson
Conifer CDCF 172 [D] **F**

Clarinet Concerto No. 2; Flute Concerto No. 2; Horn Concerto No. 1; Piano Duo Concerto Collins (cl), Jones (fl), Watkins (hn), Nettle & Markham (pno duo) London Musici, Stephenson
Conifer CDCF 228 [D] **F**

Viola Concerto, Op. 108; Concerto for 28 Players; Larch Trees; Serenade for Small Orchestra, Op. 26 Golani (vla), London Musici, Stephenson
Conifer CDCF 211 [D] **F**

4 Cornish Dances, Op. 91; 8 English Dances Opp. 27 & 33; 4 Irish Dances, Op. 126; 4 Scottish Dances, Op. 59; Solitaire (ballet): Sarabande and Polka LPO, Arnold
Lyrita SRCD 201 [A] **F**

Overtures: *Beckus the Dandipratt, Op. 5; Commonwealth Christmas, Op. 64; The Fair Field, Op. 110; The Smoke, Op. 21; A Sussex Overture, Op. 31* LPO, Arnold
Reference RRCD-48 [D] **F**

Sinfoniettas Nos. 1–3; Flute Concerto No. 1; Oboe Concerto Beckett (fl), Messiter (ob), London Festival O, Pople
Hyperion CDA 66332 [D] **F**

The Sound Barrier, Op. 38 RPO, Alwyn
(+ Bax: *Malta G.C.; Oliver Twist: Suite*)
ASV CDWHL 2058 [D] **M**

Symphony No. 1, Op. 22; Double Piano Concerto, Op. 104; English Dances Nos. 3 & 5; Solitaire (ballet): Sarabande and Polka; Tam O'Shanter (overture), Op. 51 Sellick (pno), Smith (pno), CBSO; Bournemouth SO; Philharmonia O, Arnold
EMI CDM7 64044-2 [A] **M**

*Symphonies: No. *2, Op. 40; No. 5, Op. 74; Peterloo Overture, Op. 97* CBSO, Arnold; *Bournemouth SO, Groves
EMI CDM7 63368-2 [A] **M**

Symphony No. 4, Op. 71 LPO, Arnold
Lyrita SRCD 200 [D] **F**

EDITORS' CHOICE (see page 14): *Symphony No. 6; *Fantasy on a Theme of John Field; Sweeney Todd Suite; Tam O'Shanter Overture* *Lill (pno), RPO, Handley
Conifer CDCF 224 [D] **F**

Symphonies: Nos. 7, Op. 113; No. 8, Op. 124 RPO, Handley
Conifer CDCF 177 [D] **F**

○ *Divertimento, Op. 37; Duo, Op. 10; Flute Sonata, Op. 121; Oboe Quartet, Op. 61; Quintet, Op. 7; 3 Shanties, Op. 4* Nash Ensemble
Hyperion CDA 66173 [D] **F**

Duo for 2 Cellos, Op. 85; Piano Trio, Op. 54; Viola Sonata No. 1, Op. 17; 5 Violin Pieces, Op. 84; Violin Sonatas: No. 1, Op. 15; No. 2, Op. 43 Nash Ensemble
Hyperion CDA66171 [D] **F**

Clarinet Sonatina; Bassoon Fantasia, Op. 86; Clarinet Fantasia, Op. 87; Flute Fantasia, Op. 89; Horn Fantasia, Op. 88; Oboe

Fantasia, Op. 90; Flute Sonatina, Op. 19; Oboe Sonatina, Op. 28; Recorder Sonatina, Op. 41; Trio, Op. 6 Nash Ensemble
Hyperion CDA66172 [D] **F**

C *String Quartets: No. 1, Op. 23; No. 2, Op. 118* McCapra Quartet
Chandos CHAN 9112 [D] **F**

ARRIAGA, Juan (1806–1826) SPAIN

C *String Quartets: No. 1 in D min.; No. 2 in A; No. 3 in E♭*
Chilingirian Quartet
(+ Wikmanson: *Quartet No. 2*)
CRD 3312/3, 2CDs [A] **F**

AUBER, Daniel (1782–1871) FRANCE

O Opera Overtures: *The Bronze Horse; Fra Diavolo; La Muette de Portici* Detroit SO, Paray
(+ Suppé: *Overtures*)
Philips Mercury 434 309-2 [A] **M**

AVISON, Charles (1709–1770) ENGLAND

O *12 Concerti after Domenico Scarlatti* ASMF, Marriner
Philips 438 806-2, 2 CDs [A] **B**

BACH, Carl Philipp Emanuel (1714–1788) GERMANY

O *Cello Concertos: in A min., H432; in B♭, H436; in A, H439*
Bylsma (vcl), Age of Enlightenment O, Leonhardt
◇ Virgin VC7 59541-2 [D] **F**

Flute Concertos: in D min., H426; in G, H445; in A, H438
Stinton (fl), St. John's O, Lubbock
Collins 13732 [D] **F**

Double Harpsichord Concerto, H410; Harpsichord and Fortepiano Concerto in E♭, H479 Koopman (hpd/dir), Mathot (hpd/fpno), Amsterdam Baroque O
◇ Erato 2292-45306-2 [D] **F**

Sinfonias: in C, H649; in E min., H653; in F, H650; in E♭, H654; in F, H656 C.P.E. Bach CO, Haenchen
Capriccio 10 103 [D] **F**

6 Sinfonias, H657–62: in G; in B♭; in C; in A; in B min.; in E English Concert, Pinnock
◇ DG Archiv 415 300-2 [D] **F**

4 Sinfonias, H663–6: in D; in E♭; in F; in G Amsterdam Baroque O, Koopman
◇ Erato 2292-45361-2 [D] **F**

C *3 Flute Quartets (Trio Sonatas), H537–9: in A min.; in D; in G; Flute Sonata in G, H564* Les Adieux
◇ DHM GD 77052 [A] **M**

The Complete Flute Sonatas B. Kuijken (fl), van Asperen (hpd)
◇ Sony CD 53964, 2 CDs [D] **F**

Sinfonia a tre voci in D, H585; Trio Sonatas: in B♭, H584; in C min., H579; Viola da Gamba Sonata in D, H559; 12 Variations in D min. on La Folia, H263 Purcell Quartet
◇ Hyperion CDA 66239 [D] **F**

Violin Sonatas: in B min., H512; in C min., H514; in F♯ min. (Phantasie), H536 Melkus (vln), Dreyfus (hpd)
Denon CO-72434 [D] **F**

S *Fantasias: in C, H291; in F♯ min. (Freye Fantasie), H300; Rondo in C min., H283; Keyboard Sonatas: in A min., H30; in E min., H281; in C, H47; 12 Variations in D min. on La Folia, H263* Staier (hpd)
DHM RD 77025 [A] **F**

6 Keyboard Sonatas (Prussian), H24–2 ; 6 Keyboard Sonatas (Wurttemberg), H30–34 & 36 van Asperen (hpd)
Teldec 9031 77623-2, 2 CDs [A] **M**

Organ Sonatas: H84–87 & 134; Adagio, H352; Fantasia and Fugue in C min., H103 Danby (org)
Virgin VC7 59277-2 [D] **F**

V *Die Auferstehung und Himmelfahrt Jesu (The Resurrection and Ascension of Jesus)* (oratorio), *H177* Martinpelto (sop), Prégardien (ten), Harvey (bass), Collegium Vocale Ch, Age of Enlightenment O, Herreweghe
✧ Virgin VC7 59069-2 [D] **F**

Die lezten Leiden des Erlösers (The Last Sufferings of the Saviour) (Passion cantata), *H776* Schlick (sop), de Reyghere (sop), Patriasz (cont), Prégardien (ten), van Egmond (bass), Ghent Collegium Vocale, La Petite Bande, Kuijken
✧ DHM GD 77042, 2CDs [A] **M**

Magnificat in D, H772 Palmer (sop), Watts (cont), Tear (ten), Roberts (bs), King's College Ch, ASMF, Ledger
(+ J.S. Bach: *Magnificat*)
Decca 421 148-2 [A] **M**

BACH, Johann Christian (1735–1782) GERMANY

O *6 Keyboard Concertos, Op. 1; 6 Keyboard Concertos, Op. 7* Haebler (fpno), Vienna Capella Academica, Melkus
Philips 438 712-2, 2 CDs [A] **M**

Sinfonia Concertantes: in A, T284/4; in E♭, T888/7; in E♭, T290/9; in G, T284/1 London Festival O, Pople
ASV CDDCA 651 [D] **F**

6 Symphonies, Op. 3 ASMF, Marriner
Philips 422 498-2 [A] **M**

Symphonies: in E♭, Op. 18/1, in D, Op. 18/4; in G min., Op. 6/6; Sinfonia Concertante in C, T289/4; Adriano in Siria (opera): *Overture* AAM, Standage
✧ Chandos CHAN 0540 [D] **F**

C *Quintets, T301/1: No. 1 in C; No. 6 in D; T304/6: No. 1 in D; Sextet in C, T302/1* English Concert
✧ DG Archiv 423 385-2 [D] **F**

S *6 Sonatas, Op. 17* Wooley (fpno)
✧ Chandos CHAN 0543 [D] **F**

6 Keyboard Sonatas, T338/1: No. 5 in E; No. 6 in C min.; 6 Keyboard Sonatas, T341/1: No. 2 in C min.; No. 3 in E♭; No. 5 in A Black (hpd)
CRD 3453 [D] **F**

BACH, Johann Christoph Friedrich (1732–1795) GERMANY

C *Cello Sonata in A* Bylsma (vcl), van Asperen (hpd)
(+ J.S. Bach: *Viola da Gamba Sonatas Nos. 1–3*)
✧ Sony CD 45945 [D] **F**

BACH, Johann Sebastien (1685–1750) GERMANY

O *Brandenburg Concertos Nos. 1–6, BWV1046–51* Brandenburg
   Consort, Goodman
   ◇ Hyperion CDA 66711/2, 2CDs [D] **F**

   Brandenburg Concertos Nos. 1–6, BWV1046–51 Orpheus CO
   DG 431 660-2 [D] **F**

   Harpsichord Concerti Nos. 1–8 Koopman (hpd/dir), Amsterdam
   Baroque O
   ◇ Erato 4509 91930-2, 2 CDs [D] **B**

   *Double Harpsichord Concerti Nos. 1–3; Triple Harpsichord
   Concerti Nos. 1 & 2; Triple Concerto for Flute, Violin &
   Harpsichord in A min., BWV1044; Quadruple Harpsichord
   Concerto in A min., BWV1065* Koopman (hpd/dir), Mathot,
   Marisaldi, Mustonen (hpds), Manze (vln), Hazelzet (fl),
   Amsterdam Baroque O
   ◇ Erato 4509 91929-2, 2 CDs [D] **B**

   *Violin Concertos Nos. 1 in A min., BWV1041, & 2 in E, BWV1042;
   *Double Violin Concerto in D min., BWV1043; **Violin and Oboe
   Concerto in D min., BWV1060* Grumiaux (vln), *Krebbers (vln),
   **Holliger (ob), Solistes Romands, Gerecz; **NPO, De Waart
   Philips 420 700-2 [A] **M**

   *Violin Concertos: No. 1 in A min., BWV1041, & 2 in E, BWV1042;
   *Double Violin Concerto in D min., BWV1043; **Triple Violin
   Concerto in D, BWV1064* Wallfisch (vln), *Bury (vln),
   **Beznosiuk (vln), **Mackintosh (vln), Age of
   Enlightenment O
   ◇ Virgin VC7 59319-2 [D] **F**

   Musical Offering, BWV1079 VCM, Harnoncourt
   ◇ Teldec 2292-42748-2 [A] **M**

   Orchestral Suites Nos. 1–4, BWV1066–9 Amsterdam Baroque O,
   Koopman
   ◇ DHM RD 77864, 2CDs [D] **F**

C *Flute Sonatas Nos. 1–6, BWV1030–35; Flute Partita in A min.,
   BWV1013* Stephen Preston (fl), Pinnock (hpd), Savall (gmba)
   ◇ CRD 3314/5, 2CDs [A] **F**

   Trio Sonatas Nos. 1–4, BWV1036–9 London Baroque
   ◇ HM HMC 90 1173 [D] **F**

   Viola da Gamba Sonatas Nos. 1–3, BWV1027–9 Bylsma (vcl),
   van Asperen (hpd)
   (+ J.C.F. Bach: *Cello Sonata in A*)
   ◇ Sony CD 45945 [D] **F**

   Viola da gamba Sonatas Nos. 1–3, BWV1027–9 Maisky (vcl),
   Argerich (pno)
   DG 415 471-2 [D] **F**

   10 Violin Sonatas, BWV1014–1023 Grumiaux (vln), Jaccotet
   (hpd)
   Philips 426 452-2, 2 CDs [A] **M**

S *Cello Suites Nos. 1–6, BWV1007–12*
   Schiff (vcl)
   EMI CDS7 47471-8, 2CDs [D] **F**
   Bylsma (vcl)
   ◇ Sony CD 48047, 2CDs [D] **F**

Lute Suites Nos. 1–4, BWV995–7; 1006a; Fugue, BWV1000; Prelude, Fugue and Allegro, BWV998; Prelude, BWV999
Kirchhof (lte)
◇ Sony CD 45858, 2CDs [D] **F**

Solo Violin Sonatas and Partitas Nos. 1–6, BWV1001–6
Grumiaux (vln)
Philips 438 736-2, 2 CDs [A] **B**

The Art of Fugue, BWV1080 Moroney (hpd)
◇ HM HMC 901169/70, 2CDs [D] **F**

Chromatic Fantasia and Fugue in D min., BWV903; Fantasias: in C min., BWV906; in G min., BWV917; in C min., BWV919; Fantasia and Fugue in A min., BWV904; Preludes: in A min., BWV922; in C min., BWV921; Preludes and Fugues: in A min., BWV894; in F, BWV901; in G, BWV902a Staier (hpd)
DHM RD 77039 [A] **F**

Chromatic Fantasia and Fugue in D min., BWV903; 4 Duets, BWV802–5; Italian Concerto in F, BWV971; Partita in B min., BWV831 Rousset (hpd)
L'Oiseau-Lyre 433 054-2 [D] **F**

English Suites Nos. 1–6, BWV806–11 Gilbert (hpd)
HM HMC 90 1074/5, 2CDs [D] **F**

French Suites Nos. 1–6, BWV812–7; Suite in A min., BWV818a; Suite in Eb, BWV819 Moroney (hpd)
Virgin VCD7 59011-2, 2CDs [D] **F**

Goldberg Variations, BWV988
Leonhardt (hpd)
DHM GD 77149 [A] **M**
EDITORS' CHOICE (see page 14): Gavrilov (pno)
DG 435 436-2 [D] **F**

Goldberg Variations, BWV988; Adagio in G, BWV968; Chromatic Fantasia and Fugue in D min., BWV903; Fantasia in C min., BWV906; Prelude in G, BWV902 Black (hpd)
Collins 70032, 2CDs [D] **F**

15 Inventions in 2 Parts, BWV772–86; 15 Inventions in 3 Parts, BWV787–801; 6 Little Preludes, BWV933–8 Koopman (hpd)
Capriccio 10 210 [D] **F**

15 Inventions in 2 Parts, BWV772–86; 15 Inventions in 3 Parts, BWV787–801 Gould (pno)
Sony CD 52596 [A] **M**

Partitas Nos. 1–6, BWV825–30 Pinnock (hpd)
DG Archiv 415 493-2, 2CDs [D] **F**

Partitas Nos. 1–6, BWV825–30; Preludes & Fugues Gould (pno)
Sony CD 52597, 2 CDs [A] **M**

The Well-tempered Clavier: Books Nos. 1 & 2, BWV846–893
Tilney (cvd)
Hyperion CDA 66351/4, 4CDs [D] **F**

The Well-Tempered Clavier: Books Nos. 1 & 2, BWV846–893
Gould (pno)
Book. 1:
Sony CD 52600, 2 CDs [A] **M**
Book. 2:
Sony CD 52603, 2 CDs [A] **M**

S *Keyboard transcriptions by Busoni, Le Fleming, Hess, Kempff, Liszt, Lord Berners and Rachmaninov* Fergus-Thompson (pno)
ASV CDDCA 759 [D] **F**

Complete Organ Works Vol. 1: 3 Fantasias, BWV562, 570, 572; 3 Fantasias and Fugues, BWV537, 542, 561; 6 Fugues, BWV575–7, 579 (On a Theme of Corelli), 581, 946; Kleines harmonisches Labyrinth; Passacaglia and Fugue in C min.; Pedal-Exercitium; 8 Preludes and Fugues, BWV531–3, 535, 548–551; Toccata, Adagio and Fugue in C; 3 Toccatas and Fugues, BWV538 (Dorian), 540, 565 (in D min.); 2 Trios, BWV583, 585 Hurford (org)
Decca 421 337-2, 3CDs [A] **M**

Complete Organ Works Vol. 2: 20 Chorale Preludes, BWV669–678, 680–689; 24 Kirnberger Chorale Preludes, BWV690–713; Prelude and Fugue in E♭ (St. Anne), BWV552; 6 Trio Sonatas, BWV525–530 Hurford (org)
Decca 421 341-2, 3CDs [A] **M**

Complete Organ Works Vol. 3: Canonic Variations on 'Von Himmel Hoch'; 3 Chorale Partitas, BWV766-8; 21 Chorale Preludes, BWV645-650 (Schubler), 726–740; 2 Chorale Variations, BWV770–1; Organ Concertos Nos. 1–6, BWV592–597 Hurford (org)
Decca 421 617-2, 3CDs [A] **M**

Complete Organ Works Vol. 4: 35 Chorale Preludes, BWV714, 719, 742, 957, 1090–1120 (Arnstadt/Yale Manuscript); 18 Chorale Preludes, BWV651–658 (Leipzig), 663–668, 714–725 Hurford (org)
Decca 421 621-2, 3CDs [D/A] **M**

Complete Organ Works Vol. 5: Allabreve in D, BWV589; Aria in F, BWV587; Canzona in D min., BWV588; 2 Fantasias, BWV563, 571; 3 Fugues, BWV574, 578, 580; Pastorale in F, BWV590; 3 Preludes, BWV567–9); 10 Preludes and Fugues, BWV534, 535a (unfinished), 536, 539, 541, 543–7; 8 Short Preludes and Fugues, BWV553–60; Prelude, Trio and Fugue in B♭; Toccata and Fugue in E; 3 Trios, BWV584, 586, 1027a; Ricercare (Musical Offering) Hurford (org)
Decca 425 631-2, 3CDs [A] **M**

Complete Organ Works Vol. 6: Orgelbüchlein (46 Chorale Preludes) BWV599–644; 22 Chorale Preludes, BWV620a, 741-8, 751-2, 757-763, 765, Anh. 55; Fugue in G min. Hurford (org)
Decca 425 635-2, 2CDs [A] **M**

Aus tiefer Not, BWV1099; Concerto in G, BWV592; Erbarme dich, BWV721; Fantasia and Fugue in G min., BWV542; Pastorale in F, BWV590; Trio Sonata in E♭, BWV525; Toccata and Fugue in B min., BWV565 Bowyer (org)
Nimbus NI 5280 [D] **F**

Organ Concertos Nos. 1–5, BWV592–6 Simon Preston (org)
DG 423 087-2 [D] **F**

Organ Concerto No. 5 in D min., BWV596; Partita on 'Sei gegrüsset', BWV768; Preludes and Fugues: in F min., BWV534; in A min., BWV543; Trio Sonata No. 2 in C min., BWV526 Bowyer (org)
Nimbus NI 5290 [D] **F**

Fantasia in G, BWV572; Fantasia and Fugues in C min., BWV537; in G min., BWV542; in C min., BWV562; Preludes and Fugues in D, BWV 532; in F min., BWV534; in A, BWV536; in G,

BWV541; in A min., BWV543; in B min., BWV544; in C, BWV545; in C min., BWV546; in C, BWV547; in E min. (Wedge), BWV548; in E♭ (St. Anne), BWV552 Herrick (org)
Hyperion CDA 66791/2, 2 CDs [D] **F**

Fantasia and Fugue in G min., BWV542; Passacaglia & Fugue in C min., BWV582; 6 Schubler Chorales, BWV645–50; Toccata, Adagio & Fugue in C, BWV564; Toccata & Fugue in F, BWV540 Simon Preston (org)
DG 435 381-2 [D] **F**

Fantasia con imitatione in B min., BWV563; Fugue in A, BWV950; Fugue in B min., BWV951; Fugue in C min., BWV575; 8 'Short' Preludes and Fugues, BWV553–560; Toccata in G min., BWV915; Toccata in G, BWV916 Bowyer (org)
Nimbus NI 5377 [D] **F**

Orgelbüchlein, BWV599–644 Simon Preston (org)
DG 431 816-2 [D] **F**

Partitas, BWV766–768 & 770 Simon Preston (org)
DG 429 775-2 [D] **F**

Passacaglia and Fugue in C min., BWV582; Toccata, Adagio and Fugue in C, BWV564; Toccatas and Fugues: in D min., BWV565; in F, BWV540; in D min. (Dorian), BWV538 Herrick (org)
Hyperion CDA 66434 [D] **F**

Prelude and Fugue in E min., BWV548; Passacaglia in C min., BWV582; Pastorella, BWV590; Piece d'orgue, BWV572; 3 Choral Preludes, BWV691, 727 & 734 Kee (org)
Chandos CHAN 0510 [D] **F**

Prelude and Fugues: in D, BWV532; in A, BWV536; in G, BWV541; Fugue in G, BWV577; Trio Sonata No. 5 in C, BWV529; Chorale Preludes: Ein feste Burg, BWV720; Gelobet seist du, BWV697 & 722; In dulci jubilo, BWV751 & 729; Von Himmel hoch, BWV738 Bowyer (org)
Nimbus NI 5289 [D] **F**

6 Trio Sonatas, BWV525–530 Simon Preston (org)
DG 437 835-2 [D] **F**

Toccata and Fugue in D min., BWV565; Passacaglia and Fugue in C min., BWV582; Prelude and Fugue in G, BWV541; Fugues: in G (Gigue), BWV577; in B min., BWV579; Pastorale in F, BWV590; 4 Chorale Preludes Hurford (org)
EMI Eminence CD-EMX 2218 [D] **F**

Ascension Oratorio; Cantatas Nos. 43 & 44 Schlick (sop), Patriasz (mez), Prégardien (ten), Kooy (bs), Collegium Vocale, Herreweghe
✧ HM HMC 901479 [D] **F**

Complete Cantatas Various artists accompanied by either VCM, Harnoncourt, or Leonhardt Consort, Leonhardt

Volume 1, BWV1–4
✧ Teldec 2292-42497-2, 2CDs [A] **M**

Volume 2, BWV5–8
✧ Teldec 2292-42498-2, 2CDs [A] **M**

Volume 3, BWV9–11
✧ Teldec 2292-42499-2, 2CDs [A] **M**

Volume 4, BWV12–16
✧ Teldec 2292-42500-2, 2CDs [A] **M**

V *Volume 5, BWV17–20*
◇ Teldec 2292-42501-2, 2CDs [A] **M**

Volume 6, BWV21–23
◇ Teldec 2292-42502-2, 2CDs [A] **M**

Volume 7, BWV24–27
◇ Teldec 2292-42503-2, 2CDs [A] **M**

Volume 8, BWV28–30
◇ Teldec 2292-42504-2, 2CDs [A] **M**

Volume 9, BWV31–34
◇ Teldec 2292-42505-2, 2CDs [A] **M**

Volume 10, BWV35–38
◇ Teldec 2292-42506-2, 2CDs [A] **M**

Volume 11, BWV39–42
◇ Teldec 2292-42556-2, 2CDs [A] **M**

Volume 12, BWV43–46
◇ Teldec 2292-42559-2, 2CDs [A] **M**

Volume 13, BWV47–50
◇ Teldec 2292-42560-2, 2CDs [A] **M**

Volume 14, BWV51–56
◇ 2292-42422-2, 2CDs [A] **M**

Volume 15, BWV57–60
◇ Teldec 2292-42423-2, 2CDs [A] **M**

Volume 16, BWV61–64
◇ Teldec 2292-42565-2, 2CDs [A] **M**

Volume 17, BWV65–68
◇ Teldec 2292-42571-2, 2CDs [A] **M**

Volume 18, BWV69–72
◇ Teldec 2292-42572-2, 2CDs [A] **M**

Volume 19, BWV73–75
◇ Teldec 2292-42573-2, 2CDs [A] **M**

Volume 20, BWV76–79
◇ Teldec 2292-42576-2, 2CDs [A] **M**

Volume 21, BWV80–83
◇ Teldec 2292-42577-2, 2CDs [A] **M**

Volume 22, BWV84–90
◇ Teldec 2292-42578-2, 2CDs [A] **M**

Volume 23, BWV91–94
◇ Teldec 2292-42582-2, 2CDs [A] **M**

Volume 24, BWV95–98
◇ Teldec 2292-42583-2, 2CDs [A] **M**

Volume 25, BWV99–102
◇ Teldec 2292-42584-2, 2CDs [A] **M**

Volume 26, BWV103–106
◇ Teldec 2292-42602-2, 2CDs [A] **M**

Volume 27, BWV107–110
◇ Teldec 2292-42603-2, 2CDs [A] **M**

Volume 28, BWV111–114
◇ Teldec 2292-42606-2, 2CDs [A] **M**

Volume 29, BWV115–119
✧ Teldec 2292-42608-2, 2CDs [A] **M**

Volume 30, BWV120–123
✧ Teldec 2292-42609-2, 2CDs [A] **M**

Volume 31, BWV124–127
✧ Teldec 2292-42615-2, 2CDs [A] **M**

Volume 32, BWV128–131
✧ Teldec 2292-42617-2, 2CDs [A] **M**

Volume 33, BWV132–135
✧ Teldec 2292-42618-2, 2CDs [A] **M**

Volume 34, BWV136–139
✧ Teldec 2292-42619-2, 2CDs [A] **M**

Volume 35, BWV140–146
✧ Teldec 2292-42630-2, 2CDs [D] **M**

Volume 36, BWV147–151
✧ Teldec 2292-42631-2, 2CDs [D] **M**

Volume 37, BWV152–156
✧ Teldec 2292-42632-2, 2CDs [D] **M**

Volume 38, BWV157–163
✧ Teldec 2292-42633-2, 2CDs [D] **M**

Volume 39, BWV164–169
✧ Teldec 2292-42634-2, 2CDs [D] **M**

Volume 40, BWV170–174
✧ Teldec 2292-42635-2, 2CDs [D] **M**

Volume 41, BWV175–179
✧ Teldec 2292-42428-2, 2CDs [D] **M**

Volume 42, BWV180–184
✧ Teldec 2292-42738-2, 2CDs [D] **M**

Volume 43, BWV185–188
✧ Teldec 2292-44179-2, 2CDs [D] **M**

Volume 44, BWV192–195
✧ Teldec 2292-44193-2, 2CDs [D] **M**

Volume 45, BWV196–198
✧ Teldec 2292-44194-2, 2CDs [D] **M**

Cantatas: The Complete Archiv Series Various Artists, Munich Bach O & Ch, Richter
DG Archiv 439 368-2, 26 CDs [A] **M**

Cantatas: BWV4, 56 & 82 Fischer-Dieskau (bar), Munich Bach O & Ch, Richter
DG Archiv 427 128-2 [A] **M**

Cantatas: BWV8, 78 & 99 Bach Ensemble, Rifkin
✧ L'Oiseau-Lyre 421 728-2 [D] **F**

Cantatas: BWV26, 80 & 116 Mathis (sop), Schmidt (sop), Schreier (ten), Fischer-Dieskau (bar), Munich Bach O & Ch, Richter
DG Archiv 427 130-2 [A] **M**

Cantatas: BWV34, 50 & 147 Fisher (sop), James (alt), Partridge (ten), George (bs), Sixteen O & Ch, Christophers
✧ Collins 13172 [D] **F**

V *Cantatas: BWV36, 61 & 62* Argenta (sop), Lang (mez), Rolfe Johnson (ten), Bär (bar), Monteverdi Ch, EBS, Gardiner
✧ DG Archiv 437 327-2 [D] **F**

EDITORS' CHOICE (see page 12): *Cantatas: BWV39, 93 & 107* Mellon (sop), Brett (alto), Crook (ten), Kooy (bs), Collegium Vocale, Herreweghe
✧ Virgin VC7 59320-2 [D] **F**

Cantatas: BWV51 & 140 Bach Ensemble, Rifkin
✧ L'Oiseau-Lyre 417 616-2 [D] **F**

Cantatas: BWV54, 169 & 170 Bowman (alt), King's Consort, King
✧ Hyperion CDA 66326 [D] **F**

Cantatas: BWV73, 105 & 131 Mellon (sop), Lesne (alt), Crook (ten), Kooy (bs), Collegium Vocale, Herreweghe
✧ Virgin VC7 59237-2 [D] **F**

Cantatas: BWV82, 159 & 170 Baker (mez), Tear (ten), Shirley-Quirk (bar), ASMF, Marriner
Decca 430 260-2 [A] **M**

Cantatas: BWV106, 118 & 198 Argenta (sop), Chance (alt), Rolfe Johnson (ten), Varcoe (bar), Monteverdi Ch, EBS, Gardiner
✧ DG Archiv 429 782-2 [D] **F**

Cantatas: BWV140 & 147 Holton (sop), Chance (alt), Rolfe Johnson (ten), Varcoe (bar), Monteverdi Ch, EBS, Gardiner
✧ DG Archiv 431 809-2 [D] **F**

Cantatas: BWV202 (Wedding), 209, 211 (Coffee) & 212 (Peasant) Ameling (sop), English (ten), Nimsgern (bs), Collegium Aureum
✧ DHM GD 77151, 2CDs [A] **M**

Cantata: BWV205: Der Zufriedengestelle Äolus Kenny (sop), Lipovsek (cont), Equiluz (ten), Holl (bs), Arnold Schoenberg Ch, VCM, Harnoncourt
✧ Teldec 2292-42957-2 [D] **M**

Cantatas: BWV206 & 207a Ziesak (sop), Chance (alt), Prégardien (ten), Kooy (bs), Stuttgart Chamber Ch, Concerto Cologne, Bernius
✧ Sony CD 46492 [D] **F**

Cantata: BWV208: Was mir behagt (Hunt) Smith (sop), Kirkby (sop), Davies (ten), George (bs), Parley of Instruments, Goodman
✧ Hyperion CDA 66169 [D] **F**

Christmas Oratorio, BWV248 Rolfe Johnson (ten), Argenta (sop), von Otter (mez), Blochwitz (ten), Bär (bar), Monteverdi Ch, EBS, Gardiner
✧ DG Archiv 423 232-2, 2CDs [D] **F**

*Easter Oratorio, BWV249; *Cantata No. 4* van Evera (sop), Trevor (cont), Daniels (ten), Kooy (bar), *Thomas (bs), Taverner Consort & Players, Parrott
✧ Virgin VC5 45011-2 [D] **F**

20 Lieder from Schmelli's Song-book Schreier (ten), Richter (org)
DG 427 131-2 [A] **M**

Magnificat in D, BWV243
Kirkby (sop), Bonner (sop), Chance (alt), Ainsley (ten), Varcoe

(bar), Collegium Musicum 90 O & Ch, Hickox
(+ Vivaldi: *Gloria in D, RV589; Ostro picta*)
◇ Chandos CHAN 0518 [D] **F**
Palmer (sop), Watts (cont), Tear (ten), Roberts (bs), King's
College Ch, ASMF, Ledger
(+ C.P.E. Bach: *Magnificat*)
Decca 421 148-2 [A] **M**

Mass in A, BWV234; Mass in G min., BWV235; Sanctus, BWV238
Mellon (sop), Lesne (alt), Prégardien (ten), Kooy (bs),
Collegium Vocale, Herreweghe
◇ Virgin VC7 59587-2 [D] **F**

Mass in B min., BWV232 Argenta (sop), Dawson (sop), Hall
(sop), Kwella (sop), Morgan (mez), Chance (alt), Stafford (alt),
Milner (ten), Evans (ten), Varcoe (bar), Monteverdi Ch, EBS,
Gardiner
◇ DG Archiv 415 514-2, 2CDs [D] **F**

Mass in F, BWV233; Mass in G, BWV236 Mellon (sop), Lesne
(alt), Prégardien (ten), Kooy (bs), Collegium Vocale,
Herreweghe
◇ Virgin VC7 59634-2 [D] **F**

Motets, BWV225–230 Stuttgart Chamber Ch, Stuttgart
Baroque O, Bernius
◇ Sony CD 45859 [D] **F**

St. John Passion, BWV245
Schlick (sop), Wessel (cont), de Mey (ten), Kooy (bs),
Netherlands Bach Ch, Amsterdam Baroque O, Koopman
◇ Erato 4509 94675-2, 2 CDs [D] **F**
Wunderlich (ten), Fischer-Dieskau (bar), Grummer (sop),
Ludwig (mez), Traxel (ten), St. Hedwig's Cathedral Ch,
Berlin SO, Forster
EMI CMS7 64234-2, 2 CDs [A] **M**

St. Matthew Passion,
BWV244 Rolfe Johnson (ten), Schmidt (bar), Bonney (sop),
Monoyios (sop), von Otter (mez), Chance (alt), Crook (ten),
Bär (bar), Hauptmann (bs), Monteverdi Ch, EBS, Gardiner
◇ DG Archiv 427 648-2, 3CDs [D] **F**
Pears (ten), Fischer-Dieskau (bar), Schwarzkopf (sop),
Ludwig (mez), Gedda (ten), Berry (bs), Philharmonia Ch & O,
Klemperer
EMI CMS7 63058-2, 3 CDs [A] **M**

BALAKIREV, Mily (1837–1910) RUSSIA

Piano Concertos: No. 1 in F# min., No. 2 in E♭ Binns (pno),
English Northern PO, Lloyd-Jones
(+ Rimsky-Korsakov: *Piano Concerto*)
Hyperion CDA 66640 [D] **F**

Piano Concerto No. 1 in F# min., Op. 1 Zhukov (pno), USSR
TV & Radio Large O, Dmitriev
(+ Medtner: *Piano Concerto No. 1;* Rimsky-Korsakov: *Piano
Concerto*)
Mezhdunarodnaya Kniga MK 417087 [A] **F**

Symphony No. 1 in C; Second Overture on Russian Themes
Philharmonia O, Svetlanov
Hyperion CDA 66493 [D] **F**

O *Symphony No. 2 in D min.; Tamara* (symphonic poem); *Overture on 3 Russian Themes* Philharmonia O, Svetlanov
Hyperion CDA 66586 [D] **F**

S *Islamey* Gavrilov (pno)
(+ Prokofiev: *Piano Concerto No. 1, etc.;* Tchaikovsky: *Piano Concerto No. 1, etc.*)
EMI CDM7 64329-2 [A] **M**

Mazurkas Nos. 1–7; Scherzi Nos. 1–3 Banowetz (pno)
Marco Polo 8.220447 [D] **F**

Piano Sonata in Bb min.; The Lark Fergus-Thompson (pno)
(+ Scriabin: *2 Poems; Piano Sonata No. 3; Vers la flamme*)
Kingdom KCLCD 2001 [D] **F**

BANTOCK, Granville (1868–1946) ENGLAND

O *Celtic Symphony; Hebridean Symphony; The Sea Reivers; The Witch of Atlas* RPO, Handley
Hyperion CDA 66450 [D] **F**

Pagan Symphony; Fifne at the Fair; 2 Heroic Ballads RPO, Handley
Hyperion CDA 66630 [D] **F**

BARBER, Samuel (1910–1981) USA

O *Adagio for Strings, Op. 11; *Piano Concerto, Op. 38; Medea's Meditation and Dance of Vengeance, Op. 23a* *Joselson (pno), LSO, Schenck
ASV CDDCA 534 [D] **F**

Cello Concerto, Op. 22 Ma (vcl), Baltimore SO, Zinman
(+ Britten: *Cello Symphony*)
Sony/CBS CD 44900 [D] **F**

Violin Concerto, Op. 14 Kun (vln), English SO, Boughton
(+ Bernstein: *Serenade*)
Nimbus NI 5329 [D] **F**

Essays for Orchestra Nos. 1–3 Detroit SO, Järvi
(+ Ives: *Symphony No. 1*)
Chandos CHAN 9053 [D] **F**

Medea (ballet), Op. 23: Suite Eastman-Rochester O, Hanson
(+ Gould: *Fall River Legend: Suite; Spirituals*)
Philips Mercury 432 016-2 [A] **M**

Souvenirs (ballet), Op. 28: Suite New Zealand SO, Schenck
(+ Menotti: *Amahl and the Night Visitors: Suite; Sebastian: Suite*)
Koch 37005-2 [D] **F**

Symphony No. 1, Op. 9; Adagio for Strings, Op. 11; Essays Nos. 1 & 2; Music for a Scene from Shelley, Op. 7; School for Scandal Overture Baltimore SO, Zinman
Argo 436 288-2 [D] **F**

Symphony No. 2, Op. 19; Adagio for Strings, Op. 11 Detroit SO, Järvi
(+ Bristow: *Symphony in F# min.*)
Chandos CHAN 9169 [D] **F**

C *String Quartet, Op. 11* Emerson Quartet
(+ Ives: *String Quartets Nos. 1 & 2*)
DG 435 864-2 [D] **F**

S *The Complete Piano Music* Parkin (pno)
Chandos CHAN 9177 [D] **F**

S *Piano Sonata in E♭, Op. 26* Lawson (pno)
(+ Carter: *Piano Sonata;* Copland: *Piano Sonata;* Ives: *Three-page Sonata*)
Virgin VC7 59008-2 [D] **F**

W *Agnus Dei* Corydon Singers, Best
(+ Bernstein: *Chichester Psalms;* Copland: *In the Beginning, etc.*)
Hyperion CDA 66219 [D] **F**

The Complete Songs Studer (sop), Hampson (bar), Browning (pno), Emerson Quartet
DG 435 867-2, 2 CDs [D] **F**

BARTÓK, Béla (1881–1945) HUNGARY/USA

O *Concerto for Orchestra; *Dance Suite; *2 Portraits; *Mikrokosmos* (arr.): *Bourée; From the Diary of a Fly* LSO, *Philharmonia Hungarica, Dorati
Philips Mercury 432 017-2 [A] **M**

Concerto for Orchestra; 4 Pieces, Op. 12 CSO, Boulez
DG 437 826-2 [D] **F**

Piano Concertos Nos. 1–3 Donohoe (pno), CBSO, Rattle
EMI CDC7 54871-2 [D] **F**

Viola Concerto; Music for Strings, Percussion and Celeste Christ (vla), BPO, Ozawa
DG 437 993-2 [D] **F**

Violin Concertos Nos. 1 & 2 Midori (vln), BPO, Mehta
Sony CD 45941 [D] **F**

Violin Concerto No. 2; Rhapsodies Nos. 1 & 2 Takezawa (vln), LSO, Tilson Thomas
RCA 09026 61675-2 [D] **F**

Divertimento for Strings; Music for Strings, Percussion and Celeste; 2 Portraits, Op. 5; The Wooden Prince (ballet): Suite Hetzel (vln), Hungarian State SO, Fischer
Nimbus NI 6362/3, 2 CDs [D] **M**

Divertimento for Strings; Romanian Folkdances Orpheus CO
(+ Janáček: *Mladi*)
DG 415 668-2 [D] **F**

Hungarian Sketches; Romanian Folkdances Minneapolis SO, Dorati
(+ Kodály: *Dances from Galanta, etc*)
Philips Mercury 432 005-2 [A] **M**

Miraculous Mandarin (pantomime in 1 act); *Two Pictures* *Mintz (vln), Ambrosian Singers, LSO, Abbado
(+ Prokofiev: *Scythian Suite*)
DG 410 598-2 [D] **F**

Music for Strings, Percussion and Celeste; Divertimento; Miraculous Mandarin (ballet): *Suite* CSO, Solti
Decca 430 352-2 [D] **F**

The Wooden Prince (ballet); *Cantata profana* Aler (ten), Tomlinson (bar), CSO & Ch, Boulez
DG 435 863-2 [D] **F**

: *Contrasts; Rhapsodies Nos. 1 & 2; Romanian Folkdances; Solo Violin Sonata* Collins (cl), Ososowicz (vln), Tomes (pno)
Hyperion CDA 66415 [D] **F**

C   *44 Duos* Kiss (vln), Balogh (vln)
Hyperion CDA 66453 [D] **F**

15 Hungarian Peasant Songs (arr. Arma) Hall (fl), Jacobson (pno)
(+ Martinů: *Flute Sonata;* Prokofiev: *Flute Sonata*)
Pickwick MCD 26 [D] **B**

String Quartets Nos. 1–6 Emerson Quartet
DG 423 657-2, 2CDs [D] **F**

Violin Sonata No. 1 Kremer (vln), Argerich (pno)
(+ Janáček: *Sonata;* Messiaen: *Theme & Variations*)
DG 427 351-2 [D] **F**

Sonata for 2 Pianos and Percussion Alfons Kontarsky (pno),
Aloys Kontarsky (pno), Caskel (perc), König (perc)
(+ Stravinsky: *Concerto for 2 Pianos; Sonata for 2 Pianos*)
DG 437 027-2 [A] **M**

S   *14 Bagatelles; 2 Elegies; 3 Hungarian Folk Tunes; 6 Romanian
Folk Dances; Sonatina* Kocsis (pno)
Philips 434 104-2 [D] **F**

Mikrokosmos (complete); *For Children* Ranki (pno)
Teldec 9031-76139-2, 3CDs [D] **F**

BAX, Arnold (1883–1953) ENGLAND

O   **Cello Concerto; Cortège; Mediterranean; Overture to a Picaresque
Comedy; Prelude for a Solemn Occasion* *R. Wallfisch (vcl), LPO,
Thomson
Chandos CHAN 8494 [D] **F**

*Violin Concerto; A Legend; Romantic Overture; Golden Eagle
(incidental music) *Mordkovitch (vln), LPO, Thomson
Chandos CHAN 9003 [D] **F**

From Dusk Until Dawn (ballet); *The Truth About the Russian
Dancers* (incidental music) LPO, Thomson
Chandos CHAN 8863 [D] **F**

*The Garden of Fand; The Happy Forest; November Woods; Summer
Music* Ulster O, Thomson
Chandos CHAN 8307 [D] **F**

Tone poems: *In the Faery Hills; Into the Twilight; Roscatha; The
Tale the Pine-trees knew* Ulster O, Thomson
Chandos CHAN 8367 [D] **F**

Malta G.C. (film score); **Oliver Twist* (film score): *Suite*
*Parkin (pno), RPO, Alwyn
(+ Arnold: *The Sound Barrier*)
ASV CDWHL 2058 [D] **M**

Morning Song (Maytime in Sussex); Symphonic Variations
Fingerhut (pno), LPO, Thomson
Chandos CHAN 8516 [D] **F**

Northern Ballad No. 2; Spring Fire; Symphonic Scherzo RPO,
Handley
Chandos CHAN 8464 [D] **F**

Saga Fragment; Winter Legends Fingerhut (pno), LPO,
Thomson
Chandos CHAN 8484 [D] **F**

Symphonies Nos. 1–7 LPO, Ulster O, Thomson
Chandos CHAN 8906/10 [D] **M**

o *Symphony No. 1 in E♭; Christmas Eve on the Mountains* (tone poem) LPO, Thomson
Chandos CHAN 8480 [D] **F**

Symphony No. 2 in E min./C; Nympholept (tone poem) LPO, Thomson
Chandos CHAN 8493 [D] **F**

Symphony No. 3; 4 Orchestral Sketches: Dance of Wild Irravel; Paean LPO, Thomson
Chandos CHAN 8454 [D] **F**

Symphony No. 4; Tintagel (tone poem) Ulster O, Thomson
Chandos CHAN 8312 [D] **F**

Symphony No. 5 in C♯ min.; Russian Suite LPO, Thomson
Chandos CHAN 8669 [D] **F**

Symphony No. 6; Festival Overture LPO, Thomson
Chandos CHAN 8586 [D] **F**

Symphony No. 7; Songs: Eternity; Glamour; A Lyke-Wake; Slumber Song Hill (ten), LPO, Thomson
Chandos CHAN 8628 [D] **F**

*Tintagel; Christmas Eve; Festival Overture; Nympholept; 4 Orchestral Sketches: Dance of the Wild Irravel; Paean LPO,*Ulster O, Thompson
Chandos CHAN 9168 [D] **F**

c *Cello Sonata on E♭; | Sonatina in D; Legend-Sonata in F♯ min.; Folk-Tale* Gregor-Smith (vcl), Wrigley (pno)
ASV CDDCAA 896 [D] **F**

Piano Trio in B♭ Borodin Trio
(+ Bridge: *Piano Trio No. 2*)
Chandos CHAN 8495 [D] **F**

Harp Quintet; Piano Quintet; String Quartet No. 1 Kanga (hp), McCabe (pno), English Quartet
Chandos CHAN 8391 [D] **F**

Oboe Quintet Francis (ob), English Quartet
(+ Holst: *Air and Variations; 3 Pieces;* Jacob: *Oboe Quartet;* Moeran: *Fantasy Quartet*)
Chandos CHAN 8392 [D] **F**

Clarinet Sonata Hilton (cl), Swallow (pno)
(+ Bliss: *Clarinet Quintet;* Vaughan Williams: *6 Studies*)
Chandos CHAN 8683 [D] **F**

Violin Sonatas: No. 1 in E; No. 2 in D Gruenberg (vn), McCabe (pno)
Chandos CHAN 8845 [D] **F**

String Quartet No. 2; *Piano Quintet Norris (pno), Mistry Quartet
Chandos CHAN 8795 [D] **F**

s *Apple Blossom Time; Burlesque; The Maiden with the Daffodil; Nereid; O Dame Get Up and Bake Your Pies; On a May Evening; The Princess's Rose Garden; Romance; 2 Russian Tone Pictures; Sleepy Head* Parkin (pno)
Chandos CHAN 8732 [D] **F**

Country Tune; Lullaby; Piano Sonatas Nos. 1 & 2; Winter Waters Parkin (pno)
Chandos CHAN 8496 [D] **F**

S *A Hill Tune; In a Vodka Shop; Piano Sonatas Nos. 3 & 4; Water Music* Parkin (pno)
Chandos CHAN 8497 [D] **F**

Rhapsodic Ballad R. Wallfisch (vcl)
(+ Bridge: *Cello Sonata;* Delius: *Cello Sonata;* Walton: *Passacaglia*)
Chandos CHAN 8499 [D] **F**

BEASER, Robert (born 1954) USA

O *Chorale Variations; *The Seven Deadly Sins; **Piano Concerto*
*Opalach (bs), **Paul (pno), American Composers O, Davies
Argo 440 337-2 [D] **F**

BEETHOVEN, Ludwig van (1770–1827) GERMANY

O *Piano Concertos Nos. 1–5; *Triple Concerto in C, Op. 56* Fleisher (pno), Cleveland O, Szell; *Stern (vln), Rose (vcl), Istomin (pno), Philadelphia O, Ormandy
Sony CD 48397, 3CDs [A] **B**

Piano Concertos Nos. 1–5 Pollini (pno), BPO, Abbado
DG 439 770-2, 3 CDs [D] **F**

Piano Concertos: No. 1 in C, Op. 15; No. 2 in B♭, Op. 19
Kovacevich (pno), BBC SO, C. Davis
Philips 422 968-2 [A] **B**

Piano Concertos: No. 2 in B♭, Op. 19; No. 4 in G, Op. 58 Fleisher (pno), Cleveland O, Szell
Sony CD 48165 [A] **B**

Piano Concertos: No. 3 in C min., Op. 37; No. 4 in G, Op. 58
Kovacevich (pno), BBC SO, C. Davis
Philips 426 062-2 [A] **B**
Kempff (pno), BPO, Leitner
DG 419 467-2 [A] **M**

*Piano Concerto No. 5 in E♭ (Emperor), Op. 73; *Triple Concerto in C, Op. 56* Fleisher (piano), Cleveland O, Szell; *Stern (vln), Rose (vcl), Istomin (pno), Philadelphia O, Ormandy
Sony CD 46549 [A] **B**

*Piano Concerto No. 5 in E♭ (Emperor), Op. 73; *Fantasia in C min., Op. 80* Tan (fpno), *Schütz Ch, LCP, Norrington
✧ EMI CDC7 49965-2 [D] **F**

*Piano Concerto in D (arr. of Violin Concerto), Op. 61a; *2 Violin Romances, Opp. 40 & 50* Barenboim (pno/dir), ECO; *Zukerman (vln), LPO, Barenboim
DG 429 179-2 [A] **M**

The Creatures of Prometheus (ballet) Orpheus CO
DG 419 608-2 [D] **F**

Complete Overtures: *Consecration of the House, Op. 124; Coriolan, Op. 62; The Creatures of Prometheus* (incidental music), *Op. 43; Egmont* (incidental music), *Op. 84; Fidelio* (opera); *King Stephen* (incidental music), *Op. 117; Leonores Nos. 1–3 (from Fidelio); Name Day, Op. 115; The Ruins of Athens* (incidental music), *Op. 113* BPO, Karajan
DG 427 256-2, 2CDs [A] **M**

Overtures: *Consecration of the House, Op. 124; Coriolan, Op. 62; The Creatures of Prometheus* (incidental music), *Op. 43; Egmont* (incidental music), Op. 84; *Fidelio* (opera); *King Stephen* (incidental music), *Op. 117; Leonore No. 2 (from Fidelio); The*

Ruins of Athens (incidental music), *Op. 113* Hanover Band,
Goodman, Huggett
◇ Nimbus NI 5205 [A] **F**

○ *Symphonies Nos. 1–9*
Margiono (sop), Remmert (cont), Schasching (ten), Holl (bs),
A. Schoenberg Ch, COE, Harnoncourt
Teldec 2292-46452-2, 5CDs [D] **F**
Addison (sop), Hobson (cont), Lewis (ten), Bell (bar),
Cleveland O & Ch, Szell
Sony CD 48396, 5CDs [A] **B**

Symphonies: No. 1 in C, Op. 21; No. 6 in F (Pastoral), Op. 68
Chicago SO, Reiner
RCA GD 60002 [A] **M**

Symphonies: No. 2 in D, Op. 36; No. 4 in B♭, Op. 60
Philharmonia O, Klemperer
EMI CDM7 63355-2 [A] **M**

Symphonies: No. 2 in D, Op. 36; No. 7 in A, Op. 92 BPO, Karajan
DG 419 050-2 [A] **M**

Symphonies: No. 2 in D, Op. 36; No. 8 in F, Op. 93 LCP,
Norrington
◇ EMI CDC7 47698-2 [D] **F**

Symphony No. 3 in E♭ (Eroica), Op. 55; Grosse Fuge in B♭, Op. 133
Philharmonia O, Klemperer
EMI CDM7 63356-2 [A] **M**

*Symphony No. 3 in E♭ (Eroica), Op. 55; Overtures: Fidelio, Op.
72b; Coriolan, Op. 62* Chicago SO, Reiner
RCA 09026-60962-2 [A] **M**

*Symphony No. 4 in B♭, Op. 60; Symphony No. 7 in A, Op. 92; King
Stephen (incidental music), Op. 117: Overture* Cleveland O,
Szell
Sony CD 48158 [A] **B**

Symphony No. 5 in C min., Op. 67 VPO, C. Kleiber
DG 415 861-2 [A] **F**

Symphonies: No. 5 in C min., Op. 67; No. 7 in A, Op. 92 RLPO,
Mackerras
EMI Eminence CD-EMX 2212 [D] **M**

Symphonies: No. 6 in F (Pastoral), Op. 68; No. 8 in F, Op. 93
COE, Harnoncourt
Teldec 9031-75709-2 [D] **F**

Symphony No. 7 in A, Op. 92 VPO, C. Kleiber
DG 415 862-2 [A] **F**

Symphony No. 9 in D min. (Choral), Op. 125
Tomowa-Sintow (sop), Baltsa (mez), Schreier (ten), van Dam
(bs-bar), Vienna Singverein, BPO, Karajan
DG 415 832-2 [A] **M**

*Wellingtons Sieg, Op. 91; *Egmont: Incidental Music; **Marches:
WoO29 in B♭; WoO24 in D; WoO18 in F; WoO19 in F; WoO20 in
C; Ecossaise in D; WoO22* *Janowitz (sop), BPO, Karajan;
**BPO Wind Ensemble, Priem-Bergrath
DG 419 624-2 [A] **F**

○ *Cello Sonatas: No. 1 in F, Op. 5/1; No. 2 in G min., Op. 5/2; 12
Variations on 'Ein Mädchen oder Weibchen' from Mozart's 'Die
Zauberflöte'; 7 Variations on 'Bei Männern, welche Liebe' from*

Mozart's 'Die Zauberflöte' Maisky (vcl), Argerich (pno)
DG 431 801-2 [D] **F**

C   *Cello Sonatas Nos. 3–5* Bylsma (vcl), Bilson (fpno)
◇ Elektra-Nonesuch 7559-79236-2 [D] **F**

Cello Sonatas Nos. 3–5; Variations on Handel, WoO45 Maisky (vcl), Argerich (pno)
DG 437 514-2 [D] **F**

Piano Quartet in E♭, Op. 16 Ax (pno), Stern (vln), Laredo (vla), Ma (vcl),
(+ Schumann: *Piano Quartet*)
Sony CD 53339 [D] **F**

Piano and Wind Quintet, Op. 16 Perahia (pno), Black (ob), King (cl), Halstead (hn), Sheen (bsn)
(+ Mozart: *Piano and Wind Quintet*)
Sony CD 42099 [D] **F**

Piano Trios Nos. 1–11 Istomin (pno), Stern (vln), Rose (vcl)
Sony CD 46738, 4CDs [A] **M**

Piano Trios: No. 1 in E♭, Op. 1/1; No. 3 in C min., Op. 1/3; Variations, Op. 44 Castle Trio
◇ Virgin VC7 59590-2 [D] **F**

Piano Trios: No. 2 in G, Op. 1/2; No. 4 in B♭, Op. 11; in E♭ WoO 38 Castle Trio
◇ Virgin VC7 59220-2 [D] **F**

Piano Trios: No. 4 in D (Ghost), Op. 70/1; No. 6 in B♭ (Archduke), Op. 97 Kempff (pno), Szeryng (vln), Fournier (vcl)
DG 429 712-2 [A] **M**

String Quartets: Nos. 1–6, Op. 18; No. 10 in E♭ (Harp), Op. 74; No. 11 in F Min., Op. 95 Lindsay Quartet
ASV CDDCS 305, 3CDs [A] **F**

*String Quartets: Nos. 1–6, Op. 18; *String Quintet in C Op. 29* Tokyo String Quartet; *Zukerman (vla)
RCA 09026 61286-2, 3CDs [D] **F**

String Quartets: Nos. 7–11, Opp. 59/1–3 (Rasumovsky); 74; 95 Italian Quartet
Philips 420 797-2, 3CDs [A] **M**

String Quartet No. 7 in F, Op. 59/1 (Rasumovsky) Lindsay Quartet
ASV CDDCA 553 [D] **F**

String Quartets (Rasumovsky): No. 8 in E min., Op. 59/2; No. 9 in C, Op. 59/3 Lindsay Quartet
ASV CDDCA 554 [D] **F**

String Quartets: No. 11 in F min., Op. 95; No. 12 in E♭., Op. 127; Grosse Fuge in B♭, Op. 133 Végh Quartet
Calliope CAL 9635 [A] **F**

String Quartet No. 11 in F minor Op. 95 (arr. Mahler) Moscow Soloists, Bashmet
(+ Schubert: *String Quartet No.14* arr. Mahler)
RCA RD 60988 [D] **F**

String Quartets: Nos. 12–16, Opp. 127, 130–132, 135; Grosse Fuge in B♭, Op. 133
Lindsay Quartet
ASV CDDCS 403, 4CDs [D] **F**

c *String Quartet No. 13 in B♭, Op. 130; Grosse Fuge in B♭, Op. 133*
Végh Quartet
Auvidis V4407 [A] **F**
Lindsay Quartet
ASV CDDCA 602 [D] **F**

String Quartets: No. 14 in C♯ min., Op. 131; No. 16 in F, Op. 135
Végh Quartet
Auvidis V4408 [A] **F**
(arr.) VPO, Bernstein
DG 435 779-2 [A/D] **F**

String Quartets: No. 15 in A min., Op. 132; No. 16 in F, Op. 135
Lindsay Quartet
ASV CDDCA 604 [D] **F**

String Quintet in C, Op. 29; Septet in E♭, Op. 20 Hausmusik
✧ EMI CDC7 54656-2 [D] **F**

String Trio in E♭, Op. 3; Serenade in D, Op. 8 Cummings Trio
Unicorn DKPCD 9059 [D] **F**

3 String Trios, Op. 9: No. 1 in G; No. 2 in D; No. 3 in C min.
L'Archibudelli
✧ Sony CD 48190 [D] **F**

Violin Sonatas Nos. 1–10 Perlman (vln), Ashkenazy (pno)
Decca 421 453-2, 4CDs [A] **M**

Violin Sonatas Nos. 1–3 Kremer (vln), Argerich (pno)
DG 415 138-2 [D] **F**

Violin Sonatas: No. 4 in A min., Op. 23; No. 5 in F (Spring), Op. 24 Kremer (vln), Argerich (pno)
DG 419 787-2 [D] **F**

Violin Sonatas: No. 5 in F (Spring), Op. 24; No. 8 in G, Op. 30/3; No. 9 in A (Kreutzer), Op. 47 Zukerman (vln), Barenboim (pno)
EMI CDM7 64631-2 [A] **M**

Wind Octet in E♭, Op. 103; Wind Quintet in E♭ Hess 19; Rondino in E♭, WoO 25; Wind Sextet in E♭, Op. 71 COE Wind Soloists
ASV CDCOE 807 [D] **F**

s *Bagatelles Nos. 1–24* Kovacevich (pno)
Philips 426 976-2 [A] **B**

14 Bagatelles, Opp. 33 & 126; 6 Variations on an Original Theme in F, Op. 34; 32 Variations in C min., WoO80; 15 Variations and Fugue on an Original Theme (Eroica), Op. 35 Gould (pno)
Sony CD 52646 [A] **F**

Piano Sonatas Nos. 1–32 (complete)
Barenboim (pno)
EMI CZS7 62863-2, 10CDs [A] **M**
Roberts (pno)
Nimbus NI 1792, 11CDs [D] **M**

Piano Sonatas Nos. 1–3, Op. 2 Tan (fpno)
✧ EMI CDC7 54657-2 [D] **F**

Piano Sonatas: No. 2 in A, Op. 2/2; No. 4 in E♭, Op. 7 Gilels (pno)
DG 415 481-2 [D] **F**

Piano Sonatas: No. 3 in C, Op. 2/3; No. 4 in E♭, Op. 7; No. 27 in E min., Op. 90 Richter (pno)
Olympia OCD 336 [D] **F**

S *Piano Sonatas: No. 5 in C min., Op. 10/1; No. 10 in G, Op. 14/2; No. 19 in G min., Op. 49/1; No. 20 in G, Op. 49/2* Gilels (pno)
DG 419 172-2 [D] **F**

Piano Sonatas: Nos. 5–7, Op. 10/1–3; No. 25 in G, Op. 79
Tan (fpno)
◇ EMI CDC7 54207-2 [D] **F**

Piano Sonatas: Nos. 5–7, Op. 10 Lortie (pno)
Chandos CHAN 9101 [D] **F**

Piano Sonatas: No. 7 in D, Op. 10/3; No. 18 in E♭, Op. 31/3; 15 Variations and Fugue on an Original Theme in E♭ (Eroica), Op. 35 Gilels (pno)
DG 423 136-2 [D] **F**

Piano Sonatas: No. 8 in C min. (Pathétique), Op. 13; No. 13 in E♭, Op. 27/1; No. 14 in C♯ min. (Moonlight), Op. 27/2 Gilels (pno)
DG 400 036-2 [D] **F**

Piano Sonatas: Nos. 9 & 10, Op. 14/1 & 2; No. 24 in F♯, Op. 78; No. 27 in E min., Op. 90; No. 28 in A, Op. 101 Jando (pno)
Naxos 8.550162 [D] **B**

Piano Sonatas: No. 13 in E♭, Op. 27/1; No. 14 in C♯ min. (Moonlight), Op. 27/2; No. 15 in D (Pastoral), Op. 28 Pollini (pno)
DG 427 770-2 [D] **F**

Piano Sonatas: No. 14 in C♯ min. (Moonlight), Op. 27/2; No. 21 in C (Waldstein), Op. 53; No. 23 in F min. (Appassionata), Op. 57 Pletnev (pno)
Virgin VC7 59247-2 [D] **F**

Piano Sonatas: No. 15 in D (Pastoral), Op. 28; No. 17 in D min. (Tempest), Op. 31/2 Gilels (pno)
DG 419 161-2 [A] **F**

Piano Sonatas: Nos. 16–18, Op. 31 Tan (fpno)
◇ EMI CDC7 54337-2 [D] **F**

Piano Sonatas: Nos. 17 in D min. (Tempest), & 18 in E♭, Op. 31/2 & 3; No. 26 in E♭ (Les adieux), Op. 81a Perahia (pno)
Sony/CBS CD 42319 [D] **F**

Piano Sonatas: No. 17 in D min. (Tempest), Op. 31/2; No. 25 in G, Op. 79; No. 28 in A, Op. 101 Gelber (pno)
Denon CO-75245 [D] **F**

Piano Sonatas: No. 21 in C (Waldstein), Op. 53; No. 23 in F min. (Appassionata), Op. 57; No. 26 in E♭ (Les adieux), Op. 81a Gilels (pno)
DG 419 162-2 [A] **F**

EDITORS' CHOICE (see page 13): *Piano Sonatas: No. 21 in C (Waldstein), Op. 53; No. 22 in F, Op. 54; No. 28 in A, Op. 101; Andante in F, WoO57* Brendel (pno)
Philips 438 472-2 [D] **F**

Piano Sonata No. 23 in F minor, Op. 57 (Appassionata) Richter (pno)
(+ Brahms: *Piano Concerto No. 2*)
RCA 07863 56519-2 [A] **M**

Piano Sonatas: No. 27 in E min., Op. 90; No. 28 in A, Op. 101; No. 32 in C min., Op. 111 Kovacevich (pno)
EMI CDC7 54599-2 [D] **F**

Piano Sonatas: Nos. 28–32 Pollini (pno)
DG 419 199-2, 2CDs [A] **F**

Piano Sonata No. 29 in Bb (Hammerklavier), Op. 106 Gilels (pno)
DG 410 527-2 [A] **F**

Piano Sonatas: No. 30 in E, Op. 109; No. 31 in Ab, Op. 110
Gilels (pno)
DG 419 174-2 [A] **F**

33 Variations on a Waltz by Diabelli, Op. 120
Kovacevich (pno)
Philips 422 969-2 [A] **B**
Hill (pno)
Unicorn-Kanchana DKPCD 9084 [D] **F**

*6 Variations on an Original Theme in F, Op. 34; 15 Variations and
a Fugue on an Original Theme in Eb (Eroica), Op. 35; 2 Rondos,
Op. 51; Bagatelle No. 25 in A min., Für Elise, WoO59* Lortie (pno)
Chandos CHAN 8616 [D] **F**

An die ferne Geliebte (song cycle), *Op. 98; 8 Lieder* Fischer-
Dieskau (bar), Demus (pno)
(+ Brahms: *Lieder*)
DG 415 189-2 [A] **F**

An die ferne Geliebte (song cycle), *Op. 98; 21 Lieder* Bär (bar),
Parsons (pno)
EMI CDC7 54879-2 [D] **F**

Bundeslied, Op. 122; Elegischer Gesang, Op. 118; King Stephen
(incidental music), *Op. 117; Meeresstille und glückliche Fahrt*
(cantata), *Op. 112; Opferlied, Op. 121b* Ambrosian Singers,
LSO, Tilson Thomas
Sony/CBS CD 76404 [D] **F**

Mass in C, Op. 86; Meeresstille und glückliche Fahrt (cantata), *Op.
112* Dunn (sop), Zimmermann (mez), Beccaria (ten), Krause
(bar), Ernst-Senff Chamber Ch, Berlin RSO & Ch, Chailly
Decca 417 563-2 [D] **F**

Missa Solemnis in D, Op. 123
Janowitz (sop), Ludwig (mez), Wunderlich (ten), Berry (bs),
Vienna Singverein, BPO, Karajan
(+ Mozart: *Mass No. 16*)
DG 423 913-2, 2CDs [A] **M**
Margiano (sop), Robbin (mez), Kendall (ten), Miles (bs),
Monteverdi Ch, Orchestre revolutionaire et romantique,
Gardiner
◇ DG Archiv 429 779-2 [D] **F**

BELLINI, Vincenzo (1801–1835) ITALY

Oboe Concerto in Eb Lord (ob) ASMF, Marriner
(+ Cherubini: *Horn Sonata;* Donizetti: *String Quartet;* Rossini:
String Sonatas)
Decca 430 563-2, 2CDs [A] **M**

BEN-HAIM, Paul (1897–1974) GERMANY/ISRAEL

Violin Concerto Perlman (vln), Israel PO, Mehta
(+ Castelnuovo-Tedesco: *Violin Concerto No. 2*)
EMI CDC7 54296-2 [D] **F**

Sweet Psalmist of Israel Marlowe (hpd), Stavrache (hp), NYPO,
Bernstein
(+ Bloch: *Sacred Service;* Foss: *Song of Songs*)
Sony CD 47533, 2CDs [A] **M**

BENJAMIN, George (born 1960) ENGLAND

O   *Antara* London Sinfonietta, Benjamin
(+ Boulez: *Dérive; Mémoriale;* Harvey: *Song Offerings*)
Nimbus NI 5167 [D] **F**

*At First Light; **A Mind of Winter; ***Ringed by the flat Horizon
*Hulse (ob), **Walmsley-Clark (sop), **Archibald (cl),
London Sinfonietta, Benjamin; ***Pople (vcl), BBC SO,
Elder
Nimbus NI 5075 [D] **F**

S   *Piano Sonata* Benjamin (pno)
Nimbus NI 1415 [D] **M**

BERG, Alban (1885–1935) AUSTRIA

O   *Chamber Concerto; *4 Clarinet Pieces; Piano Sonata* Barenboim
(pno), Zukerman (vln), *Pay (cl), Ensemble
InterContemporain, Boulez
DG 423 237-2 [A] **M**

Violin Concerto Szeryng (vln), Bavarian RSO, Kubelik
(+ Schoenberg: *Piano and Violin Concertos*)
DG 431 740-2 [A] **M**

Lyric Suite; 3 Orchestral Pieces, Op. 6 BPO, Karajan
(+ Schoenberg: *Pelleas und Melisande etc;* Webern: *5 Movements,
etc.*)
DG 427 424-2, 3CDs [A] **M**

3 Orchestral Pieces, Op. 6; *Lulu: Symphonic Suite *Pilarczyk
(sop), LSO, Dorati
(+ Schoenberg: *5 Pieces;* Webern: *5 Pieces*)
Philips Mercury 432 006-2 [A] **M**

*3 Orchestral Pieces Op. 6; *Lulu: Symphonic Suite; 5 Orchestral
Songs Op. 4* Price (sop), LSO, Abbado
DG 423 238-2 [A] **M**

C   *Lyric Suite; String Quartet, Op. 3* LaSalle Quartet
(+ Schoenberg: *String Quartets Nos. 1–4, etc;* Webern: *6
Bagatelles, etc*)
DG 419 994-2, 4CDs [A] **M**

V   *4 Lieder, Op. 2* Fischer-Dieskau (bar), Reimann (pno)
(+ Schoenberg: *Gurrelieder etc.;* Webern: *Lieder*)
DG 431 744-2, 2 CDs [A] **M**

BERIO, Luciano (born 1925) ITALY

O   *Chemins Nos. II & IV; Corale; Points on the Curve to Find; Ritorno
degli snovidenia* Ensemble InterContemporain, Boulez
Sony CD 45862 [D] **F**

Corale; Requies; Voci Chiarappa (vln), London Sinfonietta,
Berio
RCA RD 87898 [D] **F**

Eindrücke; *Sinfonia Pasquier (vln), *New Swingle Singers,
FNO, Boulez
Erato 2292-45228-2 [D] **F**

V   *Formazione; *Folk Songs; **Sinfonia* *van Nes (mez),
**Electric Phoenix, Royal Concertgebouw O, Chailly
Decca 425 832-2 [D] **F**

Coro Cologne Radio Ch & SO, Berio
DG 423 902-2 [A] **F**

BERKELEY, Lennox (1903–1989) ENGLAND

○ *Symphony No. 3; Canzonetta; Divertimento; Mont Juic; Partita; Serenade* LPO, Berkeley
Lyrita SRCD 226 [A] **F**

BERKELEY, Michael (born 1948) ENGLAND

○ *Clarinet Concerto; Flighting; *'Pere du doux repos . . .'* Johnson (cl), *Herford (bar), Northern Sinfonia, Edwards
ASV CDDCB 1101 [D] **M**

BERLIOZ (1803–1869) FRANCE

○ *Béatrice et Bénédict* (opera): *Overture* Boston SO, Monteux
(+ d'Indy: *Symphonie sur un chant;* Franck: *Symphony in D min.*)
RCA GD 86805 [A] **M**

Harold in Italy; Roman Carnival Overture *Christ (vla), BPO, Maazel
DG 415 109-2 [A] **F**

Overtures: *Béatrice et Bénédict; Benvenuto Cellini; Le Carnaval romain; Le Corsaire; Les Troyens* (exerpts); *Roméo et Juliette: Queen Mab Scherzo* Boston SO, Munch
(+ Saint-Saëns: *Le rouet d'Omphale*)
RCA 09026 61400-2 [A] **M**

Roméo et Juliette (dramatic symphony), *Op. 17; Symphonie funèbre et triomphale, Op. 15* *Quivar (sop), *Cupido (ten), *Krause (bar), Tudor Singers, Montreal SO & Ch, Dutoit
Decca 417 302-2, 2CDs [D] **F**

Symphonie fantastique; Overtures: *Le Corsaire; Le Carnaval romain; Hungarian March; Trojan March* Detroit SO, Paray
Philips Mercury 434 328-2 [A] **M**

*Symphonie fantastique, Op. 14; *Lélio, Op. 14b* Topart (narr), *Burles (ten), *Gedda (ten), ORTF, Martinon
EMI CZS7 62739-2, 2CDs [A] **M**

Symphonie fantastique, Op. 14
LCP, Norrington
◇ EMI CDC7 49541-2 [D] **F**
BPO, Karajan
DG 415 325-2 [A] **F**

✓ *Complete Songs* von Otter (mez), Pollet (sop), Aler (ten), Allen (bar), Garben (pno), Muhlbach (hp), Sollscher (gtr), Thedeen (vcl), Schenk (hn), Gast (hn), Stockholm Royal Opera Ch.
DG 435 860-2, 3 CDs [D] **F**

La Damnation de Faust (dramatic legend), *Op. 24* Veasey (mez), Gedda (ten), Bastin (bs), Ambrosian Singers, Wandsworth School Boys' Ch, LSO & Ch, C. Davis
Philips 416 395-2, 2CDs [A] **F**

L'Enfance du Christ (sacred trilogy), *Op. 25* Murray (mez), Tear (ten), Wilson-Johnson (bar), Best (bs), King's College Ch, RPO, Cleobury
EMI CDS7 49935-2, 2CDS [D] **F**

Messe solenelle Brown (sop), Viala (ten), Cachemaille (bar), Monteverdi Ch, Orchestre revolutionaire et romantique, Gardiner
Philips 442 137-2 [D] **F**

V *La Mort de Cléopâtre; *Herminie; Overtures: Béatrice et Bénédict;
Le Roi Lear *Plowright (sop), Philharmonia O, Rouchon
ASV CDDCA 895 [D] **F**

Requiem mass (Grande messe des morts), Op. 5; Overtures:
Benvenuto Cellini; Le Carnaval romain, Op. 9; Le Corsaire, Op. 21
Pavarotti (ten), Ernst-Senff Ch, BPO, Levine
DG 429 724-2, 2CDs [D] **F**

Les Nuits d'été, Op. 7; La belle voyageuse, Op. 2/4; La captive, Op.
12; Le chasseur danois, Op. 19/6; Le jeune pâtre breton, Op. 13/4;
Tristia, Op. 18: La mort d'Ophélie; Zaïde, Op. 19/1 Fournier
(sop), Montague (mez), Robbin (mez), Crook (ten),
Cachemaille (bar), Lyon Opera O, Gardiner
Erato 2292-45517-2 [D] **F**

Te deum, Op. 22 Araiza (ten), LSO Ch, LPO Ch, European
Community YO, Abbado
DG 410 696-2 [D] **F**

BERNSTEIN, Leonard (1918–1990) USA

O Candide Overture; Facsimile; Fancy Free; On the Town: 3 Dance
Episodes & Complete; On the Waterfront; *Trouble in Tahiti; West
Side Story: Symphonic Dances Various artists, NYPO,
*Columbia Wind Ensemble, Bernstein
Sony CD 47154, 3CDs [A] **M**

Divertimento; *Halil (Nocturne); **3 Meditations from Mass; On
the Town: 3 Dance Episodes *Rampal (fl), **Rostropovich (vcl),
Israel PO, Bernstein
DG 415 966-2 [A] **F**

Prelude, Fugue and Riffs Stolzman (cl), LSO, Leighton-Smith
(+ Copland: Clarinet Concerto; Corigliano: Clarinet Concerto;
Stravinsky: Ebony Concerto)
RCA 09026 61360-2 [D] **F**

*Serenade (after Plato's Symposium) Kun (vln), English SO,
Boughton
(+ Barber: Violin Concerto)
Nimbus NI 5329 [D] **F**

Symphonies Nos. 1–3; Prelude, Fugue and Riffs; Serenade;
Chichester Psalms Various artists, NYPO, Bernstein
Sony CD 47162, 3CDs [A] **M**

Symphonies Nos. 1 (Jeremiah) & *2 (The Age of Anxiety) *Foss
(pno), Israel PO, Bernstein
DG 415 964-2 [A] **F**

V Chichester Psalms Corydon Singers, Best
(+ Barber: Agnus Dei; Copland: In the Beginning, etc.)
Hyperion CDA 66219 [D] **F**

Dybbuk; *Mass (for the death of President Kennedy) Johnson (bar),
Ostendorf (bs), NY City Ballet O; *Titus (bar), Scribner Ch,
Berkshire Boys' Ch, Studio Orchestra, Bernstein
Sony CD 47158, 3CDs [A] **M**

BERWALD, Franz (1796–1868) SWEDEN

O Piano Concerto in D; Violin Concerto, Op. 2; Festival of the
Bayaderes; Serious & Joyful Fancies; The Queen of Golconda:
Overture Migdal (pno), Tellefson (vln), RPO, Björlin
EMI CDM5 65073-2 [A] **M**

> *Symphonies Nos. 1–4* Gothenburg SO, Järvi
DG 415 502-2, 2CDs [D] **F**

Piano Trios Nos. 1–3 Prunyi (pno), Kiss (vln), Onczay (vcl)
Marco Polo 8.223170 [D] **F**

Grand Septet in B♭ Nash Ensemble
(+ Hummel: *Septet in D min.*)
CRD 3344 [A] **F**

BIBER, Heinrich (1644–1704) BOHEMIA

Mensa sonara; Sonata violino representativa in A Goebel
(vln/dir), Cologne Musica Antiqua
✧ DG Archiv 423 701-2 [D] **F**

7 Sonatas New London Consort, Pickett
(+ Schmelzer: *2 Balletos and 3 Sonatas*)
✧ L'Oiseau-Lyre 425 834-2 [D] **F**

Mystery Sonatas Holloway (vln), Moroney (hpd),
Tragicomedia
✧ Virgin VCD7 59551-2, 2CDs [D] **F**

BIRTWISTLE, Harrison (born 1934) ENGLAND

> *Carmen Arcadiae Mechanicae Perpetuum; Secret Theatre; Silbury
Air* London Sinfonietta, Howarth
Etcetera KTC 1052 [D] **F**

The Triumph of Time; Gawain's Journey Philharmonia O,
Howarth
Collins 13872 [D] **F**

Earth Dances BBCSO, Eotvos
Collins 20012 [D] **M**

BIZET, Georges (1838–1875) FRANCE

> *L'Arlésienne* (incidental music); *Jeux d'enfants* Consort of
London, Haydon Clark
Collins 11412 [D] **F**

L'Arlésienne (incidental music): *Suites Nos. 1 & 2; Carmen*
(opera): *Suites Nos. 1 & 2* Montreal SO, Dutoit
Decca 417 839-2 [D] **F**

Jeux d'enfants; La Jolie fille de Perth (opera): *Suite; Symphony in C*
OSR, Ansermet
(+ Ravel: *Le Tombeau de Couperin*)
Decca 433 721-2 [A] **F**

Symphony in C ASMF, Marriner
(+ Prokofiev: *Symphony No. 1;* Stravinsky: *Pulcinella Suite*)
Decca 417 734-2 [A] **M**

Nocturne No. 1 in D; Variations chromatiques, Op. 3 Gould (pno)
(+ Grieg: *Piano Sonata;* Sibelius: *3 Lyric Pieces, Op. 41; Sonatines
Nos. 1–3, Op. 67*)
Sony CD 52654, 2CDs [A] **M**

BLAKE, Howard (born 1938) ENGLAND

Clarinet Concerto King (cl), ECO, Blake
(+ Lutosławski: *Dance Preludes;* Seiber: *Clarinet Concertino*)
Hyperion CDA 66215 [D] **F**

BLISS, Arthur (1891–1975) ENGLAND

Adam Zero (ballet): *excerpts; Hymn to Apollo; Mêlée Fantasque;
Rout; *Serenade; **The World is Charged with the Grandeur of God*

LSO, Bliss, *Priestman; **Woodland (sop), Shirley-Quirk (bar), LSO Wind & Brass Ensemble, Ambrosian Singers, Ledger
Lyrita SRCD 225 [A] **F**

O *Checkmate* (ballet): *Suite* English Northern PO, Lloyd-Jones (+ Lambert: *Horoscope;* Walton: *Façade*)
Hyperion CDA 66436 [D] **F**

A Colour Symphony; Metamorphic Variations BBC Welsh SO, Wordsworth
Nimbus NI 5294 [D] **F**

Cello Concerto; Hymn to Apollo; **The Enchantress* *R. Wallfisch (vcl), **Finnie (sop), Ulster O, Handley
Chandos CHAN 8818 [D] **F**

Cello Concerto; Introduction & Allegro; Meditations on a Theme of John Blow *Cohen (vcl), RPO, Wordsworth
Argo 443 170-2 [D] **F**

Piano Concerto; March (Homage to a Great Man) *Fowke (pno) RLPO, Atherton
Unicorn-Kanchana UKCD 2029 [D] **M**

*Music for Strings; *Pastorale (Lie strewn the white flocks)* *Jones (sop), Haslam (fl), Sinfonia Ch, Northern Sinfonia, Hickox
Chandos CHAN 8886 [D] **F**

C *Conversations; Oboe Quintet; *Rhapsody; **Rout; **The Women of Yueh* */**Gale (sop), *Rolfe Johnson (ten), Nash Ensemble, Friend
Hyperion CDA 66137 [D] **F**

2 Pieces: Pastoral King (cl), Benson (pno)
(+ Cooke: *Clarinet Sonata;* Howells: *Clarinet Sonata;* Reizenstein: *Arabesques*)
Hyperion CDA 66044 [D] **F**

Clarinet Quintet Hilton (cl), Lindsay Quartet
(+ Bax: *Clarinet Sonata;* Vaughan Williams: *6 Studies*)
Chandos CHAN 8683 [D] **F**

String Quartets: No. 1 in B♭; No. 2 Delmé Quartet
Hyperion CDA 66178 [D] **F**

Viola Sonata; Piano works: 2 Interludes; 4 Masks; Toccata; Triptych Vardi (vla), Sturrock (pno)
Chandos CHAN 8770 [D] **F**

S *Bliss (a one-step); Miniature Scherzo; The Rout Trot; Piano Sonata; Study; Suite; Triptych* Fowke (pno)
Chandos CHAN 8979 [D] **F**

V *A Birthday Song for a Royal Child; *Mar Portugues; River Music; **The Shield of Faith; ***The World is Charged with the Grandeur of God* *Hay (sop), *Carter (alt), **Bowen (ten), ***Finzi Wind Ensemble, Finzi Singers, Spicer
Chandos CHAN 8980 [D] **F**

Morning Heroes Westbrook (narr), RLPO & Ch, Groves
EMI CDM7 63906-2 [A] **M**

BLOCH, Ernest (1880–1959) SWITZERLAND/USA

O *Concerti grossi Nos. 1 & 2; *Schelomo* *Miquelle (vcl), Eastman-Rochester O, Hanson
Philips Mercury 432 718-2 [A] **M**

Violin Concerto; Baal Shem Guttman (vln), RPO, Serebrier
(+ Serebrier: *Momento psicologico; Poema elegiaca*)
ASV CDDCA 785 [D] **F**

An Epic Rhapsody for Orchestra; Concerto Grosso for Strings and Piano Seattle Symphony & Chorale, Schwarz
Delos DE 3135 [D] **F**

3 Jewish Poems VSO, Hendl
(+ Thomson: *Portraits Nos. 1, 17 & 21 etc*)
Bay Cities BCD-1006 [A] **F**

Schelomo; Hebrew Rhapsody Harnoy (vcl), LPO, Mackerras
(+ Bruch: *Adagio on Celtic Themes, etc*)
RCA RD 60757 [D] **F**

Symphony in C# minor; Schelomo Thedeen (vcl), Malmo SO, Markiz
BIS CD 576 [D] **F**

Violin Sonatas Nos. 1 & 2; Baal Shem Friedman (vln), Schiller (pno)
ASV CDDCA 714 [D] **F**

Sacred Service Merrill (bar), Metropolitan Synagogue & New York Community Church Chs, NYPO, Bernstein
(+ Ben-Haim: *Sweet Psalmist of Israel;* Foss: *Song of Songs*)
Sony CD 47533, 2CDs [A] **M**

BOCCHERINI, Luigi (1743–1805) ITALY

Cello Concertos Nos. 1–12 Geringas (vcl), Padua CO, Giuranna
Claves CD50-88146, 4CDs [D] **F**

Cello Concertos: No. 3 in D, G476; No. 11 in C, G573; Symphony in C min., G519; Symphony in D, G521; Notturno (Octet) No. 4 in G Bylsma (vcl), Tafelmusik, Lamon
✧ Sony CD 53121 [D] **F**

Symphonies: in D min. (La casa del diavolo), G506; in A, G498; in A, G508 London Festival O, Pople
Hyperion CDA 66236 [D] **F**

Guitar Quintets: No. 3 in B♭, G447; No. 9 in C, G453 Romero (gtr), ASMF Chamber Ensemble
Philips 426 092-2 [A] **M**

6 Oboe Quintets, G431–6 Francis (ob), Allegri Quartet
Decca 433 173-2 [A] **M**

Piano Quintets: in E♭, G410; in A min., G412; in E min., G415; in C, G418 Les Adieux
✧ DHM GD 77053 [D] **M**

String Quintets: in F min., G274; in E, G275; in D, G276 Smithsonian Chamber Players
✧ DHM RD 77159 [D] **F**

*Cello Sonatas: Nos. 2 & 8–11; *6 Fugues for 2 Cellos, G73* Bylsma (vcl), *Slowik (vcl), van Asperen (hpd)
✧ Sony CD 53362 [D] **F**

BORODIN, Alexander (1833–1887) RUSSIA

Prince Igor (opera): *Polovtsian Dances* LSO, Dorati
(+ Rimsky-Korsakov: *Capriccio espagnol, etc.*)
Philips Mercury 434 308-2 [A] **M**

Symphonies Nos. 1–3; In the Steppes of Central Asia; Nocturne for Strings (arr.); *Prince Igor: Overture & Polovtsian Dances*

Gothenburg SO, Järvi
DG 435 757-2, 2CDs [D] **F**

O *Symphonies: No. 1 in E♭; No. 2 in B min.; In the Steppes of Central Asia* RPO, Ashkenazy
Decca 436 651-2 [D] **F**

C *Piano Quintet; String Quintet; Cello Sonata* Prunyi (pno), Kertész (vcl), New Budapest Quartet
Marco Polo 8.223172 [D] **F**

String Quartets Nos. 1 & 2 Borodin Quartet
EMI CDC7 47795-2 [A] **F**

V *Complete Songs; Prince Igor (without Act 3)* Christoff (bs), Tcherepnin (pno), Lamoureux O, Tzipine
EMI CMS7 63386-2, 3CDs [A] **M**

BORTKIEWICZ, Sergei (1877–1952) RUSSIA/AUSTRIA

O *Piano Concerto No. 1 in B♭, Op. 16* Coombs (pno), BBC Scottish SO, Maksymiuk
(+ Arensky: *Piano Concerto; Fantasia on Russian Folksongs*)
Hyperion CDA 66624 [D] **F**

BOUGHTON, Rutland (1878–1960) ENGLAND

O **Oboe Concerto; Symphony No. 3 in B min.* *Francis (ob), RPO, Handley
Hyperion CDA 66343 [D] **F**

BOULEZ, Pierre (born 1925) FRANCE

O *Dérive; *Mémoriale* *Bell (fl), London Sinfonietta, Benjamin
(+ Benjamin: *Antara;* Harvey: *Song Offerings*)
Nimbus NI 5167 [D] **F**

Éclat-Multiples; *Rituel: In memoriam Bruno Maderna
Ensemble InterContemporain, *BBC SO, Boulez
Sony CD 45839 [A] **M**

Figures, Doubles, Prismes; *Le Soleil des eaux; **Le Visage nuptial
*/**Bryn-Julson (sop), **Laurence (mez), */**BBC Singers, BBC SO, Boulez
Erato 2292-45494-2 [D] **F**

Messagesquisse; Notations Nos. 1–4; Rituel Paris O, Barenboim
Erato 2292-45493-2 [D] **F**

S *Piano Sonatas Nos. 1–3* Helffer (pno)
Astrée (Auvidis) E7716 [A] **F**

Piano Sonata No. 2 Pollini (pno)
(+ Prokofiev: *Piano Sonata No. 7;* Stravinsky: *3 Movements from Petrushka;* Webern: *Variations*)
DG 419 202-2 [A] **F**

V *Le Marteau sans maître; Notations pour piano; Structures pour deux pianos; Livre II* Ensemble InterContemporain, Boulez
Sony/CBS CD 42619 [D] **F**

Pli selon pli Bryn-Julson (sop), BBC SO, Boulez
Erato 2292-45376-2 [D] **F**

BOUZIGNAC, Guillaume (before 1592–after 1641) FRANCE

V *Te Deum; 16 Motets* Les Arts Florissants, Christie
HM HMC 901471 [D] **F**

BOYCE, William (1711–1779) ENGLAND

○ *12 Overtures: Nos. 1–9* Cantilena, Shepherd
Chandos CHAN 6531 [A] **M**

12 Overtures: Nos. 10–12; Concerti grossi: in Bb; in B min.; in Eb
Cantilena, Shepherd
Chandos CHAN 6541 [A] **M**

8 Symphonies, Op. 2 English Concert, Pinnock
✧ DG Archiv 419 631-2 [D] **F**

♩ Anthems: *By the waters of Babylon; I have surely built thee an
house; The Lord is King; O give thanks; O praise the Lord; O where
shall wisdom be found?; Turn thee unto me; Wherewithal shall a
young man* New College Ch, Higginbottom
CRD 3483 [D] **F**

Solomon (serenata) Mills (sop), Crook (ten), Parley of
Instruments & Ch, Goodman
✧ Hyperion CDA 66378 [D] **F**

BRAHMS, Johannes (1833–1897) GERMANY

○ *Piano Concertos Nos. 1 & 2; 7 Fantasias Op. 116* Gilels (pno),
BPO, Jochum
DG 419 158-2, 2 CDs [A] **F**

*Piano Concertos Nos. 1 & 2; Ballades, Op. 10; Piano Pieces, Op.
76; Scherzo, Op. 4* Kovacevich (pno), LSO, C. Davis
Philips 442 109-2, 2 CDs [A] **F**

*Piano Concerto No. 1 in D min., Op. 15; *2 Lieder, Op. 91*
Kovacevich (pno), LPO, Sawallisch; *Murray (mez), Imai
(vla), Kovacevich (pno)
EMI CDC7 54578-2 [D] **F**

Piano Concerto No. 2 in Bb, Op. 83
Gilels (pno), BPO, Jochum
(+ *7 Piano Pieces, Op. 116*)
DG 435 588-2 [A] **M**

Piano Concerto No. 2 in Bb, Op. 83 Richter (pno), CSO,
Leinsdorf
(+ Beethoven: *Piano Sonata No. 23*)
RCA 07863 56519-2 [A] **M**

*Violin Concerto in D, Op. 77; *Double Concerto in A min., Op. 102*
Stern (vln), *Rose (vcl), Philadelphia O, Ormandy
Sony CD 46335 [A] **B**

Violin Concerto in D, Op. 77
Little (vln), RLPO, Handley
(+ Sibelius: *Violin Concerto*)
EMI Eminence CD-EMX 2203 [D] **M**
Szeryng (vln), LSO, Dorati
(+ Khachaturian: *Violin Concerto*)
Philips Mercury 434 318-2 [A] **M**

21 Hungarian Dances VPO, Abbado
DG 410 615-2 [D] **F**

16 Hungarian Dances; Variations on a Theme by Haydn, Op. 56a
LSO, Dorati
(+ Enescu: *Romanian Rhapsody No. 2*)
Philips Mercury 434 326-2

O *Serenades: No. 1 in D, Op. 11; No. 2 in A, Op. 16*
Concertgebouw O, Haitink
Philips 432 510-2 [A] M

*Symphonies Nos. 1–4; Tragic Overture, Op. 81; Academic Festival
Overture, Op. 80; Variations on a Theme by Haydn, Op. 56a*
Cleveland O, Szell
Sony CD 48398, 3CDs [A] B

Symphony No. 1 in C min., Op. 61
Philharmonia O, Klemperer
(+ *Academic Festival & Tragic Overtures*)
EMI CDM7 69651-2 [A] M

*Symphony No. 2 in D, Op. 73; *Alto Rhapsody, Op. 53*
*Lipovsek (cont), *Ernst-Senff Ch, BPO, Abbado
DG 427 643-2 [D] F
*Ludwig (mez), Philharmonia O & *Ch, Klemperer
EMI CDM7 69650-2 [A] M

Symphonies: No. 3 in F, Op. 90; No. 4 in E min., Op. 98
BPO, Karajan
DG 437 645-2 [A] M

*Symphony No. 3 in F, Op. 90; Tragic Overture, Op. 81;
Schicksalslied, Op. 54 Ernst-Senff Ch, BPO, Abbado
DG 429 765-2 [D] F

Symphony No. 4 in E min., Op. 98 VPO, C. Kleiber
DG 400 037-2 [A] F

C *Cello Sonatas: No. 1 in E min., Op. 38; No. 2 in F, Op. 99* Ma
(vcl), Ax (pno)
RCA 09026 61355-2 [A] M

Clarinet Quintet in B min., Op. 115 de Peyer (cl), Melos
Ensemble
(+ *Mozart: Clarinet Quintet*)
EMI CDM7 63116-2 [A] M

*Clarinet Sonatas: No. 1 in F min., Op. 120/1; No. 2 in E♭, Op.
120/2* de Peyer (cl), Pryor (pno)
Chandos CHAN 8563 [D] F

*Clarinet Trio, Op. 114; Horn Trio, Op.40; *Piano Trios Nos. 1–3
Opp. 8, 87 & 101* Leister (cl), Donderer (vcl), Seifert (hn),
Eschenbach (pno), Drolc (vln), *Trio di Trieste
DG 437 131-2, 2CDs [A] M

Horn Trio in E♭, Op. 40 Tuckwell (hn), Perlman (vln),
Ashkenazy (pno)
(+ *Franck: Violin Sonata;* Saint-Saëns: *Romance;* Schumann:
Adagio and Allegro)
Decca 433 695-2 [A] M

Hungarian Dances Nos. 1–21 Alfons & Aloys Kontarsky (pno
duo)
DG 429 180-2 [A] M

Piano Quartets Nos. 1–3 Ax (pno), Stern (vln), Laredo (vla),
Ma (vcl)
Sony CD 45846, 2CDs [D] F

Piano Quintet in F min., Op. 34 Pollini (pno), Italian Quartet
DG 419 673-2 [A] F

Piano Trios Nos. 1–4 Trio Fontenay
Teldec 9031-76036-2, 2CDs [D] F

c *Piano Trio in A, Op. posth.* Trio Fonteney
(+ Schumann: *Piano Trio No. 1*)
Teldec 2292-44927-2 [D] **F**

String Quartets Nos. 1–3 Melos Quartet
(+ Schumann: *String Quartets Nos. 1–3*)
DG 423 670-2, 3CDs [D] **F**

String Quartets Nos. 1 & 2, Op. 51 Gabrieli Quartet
Chandos CHAN 8562 [D] **F**

String Quartets: No. 1 in C min., Op. 51/1; No. 3 in Bb, Op. 67
Borodin Quartet
Teldec 4509 09889-2 [D] **F**

String Quintets: No. 1 in F, Op. 88; No. 2 in G, Op. 111 BPO
Octet
Philips 426 094-2 [A] **M**

String Sextets: No. 1 in Bb, Op. 18; No. 2 in G, Op. 36
Raphael Ensemble
Hyperion CDA 66276 [D] **F**

Viola Sonatas: No. 1 in F min., Op. 120/1; No. 2 in Eb, Op. 120/2;
*Scherzo (from the FAE Sonata) Zukerman (vla/*vln),
Barenboim (pno)
DG 437 248-2 [A] **M**

Violin Sonatas Nos. 1–3 Suk (vln), Katchen (pno)
Decca 421 092-2 [A] **M**

s *Complete Piano Music*
Katchen (pno)
Decca 430 053-2, 6CDs [A] **M**
Jones (pno)
Nimbus NI 1788, 6 CDs [D] **F**

4 Ballades, Op. 10 Michelangeli (pno)
(+ Schubert: *Piano Sonata No. 4*)
DG 400 043-2 [D] **F**

7 Piano Pieces, Op. 116; 3 Piano Pieces, Op. 117; 4 Piano Pieces,
Op. 119 Kovacevich (pno)
Philips 411 137-2 [D] **F**

6 Piano Pieces, Op. 118; 2 Rhapsodies, Op. 79; 16 Waltzes, Op. 39
Kovacevich (pno)
Philips 420 750-2 [D] **F**

Piano Pieces, Opp. 116–9 Kempff (pno)
DG 437 249-2 [A] **M**

3 Piano Pieces, Op. 117; 6 Piano Pieces, Op. 118; 4 Piano Pieces,
Op. 119; 2 Rhapsodies, Op. 79 Lupu (pno)
Decca 417 599-2 [A] **F**

Piano Sonatas: No. 1 in C, Op. 1; No. 2 in F# min., Op. 2
Richter (pno)
Decca 436 457-2 [A] **F**

Piano Sonata No. 3 in F min., Op. 5; Theme and Variations in
D min. Lupu (pno)
Decca 417 122-2 [A] **F**

Piano Sonata No. 3 in F min., Op. 5; 3 Intermezzi, Op. 117
Ax (pno)
Sony CD 45933 [D] **F**

S *25 Variations and Fugue on a Theme by G.F. Handel, Op. 24; 6 Piano Pieces, Op. 118; 2 Rhapsodies, Op. 79* Ax (pno)
Sony CD48046 [D] **F**

11 Chorale Preludes, Op. 122; O Traurigkeit (chorale prelude and fugue in A min., with original version)*; Fugue in A♭ min.* (with original version)*; Preludes and Fugues in A min. & G min.* Bowyer (org)
Nimbus NI 5262 [D] **F**

V *Begräbnisgesang, Op. 13; Gesang der Parzen, Op. 89; Nänie, Op. 82; Alto Rhapsody, Op. 53; Schicksalslied, Op. 54* van Nes (cont), SFSO & Ch, Blomstedt
Decca 430 281-2 [D] **F**

Dein blaues Auge; Dort in den Weiden; Immer leiser wird mein Schlummer; Klage I & II; Liebestreu; Des Liebsten Schwur; Das Mädchen; Das Mädchen spricht; Regenlied; Romanzen und Lieder, Op.84; Salome; Sapphische Ode; Der Schmied; *2 Songs with Viola, Op. 91; Therese, Vom Strande; Wie Melodien; Ziguenerlieder Norman (sop), *Christ (vla), Barenboim (pno)
DG 413 311-2 [D] **F**

Deutsche Volkslieder Schwarzkopf (sop), Fischer-Dieskau (bar), Moore (pno)
EMI CDS7 49525-2, 2CDs [A] **F**

4 Ernste Gesänge; Alte liebe; Auf dem Kirchofe; Feldeinsamkeit; Heimweh II; Nachklang; Verzagen Fischer-Dieskau (bar), Demus (pno)
(+ Beethoven: *Lieder*)
DG 415 189-2 [A] **F**

German Requiem, Op. 45
Margiono (sop), Gilfry (bar), Monteverdi Ch, Orchestre Révolutionaire et Romantique, Gardiner
◇ Philips 432 140-2 [D] **F**
Schwarzkopf (sop), Fischer-Dieskau (bar), Philharmonia O & Ch, Klemperer
EMI CDC7 47238-2 [A] **F**

18 Liebeslieder Wältzer, Op. 52; 15 Neue Liebeslieder Wältzer, Op. 56; 3 Quartets, Op. 64 Mathis (sop), Fassbaender (mez), Schreier (ten), Fischer-Dieskau (bar), Engel (pno), Sawallisch (pno)
DG 423 133-2 [D] **F**

25 Lieder Ameling (sop), Jansen (pno)
Hyperion CDA 66444

25 Lieder von Otter (mez), Forsberg (pno)
DG 429 727-2 [D] **F**

Motets: *Opp. 10, 12, 27, 30, 37, 74, 109–110* (complete)
Corydon Singers, Best
Hyperion CDA 66389 [D] **F**

BRIAN, Havergal (1876–1972) ENGLAND

O *Symphony No. 1 (Gothic)* Jenisová (sop), Pecková (cont), Dolezal (ten), Mikuláš (bs), various choirs, Czech RSO (Bratislava), Slovak PO, Lenárd
Marco Polo 8.2323280/1, 2CDs [D] **F**

Symphony No. 3 BBC SO, Friend
Hyperion CDA 66334 [D] **F**

○ *Symphonies Nos. 7 & 31; The Tinker's Wedding* RLPO, Groves
EMI CDM7 64717-2 [A] **M**

*Symphonies Nos. 10 & *21* Leicestershire Schools SO,
Loughran, *Pinckett
Unicorn-Kanchana UKCD 2027 [A] **M**

BRIDGE, Frank (1879–1941) ENGLAND

○ *Enter Spring* (rhapsody); *Oration (Concerto elegiaco)* *Baillie
(vcl), Cologne RSO, Carewe
Pearl SHECD 9601 [A] **F**

2 Entr'actes; Heart's Ease (arr.); *Norse Legend; *Suite for Cello and
Orchestra* (arr.); *Threads* (incidental music): *2 Intermezzi; The
Turtle's Retort* (arr.); *Vignettes de danse* *Blake (vcl), Chelsea
Opera Group O, Williams
Pearl SHECD 9600 [A] **F**

Suite for Strings
ECO, Garforth
(+ Ireland: *Downland Suite, etc*)
Chandos CHAN 8390 [D] **F**
English String O, Boughton
(+ Butterworth: *The Banks of Green Willow, etc;* Parry: *Lady
Radnor's Suite*)
Nimbus NI 5068 [D] **F**

Phantasm Stott (pno), RPO, Handley
(+ Ireland: *Piano Concerto;* Walton: *Sinfonia Concertante*)
Conifer CDCF 175 [D] **F**

⊂ *Cello Sonata in D min.* R. Wallfisch (vcl), P. Wallfisch (pno)
(+ Bax: *Rhapsodic Ballad;* Delius: *Cello Sonata;* Walton:
Passacaglia)
Chandos CHAN 8499 [D] **F**

*Cherry Ripe; An Irish Melody (Londonderry Air); Sally in our Alley;
Sir Roger de Coverley; String Quartet No. 2 in G min.* Delmé
Quartet
Chandos CHAN8426 [D] **F**

Elegy; Scherzetto Lloyd Webber (vcl), McCabe (pno)
(+ Ireland: *Cello Sonata;* Stanford: *Cello Sonata No. 2*)
ASV CDDCA 807 [D] **F**

Phantasie Trio in C min. Hartley Piano Trio
(+ Clarke: *Piano Trio;* Ireland: *Phantasie Trio*)
Gamut GAMCD 518 [D] **F**

Piano Quintet in D min. Schiller (pno), Coull Quartet
(+ Elgar: *Piano Quintet*)
ASV CDDCA 678 [D] **F**

Piano Trio No. 2 Borodin Trio
(+ Bax: *Piano Trio in B♭*)
Chandos CHAN 8495 [D] **F**

String Quartets: No. 1 in E min.; No. 3 Brindisi Quartet
Continuum CCD 1035 [D] **F**

String Quartets: No. 2 in G min.; No. 4 Brindisi Quartet
Continuum CCD 1036 [D] **F**

▪ *Arabesque; Capriccios Nos. 1 & 2; A Dedication; A Fairy Tale
(Suite); Gargoyle; Hidden Fires; 3 Improvisations; In Autumn; 3
Miniature Pastorals Sets Nos. 1 & 2; A Sea Idyll; Winter Pastoral*

Jacobs (pno)
Continuum CCD 1016 [D] **F**

S *Berceuse; Canzonetta (Happy South); 4 Characteristic Pieces;*
Dramatic Fantasia; Étude rhapsodique; Lament; Pensées fugitives 1,
3 Pieces; 3 Poems; Scherzettino; Vignettes de Marseille (Suite)
Jacobs (pno)
Continuum CCD 1018 [D] **F**

Graziella; The Hour-glass (Suite); 3 Lyrics; 3 Miniature Pastorals
Set 3; Miniature Suite; 3 Sketches; Piano Sonata Jacobs (pno)
Continuum CCD 1019 [D] **F**

BRITTEN, Benjamin (1913–1976) ENGLAND

O *An American Overture, Op. 27; *Ballad of Heroes; The Building of*
the House (overture), *Op.97; Canadian Carnival* (overture), *Op.*
19; **4 Chansons françaises; ***Diversions; Occasional Overture,
Op. 38; Praise we great men; ***/****Scottish Ballad, Op. 26;
Sinfonia da Requiem, Op. 20; Suite on English Folktunes, Op. 90;
***Young Apollo, Op. 16 *Tear (ten), **Gomez (sop),
***Donohoe (pno), Hargan (sop), King (mez), White (bs),
****Fowke (pno),
CBSO & Ch, Rattle
EMI CDS7 54270-2, 2CDs [D] **F**

Cello Symphony, Op. 68 Ma (vcl), Baltimore SO, Zinman
(+ Barber: *Cello Concerto*)
Sony/CBS CD 44900 [D] **F**

*Cello Symphony, Op. 68; Sinfonia da Requiem, Op. 20; **Cantata
Misericordium, Op. 69 NPO, Britten; *Rostropovich (vcl),
ECO, Britten; **Pears (ten), Fischer-Dieskau (bar), LSO &
Ch, Britten
Decca 425 100-2 [A] **M**

Piano Concerto in D, Op. 13; Violin Concerto in D min., Op. 15
Richter (pno), Lubotsky (vln), ECO, Britten
Decca 417 308-2 [A] **M**

Diversions (for the Piano Left Hand) Fleisher (pno), Boston SO,
Ozawa
(+ Prokofiev: *Piano Concerto No. 4;* Ravel: *Piano Concerto for the*
Left Hand)
Sony CD 47188 [D] **F**

Peter Grimes (opera): *4 Sea Interludes and Passacaglia; Variations*
on a Theme of Frank Bridge; Young Person's Guide to the Orchestra
BBC SO, A. Davis
Teldec 9031-73162-2 [D] **F**

Prince of the Pagodas, Op. 57 (ballet in 3 acts) London
Sinfonietta, Knussen
Virgin VCD7 59578-2, 2CDs [D] **F**

Simple Symphony, Op. 4; Variations on a Theme of Frank Bridge,
Op. 10; *Young Person's Guide to the Orchestra, Op. 34 ECO,
*LSO, Britten
Decca 417 509-2 [A] **F**

C *2 Insect Pieces for Oboe and Piano; 6 Metamorphoses after Ovid for*
Solo Oboe; Suite for Harp; Tit for Tat; Folksong arrangements:
Bird Scarer's Song; Bonny at Morn; David of the White Rock;
Lemady; Lord! I married me a wife; She's like a Swallow Watkins
(ob), Ledger (pno), Ellis (hp), Shirley-Quirk (bar)
Meridian CDE 84119 [D] **F**

c *String Quartet in D; String Quartet No. 1; Simple Symphony,*
Op. 4 Britten Quartet
Collins 11152 [D] **F**

String Quartets Nos. 1 & 2 Britten Quartet
Collins 10252 [D] **F**

String Quartet No. 3, Op. 94 Lindsay Quartet
(+ Tippett: *String Quartet No. 4*)
ASV CDDCA 608 [D] **F**

*Cello Sonata, Op. 65; Cello Suites Nos. 1, Op. 72, & 2, Op. 80
Rostropovich (vcl), *Britten (pno)
Decca 421 859-2 [A] **M**

s *Cello Suite No. 3* Isserlis (vcl)
(+ Tavener: *The Protecting Veil; Thrinos*)
Virgin VC7 59052-2 [D] **F**

v *The Complete Choral Works* The Sixteen, Christophers
Volume 1
Collins 12862 [D] **F**
Volume 2
Collins 13432 [D] **F**
Volume 3
Collins 13702 [D] **F**

21 Folksong Arrangements Pears (ten), Britten (pno)
Decca 430 063-2 [A] **M**

A Birthday Hansel, Op. 92; Canticles Nos. 1–5; Sweeter than Roses
(Purcell arr. Britten) Pears (ten), Hahessy (alt), Bowman (alt),
Shirley-Quirk (bar), Tuckwell (hn), Ellis (hp), Britten (pno)
Decca 425 716-2 [A] **M**

*A Boy was Born, Op. 3; Festival Te Deum, Op. 32; Rejoice in the
Lamb, Op. 30; A Wedding Anthem, Op. 46* Unwin (trb), Seers
(sop), Chance (alt), Coxwell (sop), Salmon (ten), Hayes (bs),
Trotter (org), Corydon Singers, Westminster Cathedral Ch,
Best
Hyperion CDA 66126 [A] **F**

**Cantata Academica, Op. 62; **Hymn to St. Cecilia, Op. 27;
***Spring Symphony, Op. 44* *Vyvyan (sop), Watts (cont),
Pears (ten), Brannigan (bs), LSO & Ch, Britten; **London
Symphony Ch, Malcolm; ***Vyvyan (sop), Proctor (cont),
Pears (ten), Emanuel School Boys' Ch, ROHO & Ch, Britten
Decca 436 396-2 [A] **M**

*Canticles Nos. 1-5; (Purcell arr. Britten) An Evening Hymn; In the
Deep, Dismal Dungeon of Despair; Let the Dreadful Engines*
Chance (alt), Rolfe Johnson (ten), Opie (bar), Williams (hp),
Thompson (hn), Vignoles (pno)
Hyperion CDA 66498 [D] **F**

*A Ceremony of Carols, Op. 28; Deus in adjutorium; Hymn of St.
Columba; Hymn to the Virgin; Jubilate Deo in Eb; Missa Brevis in D*
Williams (hp), O'Donnel (org), Westminster Cathedral Ch, Hill
Hyperion CDA 66220 [D] **F**

**A Ceremony of Carols; *Hymn to St. Cecilia; Jubilate Deo in C;
Missa brevis in D; Rejoice in the Lamb; Te Deum in C King's
College Ch, Cambridge, Ledger, *Willcocks
EMI CDM7 64653-2 [A] **M**

*Les Illuminations, Op. 18; *Nocturne, Op. 60; **Serenade for
Tenor, Horn and Strings, Op. 31* Pears (ten), ECO; *Wind

soloists, LSO strings; **Tuckwell (hn), Britten
Decca 436 395-2 [A] **F**

V *Saint Nicholas, Op. 42; Hymn to St. Cecilia, Op. 27* Rolfe
Johnson (ten), Corydon Singers, Warwick University Ch,
ECO, Best
Hyperion CDA 66333 [D] **F**

Spring Symphony; Peter Grimes (opera): Four Sea Interludes
Armstrong (sop), Baker (mez), Tear (ten), LSO & Ch, Previn
EMI CDM7 64736-2 [A] **M**

War Requiem, Op. 66 Vishnevskaya (sop), Pears (ten), Fischer-
Dieskau (bar), Bach Ch, Highgate School Ch, Melos
Ensemble, LSO & Ch, Britten
Decca 414 383-2, 2CDs [A] **F**

War Requiem, Op. 66; Sinfonia da Requiem; *Ballad of Heroes
Harper (sop), Langridge (ten), Shirley-Quirk (bar), *Hill (ten),
St. Paul's Cathedral Choristers, LSO & Ch, Hickox
Chandos CHAN 8983/4, 2CDs [D] **F**

BRUCH, Max (1838–1920) GERMANY

O *Adagio on Celtic Themes, Op. 56; Ave Maria, Op. 61; Canzone.
Op. 55; Kol Nidrei, Op. 47* Harnoy (vcl), LPO, Mackerras
(+ Bloch: *Schelemo; Hebrew Rhapsody*)
RCA RD 60757 [D] **F**

*Violin Concertos Nos. 1–3; Adagio appassionato, Op. 57; In
Memoriam, Op. 65; Konzertstücke, Op. 84; Romanze, Op. 41;
Scottish Fantasy, Op. 46; Serenade, Op. 75* Accardo (vln), LGO,
Masur
Philips 432 282-2, 3CDs [A] **M**

Violin Concerto No. 1 in G min., Op. 26 Stern (vln), Philadelphia
O, Ormandy
(+ Lalo: *Symphonie espagnole*)
Sony/CBS CD 45555 [A] **M**

Violin Concerto No. 1 in G min., Op. 26; Scottish Fantasy, Op. 46
Lin (vln), CSO, Slatkin
Sony CD 42315 [D] **F**

Violin Concerto No. 2 in D min., Op. 44; Scottish Fantasy, Op. 46
Perlman (vln), Israel PO, Mehta
EMI CDC7 49071-2 [D] **F**

Kol Nidrei, Op. 47 Haimowitz (vcl), CSO, Levine
(+ Lalo: *Cello Concerto;* Saint-Saëns: *Cello Concerto No. 1*)
DG 427 323-2 [D] **F**

Symphonies Nos. 1–3; Swedish Dances, Op. 63 (7 only) LGO,
Masur
Philips 420 932-2, 2CDs [D] **F**

BRUCKNER, Anton (1824–1896) AUSTRIA

O *Symphonies Nos. 1–9*
BPO, Karajan
DG 429 648-2, 9CDs [A] **M**
BPO, Bavarian RSO, Jochum
DG 429 079-2, 9CDs [A] **M**

Symphony in F min. Frankfurt RSO, Inbal
Teldec 2292 72300-2 [D] **F**

Symphony No. 0 in D min.; Overture in G min. Berlin RSO, Chailly
Decca 421 593-2 [D] **F**

*Symphonies: No. 1 in C min.; *No. 5 in Bb* BPO, Karajan
DG 415 985-2, 2CDs [D/*A] **F**

Symphony No. 1 in C min. Berlin RSO, Chailly
Decca 421 091-2 [D] **F**

Symphony No. 2 in C min. BPO, Karajan
DG 415 988-2 [D] **F**

Symphony No. 3 in D min.
VPO, Böhm
Decca 425 032-2 [A] **M**
BPO, Karajan
DG 413 362-2 [A] **F**

Symphony No. 4 in Eb (Romantic)
BPO, Barenboim
Teldec 9031 73272-2 [D] **F**
VPO, Böhm
Decca 425 036-2 [A] **M**

*Symphony No. 5 in Bb; *Te Deum* *Mattila (sop), *Mentzer
(mez), *Cole (ten), *Holl (bs), *Bavarian Radio Ch, VPO,
Haitink
Philips 422 342-2, 2CDs [D] **F**

Symphony No. 6 in A NPO, Klemperer
EMI CDM7 63351-2 [A] **M**

Symphony No. 7 in E
BPO, Barenboim
Teldec 9031-77118-2 [D] **F**
VPO, Karajan
DG 429 226-2 [D] **F**

Symphony No. 8 in C min.
VPO, Karajan
DG 427 611-2, 2CDs [D] **F**

Symphony No. 9 in D min.
BPO, Barenboim
Teldec 9031-72140-2 [D] **F**

Symphony No. 9 BPO, Karajan
DG 429 904-2 [A] **M**

String Quintet in F VPO Quintet
(+ Schmidt: *Piano Quintet*)
Decca 430 296-2 [A] **M**

*Masses Nos.1–3; Afferentur regi; Ave Maria; Christus factus est; Ecce
sacerdos magnus; Locus iste; Os justi; Pange lingua; Psalm 150; Te
deum; Tota pulchra es; Vexilla regis; Virga Jesse* Various artists,
Berlin Deutsche Opera Ch, Bavarian RSO & Ch, BPO,
Jochum
DG 423 127-2, 4CDs [A] **M**

EDITORS' CHOICE (see page 15): *Mass No. 1 in D min.; Te Deum*
Rodgers (sop), Wyn-Rogers (cont), Lewis (ten), Miles (bs),
O'Donnell (org), Corydon Singers & O, Best
Hyperion CDA 66650 [D] **F**

*Mass No. 2 in E min.; Libera me; *2 Aequali* *Sheen (tbn),
*Brenner (tbn), *Brown (tbn), ECO Wind Ensemble,
Corydon Singers, Best
Hyperion CDA 66177 [D] **F**

v *Mass No. 3 in F min.; Psalm 150* Booth (sop), Rigby (mez), Ainsley (ten), Howell (bs), Corydon Singers & O, Best
Hyperion CDA 66599 [D] **F**

Motets: Afferentur regi; Ave Maria (1861); Christus factus est; Ecce sacerdos magnus; Inveni David; Locus iste; Os justi; Pange lingua; Tota pulchra es; Vexilla regis; Virga Jesse Corydon Singers, Best
Hyperion CDA 66062 [D] **F**

Requiem in D min.; Psalms 112 & 114 Rodgers (sop), Denley (mez), Davies (ten), George (bs), Trotter (org), Corydon Singers, ECO, Best
Hyperion CDA 66245 [A] **F**

BRUMEL, Antoine (c.1460–c.1515)

v *Missa 'Et ecce terrae motus'; Sequentia 'Dies irae'* Huelgas Ensemble, van Nevel
Sony CD 46348 [D] **F**

BURGON, Geoffrey (born 1941) ENGLAND

v *At the round Earth's imagined corners; But have been found again; Laudate Dominum; Magnificat; Nunc dimittis; A Prayer to the Trinity; Short Mass; This World; Two Hymns to Mary* Chichester Cathedral Ch, Thurlow
Hyperion CDA 66123 [D] **F**

BUSH, Geoffrey (born 1920) ENGLAND

c *Air and Round-O; Dialogue; Trio; Wind Quintet* Bennett (fl), Black (ob), King (cl), Sheen (bsn), O'Neill (bsn), Lloyd (hn), Bush (pno)
Chandos CHAN 8819 [D] **F**

v *The End of Love* (song cycle); *Greek Love Songs; A Little Love Music; 3 Songs of Ben Jonson; Songs of Wonder* Luxon (bar), Cahill (mez), Partridge (ten), Bush (pno)
Chandos CHAN 8830 [D] **F**

Farewell, Earth's Bliss; A Menagerie; 4 Songs from 'The Hesperides'; A Summer Serenade Varcoe (bar), Thomson (ten), Parkin (pno), Westminster Singers, City of London Sinfonia, Hickox
Chandos CHAN 8864 [D] **F**

BUSONI, Ferruccio (1866–1924) ITALY/GERMANY

o *Piano Concerto, Op. 39* Ogdon (pno), John Alldis Ch, RPO, Revenaugh
EMI CDM7 69850-2 [A] **M**

Turandot Suite, Op. 41 La Scala PO, Muti
(+ Casella: *Paganiniana;* Martucci: *Giga, Notturno; Novelette*)
Sony CD 53280 [D] **F**

c *Violin Sonatas: No. l in E min., Op. 29; No. 2 in E min. Op. 36a* Mordkovitch (vln), Postnikova (pno)
Chandos CHAN 8868 [D] **F**

s *Fantasia contrappuntistica; Fantasia after J.S. Bach; Toccata* Ogdon (pno)
Altarus AIR-2-9074 [A] **F**

Suite Campestre; Berceuse; Elegy No. 1; Klavierstuck, Op. 33b/4; Nach der Wendung; Machiotte Medioevali; Sonatatinas Nos. 4 & 6; 2 Bach Chorale Transcriptions Stephenson (pno)
Olympia OCD 461 [D] **F**

BUTTERWORTH, George (1885–1916) ENGLAND

O *The Banks of Green Willow; 2 English Idylls; A Shropshire Lad*
(rhapsody) English String O, Boughton
(+ Bridge: *Suite for Strings;* Parry: *Lady Radnor's Suite*)
Nimbus NI 5068 [D] **F**

V *A Shropshire Lad* (song cycle) Luxon (bar), Willison (pno)
(+ Vaughan Williams: *10 Blake Songs, etc*)
Decca 430 368-2 [A] **M**

BUXTEHUDE, Dietrich (c.1637–1707) GERMANY/DENMARK

C *Trio Sonatas, Op. 1 Nos. 2, 4 & 6; Op. 2 Nos. 2 & 3* Trio
Sonnerie
◇ ASV CDGAU 110 [D] **F**

S *The Complete Organ Works* Saorgin (org)
HM HMX 2901484/8, 5 CDs [A] **B**

V *15 Cantatas* Schlick (sop), Frimmer (sop), Chance (alt), Jacobs
(alt), Prégardien (ten), Kooy (bs), Hannover Knabenchor,
Amsterdam Baroque O, Koopman
◇ Erato 2292-45294-2 [D] **F**

BYRD, William (1543–1623) ENGLAND

S *Galliards: BK 34, 53 & 55; Pavans: BK 17, 54 & 74; Pavans and
Galliards: BK 2–3, 14, 29–32, 60, 70–71 & 114; Preludes: BK 1 &
115* Moroney (hpd)
HM HMC 90 1241-2, 2CDs [A] **F**

My Lady Nevells Booke (complete) Hogwood (hpd)
L'Oiseau-Lyre 430 484-2, 3 CDs [A] **F**

V 3 Anthems: *Praise our Lord; Sing joyfully; Turn our Capacity;* 15
Motets: *Attolite portas; Ave verum corpus; Beata virgo; Christus
resurgens; Emendemus in melius; Laudibus in sanctis; Mass Propers
Nos. 1 (Gaudeamus omnes) & 3 (Justorum animae); Non vos
relinquam; O magnum misterium; O quam suavis; Plorans plorabit;
Siderum rector; Solve iubente Deo; Veni sancte spiritus; Visita
quaesumus* Cambridge Singers, Rutter
Collegium COLCD 110 [D] **F**

Cantiones sacrae: Book 1 New College Ch, Higginbottom
CRD 3420 [D] **F**

Cantiones sacrae: Book 2 New College Ch, Higginbottom
CRD 3439 [D] **F**

Complete Consort Music Wilson (lte) Fretwork
Virgin VC5 45031 2 [D] **F**

Gradualia William Byrd Ch, Turner
Hyperion CDA 66451 [D] **F**

*Great Service in F; Lift up your heads; O clap your hands; O Lord,
make thy servant; Sing joyfully unto God* King's College Ch,
Farnes (org), Cleobury
EMI CDC7 47771-2 [D] **F**

Masses for 3, 4 and 5 Voices
Westminster Cathedral Ch, Hill
Argo 430 164-2 [D] **F**
Tallis Scholars, Phillips
(+ *Ave verum corpus*)
Gimell CDGIM 345 [D] **F**

CAGE, John (1912–1992) USA

C *Amores; Double Music; Third Construction; 4' 33"* Kocsis (pno),
Amadinda Percussion Group
(+ Chavez: *Toccata;* Varèse: *Ionisation*)
Hungaroton HCD 12991 [D] **F**

String Quartet LaSalle Quartet
(+ Lutoslawski: *String Quartet;* Mayuzami: *Prelude;* Penderecki:
String Quartet)
DG 423 245-2 [A] **M**

S *Sonatas and Interludes for Prepared Piano* Takahashi (pno)
Denon C37-7673 [D] **F**

CALDARA, Antonio (c.1670–1736) ITALY

V *4 Cantatas; 2 Sonatas da camera* Lesne (alt), Il Seminario
musicale
Virgin VC7 59058-2 [D] **F**

CANTELOUBE, Joseph (1879–1957) FRANCE

V *Chants d'Auvergne: Series 1–5; *Chants des Pays basques; *Chants
du Languedoc; *Chants paysans* Davrath (sop), studio O, de la
Roche, *Kinsley
Vanguard 08.8002.72 [A] **M**

Chants d'Auvergne (selection) Gomez (sop), RLPO,
Handley
EMI Eminence CD-EMX 9500 [D] **M**

CARPENTER, John Alden (1876–1951) USA

S *Danza; 5 Diversions; Impromptu; Little Dancer; Little Indian;
Minuet; Nocturne; Piano Sonata; Polonaise américaine; Tango
américaine; Twilight Reverie* Oldham (pno)
New World NWCD 328/9-2, 2CDs [D] **F**

CARTER, Elliot (born 1908) USA

O **Oboe Concerto; **Esprit rude/Esprit doux; Penthode; ***A Mirror
on which to Dwell* *Holliger (ob), **Trouttet (cl), **Cherrier
(fl), ***Bryn-Julson (sop), Ensemble InterContemporain,
Boulez
Erato 2292-45364-2 [D] **F**

*Piano Concerto; Variations for Orchestra *Oppens (pno),
Cincinnati SO, Gielen
New World NWCD 347-2 [A] **F**

Concerto for Orchestra; *Violin Concerto; Three Occasions *Bohn
(vln), London Sinfonietta, Knussen
Virgin VC7 59271-2 [D] **F**

C *String Quartets Nos. 1–4; *Duo for Violin and Piano* Juilliard
Quartet; *Mann (vln), Oldfather (pno)
Sony CD 47229, 2CDs [D] **F**

S *Piano Sonata* Lawson (pno)
(+ Barber: *Piano Sonata;* Copland: *Piano Sonata;* Ives: *Three-
page Sonata*)
Virgin VC7 59008-2 [D] **F**

CARVER, Robert (c.1490–1550) SCOTLAND

V *Complete Sacred Choral Music* Capella Nova, Tavener
ASV CDGAX 319, 3CDs [D] **F**

CASELLA, Alfredo (1883–1947) ITALY

○ *Paganiniana, Op. 65* La Scala PO, Muti
(+ Busoni: *Turandot Suite;* Martucci: *Giga, Notturno; Novelette*)
Sony CD 53280 [D] **F**

CASTELNUOVO-TEDESCO, Mario (1895–1968) ITALY/USA

○ *Guitar Concerto No. 1, Op. 99* Hall (gtr), LMP, Litton
(+ Paganini: *Violin Concerto No. 2;* Sarasate: *Ziguenerweisen*)
Decca 440 293-2 [D] **F**

*Guitar Concertos: No. 1, Op. 99; No. 2, Op. 160; *Double Guitar Concerto, Op. 201* K. Yamashita (gtr), *N. Yamashita (gtr), LPO, Slatkin
RCA RD 60355 [D] **F**

Violin Concerto No. 2 (I Profeti) Perlman (vln), Israel PO, Mehta
(+ Ben-Haim: *Violin Concerto*)
EMI CDC7 54296-2 [D] **F**

CENTER, Ronald (1913–1973) SCOTLAND

♪ *6 Bagatelles; Piano Sonata; Suite: Children at Play* McLachlan (pno)
(+ piano works by Scott and Stevenson)
Olympia OCD 264 [D] **F**

CHABRIER, Emmanuel (1841–1894) FRANCE

○ *Bourrée fantasque; España; Gwendoline* (opera): *Overture; Marche joyeuse; Le Roi malgré lui; Danse slave; Fête polonaise; Suite pastorale* Detroit SO, Paray
(+ Roussel: *Suite in F*)
Philips Mercury 434 303-2 [A] **M**

Dix Pieces pittoresques; Bourree fantasque; habanera; Impromptu; Cinq pieces posthumes Planes (pno)
HM HMC 901465 [D] **F**

CHAMINADE, Cécile (1857–1944) FRANCE

Piano Trio No. 1 in G min., Op. 11 Rembrandt Trio
(+ Saint-Saëns: *Piano Trio No.1;* Ravel: *Piano Trio*)
Dorian DOR 90187 [D] **F**

Air à danser; Air de ballet; Contes bleues No. 2; Danse créole; 6 Études de concert: Autumne; Feuillets d'album: Valse arabesque; Guitare; Lisonjera; Lolita; Minuetto; Pas d'écharpes; Pas des sylphes; 6 Pièces humoristiques: Autrefois; Pierette; 6 Romances sans paroles: Souvenance, Idylle, & Meditation; Sérénade; Sous le masque; Toccata Parkin (pno)
Chandos CHAN 8888 [D] **F**

CHARPENTIER, Marc-Antoine (1643–1704) FRANCE

Andromède; Sonate à 8; Suite à 4 London Baroque, Medlam
✧ HM HMC 901244 [D] **F**

Motets: Alma Redemptoris; Amicus meus; Ave regina; Ecce panis angelorum; Hei mihi infelix; O crux ave spes unica; O vere, o bone; O vos omnes; Popule meus; Salve regina; Solva vivebat I and II Concerto vocale
✧ HM HMC90 1149 [A] **F**

Caecilia, virgo et martyr; Filius prodigus; Magnificat Benet (sop), Laplénie (ten), Reinhard (bs), Les Arts Florissants, Christie
✧ HM HMC90 066 [D] **F**

V *In nativitatem Domini nostri Jesus Christi, H414; Pastorale sur la naissance de notre Seigneur Jésus Christ, H483* Les Arts Florissants Vocal & Instrumental Ensembles, Christie
✧ HM HMC90 1082 [A] **F**

In nativitatem Domini nostri Jesus Christi, H416; Pastorale sur la naissance de notre Seigneur Jésus Christ, H482 Les Arts Florissants Vocal & Instrumental Ensembles, Christie
✧ HM HMC90 5130 [A] **F**

3 Leçons de Ténèbres, H96–98; 9 Tenebrae Responsaries Nos. 1–3, H111–113 Concerto Vocale
✧ HM HMC90 1005 [A]

5 Leçons de Ténèbres du Jeudi Sainct: Nos. 1 (De lamentatione Jeremiae), 2 (Matribus suis) & 5 (Ergo vir videns) Concerto Vocale
✧ HM HMC90 1006 [A] **F**

3 Leçons de Ténèbres du Vendredy Sainct, H105–6 & 110 Concerto Vocale
✧ HM HMC90 1007 [A] **F**

Litanies de la Vierge, H83; Missa Assumpta est Maria, H11; Te Deum, H146 Les Arts Florissants Vocal & Instrumental Ensembles, Christie
✧ HM HMC90 1298 [D] **F**

Miserere; O Deus, O salvator noster; Oculi omnium; Paravit Dominus in judico Mellon (sop), Poulenard (sop), Ledroit (sop), Kendall (ten), Kooy (bs), Chapelle Royale O & Ch, Herreweghe
✧ HM HMC90 1185 [D] **F**

CHAUSSON, Ernest (1855–1899) FRANCE

O *Poème, Op. 25*
Perlman (vln), NYPO, Mehta
(+ Ravel:*Tzigane*; Saint-Saëns: *Havanaise; Introduction and Rondo capriccioso*; Sarasate: *Carmen Fantasy*)
DG 423 063-2 [D] **F**
Kremer (vln), LSO, Chailly
(+ Milhaud: *Le Boeuf sur le toit: Le Printemps*; Satie: *Choses vues à droite et à gauche*; Vieuxtemps: *Fantasia appassionata*)
Philips 432 513-2 [A] **M**

*Symphony in B♭, Op. 20; *Poème, Op. 25* *Oistrakh (vln), Boston SO, Munch
(+ Saint-Saëns: *Introduction and Rondo capriccioso*)
RCA GD 60683 [A] **M**

C *Concerto for Piano, Violin and String Quartet, Op. 21* Maazel (vln), Margalit (pno), Cleveland O Quartet
Telarc CD 80046 [D] **F**

Piano Quartet in A, Op. 30; Piano Trio in G min., Op. 3 Les Musiciens
HM HMA90 1115 [A] **M**

S *Quelques Danses, Op. 26; Paysage, Op. 38* Hubeau (pno)
(+ Franck: *Prelude, Aria et Finale, etc*)
Erato 4509 92402-2 [D] **F**

V **Chanson perpétuelle; **Poème de l'amour et de la mer; ***5 Mélodies, Op. 2: Le charme, Le colibri, La dernière feuille, Sérénade italienne, Les papillons* Norman (sop), *Monte Carlo Quartet,

Dalberto (pno); **Monte Carlo PO, Jordan; ***Dalberto (pno)
Erato 2292-45368-2 [D] **F**

CHAVEZ, Carlos (1899–1978) MEXICO

○ *Symphonies Nos. 1 (Sinfonia de Antigona) & 4 (Romantic)* RPO,
Bátiz
(+ Revueltas: *Caminos; Musica para charlar; Ventanas*)
ASV CDDCA 653 [D] **F**

C *Toccata* Amadinda Percussion Group
(+ Cage: *Amores etc;* Varèse: *Ionisation*)
Hungaroton HCD 12991 [D] **F**

CHERUBINI, Luigi (1760–1842) ITALY

○ Overtures: *Les Abencérages; Elisa; Les deux journées; Medée;
Overture in G* ASMF, Marriner
EMI CDC7 54438-2 [D] **F**

C *Horn Sonata No. 2 in F* Tuckwell (hn), ASMF, Marriner
(+ Bellini: *Oboe Concerto;* Donizetti: *String Quartet;* Rossini:
String Sonatas)
Decca 430 563-2, 2CDs [A] **M**

String Quartets Nos. 1–6 Melos Quartet
DG 429 185-2, 3CDs [A] **M**

V *Coronation Mass in A; *Coronation Mass in G; Marche religieuse;
Requiem in C min.; **Requiem in D min.* Ambrosian Singers,
Philharmonia Ch, Philharmonia O, *LPO & Ch, **NPO, Muti
EMI CMS7 63161-2, 4CDs [D/A] **M**

Requiem Mass No. 1 in C min. Berlin Radio Ch, Berlin RSO,
Flor
RCA RD 60059 [D] **F**

CHOPIN, Frédéric (1810–1849) POLAND

○ *Piano Concertos Nos. *1 & **2; Andante Spianato et Grande
Polonaise* (solo version); *4 Ballades; Barcarolle* (mono and stereo
versions); *Berceuse* (mono and stereo versions); *Bólero;
Fantaisie; Fantaisie-impromptu; 3 Impromptus; 51 Mazurkas; 21
Nocturnes; 3 Nouvelles études; 6 Polonaises; Polonaise-fantaisie; 24
Préludes; 4 Scherzi; Piano Sonatas Nos. 2 (mono and stereo
versions) & 3; Tarantelle; 19 Waltzes* Rubinstein (pno), *New
SO of London, Skrowaczewski; **Symphony of the Air,
Wallenstein
RCA GD 60822, 11CDs [A] **M**

*Piano Concerto No. 1 in E min., Op. 11; Ballade No. 1 in G min.,
Op. 23; Nocturnes Nos. 4, 5, 7 & 8; Polonaise No. 6 in A♭, Op. 53*
Pollini (pno), *Philharmonia O, Kletzki
EMI CDM7 64354-2 [A] **M**

*Piano Concerto No. 2 in F min., Op. 21; Andante Spianato et
Grande Polonaise, Op. 22; Krakowiak, Op. 14* Arrau (pno), LPO,
Inbal
Philips 420 654-2 [A] **M**

Les Sylphides (ballet arr.) National PO, Bonynge
(+ Respighi: *Boutique fantasque*)
Decca 430 723-2 [D] **M**

C *Cello Sonata in G min., Op. 65* Hoffman (vcl), Collard (pno)
(+ Rachmaninov: *Cello Sonata*)
EMI CDC7 54819-2 [D] **F**

C *Piano Trio in G min., Op. 8* Fontenay Trio
(+ Smetana: *Piano Trio*)
Teldec 2292-43715-2 [D] **F**

S *Albumleaf; Allegro de concert; Andantino; Barcarolle; Berceuse;
Bólero; 2 Bourées; Cantabile; Contredanse; 3 Écossaises; Fugue in A
min.; *Funeral March; Galop maquis; Hexameron Variations;
Introduction and Allegro in E; Introduction and Rondo;
*Introduction and Variations (1826) for 2 pianos; Introduction and
Variations, Op. 12; Largo; 3 Nouvelles études; Rondos, Opp. 1 & 5;
Rondo in C; Piano Sonata No. 1; Souvenir de Paganini; Tarantelle*
Vladimir Ashkenazy (pno), *Vovka Ashkenazy (pno)
Decca 421 035-2, 2CDs [A/D] **F**

*Ballades Nos. 1–4; Barcarolle; 27 Etudes; 10 Mazurkas; 12
Nocturnes; 2 Polonaises; 25 Preludes; Scherzo No. 3; Piano Sonatas
Nos. 2 & 3; Tarantelle* Perlemuter (pno)
Nimbus NI 1787 [A/D] **F**

*Ballades Nos. 1–4; Barcarolle in F♯, Op. 60; Fantaisie in F min.,
Op. 49* Zimerman (pno)
DG 423 090-2 [D] **F**

Ballades Nos. 1–4; Piano Sonata No. 3 in B min., Op. 58
Demidenko (pno)
Hyperion CDA 66577 [D] **F**

Études, Opp. 10 & 25 Pollini (pno)
DG 413 794-2 [A] **F**

Études, Opp. 10 & 25; Polonaises Nos. 1–7; 24 Préludes, Op. 28
Pollini (pno)
DG 431 221-2, 3CDs [A] **M**

*12 Etudes, Op. 10; Ballades Nos. 1 & 4; Berceuse; Scherzo No. 4; 3
Waltzes Op. 64* Donohoe (pno)
EMI CDC7 54416-2 [D] **F**

*Impromptus Nos. 1–3; Fantaisie-impromptu, Op. 66; Andante
Spianato et Grande Polonaise, Op. 22; Barcarolle, Op. 60; Berceuse
Op. 57; Bólero, Op. 19; 3 Nouvelles études; Tarantelle, Op. 43*
Rubinstein (pno)
RCA RD 89911 [A] **F**

Mazurkas Nos. 1–51 Rubinstein (pno)
RCA RD 85171, 2CDs [A] **F**

Nocturnes Nos. 1–21 Barenboim (pno)
DG 423 916-2, 2CDs [A] **M**

Nocturnes Nos. 1–19 Rubinstein (pno)
RCA RD 89563, 2CDs [A] **F**

Polonaises Nos. 1–16 Ashkenazy (pno)
Decca 421 032-2, 2CDs [D] **M**

Preludes Nos. 1–26; Barcarolle; Polonaise No. 6 Argerich (pno)
DG 415 836-2 [A] **M**

24 Preludes, Op. 28 Pollini (pno)
DG 413 796-2 [A] **F**

*Scherzi Nos. 1–4; Introduction and Variations on a German air
(Der Schweizerbub); Variations on 'Là ci darem la mano', Op. 2*
Demidenko (pno)
Hyperion CDA 66514 [D] **F**

S *Piano Sonatas: Nos. 1–3; 4 Mazurkas, Op. 17; 5 Études*
Andsnes (pno)
Virgin VCK7 59072-2, 2CDs [D] **B**

Piano Sonatas: No. 2 in B♭ min., Op. 35; No. 3 in B min., Op. 58
Pollini (pno)
DG 415 346-2 [D] **F**

Souvenir de Paganini Petrov (pno)
(+ Liszt: *6 Études d'exécution transcendante d'après Paganini*;
Schumann: *6 Studies on Caprices by Paganini, Op. 3*)
Olympia OCD 144 [A]

Waltzes Nos. 1–18 Pommier (pno)
Erato 4509 92887-2 [D] **F**

Collection Various artists
Classics for Pleasure CD-CFP 4501 [A] **B**

CLARKE, Rebecca (1886–1979) ENGLAND

C *Piano Trio* Hartley Piano Trio
(+ Bridge: *Phantasie Trio in C min.*; Ireland: *Phantasie Trio*)
Gamut GAMCD 518 [D] **F**

CLEMENTI, Muzio (1752–1832) ITALY/ENGLAND

O **Piano Concerto in C; 2 Symphonies, Op. 18; Menuetto pastorale*
*Spada (pno), Philharmonia O, D'Avalos
ASV CDDCA 802 [D] **F**

Symphonies: No. 1 in C; No. 3 (Great National); Overture in C
Philharmonia O, D'Avalos
ASV CDDCA 803 [D] **F**

Symphonies: No. 2 in D; No. 4 in D; Overture in D Philharmonia
O, D'Avalos
CDDCA 804 [D] **F**

*Keyboard Sonatas: in F min., Op. 13/6; in B♭, Op. 24/2 (Rondo); in
F♯ min., Op. 25/5; in A, Op. 33/3; in G min., Op. 34/2; Sonatina in
C, Op. 36/3* Horowitz (pno)
RCA GD 87753 [A] **M**

*Keyboard Sonatas: in F♯ min., Op. 25/5; in B♭, Op. 24/2; in G
min., Op. 7/3; in D, Op. 25/6; in F min., Op. 13/6* Katin (fpno)
✧ Athene ATH CD4 [D] **F**

CLÉRAMBAULT, Louis-Nicolas (1676–1749) FRANCE

Premier livre d'orgue: Suite de deuxième ton Alain (org)
(+ Couperin: *Messe à l'usage ordinaire des paroisses, etc*)
Erato 2292-45460-2, 2CDs [D] **F**

*Cantatas: La Mort d'Hercule; La Muse de l'Opéra; Orphée; Pirame
et Tisbé* Rime (sop), Rivenq (bar), Fouchécourt (bs), Les Arts
Florissants O, Christie
✧ HM HMC90 1329 [D] **F**

COATES, Eric (1886–1957) ENGLAND

*Ballad; By the Sleepy Lagoon; London Suite; Three Bears Phantasy;
Three Elizabeths Suite* East of England O, Nabarro
ASV CDWHL 2053 [D] **M**

*By the Sleepy Lagoon; Calling all Workers; Cinderella; Dambusters
March; From Meadow to Mayfair Suite; London Again; London
Suite; The Merrymakers; Music Everywhere; *Saxo-Rhapsody;
Summer Days Suite: At the Dance; Three Bears Phantasy; Three
Elizabeths Suite; The Three Men: Man From the Sea; Wood Nymphs*

    *Brymer (sax), RLPO, Groves; CBSO, Kilbey; LSO, Mackerras
Classics for Pleasure CD-CFPD 4456, 2CDs [A] B

V   *20 Songs* Rayner Cook (bar), Terroni (pno)
ASV CDDCA 567 [D] **F**

COLERIDGE-TAYLOR, Samuel (1875–1912) ENGLAND

V   *Scenes from 'The Song of Hiawatha'* (cantata), *Op. 30* Field (sop), Davies (ten), Terfel (bs-bar), Welsh National Opera O & Ch, Alwyn
Argo 430 356-2, 2CDs [D] **F**

CONUS, George (1862–1933) RUSSIA

O   *Violin Concerto in E min.* Stadler (vln), Leningrad PO, Ponkin
(+ Glière: *Solemn Overture;* Tcherepnin: *Pavillon d'Armide: Suite*)
Olympia OCD 151 [A] **F**

COOKE, Arnold (born 1906) ENGLAND

C   *Clarinet Quintet* King (cl), Britten Quartet
(+ Frankel: *Clarinet Quintet;* Maconchy: *Clarinet Quintet;* Holbrooke: *Eilen Shona*)
Hyperion CDA 66428 [D] **F**

    Clarinet Sonata King (cl), Benson (pno)
(+ Bliss: *2 Pieces;* Howells: *Clarinet Sonata;* Reizenstein: *Arabesques*)
Hyperion CDA 66044 [D] **F**

COPLAND, Aaron (1900–1990) USA

O   *Las Agachadas; Appalachian Spring; Billy the Kid (Suite);*
*Clarinet Concerto; Danzón Cubano; El Salón Mexico; Fanfare for the Common Man; John Henry; Letter from Home; **Lincoln Portrait; Music for Movies; Our Town; Outdoor Overture; Quiet City; Rodeo: 4 Dance Episodes; Symphony No. 3 *Goodman (cl), **Fonda (narr), New England Conservatory Ch, LSO, NPO, Columbia SO, Copland
Sony CD 46559, 3CDs [A] **M**

    Appalachian Spring; Billy the Kid; *Danzón Cubano; *El Salón Mexico LSO, *Minneapolis SO, Dorati
Philips Mercury 434 301-2 [A] **M**

    Appalachian Spring; 3 Latin-American Sketches; Music for the Theatre; Quiet City St. Paul CO, Wolff
Teldec 2292-46314-2 [D] **F**

    Billy the Kid (ballet); *Rodeo* (ballet) St. Louis SO, Slatkin
EMI CDC7 47382-2 [D] **F**

    Clarinet Concerto Stolzman (cl), LSO, Leighton-Smith
(+ Bernstein: *Prelude, Fugue & Riffs;* Corigliano: *Clarinet Concerto;* Stravinsky: *Ebony Concerto*)
RCA 09026 61360-2 [D] **F**

    *Piano Concerto; Dance Symphony; Music for the Theatre; **Organ Symphony; 2 Pieces for Strings; Short Symphony; Statements; Symphonic Ode *Bernstein (pno), **Power Biggs (org), NYPO, LSO, Copland, Bernstein
Sony CD 47232, 2CDs [A] **M**

    Connotations; Dance Panels; Down a Country Lane; Inscape; Latin American Sketches; Music for a Great City; Orchestral Variations;

Preamble for a Solemn Occasion; *Red Pony Suite NPO, LSO, Copland; **NYPO, Bernstein
Sony CD47236, 2CDs [A/D] **M**

○ *Film Music from: The Red Pony; The City; Of Mice and Men; Our Town; North Star; The Heiress; Prairie Journal* (Music for Radio) St. Louis SO, Slatkin
RCA 09026 61699 2 [D] **F**

Symphony No. 3; Music for a Great City St. Louis SO, Slatkin
RCA RD 60149 [D] **F**

S *Old American Songs* (transcribed Marks); *4 Piano Blues; Rodeo; Variations* Marks (pno)
Nimbus NI 5267 [D] **F**

Piano Sonata Lawson (pno)
(+ Barber: *Piano Sonata;* Carter: *Piano Sonata;* Ives: *Three-page Sonata*)
Virgin VC7 59008-2 [D] **F**

♪ *Alone; My Heart is in the East; Night; Old American Songs: Sets 1 & 2; Old Poem; Pastorale; 12 Poems of Emily Dickinson; Poet's Song; A Summer Vacation* Alexander (sop), Vignoles (pno)
Etcetera KTC 1100 [D] **F**

In the Beginning; Motets: *Help us, O Lord; Have Mercy on us, O my Lord; Sing ye praises to our King* Corydon Singers, Best
(+ Barber: *Agnus Dei;* Bernstein: *Chichester Psalms*)
Hyperion CDA 66219 [D] **F**

CORELLI, Arcangelo (1653–1713) ITALY

○ *12 Concerti grossi, Op. 6*
English Concert, Pinnock
♦ DG Archiv 423 626-2, 2CDs [D] **F**
ASMF, Marriner
Decca 430 560-2, 2CDs [A] **M**

: *12 Trio Sonatas, Op. 1; 12 Trio Sonatas, Op. 2* Purcell Quartet, Lindberg Trio
♦ Chandos CHAN 0515/ CHAN 0516, 2 separate CDs [D] **F**

12 Sonatas from Opp. 3 & 4 Purcell Quartet
♦ Chandos CHAN 0526 [D] **F**

12 Violin Sonatas, Op. 5 Locatelli Trio
♦ Hyperion CDA 66381/2, 2CDs [D] **F**

CORIGLIANO, John (born 1938) USA

Clarinet Concerto Stolzman (cl), LSO, Leighton-Smith
(+ Bernstein: *Prelude, Fugue & Riffs;* Copland: *Clarinet Concerto;* Stravinsky: *Ebony Concerto*)
RCA 09026 61360-2 [D] **F**

Flute Concerto; Voyage Galway (fl), Eastman PO, Effron
RCA 07863-56602-2 [D] **F**

Symphony No. 1 CSO, Barenboim
Erato 2292-45601-2 [D] **F**

COUPERIN, François (1668–1733) FRANCE

4 Concerts royaux Trio Sonnerie
♦ ASV CDGAU 101 [D] **F**

Les Nations Cologne Musica Antiqua
♦ DG Archiv 427 164-2, 2CDs [D] **M**

S *L'Art de toucher le clavecin; Livre de clavecin – Book 1 (Ordres 1–5)*
Gilbert (hpd)
HM HMA 190 351/3, 3CDs [A] **M**

Livre de clavecin – Book 2 (Ordres 6–12) Gilbert (hpd)
HM HMA 190 354/6, 3CDs [A] **M**

Livre de clavecin – Book 3 (Ordres 13–19)
Gilbert (hpd)
HM HMA 190 357/8, 2CDs [A] **M**
Baumont
Erato 4509 92859-2, 2 CDs [D] **F**

Livre de clavecin – Book 4 (Ordres 20–27) Gilbert (hpd)
HM HMA 190 359/60, 2CDs [A] **M**

V *Messe à l'usage ordinaire des paroisses; Messe pour les convents de
religieux et religieuses* Alain (org)
(+ Clérambault: *Premier livre d'orgue*)
Erato 2292-45460-2, 2CDs [D] **F**

*Domine salvum; Doux liens de mon coeur; Jacunda vox Ecclesiae;
Laetentur coeli et exultet; Lauda Sion; Magnificat; O misterium
ineffabile; Regina coeli laetare; Tantum ergo; Venite exultemus;
Victoria! Christo resurgenti* Feldman (sop), Poulenard (sop),
Reinhart (bs), Linden (gmba), Moroney (hpd)
✧ HM HMA 190 1150 [A] **F**

3 Leçons de ténèbres; Magnificat; Victoria! Christo resurgenti
van der Sluis (sop), Laurens (mez), Monteilhet (lte), Muller
(gmba), Boulay (hpd)
✧ Erato 2292-45012-2 [D] **F**

COUPERIN, Louis (c.1626–1661) FRANCE

S *Complete Harpsichord Works (Volumes 1–5)* Maroney (hpd)
HM HMA 190 1124/7, 4CDs [D] **M**

Harpsichord Suites: in A min.; C; F; Pavane in F♯
Leonhardt (hpd)
DHM GD 77058 [A] **M**

CROFT, William (1678–1727) ENGLAND

V *Burial Service; Rejoice in the Lord; Te Deum and Jubilate in D*
St. Paul's Cathedral Ch, Parley of Instruments, Scott
Hyperion CDA 66606 [D] **F**

CRUMB, George (born 1929) USA

C *Madrigals – 4 Books; Music for a Summer Evening (Makrokosmos
III)* Musica Varia, Dahlman (pno), Lindgren (pno), Asikainen
(perc), Kuisma (perc)
BIS BIS-CD 261 [D] **F**

CRUSELL, Bernhard (1775–1838) FINLAND/SWEDEN

O *Bassoon Concertino in B♭; *Introduction, Theme and Variations on
a Swedish Air, Op. 12; Sinfonia Concertante for Bassoon, Clarinet
and Horn in B♭, Op. 3* Hara (bsn), *Korsimaa-Hursti (cl),
Lanzky-Otto (hn), Tapiola Sinfonietta, Vänskä
BIS BIS-CD 495 [D] **F**

*Clarinet Concertos: No. 1 in E♭, Op. 1; *No. 2 in F min., Op. 5;
**No. 3 in B♭, Op. 11* Johnson (cl), RPO, Herbig; *ECO,
Groves; **ECO, Schwarz
ASV CDDCA 784 [D] **F**

O *Clarinet Concertos: No. 1 in E♭, Op. 1; No. 2 in F min., Op. 5; No. 3 in B♭, Op. 11* Pay (cl), Age of Enlightenment O
◇ Virgin VC7 59287-2 [D] **F**

C *Clarinet Quartets Nos. 1–3* King (cl), Members of the Allegri Quartet
Hyperion CDA 66077 [A] **F**

CZERNY, Carl (1791–1857) AUSTRIA

C *Fantaisie in F min., Op. 226; Grande sonate brillante in C, Op. 10; Grande sonate in F min., Op. 178; Ouverture caractéristique et brillante in B min., Op. 54* Tal, Groethuysen (pno duo)
Sony CD 45936 [D] **F**

DARGOMIZHSKY, Alexander (1813–1869) RUSSIA

O *Baba-Yaga* (fantasia); *Bolero; Finnish Fantasy; Kazochok* (fantasia); **13 Petersburg Serenades* USSR Academy SO, Svetlanov; *Leningrad Radio & Television Ch, Sandler
Olympia OCD 216 [A] **F**

DAWSON, William Levi (born 1899) USA

O *Negro Folk Symphony* Detroit SO, Jarvi
(+ Ellington: *Harlem*; Still: *Symphony No. 2*)
Chandos CHAN 9226 [D] **F**

DEBUSSY, Claude (1862–1918) FRANCE

O *La Boîte à joujoux* Ulster O, Tortelier
(+ Ravel: *Ma Mère l'Oye*)
Chandos CHAN 8711 [D] **F**

Images; Nocturnes Montreal SO, Dutoit
Decca 425 502-2 [D] **F**

Images; Prélude à l'après-midi d'un faune; Printemps Cleveland O, Boulez
DG 435 766-2 [D] **F**

Images: Iberia (only) CSO, Reiner
(+ Ravel: *Alborada, etc.*)
RCA GD 60179 [A] **M**

Jeux; La Mer; Prélude à l'après-midi d'un faune LPO, Baudo
EMI Eminence CD-EMX 9502 [D] **M**

Jeux; Prélude à l'après-midi d'un faune; La Boîte à joujoux LSO, Tilson Thomas
Sony CD 48231 [D] **F**

La Mer; *Berceuse heroïque; Danse sacrée et danse profane; Jeux; Images; Marche écossaise; Nocturnes; Prélude à l'après-midi d'un faune; Première rhapsodie Concertgebouw O, Haitink, *van Beinum
Philips 438 742-2, 2 CDs [A] **B**

La Mer; Prélude à l'après-midi d'un faune BPO, Karajan
(+ Ravel: *Boléro; Daphnis et Chloë Suite No. 2*)
DG 427 250-2 [A] **M**

La Mer CSO/Reiner
(+ Rimsky-Korsakov: *Sheherazade*)
RCA GD 60875 [A] **M**

Nocturnes; Le Martyre de Saint Sébastien: 2 Fanfares and Symphonic Fragments; Printemps Orchestre & Ch de Paris, Barenboim
DG 435 069-2 [A] **M**

O *Petite Suite; Children's Corner Suite* (orch. Caplet) Ulster O, Tortelier
(+ Ravel: *Le Tombeau de Couperin; Valses nobles et sentimentales*)
Chandos CHAN 8756 [D] **F**

C *Danse sacrée et danse profane; En blanc et noir; Linderaja; Nocturnes* (arr. Ravel); *Prélude à l'après-midi d'un faune* Coombs (pno), Scott (pno)
Hyperion CDA 66468 [D] **F**

Ballade; En blanc et noir; Cortège et air de danse; 6 Épigraphes antiques; Linderaja; Marche écossaise; Petite suite; Prélude à l'après-midi d'un faune; Symphony in B min. Alfons & Aloys Kontarsky (pno)
(+ Ravel: *Piano duet works*)
DG 427 259-2, 2CDs [A] **M**

Cello Sonata; Flute, Viola and Harp Sonata; Violin Sonata; Syrinx; Chansons de Bilitis Nash Ensemble
Virgin VC7 59604-2 [D] **F**

Cello Sonata Rostropovich (vcl), Britten (pno)
(+ Schubert: *Arpeggione Sonata;* Schumann: *5 Stücke in Volkston*)
Decca 417 833-2 [A] **M**

Piano Trio in G Borodin Trio
(+ Martin: *Piano Trio;* Turina: *Piano Trio No. 1)*
Chandos CHAN 9016 [D] **F**

String Quartet in G min. Carmina Quartet
(+ Ravel: *String Quartet*)
Denon CO-75164 [D] **F**

Violin Sonata Takezawa (vln), de Silva (pno)
(+ Ravel: *Violin Sonata [1827];* Saint-Saëns: *Violin Sonata No. 1)*
RCA 09026 61386-2 [D] **F**

S *2 Arabesques; Ballade; Feux d'artifice; L'isle joyeuse; Mouvement; Poissons d'or; Reflets dans l'eau; Suite bergamasque* Adni (pno)
EMI Eminence CD-EMX 2055-2 [A] **M**

Ballade; Berceuse héroïque; Danse (Tarantelle styrienne); Danse bohémienne; D'un cahier d'esquisses; Élégie; Hommage à Haydn; L'isle joyeuse; Masques; Mazurka; Morceau de concours; Nocturne; Page d'album; Le petit nègre; La plus que lente; Rêverie; Valse romantique Fergus-Thompson (pno)
ASV CDDCA 711 [D] **F**

Children's Corner Suite; Estampes; Images: Books I & II; Pour le piano Fergus-Thompson (pno)
ASV CDDCA 695 [D] **F**

Children's Corner Suite; Images: Books I & II Michelangeli (pno)
DG 415 372-2 [A] **F**

Études: Books I & II; Pour le piano Fergus-Thompson (pno)
ASV CDDCA 703 [D] **F**

Études: Books I & II Uchida (pno)
Philips 422 412-2 [D] **F**

Images: Books I & II; 2 Arabesques; Berceuse héroïque; D'un cahier d'esquisses; Hommage à Haydn; L'isle joyeuse; Page d'album; Rêverie Kocsis (pno)
Philips 422 404-2 [D] **F**

24 Preludes (Books 1 & 2) Zimerman (pno)
DG 435 773-2, 2 CDs [D] **F**

S *Préludes: Book 1; 2 Arabesques; Images oubliées* Fergus-Thompson (pno)
ASV CDDCA 720 [D] **F**

Préludes: Book 2; Suite bergamasque Fergus-Thompson (pno)
ASV CDDCA 723 [D] **F**

Suite bergamasque; Estampes; Images oubliées; Pour le piano Kocsis (pno)
Philips 412 118-2 [D] **F**

V *Ariettes oubliées; 5 poèmes de Charles Baudelaire; Chansons de Bilitis* Stutzmann (cont), C. Collard (pno)
(+ Ravel: *Histoires naturelles*)
RCA RD 60899 [D] **F**

*La Damoiselle élue; *L'Enfant prodigue* Cotrubas (sop), Maurice (mez), *Norman (sop), *Carreras (ten), South German Radio Women's Ch, Stuttgart RSO, Bertini
Orfeo C012 821A [D] **F**

Le Martyre de Saint Sébastien McNair (sop), Murray (mez), Stutzmann (cont), LSO & Ch, Tilson Thomas
Sony CD 48240 [D] **F**

DELALANDE, Michel-Richard (1657–1726) FRANCE

O *13 Sinfonies pour les soupers du Roi* Simphonie du Marais, Reyne
◇ HM HMC90 1337/40, 4CDs [D] **F**

V Motets: *Confitebimur tibi, Deus, S59; Jubilate Deo, S9; Te Deum, S32* van der Sluis (sop), Brunner (sop), Ragon (ten), Honeyman (ten), Delétré (bs), Nantes Vocal Ensemble, Grande Écurie, Colleaux
◇ Erato 2292-45608-2 [D] **F**

Motets: *Confitebor tibi Domine, S56; De Profundis, S23; Miserere, S120* Fisher (sop), Johnston (trb), Daniels (alt), Smith (ten), Varcoe (bar), New College Ch, King's Consort, Higginbottom
◇ Erato 2292-45014-2 [D] **F**

Motets: *Dies irae, S31; Miserere mei Deus secundum, S27* Perillo (sop), Kwella (sop), Crook (ten), Lamy (ten), Harvey (bs), Chapelle Royale O & Ch, Herreweghe
◇ HM HMC90 1352 [D] **F**

DELIBES, Léo (1836–1891) FRANCE

O EDITORS' CHOICE (see page 14): *Coppélia* (complete) Lyon Opera Orchestra, Nagano
Erato 4509 91730-2, 2 CDs [D] **F**

Sylvia (ballet) NPO, Bonynge
(+ Massenet: *Le Cid*)
Decca 425 475-2, 2CDs [A] **M**

DELIUS, Frederick (1862–1934) ENGLAND

O *Brigg Fair; Dance Rhapsody No. 2; Florida (suite); Fennimore and Gerda: Intermezzo; Irmelin: Prelude; Marche caprice; On hearing the first cuckoo in spring; Over the hills and far away; Sleigh ride; A song before sunrise; *Songs of Sunset; Summer evening; Summer night on the river* *Forrester (cont), *Cameron (bar), *Beecham Choral Society, RPO, Beecham
EMI CDS7 47509-8, 2CDs [A] **F**

Brigg Fair; Eventyr; In a summer garden; A song of summer Hallé O, Handley
Classics for Pleasure CD-CFP4568 [A] **B**

O *Brigg Fair; In a Summer Garden; On Hearing the First Cuckoo in Spring; Summer Night on the River; A Village Romeo and Juliet: Walk to the Paradise Garden* BBCSO, A. Davis
Teldec 4509 90845-2 [D] **F**

Cello Concerto; *Double Concerto; Paris (The song of a great city) R. Wallfisch (vcl), *Little (vln), RLPO, Mackerras
EMI Eminence CD-EMX 2185 [D] **F**

Violin Concerto; Legende; Suite Holmes (vln), RPO, Handley
Unicorn-Kanchana DKPCD 9040 [D] **F**

*Violin Concerto; 2 Aquarelles; Dance Rhapsodies Nos. 1 & 2; Fennimore and Gerda: Intermezzo; Irmelin: Prelude; On hearing the first cuckoo in spring; Summer night on the river *Little (vln), Welsh National Opera O, Mackerras
Argo 433 704-2 [D] **F**

Fennimore and Gerda: Intermezzo; Irmelin: Prelude; Koanga: La Calinda; On hearing the first cuckoo in spring; Sleigh ride; A Song before sunrise; Summer night on the river; A Village Romeo and Juliet: The walk to the paradise garden LPO, Handley
Classics for Pleasure CD-CFP 4304 [A] **B**

*Piano Concerto; Dance Rhapsody No. 1; Lebentanz; Paris (The song of a great city) *Fowke (pno), RPO, Del Mar
Unicorn-Kanchana DKPCD 9108 [D] **F**

Dance Rhapsody No. 2; *An Arabesque; **Songs of Sunset **Walker, */**Allen, **Ambrosian Singers, RPO, Fenby
Unicorn-Kanchana DKPCD 9063 [D] **F**

Florida (suite); North Country Sketches Ulster O, Handley
Chandos CHAN 8413 [D] **F**

C *Cello Sonata* R. Wallfisch (vcl), P. Wallfisch (pno)
(+ Bax: *Rhapsodic Ballad;* Bridge: *Cello Sonata;* Walton: *Passacaglia*)
Chandos CHAN 8499 [D] **F**

String Quartet Brodsky Quartet
(+ Elgar: *String Quartet*)
ASV CDDCA 526 [D] **F**

S Piano works: **3 Preludes; *Zum Carnival* (polka); Songs: *Autumn; Avant que ti ne t'en ailles; Chanson d'automne; Le ciel est par-dessus le toit; I-Brasil; Il pleure dans mon coeur; In the garden of the Seraglio; Irmelin Roise; Let springtime come; La lune blanche; Silken shoes; So white, so soft; To daffodils; Twilight fancies; The Violet; Young Venevil* *Parkin (pno); Lott (sop), Walker (mez), Rolfe Johnson (ten), Fenby (pno)
Unicorn-Kanchana DKPCD 2041 [D] **F**

V *Durch den Wald; Frühlingsanbruch; Midsummer Song; On Craig Ddu; Sonnenscheinlied; The Splendour Falls; 2 Unaccompanied Part-songs* CBSO Ch, Halsey
(+ Grainger: *Partsongs*)
Conifer CDCF 162 [D] **F**

Hassan (incidental music) Hill (ten), Rayner-Cook (bar), Bournemouth Sinfonietta & Ch, Handley
EMI Eminence CD-EMX 2207 [D] **M**

A Mass of Life; Songs of Sunset; An Arabesque Harper (sop), Watts (cont), Tear (ten), Luxon (bar), LPO & Ch, RLPO & Ch, Groves
EMI CMS7 64218-2, 2CDs [A] **M**

Sea Drift; Florida Suite Hampson (bar), Welsh National Opera O & Ch, Mackerras
Argo 430 206-2 [D] **F**

Song of the high hills; Songs: *The bird's story; Le ciel est par-dessus le toit; I-Brasil; Il pleure dans mon coeur; Let springtime come; La lune blanche; To daffodils; Twilight fancies; Wine roses* Lott (sop), Walker (mez), Rolfe Johnson (ten), Ambrosian Singers, RPO, Fenby
Unicorn-Kanchana DKPCD 9029 [D] **F**

DE SILVA, Andreas (c.1475/80–c.1530) SPAIN

Nigra sum sed formosa (motet) Tallis Scholars, Phillips
(+ Lhéritier: *Nigra sum;* Palestrina: *Missa Nigra sum;* Victoria: *Nigra sum*)
Gimell CDGIM 003 [D] **F**

DIAMOND, David (born 1915) USA

Concerto for Small Orchestra; Symphonies Nos. 2 & 4 Seattle SO, Schwarz
Delos DE 3093 [D] **F**

*Symphony No. 1; *Violin Concerto; The Enormous Room* *Talvi (vln), Seattle SO, Schwarz
Delos DE 3119 [D] **F**

**Kaddish; Psalm; Romeo and Juliet* (incidental music); *Symphony No. 3* *Starker (vcl), Seattle SO, Schwarz
Delos DE 3103 [D] **F**

DICKINSON, Peter (born 1934) ENGLAND

Piano works: *4 Blues; Blue Rose; Concerto Rag; Extravaganzas; Hymn-tune rag; Quartet Rag; Wild Rose;* Songs: *A Red Red Rose; So we'll go no more a-roving; Stevie's Tunes* M. Dickinson (mez), P. Dickinson (pno)
Conifer CDCF 134 [D] **F**

4 Auden Songs; 3 Comic Songs; A Dylan Thomas Cycle; An E.E. Cummings Cycle; Let the florid music praise!; The Unicorns: Lullaby; Interrupted Love Song; The Ballad of St. Brendan M. Dickinson (mez), Hill (ten), Herford (bar), Bowman (pno), P. Dickinson (pno)
Conifer CDCF 154 [D] **F**

DOHNÁNYI, Ernö (1877–1960) HUNGARY

Piano Concertos: No. 1 in E min., Op. 5; No. 2 in B min., Op. 42 Roscoe (pno), BBC Scottish SO, Glushchenko
Hyperion CDA 66684 [D] **F**

Variations on a Nursery Theme, Op. 25; 6 Concert Studies, Op. 28: No. 6 (Capriccio) in F min. Wild (pno), NPO, von Dohnányi
(+ Tchaikovsky: *Piano Concerto No. 1*)
Chesky CD 13 [A] **F**

**Piano Quintet No. 1 in C min., Op. 1; String Quartet No. 2 in Db, Op. 15* *Manz (pno), Gabrieli Quartet
Chandos CHAN 8718 [D] **F**

Pastorale; 4 Pieces, Op. 2; 3 Pieces, Op. 23; 4 Rhapsodies, Op. 11 Roscoe (pno)
ASV CDDCA 863 [D] **F**

7 Piano Pieces, Op. 32a; 4 Rhapsodies, Op. 11 Jando (pno)
Koch 3-1181-2 [D] **F**

DONIZETTI, Gaetano (1797–1848) ITALY

C *String Quartet in D* (arr. Marriner) ASMF, Marriner
(+ Bellini: *Oboe Concerto;* Cherubini: *Horn Sonata;* Rossini:
String Sonatas)
Decca 430 563-2, 2CDs [A] **M**

V *Requiem* Cortez (mez), Pavarotti (ten), Bruson (bar),
Washington (bs), Verona Areana O & Ch., Fackler
Decca 425 043-2 [A] **M**

DOWLAND, John (c.1563–1626) ENGLAND

C *Lachrimae (1604)* Fretwork
Virgin VC5 45005-2 [D] **F**

12 Pieces of Consort Music Extempore String Ensemble,
Weigand
Hyperion CDA 66010 [D] **F**

V *First Booke of Songes* Consort of Musicke, Rooley
L'Oiseau-Lyre 421 653-2 [A] **F**

Second Booke of Songes Consort of Musicke, Rooley
L'Oiseau-Lyre 425 889-2 [A] **F**

Third Booke of Songes Consort of Musicke, Rooley
L'Oiseau-Lyre 430 284-2 [A] **F**

DUKAS, Paul (1865–1935) FRANCE

O *L'apprenti sorcier* BPO, Levine
(+ Saint-Saëns: *Symphony No. 3*)
DG 419 617-2 [D] **F**

S *Piano Sonata in E♭ min.; La Plainte, au loin, du faune; Prélude
élégiaque; Variations, interlude et finale sur un thème de Rameau*
Fingerhut (pno)
Chandos CHAN 8765 [D] **F**

DUPARC, Henri (1848–1933) FRANCE

V *17 Mélodies* Walker (mez), Allen (bar), Vignoles (pno)
Hyperion CDA 66323 [D] **F**

DUPRÉ, Marcel (1886–1971) FRANCE

O *Organ Symphony in G min., Op. 25* Murray (org), RPO, Ling
(+ Rheinberger: *Organ Concerto No. 1*)
Telarc CD 80136 [D] **F**

S EDITORS' CHOICE (see page 15): *Symphonie-Passion, Op. 23;
Evocation, Op. 37* Castagnet (org)
Sony CD 57485 [D] **F**

*Chorale and Fugue, Op. 57; 2 Esquisses, Op. 41; 3 Preludes and
Fugues, Op. 7; Le Tombeau de Titelouze, Op. 38: Te lucis ante
terminum; Placare Christe servulis; Variations sur un vieux Noël,
Op. 20* Scott (org)
Hyperion CDA 66205 [D] **F**

DURUFLÉ, Maurice (1902–1986) FRANCE

S *Fugue sur le Carillon des heures de la Cathédrale de Soissons;
*Prélude, Adagio et Chorale varié sur le Veni Creator, Op. 4;
Prélude et Fugue sur le nom d'Alain; Prélude sur l'introït de
l'Épiphanie; Scherzo, Op. 2; Suite, Op. 5* *St. Paul's Men's Ch,
Scott (org)
Hyperion CDA 66368 [D] **F**

Requiem, Op. 9; 4 Motets sur des thèmes grégoriens, Op. 10 Murray (mez), Allen (bar), Trotter (org), Corydon Singers, ECO, Best
Hyperion CDA 66191 [D] **F**

USSEK, Jan (1760–1812) BOHEMIA

Piano Sonatas: in A min., Op. 18/2; in D, Op. 69/3; in F min. (L'Invocation), Op. 77 Marvin (pno)
Dorian DIS 80110 [D] **F**

UTILLEUX, Henri (born 1916) FRANCE

Cello Concerto Rostropovich (vcl), Paris O, Baudo
(+ Lutoslawski: *Cello Concerto*)
EMI CDC7 49304-2 [A] **F**

Violin Concerto (L'arbre des songes) Stern (vln), FNO, Maazel
(+ Maxwell Davies: *Violin Concerto*)
Sony/CBS CD 42449 [D] **F**

Le Loup (ballet): *Symphonic Fragments* Paris Conservatoire O, Cluytens
(+ Milhaud: *Création du Monde*; Poulenc: *Les Biches*)
EMI CDM7 63945-2 [A] **M**

Symphonies Nos. 1 & 2 BBC PO, Tortelier
Chandos CHAN 9194 [D] **F**

Sonate pour Piano; Figures de resonances; 3 Préludes; Strophes sur le nom de SACHER; 'Ainsi la nuit'; Sonnets de Jean Cassou; Les Citations Joy (pno), Dutilleux (pno), Geringas (vcl), Quatuor Sine Nomine, Cachemaille (bar), Bourgue (ob), Dreyfuss (hpd), Cazuran (db), Balet (perc)
Erato 4509 91721-2, 2CDs [D] **F**

VOŘÁK, Antonin (1841–1904) BOHEMIA

Overtures: *Carnaval; Hussite; In Nature's Realm; My Home; Othello;* Symphonic poems: *The Golden Spinning-wheel; The Noon Witch; Symphonic Variations; The Water Goblin; The Wood Dove* Bavarian RSO, Kubelik
DG 435 074-2, 2CDs [A] **M**

Cello Concerto in B min. Rostropovich (vcl), BPO, Karajan
(+ Tchaikovsky: *Variations on a Rococo Theme*)
DG 415 819-2 [A] **F**

Piano Concerto in G min. Firkušný (pno), Czech PO, Neumann
(+ Janáček: *Capriccio; Concertino*)
RCA RD 60781 [D] **F**

Violin Concerto in A min.; Romance in F min.; Carnaval Overture Midori (vln), NYPO, Mehta
Sony CD 44923 [D] **F**

Serenade for Strings in E; Serenade for Wind in D min. COE, Schneider
ASV CDCOE 801 [D] **F**

Serenade for Strings in E BPO, Karajan
(+ Tchaikovsky: *Serenade for Strings*)
DG 400 038-2 [D] **F**

Serenade for Wind in D min. Nash Ensemble
(+ Kramař: *Octet-Partitas in B♭ and E♭*)
CRD 3410 [A] **F**

16 Slavonic Dances Bavarian RSO, Kubelik
DG 419 056-2 [A] **M**

O *Symphonies Nos. 1–9; *Carnival Overture; *Scherzo capriccioso; *The Wood Dove* BPO, *Bavarian RSO, Kubelik
DG 423 120-2, 6 CDs [A] **M**

Symphony No. 1 in C min. (The Bells of Zlonice); *Legends Nos. 1– Slovak PO, *Slovak RSO, Gunzenhauser
Naxos 8.550266 [D] **B**

Symphony No. 2 in Bb; *Legends Nos. 6–10 Slovak PO, *Slovak RSO, Gunzenhauser
Naxos 8.550267 [D] **B**

Symphony No. 3 in Eb; Carnival Overture; Scherzo capriccioso RLPO, Pesek
Virgin VC7 59257-2 [D] **F**

Symphony No. 4; *10 Biblical Songs *Rayner-Cook (bar), SNO, Järvi
Chandos CHAN 8608 [D] **F**

Symphony No. 5; The Water-goblin SNO, Järvi
Chandos CHAN 8552 [D] **F**

Symphony No. 6 in D Cleveland O, Dohnányi
(+ Janacek: *Taras Bulba*)
Decca 430 204-2 [D] **F**

Symphonies: No. 7 in D min.; No. 8 in G LSO, Dorati
Philips Mercury 434 312-2 [A] **M**

Symphonies: No. 7 in D min.; No. 9 in E min. (From the New World) LPO, Mackerras
EMI Eminence CD-EMX 2202 [D] **M**

Symphony No. 8 in G; Symphonic Variations LPO, Mackerras
EMI Eminence CD-EMX 2216 [D] **M**

Symphony No. 9 in E min., Op. 95 (New World); Slavonic Dances Op. 46/1, 2, 7 & 8; Op. 72/8 Bavarian RSO, Kubelik
DG 439 436-2 [A] **B**

C *5 Bagatelles* Domus
(+ Martinů: *Piano Quartet*; Suk: *Piano Quartet*)
Virgin VC7 59245-2 [D] **F**

From the Bohemian Forest; 10 Legends Thorson, Thurber (pno duo)
Olympia OCD 363 [A] **F**

Piano Quartets: No. 1 in D; No. 2 in Eb Domus
Hyperion CDA 66287 [A] **F**

Piano Quintet in A Curzon (pno), VPO Quartet
(+ Franck: *Piano Quintet*)
Decca 421 153-2 [A] **M**

Piano Trios: No. 1 in Bb; No. 2 in G min. Suk Trio
Denon CO-1409 [D] **F**

Piano Trios: No. 3 in F min.; No. 4 in E min. (Dumky) Suk Trio
Denon CO-1410 [D] **F**

Romance in F min.; 2 Waltzes Lindsay Quartet
(+ Smetana: *String Quartets Nos. 1 & 2*)
ASV CDDCA 777 [D] **F**

4 Romantic Pieces; Violin Sonata in F; Violin Sonatina in G Suk (vln), Holaček (pno)
Supraphon 11 0703-2 [A] **M**

C *16 Slavonic Dances* Thorson, Thurber (pno duo)
Olympia OCD 362 [A] **F**

String Quartets Nos. 1–14; Andante appassionato in F; Cypresses; Quartet Movement in F; 2 Waltzes Prague Quartet
DG 429 193-2, 9CDs [A] **M**

String Quartets: No. 9 in D min.; No. 12 in F (American) Britten Quartet
EMI CDC7 54413-2 [D] **F**

String Quartets: No. 10 in Eb; No. 14 in Ab Lindsay Quartet
ASV CDDCA 788 [D] **F**

EDITORS' CHOICE (see page 14): *String Quartet No. 10 in Eb* Vanburgh Quartet
(+ Janáček: *String Quartets Nos. 1 & 2*)
Collins 13812 [D] **F**

String Quartets: No. 12 in F (American); No. 13 in G Lindsay Quartet
ASV CDDCA 797 [D] **F**

*String Quartet No. 12 in F (American); *String Quintet in Eb* Janáček Quartet, *Vienna Octet members
Decca 425 537-2 [A] **M**

String Quintet in Eb; String Sextet in A Raphael Ensemble
Hyperion CDA 66308 [D] **F**

S *Dumka in C min.; Furiant in G min.; 13 Poetic Tone Pictures; Theme with Variations; 8 Waltzes* Howard (pno)
Chandos CHAN 9044 [D] **F**

Theme & Variations, Op. 36; Poetical Tone-Pictures, Op. 85 Kvapil (pno)
Unicorn Kanchana DKCPD 9137 [D] **F**

V *10 Biblical Songs; Cypresses* (song collection) Langridge (ten), Kvapil (pno)
Unicorn-Kanchana DKPCD 9115 [D] **F**

Mass in D Ritchie (sop), Giles (alt), Byers (ten), Morton (ten), Christ Church Cathedral Ch, Cleobury (org), Preston
(+ Liszt: *Missa Choralis*)
Decca 430 364-2 [A] **M**

Requiem Lorengar (sop), Komlóssy (cont), Ilosfalvy (ten), Krause (bar), Ambrosian Singers, LSO, Kertész
(+ Kodály: *Psalmus Hungaricus; Hymn of Zrinyi*)
Decca 421 810-2, 2CDs [A] **M**

*Stabat Mater; *10 Legends* Mathis (sop), Reynolds (mez), Ochman (ten), Shirley-Quirk (bar), Bavarian RSO & Ch, Kubelik; *ECO, Kubelik
DG 423 919-2 [A] **M**

DYSON, George (1883–1964) ENGLAND

O *At the Tabard Inn Overture; *In Honour of the City; **Sweet Thames, run softly* *Roberts (bar), **RCM Chamber Ch, RPO, Willcocks
Unicorn-Kanchana UKCD 2013 [D] **M**

*Concerto da Camera; Concerto da Chiesa; *Concerto Leggiero* *Parkin (pno), City of London Sinfonia, Hickox
Chandos CHAN 9076 [D] **F**

O *Symphony in G* City of London Sinfonia, Hickox
Chandos CHAN 9200 [D] **F**

C *3 Rhapsodies (for string quartet)* Divertimenti
(+ Howells: *String Quartet*)
Hyperion CDA 66139 [D] **F**

V **Prelude and Postlude; *Psalm-tune Variations on I Was Glad;
*Voluntary of Praise; Benedicte; Evening Service in D; Hail,
Universal Lord; Live forever, glorious Lord; Morning Service in F;
Valour; Vespers* St. Catherine's College Ch, Rees (dir/*org)
Unicorn-Kanchana UKPCD 9065 [D] **F**

*The Blacksmiths; The Canterbury Pilgrims: Suite; Quo Vadis:
Nocturne; 3 Rustic Songs; Song on May Morning; A Spring
Garland; A Summer Day: Suite; To Music* Mackie (ten), RCM
Chamber Ch, RPO, Willcocks
Unicorn-Kanchana DKPCD 9061 [D] **F**

ELGAR, Edward (1857–1934) ENGLAND

O *3 Bavarian Dances, Op. 27; Chanson de matin, Op. 15 No. 2;
Chanson de nuit, Op. 15 No. 1; Dream Children, Op. 43; Salut
d'amour, Op. 12; Serenade lyrique; Soliloquy; Sospiri, Op. 70;
Sursum Corda, Op. 11* Bournemouth Sinfonietta, Del Mar,
Hurst
Chandos CHAN 6544 [A] **M**

*Cockaigne Overture, Op. 40; Introduction and Allegro, Op. 47;
Serenade in E min., Op. 20; Variations on an Original Theme
(Enigma), Op. 36* BBC SO, A. Davis
Teldec 9031-73279-2 [D] **F**

**Cello Concerto in E min.; Froissart, Op. 19; In the South (Alassio),
Op. 50; Introduction and Allegro, Op. 47* *Tortelier (vcl), LPO,
Boult
EMI CDM7 69200-2 [A] **M**

Cello Concerto in E min., Op. 85; *Sea Pictures Du Pré (vcl),
*Baker (mez), LSO, Barbirolli
EMI CDC7 47329-2 [A] **F**

EDITORS' CHOICE (see page 13): *Violin Concerto in B min.,
Op. 61; Introduction and Allegro, Op. 47* Takezawa (vln),
Bavarian RSO, C. Davis
RCA 09026 61612-2 [D] **F**

Violin Concerto in B min., Op. 61 Kennedy (vln), LPO, Handley
EMI Eminence CD-EMX 2058 [D] **M**

*Dream Children; Wand of Youth, Suites Nos. 1 & 2; Starlight
Express* Hagley (sop), Terfel (bs-bar), Welsh National Opera
O, Mackerras
Argo 433 214-2 [D] **F**

*Introduction and Allegro, Op. 47; Serenade in E min., Op. 20
*Allegri Quartet, Sinfonia of London, Barbirolli
(+ Vaughan Williams: *Fantasia on Thomas Tallis; Fantasia on
Greensleeves*)
EMI CDC7 47537-2 [A] **F**

Symphony No. 1 in A♭, Op. 55; Cockaigne Overture, Op. 40
Philharmonia O, Barbirolli
EMI CDM7 64511-2 [A] **M**

Symphony No. 2 in E♭, Op. 63; In the South, Op. 50 BBC SO,
A. Davis
Teldec 9031-74888-2 [D] **F**

Variations on an Original Theme (Enigma), Op. 36; Pomp and Circumstance Marches Nos. 1–5, Op. 39 RPO, Del Mar
DG 429 713-2 [A] **M**

Piano Quintet in A min., Op. 84 Schiller (pno), Coull Quartet
(+ Bridge: *Piano Quintet*)
ASV CDDCA 678 [D] **F**

String Quartet in E min., Op. 83 Brodsky Quartet
(+ Delius: *String Quartet*)
ASV CDDCA 526 [D] **F**

Violin Sonata in E min., Op. 82; Canto populare; Chanson de matin, Op. 15/2; Chanson de nuit, Op. 15/1; Mot d'amour; Salut d'amour, Op. 12; Sospiri, Op. 70; (6) Very easy melodious exercises in the First Position, Op. 22 Kennedy (vln), Pettinger (pno)
Chandos CHAN 8380 [A] **M**

Complete Music for Wind Quintet Athena Ensemble
Volume 1: Harmony Music Nos. 1 & 5; Intermezzo; Adagio cantabile; Andante con variazione
Chandos CHAN 6553 [A] **M**
Volume 2: Harmony Music Nos. 2–4; 6 Promenades; 4 Dances
Chandos CHAN 6554 [A] **M**

Adieu; Carissima; Chantant; Concert Allegro; Danse pensée; Dream Children; Griffinesque; In Smyrna; May Song; Minuet; Pastourelle; Presto; Serenade; Skizze; Sonatina (1889 and 1931 versions)
Pettinger (pno)
Chandos CHAN 8438 [D] **F**

Angelus, Op. 56; Ave Maria, Op. 2/2; Ave maris stella ,Op. 2/3; Ave verum corpus, Op. 2 No. 1; Ecce sacerdos magnus; Fear not; O Land; Give unto the Lord, Op. 74; Great is the Lord, Op. 67; I sing the birth; Lo! Christ the Lord is born; O hearken thou, Op. 64; O salutaris hostia I, II & III Worcester Cathedral Ch, Partington (org), Hunt
Hyperion CDA 66313 [D] **F**

The Apostles (oratorio), *Op. 49* Hargan (sop), Hodgson (cont), Rendall (ten), Roberts (bar), Terfel (bs-bar), Lloyd (bs), LSO & Ch, Hickox
Chandos CHAN 8875/6, 2CDs [D] **F**

Caractacus, Op. 35 Howarth (sop), Davies (ten), Roberts (bar), Wilson-Johnson (bar), Roberts (bs), Miles (bs) LSO & Ch, Hickox
Chandos CHAN 9156/7, 2CDs [D] **F**

*Coronation Ode, Op. 44; The Spirit of England, Op. 80 Cahill (sop), *Collins (cont), *Rolfe Johnson (ten), *Howell (bs), SNO & Ch, Gibson
Chandos CHAN 6574 [A] **M**

The Dream of Gerontius; Sea Pictures Baker (mez), Lewis (ten), Borg (bs), Hallé & Sheffield Philharmonic Chs, Ambrosian Singers, Hallé O, Barbirolli
EMI CMS7 63185-2, 2CDs [A] **M**

The Kingdom, Op. 51; Sospiri, Op. 70; Sursum corda, Op. 11 Marshall (sop), Palmer (mez), Davies (ten), Wilson-Johnson (bar), LSO & Ch, Hickox
Chandos CHAN 8788/9, 2CDs [D] **F**

The Light of Life, Op. 29 Howarth (sop), Finnie (cont), Davies (ten), Shirley-Quirk (bs), LSO & Ch, Hickox
Chandos CHAN 9208 [D] **F**

V *22 Part Songs* Finzi Singers, Spicer
Chandos CHAN 9269 [D] **F**

26 Partsongs Swallow (pno), Ballard (vln), Thurlby (vln),
Worcester Cathedral Ch, Donald Hunt Singers, Hunt
Hyperion CDA 66271/2, 2CDs [D] **F**

Scenes from the Bavarian Highlands CBSO Ch, Markham (pno),
Halsey
(+ Holst: *Dirges and Hymeneal; 2 Motets; 5 Partsongs*)
Conifer CDCF 142 [D] **F**

Sea Pictures, Op. 37; The Music Makers, Op. 69 Finnie (cont),
LPO & Ch, Thomson
Chandos CHAN 9022 [D] **F**

ELLINGTON, Duke (1899–1974) USA

O *Harlem* Detroit SO, Järvi
(+ Dawson: *Negro Folk Symphony;* Still: *Symphony No. 2*)
Chandos CHAN 9226 [D] **F**

The River: Suite (Orch. Collier) Detroit SO, Järvi
(+ Still: *Symphony No. 1*)
Chandos CHAN 9154 [D] **F**

ENESCU, George (1881–1955) ROMANIA

O *2 Romanian Rhapsodies, Op. 11: No. 1* LSO, Dorati
(+ Liszt: *Hungarian Rhapsodies Nos. 1–6*)
Philips Mercury 432 015-2 [A] **M**

Romanian Rhapsody No. 2 LSO, Dorati
(+ Brahms: *16 Hungarian Dances; Haydn Variations*)
Philips Mercury 434 326-2 [A] **M**

Symphonies Nos. 1 & 2 Monte-Carlo PO, Foster
EMI CDC7 54763-2 [D] **F**

C *Piano Quartets: No. 1 in D, Op. 16; No. 2 in D min., Op. 30*
Piedemonte (pno), Voces Quartet
Olympia OCD 412 [A] **F**

*Violin Sonatas: No. 2 in F min., Op. 6; No. 3 in A min., Op. 25;
Sonata Movement* A. Oprean (vln), J. Oprean (pno)
Hyperion CDA 66484 [D] **F**

ESHPAY, Andrey (born 1925) RUSSIA

V *Lenin is With Us* (cantata) USSR Radio Ch and SO, Gusman
(+ Prokofiev: *Festive Poem;* Shostakovich: *October*)
Olympia OCD 201 [D] **F**

FALLA, Manuel de (1876–1946) SPAIN

O *El amor brujo* (ballet); *The Three-Cornered Hat* (ballet) Boky
(sop), Tourangeau (mez), Montreal SO, Dutoit
Decca 410 008-2 [D] **F**

*Nights in the Gardens of Spain; *El amor brujo* (ballet); The Three
Cornered Hat* (ballet)*: Suite* Soriano (pno), Paris Conservatoire
O, de Burgos; *de los Angeles (mez), Philharmonia O, Giulini
EMI CDM7 64746-2 [A] **M**

S *Complete Solo Piano Works* Heisser (pno)
Erato 2292-45481-2 [D] **F**

FAURÉ, Gabriel (1845–1924) FRANCE

O **Fantaisie, Op. 79; Masques et bergamasques suite, Op. 112;
Pavane, Op. 50; Pelléas et Mélisande suite* (incidental music),

Op. 80 *Bennett (fl), ASMF, Marriner
Decca 410 552-2 [D] **F**

C *Piano Quartets: No. 1 in C min., Op. 15; No. 2 in G min., Op. 45; Piano Quintets: No. 1 in D min., Op. 89; No. 2 in C min., Op. 115; String Quartet in E min., Op. 121* Collard (pno), Dumay (vln), Pasquier (vla), Lodéon (vcl), Parrenin Quartet
EMI CMS7 62548-2, 2CDs [A] **B**

Piano Quartets: No. 1 in C min., Op. 15; No. 2 in G min., Op. 45 Ax (pno), Stern (vln), Laredo (vla), Ma (vcl)
Sony CD 48066 [D] **F**

Cello Sonata No. 2 in G min., Op. 117; Apres une reve; Berceuse, Op. 16; Elegie, Op. 24; Papillon, Op. 77; Romance, Op. 69; Sicilienne, Op. 78 Isserlis (vcl), Devoyon (pno)
Hyperion CDA 66235 [D] **F**

Violin Sonatas: No. 1, Op. 13; No. 2, Op. 108 Mintz (vln), Bronfman (pno)
DG 423 065-2 [D] **F**

Ballade in F♯, Op. 49; Mazurka in B♭, Op. 32; 3 Songs without Words, Op. 17; 4 Valses caprices Crossley (pno)
CRD 3426 [D] **F**

Barcarolles Nos. 1–13 Crossley (pno)
CRD 3422 [A] **F**

Barcarolles Nos. 1–13; *Dolly Suite, Op. 56; Impromptus Nos. 1–5; Mazurka in B♭, Op. 32; 8 Pièces brèves, Op. 84; 3 Songs without Words, Op. 17; *Souvenir de Bayreuth; 4 Valses caprices Collard (pno), *Rigutto (pno)
EMI CZS7 62687-2, 2CDs [A] **B**

Impromptus Nos. 1–5; 9 Preludes, Op. 103; Theme and Variations in C♯ min., Op. 73 Crossley (pno)
CRD 3423 [D] **F**

Nocturnes Nos. 1–13; 8 Pièces brèves, Op. 84 Crossley (pno)
CRD 1106/7, 2CDs [A] **F**

Mélodies (selection) Baker (mez), Parsons (pno)
Hyperion CDA 66320 [D] **F**

Requiem; Ave verum corpus, Op. 65/1; Cantique de Jean Racine, Op. 11; Messe basse; Tantum ergo, Op. 65/2 Seers (sop), Poulenard (sop), George (bs), Corydon Singers, Best
Hyperion CDA 66292 [D] **F**

AYRFAX, Robert (1464–1521) ENGLAND

Aeternae laudis lilium; Missa Albanus The Sixteen, Christophers
Hyperion CDA 66073 [D] **F**

ELDMAN, Morton (1926–1987) USA

EDITORS' CHOICE (see page 13): *Piano and String Quartet (1985)* Takahashi (pno), Kronos Quartet
Elektra-Nonesuch 7559 79320-2 [D] **F**

ERGUSON, Howard (born 1908) NORTHERN IRELAND

Piano Concerto Op. 12; *Amore langueo Op. 18 Shelley (pno), *Hill (ten), *London Symphony Ch, City of London Sinfonia, Hickox
(+ Finzi: *Eclogue*)
EMI CDM7 64738-2 [D] **M**

C *Octet, Op. 4; Violin Sonata No. 2, Op. 10; 5 Bagatelles, Op. 9*
Chilingirian (vln), Benson (pno), Nash Ensemble
(+ Finzi: *Elegy*)
Hyperion CDA 66192 [D] **F**

Partita for 2 pianos, Op. 5b; Piano Sonata in F min., Op. 8
Shelley (pno), *Macnamara (pno)
Hyperion CDA 66130 [D] **F**

4 Short Pieces, Op. 6 King (cl), Benson (pno)
(+ Finzi: *5 Bagatelles;* Hurlstone: *4 Characteristic Pieces;*
Stanford: *Clarinet Sonata, Op. 129*)
Hyperion CDA 66014 [D] **F**

V *The Dream of the Rood, Op. 19; Overture for an Occasion, Op. 16; 2
Ballads, Op. 1; Partita, Op. 5a* Dawson (sop), Rayner Cook
(bar), LSO & Ch, Hickox
Chandos CHAN 9082 [D] **F**

FIELD, John (1782–1837) IRELAND

S *Andante in C min.; *The Bear dance in Eb; Grand Pastorale; 3
Sonatas: No. 1 in Eb; *Variations on a Russian air; Variations on a
Russian air (Kamarinskaya); Variations on a Russian drinking
song (My dear bosom friend)* Burnett (fpno) *Fulford (fpno)
✧ Amon Ra CD-SAR 48 [D] **F**

Nocturnes Nos. 1–18 O'Rourke (pno)
Chandos CHAN 8719/20, 2CDs [D] **F**

FINZI, Gerald (1901–1956) ENGLAND

O *Cello Concerto in A min., Op. 40* R. Wallfisch (vcl), RLPO,
Handley
(+ Leighton: *Veris gratia*)
Chandos CHAN 8471 [D] **F**

Clarinet Concerto in C min., Op. 31; Love's Labours Lost
(incidental music), *Op. 21: Suite; Prelude in F min., Op. 25;
Romance in Eb, Op. 11* *Hacker (cl), English String O,
Boughton
Nimbus NI 5101 [D] **F**

Eclogue, Op. 10 Shelley (pno), City of London Sinfonia,
Hickox
(+ Ferguson: *Piano Concerto; Amore langueo*)
EMI CDM7 64738-2 [D] **M**

C *5 Bagatelles, Op. 23* King (cl), Benson (pno)
(+ Ferguson: *4 Short Pieces, Op. 6;* Hurlstone: *4 Characteristic
Pieces;* Stanford: *Clarinet Sonata, Op. 129*)
Hyperion CDA 66014 [D] **F**

Elegy in F, Op. 22 Chilingirian (vln), Benson (pno)
(+ Ferguson: *Octet, Op. 4; Violin Sonata No. 2; 5 Bagatelles*)
Hyperion CDA 66192 [D] **F**

V *All this night, Op. 33; 3 Anthems: God is gone up, Op. 27/2; Lo, the
full, final sacrifice, Op. 26; Magnificat, Op. 36; 7 Partsongs, Op. 17
3 Short elegies, Op. 5; Though didst delight mine eyes, Op. 32; White
flowering days, Op. 37* Bickett (org), Finzi Singers, Spicer
Chandos CHAN 8936 [D] **F**

Song cycles: *Before and After Summer, Op. 16; Earth and Air and
Rain, Op. 15; Till Earth Outwears, Op. 19a; I Said to Love, Op.
19b; A Young Man's Exhortation, Op. 14* Hill (ten), Varcoe (bar)
Benson (pno)
Hyperion CDA 66161/2, 2 CDs [D] **F**

v *Intimations of Immortality Op. 29; *Grand Fantasia & Toccata, Op. 38* Langridge (ten), *Shelley (pno), RLPO & Ch, Hickox
EMI CDM7 64720-2 [D] **M**

FITKIN, Graham (born 1963) ENGLAND

C *Hook; Mesh; Stub; Cud* Ensemble Bash; Icebreaker; Delata
Saxophone Quartet; John Harle Band
Argo 440 216-2 [D] **F**

Log; Line; Load Piano Circus
Argo 436 100-2 [D] **F**

FOSS, Lucas (born 1922) USA

v *Song of Songs* Tourel (sop), NYPO, Bernstein
(+ Ben-Haim: *Sweet Psalmist of Israel;* Bloch: *Sacred Service*)
Sony CD 47533, 2CDs [A] **M**

FOULDS, John (1880–1939) ENGLAND

O *April–England; Le Cabaret (overture); Hellas, a Suite of Ancient Greece; 3 Mantras; Pasquinade Symphonique No. 2* LPO,
Wordsworth
Lyrita SRCD 212 [D] **F**

Dynamic Triptych, Op. 88 Shelley (pno), RPO, Handley
(+ Vaughan Williams: *Piano Concerto*)
Lyrita SRCD 211 [A] **F**

C *String Quartets: No. 9 (Quartetto intimo), Op. 89; No. 10 (Quartetto geniale), Op. 97; Aquarelles, Op. 32* Endellion Quartet
Pearl SHECD 9564 [A] **F**

FRANÇAIX, Jean (born 1912) FRANCE

O *L'Horloge de flore (suite)* de Lancie (ob), LSO, Previn
(+ Ibert: *Symphonie Concertante;* Satie: *Gymnopédies Nos. 1 & 3;* R. Strauss: *Oboe Concerto*)
RCA GD 87989 [A] **M**

FRANCK, César (1822–1890) BELGIUM/FRANCE

O *Le chasseur maudit* (symphonic poem); *Les Éolides* (symphonic poem); *Psyché* (orchestral sections) Basle PO, Jordan
Erato 2292-45552-2 [D] **F**

**Symphonic variations; Prélude, aria et finale; Prélude, choral et fugue; Prélude, fugue et variation, Op. 18* Ciccolini (pno), *Liège O, Strauss
EMI CDM7 64561-2 [A] **M**

Symphony in D min. CSO, Monteux
(+ Berlioz: *Béatrice et Bénédict Overture;* d'Indy: *Symphonie sur un chant*)
RCA GD 86805 [A] **M**

C *Piano Quintet in F min.* Curzon (pno), VPO Quartet
(+ Dvořák: *Piano Quintet in A, Op. 81*)
Decca 421 153-2 [A] **M**

String Quartet in D Ensemble César Franck
Koch Schwann 3-1053-2 [D] **F**

Violin Sonata in A Perlman (vln), Ashkenazy (pno)
(+ Brahms: *Horn Trio;* Saint-Saëns: *Romance Op. 67;* Schumann: *Adagio and Allegro*)
Decca 433 695-2 [A] **F**

S *Prélude, aria et finale; Prélude, choral et fugue; Danse lente; Les Plaintes d'une poupée* Hubeau (pno)
(+ Chausson: *Quelques danses, etc.*)
Erato 4509 92402-2 [D] **F**

3 Chorales; Fantaisie in A; Fantaisie in C, Op. 16; Final in B♭, Op. 21; Grande pièce symphonique in F♯ min., Op. 17; Pastorale in E, Op. 19; Pièce héroïque in B min.; Prélude, fugue and variation in B min., Op. 18; Prière in C♯ min., Op. 20 Murray (org)
Telarc CD 80234, 2CDs [D] **F**

V *Les Béatitudes* (oratorio), *Op. 53* Lebrun (sop), Berbié (mez), Stutzmann (cont), Rendall (ten), Jeffes (ten), Vanaud (bar), Loup (bs), Ottevaere (bs), French Radio Ch, Nouvel PO, Jordan
Erato 2292-45553-2, 2CDs [D] **F**

FRANKEL, Benjamin (1906–1973) ENGLAND

C *Clarinet Quintet, Op. 28* King (cl), Britten Quartet
(+ Cooke: *Clarinet Quintet;* Maconchy: *Clarinet Quintet;* Holbrooke: *Eilen Shona*)
Hyperion CDA 66428 [D] **F**

FRESCOBALDI, Girolamo (1583–1643) ITALY

S *The Complete Toccatas* Hogwood (hpd)
L'Oiseau-Lyre 436 197-2, 2 CDs [D] **F**

V *Il primo libro di Capricci* Leonhardt (hpd), Van Der Kamp (bs)
DHM GD 77071 [A] **M**

FROBERGER, Johann (1616–1667) GERMANY

S *Canzon No. 2; Capriccio No. 10; Fantasia No. 4; Lamentation faite; Ricercar No. 5; Suites Nos. 2, 14 & 30; Toccatas Nos. 9, 10 & 114; Tombeau facit a Paris* Leonhardt (hpd)
DHM RD 77923 [D] **F**

FUCHS, Robert (1847–1927) GERMANY

C *Clarinet Quintet in E♭, Op. 102* King (cl), Britten Quartet
(+ Romberg: *Clarinet Quintet;* Stanford: *Fantasy Pieces*)
Hyperion CDA 66479 [D] **F**

GABRIELI, Giovanni (1557–1612) ITALY

V *Canzon in echo duodecimi toni; Canzon VII; Sonata XVIII a 14; Sonata per tre violini; Sonata pian e forte a 8; Sonata XX a 22;* Motets: *Audite principes; Dulcis Jesu patris; Hic est filius Deus; Jubilate Deo II; Miserere mei, Deus II; O Jesu mi dulcissime II* Taverner Consort, Taverner Ch, Taverner Players, Parrott
◇ EMI CDC7 54265-2 [D] **F**

GADE, Niels (1817–1890) DENMARK

O *Symphonies: No. 1 in C min., Op. 5; No. 8 in B min., Op. 47* Stockholm Sinfonietta, Järvi
BIS BIS-CD 339 [D] **F**

Symphonies: No. 2 in E, Op. 10; No. 7 in F, Op. 45 Stockholm Sinfonietta, Järvi
BIS BIS-CD 355 [D] **F**

Symphonies: No. 3 in A min., Op. 15; No. 4 in B♭, Op. 20 Stockholm Sinfonietta, Järvi
BIS BIS-CD 338 [D] **F**

O *Symphonies: *No. 5 in D min., Op. 25; No. 6 in G min., Op. 32*
*Pöntinen (pno), Stockholm Sinfonietta, Järvi
BIS BIS-CD 356 [D] **F**

C *String Quartets: in F min.; in E min.; in D, Op. 63* Kontra
Quartet
BIS BIS-CD 516 [D] **F**

V *Elverskud, Op. 30; Echoes of Ossian (overture), Op. 1; 5 Songs, Op. 13*
Johanssen (sop), Gjevang (cont), Elming (ten), Danish National
Radio Ch, Danish National RSO, Kitaienko
Chandos CHAN 9075 [D] **F**

GAUBERT, Philippe (1879–1941) FRANCE

C *Ballade; Berceuse; 2 Esquisses; Fantaisie; Madrigal; Morceau
symphonique; Nocturne et allegro scherzando; Romance; Sicilienne;
Sonatas Nos. 1–3; Sonatine; Suite; Sur l'eau* Milan (fl), Brown (pno)
Chandos CHAN 8981/2, 2CDs [D] **F**

GEMINIANI, Francesco (1687–1762) ITALY

O *6 Concerti grossi, Op. 2; 12 Concerti grossi* (based on Corelli's Op.
5): *Nos. 3 & 5* Tafelmusik, Lamon
✧ Sony CD 48043 [D] **F**

6 Concerti grossi, Op. 3 AAM, Hogwood
✧ L'Oiseau-Lyre 417 522-2 [A] **F**

6 Concerti grossi, Op. 7 ASMF, Brown
ASV CDDCA 724 [D] **F**

C *12 Concerti grossi* (based on Corelli's Op. 5): *No. 12 in D min.
(La Folia); 6 Trio Sonatas* (arr. from *Violin Sonatas, Op. 1 Nos.
7–12): *No. 3 in F; No. 5 in A min.; No. 6 in D min.; 12 Violin
Sonatas, Op. 1: No. 3 in E min.; 12 Violin Sonatas, Op. 4: No. 12
in A* Purcell Quartet
✧ Hyperion CDA 66264 [D] **F**

6 Cello Sonatas, Op. 5 Pleeth (vcl), Webb (vcl), Hogwood (hpd)
✧ L'Oiseau-Lyre 433 192-2 [A] **F**

GERMAN, Edward (1862–1936) ENGLAND

O *Welsh Rhapsody* SNO, Gibson
(+ Harty: *With the Wild Geese;* MacCunn: *Land of Mountain and
Flood;* Smyth: *The Wreckers Overture*)
Classics for Pleasure CDCFP 4635 [A] **B**

S *15 Piano Miniatures* Cuckston (pno)
Marco Polo 8.223370 [D] **F**

GERSHWIN, George (1898–1937) USA

O *An American in Paris; *Piano Concerto in F; *Rhapsody in Blue;
Variations on 'I Got Rhythm' Wild (pno), Boston Pops O,
Fiedler
RCA GD 86519 [A] **M**

Girl Crazy (musical): *Suite;* Overtures: *Funny Face; Let 'em Eat
Cake; Oh Kay; Of Thee I Sing; 3 Preludes* (arr. Stone); *Second
Rhapsody* *Votapek (pno), Boston Pops O, Fiedler
Pickwick IMPX 9013 [A] **B**

Porgy and Bess (opera): *Symphonic Picture* (arr. Bennett) Detroit
SO, Dorati
(+ Grofé: *Grand Canyon Suite*)
Decca 430 712-2 [D] **M**

O *Rhapsody in Blue; Second Rhapsody; 3 Preludes, etc.* Tilson
Thomas (pno/dir), LAPO
Sony/CBS CD 39699 [D] **F**

Rhapsody in Blue K. & M. Labèque (pnos), Cleveland O,
Chailly
(+ Addinsell: *Warsaw Concerto;* Gottschalk: *Grande fantaisie;*
Liszt: *Fantasia on Hungarian Themes;* Litolff: *Concerto
symphonique No. 4*)
Decca 430 726-2 [D] **M**

S *Gershwin Songbook; Impromptu in 2 Keys; Merry Andrew; 3
Preludes; Rialto Ripples; Three-Quarter Blues* Achatz (pno)
BIS BIS-CD 404 [D] **F**

Piano transcriptions (arr. Wild): *Fantasy on 'Porgy and Bess';
Improvisation in the form of a Theme and 3 Variations on 'Someone
to watch over me'; 7 Virtuoso Études: I Got Rhythm; Lady be Good;
Liza; Embraceable You; Somebody Loves Me; Fascinatin' Rhythm;
The Man I Love* Wild (pno)
Chesky CD 32 [D] **F**

V *Song Collection* Hendricks (sop), K. & M. Labèque (pnos)
Philips 416 460-2 [D] **F**

GESUALDO, Carlo (c.1561–1613) ITALY

V *Aestimatus sum; Astiterunt reges terrae; Ave, dulcissima Maria; Ave,
regina coelorum; Ecce quomodo moritur; Jerusalem, surge; Maria,
mater gratiae; O vos omnes; Plange quasi virgo; Precibus et meritis
beatae Maria; Recessit pastor noster; Sicut ovis; Sepulto domino*
Tallis Scholars, Phillips
Gimmell CDGIM 015 [D] **F**

41 Madrigals Cologne Collegium Vocale, Fromme
Sony CD 46467, 2CDs [D] **F**

Responsaria et alia ad Officum Hebdonadae Sanctae spectantia
(complete) Hilliard Ensemble
ECM 843 867-2, 2CDs [D] **F**

GIBBONS, Orlando (1583–1625) ENGLAND

V *Almighty and everlasting God; Come, kiss me; First Service:
Magnificat; Nunc dimittis; Hosanna to the Son of David; Lift up
your heads; Now shall the praises of the Lord; O Lord of Hosts; O
thou the central orb; Second Service: Magnificat; Nunc dimittis; See,
see the word is incarnate; Sing of joy unto the Lord; This is the record
of John;* Organ works: *Fantasia; Fantasia in D min.; Voluntary*
Butt (org), King's College Ch, London Early Music Group,
Ledger
ASV CDGAU 123 [D] **F**

GINASTERA, Alberto (1916–1983) ARGENTINA

O *Harp Concerto, Op. 25; Piano Concerto No. 1, Op. 28; Estancia*
(ballet): *Suite, Op. 8a* Allen (hp), Tarrago (pno), Mexico City
PO, Bátiz
ASV CDDCA 654 [D] **F**

Harp Concerto, Op. 25 Masters (hp), City of London Sinfonia,
Hickox
(+ Glière: *Harp Concerto; Coloratura Soprano Concerto*)
Chandos CHAN 9094 [D] **F**

S *The Complete Solo Piano Music & Chamber Music with Piano*
Natola-Ginastera (vcl), Portugheis (pno)

Volume 1
ASV CDDCA 865 [D] **F**
Volume 2
ASV CDDCA 880 [D] **F**

GIULIANI, Mauro (1781–1829) ITALY

O *Guitar Concerto in A, Op. 30* Fernández (gtr), ECO, Malcolm
(+ Vivaldi: *Concerto, RV93, etc.*)
Decca 417 617-2 [D] **F**

C *Duettino facile, Op. 77; Duo; Gran duetto concertante, Op. 52;
Grand Sonata in A, Op. 85; 12 Ländler samt Coda, Op. 75*
Helasvuo (fl), Savijoki (gtr)
BIS BIS-CD 411 [D] **F**

*Divertimenti notturni, Op. 86; Grande Serenade, Op. 82; Serenade,
Op. 127; Variations, Op. 84* Helasvuo (fl), Savijoki (gtr)
BIS BIS-CD 412 [D] **F**

*Duo concertante, Op. 25; Gran duetto concertante, Op. 52; Serenade,
Op. 19* Yamashita (gtr), Galway (fl), Swenson (vln)
RCA 09026-60237-2 [D] **F**

*Grand Potpourri, Op. 126; Grand Potpourri, Op. 53; Pièces faciles
et agréables, Op. 74; Potpourri tiré de l'opéra 'Tancredi', Op. 76; 6
Variations, Op. 81* Helasvuo (fl), Savijoki (gtr)
BIS BIS-CD 413 [D] **F**

GLASS, Philip (born 1937) USA

O *Anima Mundi* (film score) Various artists, Riesman
Elektra-Nonesuch 7559 79329-2 [D] **F**

Violin Concerto Kremer (vln), VPO, von Dohnányi
(+ Schnittke: *Concerto grosso No. 5*)
DG 437 091-2 [D] **F**

Dances 1–5 Philip Glass Ensemble, Riesman
Sony CD 44765, 2 CDs [A] **F**

Low Symphony (with Bowie & Eno) Brooklyn PO, Davies
Philips 438 150-2 [D] **F**

Itaipu; The Canyon Atlanta SO & Ch, Shaw
Sony CD 46352 [D] **F**

S *Mad Rush; Metamorphosis 1–5; Wichita Vortex Sutra* Glass (pno)
Sony CD 45576 [D] **F**

GLAZUNOV, Alexander (1865–1936) RUSSIA

O *Chant du ménestrel, Op. 71* R. Wallfisch (vcl), LPO, Thomson
(+ Kabalevsky: *Cello Concerto No. 2;* Khachaturian: *Cello
Concerto*)
Chandos CHAN 8579 [D] **F**

*Violin Concerto in A min., Op. 82 Heifetz (vln), RCA Victor
SO, Hendl
(+ Prokofiev: *Violin Concerto No. 2;* Sibelius: *Violin Concerto*)
RCA RD 87019 [A] **F**

March on a Russian Theme, Op. 76; *The Sea (fantasy), *Op. 28;
**Les Ruses d'amour* (ballet), *Op. 61* USSR Ministry of
Defence Symphonic Band, Maltsiev; *USSR Radio SO,
Provatorov, **Zuraitis
Olympia OCD 141 [A] **F**

Raymonda (ballet – highlights) SNO, Järvi
Chandos CHAN 8447 [D] **F**

O   *The Sea* (fantasy), *Op. 28; Spring, Op. 34* SNO, Järvi
    (+ Kalinnikov: *Symphony No. 1*)
    Chandos CHAN 8611 [D] **F**

    *Symphonies: No. 1 in E (Slavyanskaya), Op. 5; No. 7 in F
    (Pastoral'naya), Op. 77* USSR Ministry of Culture SO,
    Rozhdestvensky
    Olympia OCD 100 [D] **F**

    ***Symphony No. 2 in F# min., Op. 16; Intermezzo romantico, Op.
    69; *Stenka Razin (symphonic poem), Op. 13* USSR Radio SO,
    Dimitriedi; *USSR State Academy SO; **USSR Ministry of
    Culture SO, Rozhdestvensky
    Olympia OCD 119 [D] **F**

    **Symphony No. 3 in D, Op. 33; Lyric poem, Op. 12; Solemn
    Procession* USSR Radio SO, Dimitriedi; *USSR Ministry of
    Culture SO, Rozhdestvensky
    Olympia OCD 120 [D] **F**

    Symphonies: No. 4 in Eb, Op. 48; No. 5 in Bb, Op. 55 USSR
    Ministry of Culture SO, Rozhdestvensky
    Olympia OCD 101 [D] **F**

    **Symphony No. 6 in C min., Op. 58; Scènes de Ballet (suite), Op. 52*
    USSR Radio SO, *USSR Ministry of Culture SO,
    Rozhdestvensky
    Olympia OCD 104 [A/*D] **F**

    **Symphony No. 8 in Eb, Op. 83; Ballade in F, Op. 78; Slav
    Holiday in G, Op. 26a* USSR SO, Dimitriedi; *USSR Ministry
    of Culture SO, Rozhdestvensky
    Olympia OCD 130 [D] **F**

    Symphony No. 9 in D (unfinished) USSR RSO, Yudin
    (+ Kabalevsky: *Romeo and Juliet;* Lvov: *Violin Concerto*)
    Olympia OCD 147 [A] **F**

C   *Novelettes Nos. 1–4* Shostakovich Quartet
    (+ Glinka: *String Quartets*)
    Olympia OCD 524 [D] **F**

    String Quartets Nos. 2 & 4 Shostakovich Quartet
    Olympia OCD 173 [A] **F**

    String Quartets Nos. 3 & 5; Kuranta Shostakovich Quartet
    Olympia OCD 525 [D] **F**

    String Quartets Nos. 6 & 7 Shostakovich Quartet
    Olympia OCD 526 [D] **F**

S   *Grand Concert Waltz in Eb, Op. 41; Piano Sonatas: No. 1 in Bb
    min., Op. 74; No. 2 in Eb, Op. 75* Howard (pno)
    Pearl SHECD 9538 [A] **F**

GLIÈRE, Reyngo'ld (1875–1956) RUSSIA

O   *Harp Concerto; Coloratura Soprano Concerto* Masters (hp),
    Hulse (sop), City of London Sinfonia, Hickox
    (+ Ginastera: *Harp Concerto*)
    Chandos CHAN 9094 [D] **F**

    Solemn Overture, Op. 72 USSR Academy SO, Svetlanov
    (+ Conus: *Violin Concerto in E min.;* Tcherepnin: *Pavillon
    d'Armide Suite*)
    Olympia OCD 151 [A] **F**

Symphony No. 1 in E♭, Op. 8; The Red Poppy (ballet): *Suite* BBC PO, Downes
Chandos CHAN 9160 [D] **F**

Symphony No. 2 in C min., Op. 25; The Zaporozhy Cossacks, Op. 64 BBC PO, Downes
Chandos CHAN 9071 [D] **F**

Symphony No. 3 (Il'ya Mouromets), Op. 42 BBC PO, Downes
Chandos CHAN 9041 [D] **F**

GLINKA, Mikhail (1804–1857) RUSSIA

Ruslan and Lyudmila (opera): *Overture* CSO, Reiner
(+ Prokofiev: *Lieutenant Kijé; Alexander Nevsky*)
RCA GD 60176 [A] **M**

*Divertimento brillant on themes from Bellini's 'La Sonnambula'; String Quartet in F; **Valse-fantaisie in B min. *Shakin (pno), *Yakovlev (pno), Leningrad PO Quartet; **Kamishov (db)
(+ Alabiev: *Violin Sonata*)
Olympia OCD 184 [A] **F**

Grand Sextet in E♭ Capricorn
(+ Rimsky-Korsakov: *Piano and Wind Quintet*)
Hyperion CDA 66163 [A] **F**

String Quartets: in F; in D Shostakovich Quartet
(+ Glazunov: *Novelettes*)
Olympia OCD 524 [D] **F**

Viola Sonata Bashmet (vla), Muntian (pno)
(+ Roslavets: *Viola Sonata No.1;* Shostakovich: *Viola Sonata*)
RCA 09026 61273-2 [D] **F**

Trio pathétique in D min. Borodin Trio
(+ Arensky: *Piano Trio No. 1*)
Chandos CHAN 8477 [D] **F**

19 Piano Miniatures Kamishov (pno)
Olympia OCD 124 [A] **F**

GLUCK, Christoph Willibald (1714–1787) BOHEMIA

Don Juan (pantomime); *Semiramis* (ballet) Tafelmusik, Weil
✧ Sony CD 53119 [D] **F**

GODOWSKY, Leopold (1870–1938) POLAND/USA

Piano transcriptions: Godowsky: *Passacaglia; Alt Wien;* Schubert: *Das Wandern; Ungeduld; Gute Nacht; Rosamunde: Ballet Music; Moments musicaux No. 3 in F min.;* Weber: *Invitation to the Dance, J260;* J. Strauss II: *Artist's Life, Op. 316* De Waal (pno)
Hyperion CDA 66496 [D] **F**

Piano Transcriptions of Chopin's Etudes and Waltzes Bolet (pno)
Decca 425 059-2 [A] **M**

GOEHR, Alexander (born 1932) ENGLAND

...a musical offering (J.S.B. 1985), Op. 46; Lyric Pieces, Op. 35; Sinfonia, Op. 42; *Behold the Sun (concert aria) *Thames (sop), *Holland (vib), London Sinfonietta, Knussen
Unicorn-Kanchana DKPCD 9102 [D] **F**

Metamorphosis Dance, Op. 36; Romanza, Op. 24 Welsh (vcl), RLPO, Atherton
Unicorn-Kanchana UKCD 2039 [D] **M**

V *The Death of Moses* Chance (alt), Richardson (bar), Leonard (sop), Rangarajan (ten), Robinson (bs), Cambridge University Ch, Instrumental Ensemble, S. Cleobury
Unicorn-Kanchana DKPCD 9146 [D] **F**

GORECKI, Henryk (born 1933) POLAND

O *Symphony No. 1 (1959), Op. 14; Choros I, Op. 20; 3 Pieces in Olde Style* Krakow PO, Bader
Koch Schwann 310412 [D] **F**

Symphony No. 3, Op. 36 Upshaw (sop), London Sinfonietta, Zinman
Elektra-Nonesuch 7559-79282-2 [D] **F**

C *String Quartet No. 1; Already it is Dusk; *Lerchenmusik, Op. 53* *Collins (cl), *van Kampen (vcl), Kronos Quartet
Elektra-Nonesuch 7559-79257-2 [D] **F**

V *Beatus Vir; Old Polish Music; Totus Tuus* Sotrojev (bs), Prague Philharmonic Ch, Czech PO, Nelson
Argo 436 835-2 [D] **F**

GOTTSCHALK, Louis (1829–1869) USA

O *Grande fantaisie triomphale sur l'hymne national brésilien* Ortiz (pno), RPO, Atzmon
(+ Addinsell: *Warsaw Concerto;* Gershwin: *Rhapsody in Blue;* Liszt: *Fantasia on Hungarian Themes;* Litolff: *Concerto symphonique No. 4*)
Decca 430 726-2 [D] **M**

Cakewalk (ballet arr. Kay) Louisville O, Mester
(+ Piston: *The Incredible Flutist*)
Albany TROY 016-2 [A] **F**

C *Piano Music for Four Hands* Marks, Barrett (pno duo)
Nimbus NI 5324 [D] **F**

S Piano works: *Ballade; Berceuse; Caprice-Polka; Grand Scherzo; L Jota aragonese; Manchega; Marche de nuit; Misère du trovatore; Pasquinade; Polka in A♭; Polka in B♭; La Savane; Scherzo romantique; Souvenir d'Andalousie; Souvenir de Lima; Sui moi!* Ynes Martin (pno)
Hyperion CDA 66697 [D] **F**

Ballade No. 6; Le Bananier; Le Banjo; Canto del Gitano; Columbia: caprice américain; Danza; La Mancenillier; Mazurka; Minuit à Seville; Ojos Criollos; Romance; Souvenir de la Havane; Souvenir de Puerto Rico; Union Martin (pno)
Hyperion CDA 66459 [D] **F**

GOULD, Morton (born 1913) USA

O *American Symphonette No. 2; Columbia – Broadsides for Orchestra on Columbian Themes; Viola Concerto; Flourishes and Galop; Housewarming; Soundings; Symphony of Spirituals* Glazer (vla), Louisville O, Mester
Albany TROY 013/4, 2CDs [D] **F**

Fall River Legend (ballet): *Suite; Spirituals* Eastman-Rochester O, Hanson
(+ Barber: *Medea: Suite*)
Philips Mercury 432 016-2 [A] **M**

V *A capella; Of Time and the River; *Quotations* Gregg Smith Singers, Smith; *NY Society O & Ch, Goodwin
Koch 37026-2 [D] **F**

GOUNOD, Charles (1818–1893) FRANCE

> *Symphonies: No. 1 in D; No. 2 in E♭* Toulouse Capitole O,
> Plasson
> EMI CDM7 63949-2 [A] **M**

Biondina (song cycle); *29 Songs* Lott (sop), Murray (mez),
Rolfe Johnson (ten), Johnson (pno)
Hyperion CDA 66801/2, 2 CDs [D] **F**

Messe solennelle de Sainte Cécile
Seefried (sop), Stolze (ten), Uhde (bar), Czech PO & Ch,
Markevitch
DG 427 409-2 [A] **M**

Mors et vita Hendricks (sop), van Dam (bs), Denize (cont),
Aler (ten), Orféon Donostiarra, Toulouse Capitale O,
Plasson
EMI CDS7 54459-2, 2CDs [D] **F**

GOUVY, Louis Theodore (1819–1898) FRANCE

Works for Piano Duet: *Aubade; Ghiribizzi; 6 Morceaux; Scherzo;
Sonatas: in C min.; in D min.; in F* Duo Tal & Groethuysen
Sony CD 53110 [D] **F**

GRAINGER, Percy (1882–1961) AUSTRALIA/USA

*Andante con moto; Arrival Platform Humlet; Bridal Lullaby;
Children's March; Colonial Song; English Waltz; Gay but wistful;
The Gum-suckers' March; Handel in the Strand; Harvest Hymn; The
Immovable 'Do'; In a Nutshell (suite); In Dahomey; Mock Morris;
Pastoral; Peace; Sailor's Song; Saxon Twi-play; To a Nordic
Princess; Walking Tune* Jones (pno)
Nimbus NI 5220 [D] **F**

Arrangements of: Bach: *Blithe bells;* Brahms: *Cradle Song;*
Dowland: *Now, o now, I needs must part;* Elgar: *Nimrod;* Foster:
Lullaby; The rag-time girl; Gershwin: *Love walked in; The man I
love;* Rachmaninov: *Finale of the Second Piano Concerto
[abridged];* R. Strauss: *Ramble on the last love-duet from 'Der
Rosenkavalier';* Tchaikovsky: *Opening of the First Piano Concerto;
Paraphrase on the Waltz of the Flowers;* Traditional (Chinese):
Beautiful fresh flower Jones (pno)
Nimbus NI 5232 [D] **F**

29 Folksong Arrangements Jones (pno)
Nimbus NI 5244 [D] **F**

*Angelus ad virginem; Bigelow march; Eastern intermezzo;
Klavierstücke in A min., B♭, D & E; Lullaby; Tiger-tiger* Jones
(pno)
Nimbus NI 5255 [D] **F**

*Australian up-country song; Brigg Fair; Danny Deever; Irish tune
from County Derry; The lost lady found; Morning song in the jungle;
The peora hunt; Shallow Brown; Six dukes went afishin'; Skye boat
song; There was a pig* CBSO Ch, Halsey
(+ Delius: *Partsongs*)
Conifer CDCF 162 [D] **F**

GRANADOS, Enrique (1867–1916) SPAIN

*Cuentos de la juventud, Op. 1: Dedicatoria; 12 Danzas españolas
Nos. 4 & 5; 15 Tonadillas al estilo antiguo: La maja de Goya; 7
Valses poéticos* (all arr. Bream) Bream (gtr)
(+ Albéniz: *Guitar works*)
RCA 09026-61608-2 [D] **M**

S *Allegro de concierto; Capricho espagnol, Op. 39; Carezza (Valse), Op. 38; 2 Impromptus; Oriental; Rapsodia aragonesa; 7 Valses poéticos* Rajna (pno)
CRD 3323 [A] **F**

Danza lenta; 6 Escenas romanticas; 6 Piezas sobre cantos populares españoles Rajna (pno)
CRD 3322 [A] **F**

12 Danzas españolas, Op. 37 Rajna (pno)
CRD 3321 [A] **F**

Goyescas (suite) de Larrocha (pno)
Decca 411 958-2 [A] **F**

GRECHANINOV, Alexander (1864–1956) RUSSIA

C *String Quartet No. 1 in G, Op. 2* Shostakovich Quartet
(+ Tchaikovsky: *String Quartet No. 3, etc.*)
Olympia OCD 522 [A] **F**

GRIEG, Edvard (1843–1907) NORWAY

O *Piano Concerto in A min., Op. 16* Kovacevich (pno), BBC SO, C. Davis
(+ Schumann: *Piano Concerto*)
Philips 412 923-2 [A] **F**

Piano Concerto in A min., Op. 16 (original version); *Larviks-Polka; 23 Small Piano Pieces* Derwinger (pno), Norrkoping SO Hirokami
BID CD-619 [D] **F**

Cradle Song, Op. 68/5; 2 Elegiac Melodies, Op. 34; Holberg Suite, Op. 40; 2 Melodies, Op. 53; 2 Norwegian Melodies, Op. 63
Norwegian CO, Tønnesen
BIS BIS-CD 147 [D] **F**

Holberg Suite, Op. 40; 2 Norwegian Melodies, Op. 63 Moscow Soloists, Bashmet
(+ Tchaikovsky: *Serenade for Strings*)
RCA RD 60368 [D] **F**

Lyric Suite, Op. 54; Norwegian Dances, Op. 35; Symphonic Dances, Op. 64 Gothenburg SO, Järvi
DG 419 431-2 [D] **F**

Peer Gynt (incidental music); *Sigurd Jorsalfar* (incidental music), *Op. 56* Bonney (sop), Eklof (mez), Sandve (ten), Malmberg (bar), Holmgren (bar), Gosta Ohlin's Vocal Ensemble, Pro Musica Chamber Ch, Gothenburg SO, Järvi
DG 423 079-2, 2CDs [D] **F**

Peer Gynt: Suites Nos. 1 & 2 BPO, Karajan
(+ Sibelius: *Pelléas et Mélisande*)
DG 410 026-2 [D] **F**

Symphony in C min.; Funeral March; In Autumn (concert overture), *Op. 11; Old Norwegian Melody with Variations, Op. 51* Gothenburg SO, Järvi
DG 427 321-2 [D] **F**

C *String Quartet No. 1 in G min., Op. 27; String Quartet No. 2 in F; *Andante con moto in C min. for piano trio; Fugue in F min.* *Roling (pno), Raphael Quartet
Olympia OCD 432 [D] **F**

Violin Sonatas Nos. 1–3 Turban (vln), Dunki (pno)
Claves CD50-8808 [D] **F**

Complete Piano Music Oppitz (pno)
Volume 1
RCA 09026 61568-2, 3 CDs [D] **F**
Volume 2
RCA 09026 61569-2, 4 CDs [D] **F**

*4 Album Leaves, Op. 28; 2 Improvisations on Norwegian
Folksongs, Op. 29; 25 Norwegian Folksongs and Dances, Op. 17; 3
Pictures, Op. 19* Knardahl (pno)
BIS BIS-CD 108 [D] **F**

*Ballade, Op. 24; Peer Gynt Suites Nos. 1 & 2; Sigurd Jorsalfar:
Suite* Knardahl (pno)
BIS BIS-CD 109 [D] **F**

*Elegiac Melodies; Holberg Suite; 2 Nordic Melodies, Op. 63; Olav
Trygvason; Valses Caprices, Op. 37* Knardahl (pno)
BIS BIS-CD 110 [D] **F**

6 Lyric Pieces, Op. 65; 19 Norwegian Folksongs, Op. 66
Braaten (pno)
Victoria VCD 19032 [D] **F**

*19 Norwegian Folksongs, Op. 66; 12 Song Transcriptions, Opp. 41
& 52* Knardahl (pno)
BIS BIS-CD 111 [D] **F**

*Nordraak's Funeral March; 4 Humoresques, Op. 6; 4 Piano Pieces,
Op. 1; Piano Sonata, Op. 7; 6 Tone Pictures, Op. 3* Knardahl (pno)
BIS BIS-CD 107 [D] **F**

Lyric Pieces Books 1–4 Katin (pno)
Unicorn-Kanchana UKCD 2033 [D] **M**

Lyric Pieces Books 5–7 Katin (pno)
Unicorn-Kanchana UKCD 2034 [D] **M**

Lyric Pieces Books 8–10 Katin (pno)
Unicorn-Kanchana UKCD 2035 [D] **M**

Lyric Pieces (selection) Gilels (pno)
DG 419 749-2 [A] **F**

*17 Norwegian Peasant Dances, Op. 72; Piano Pieces, Op. posth.;
Stimmungen, Op. 73* Knardahl (pno)
BIS BIS-CD 112 [D] **F**

Piano Sonata, Op. 7 Gould (pno)
(+ Bizet: *Nocturne No. 1; Variations chromatiques, Op. 3;* Sibelius:
3 Lyric Pieces, Op. 41; Sonatines Nos. 1–3, Op. 67)
Sony CD 52654, 2CDs [A] **M**

*Bergliot, Op. 42; The Mountain Thrall, Op. 32; Before a Southern
Convent, Op. 20; 7 Songs* Bonney (sop), Stene (cont), Hagegard
(bar), Tellefsen (narr), Gothenburg SO & Ch, Järvi
DG 437 519-2 [D] **F**

Olav Trygvason (operatic fragments), *Op. 50; Recognition of
Land* (cantata), *Op. 31; Peer Gynt Act V* (excerpts) Carlsen
(sop), Hanssen (mez), Hansli (bar), Oslo Philharmonic Ch,
LSO, Dreier
Unicorn-Kanchana UKCD 2056 [A] **M**

Song Recital
Von Otter (mez), Forsberg (pno)
DG 437 521-2 [D] **F**
Hagegård (bar), Jones (pno)
RCA 09026 61630-2, 2 CDs [D] **F**

v 7 *Children's Songs, Op. 61; 19 Songs from Garborg's 'Haugtassa'*
Hirsti (sop), Skram (bar), Jansen (pno)
Victoria VCD 19040 [D] **F**

GRIER, Francis (born 1956) ENGLAND

s *A Sequence for the Ascension* Grier (org), Rodolfus Ch, Allwood
Herald HAVPCD 158 [D] **F**

GRIFFES, Charles (1884–1920) USA

s *3 Fantasy Pieces, Op. 6; Piano Sonata in F♯ min.; 3 Tone Pictures,*
Op. 5 Landes (pno)
(+ Macdowell: *Piano Sonata No. 4*)
Koch 37045-2 [D] **F**

Piano Sonata in F sharp min. Lawson (pno)
(+ Ives: *Piano Sonata No. 1;* Sessions: *Piano Sonata No. 2*)
Virgin VC7 59316 [D] **F**

GROFÉ, Ferdinand (1892–1972) USA

o *Grand Canyon Suite* Detroit SO, Dorati
(+ Gershwin: *Porgy and Bess: Symphonic Picture*)
Decca 430 712-2 [D] **M**

GUBAIDULINA, Sofia (born 1931) RUSSIA

o *Offertorium (Violin Concerto); *Hommage à T.S. Eliot* Kremer
(vln), Boston SO, Dutoit; *Various artists
DG 427 336-2 [D] **F**

c *Garden of Joy and Sadness; String Trio; The Seven Last Words*
Various artists
Philips 434 041-2 [D] **F**

GURNEY, Ivor (1890–1937) ENGLAND

s *Nocturne in A♭; Nocturne in B; A Picture; Prelude in C; Prelude in*
min.; Prelude in D♭; Prelude in F♯; 5 Preludes; Revery; To E.H.M.
Gravill (pno)
Gamut GAMCD 516 [D] **F**

v Song cycles: *Ludlow and Teme; The Western Playland*
Thompson (ten), Varcoe (bar), Delmé Quartet, Burnside (sop)
(+ Vaughan Williams: *On Wenlock Edge*)
Hyperion CDA 66385 [D] **F**

HAAS, Pavel (1899–1944) CZECHOSLOVAKIA

c *String Quartets: No. 2 (From the Monkey Mountains), Op. 7; No. 3*
Op. 15 Hawthorne Quartet
(+ Krasa: *String Quartet*)
Decca 440 853-2 [D] **F**

HADLEY, Patrick (1899–1973) ENGLAND

v *Lenten Cantata; The Cup of Blessing; I Sing of a Maiden; My*
Beloved Spake; A Song for Easter Ainsley (ten), Sweeney (bs),
Gonville & Caius College Ch, Webber
(+ Rubbra: *Choral works*)
ASV CDDCA 881 [D] **F**

HAHN, Reynaldo (1875–1947) VENEZUELA/FRANCE

o *Le bal de Béatrice d'Este: Suite* New London O, Corp
(+ Poulenc: *Aubade; Sinfonietta*)
Hyperion CDA 66347 [D] **F**

v *17 Melodies* Hill (ten), Johnson (pno)
Hyperion CDA 66045 [D] **F**

HANDEL, George Frideric (1685–1759) GERMANY/ENGLAND

○ *Alcina* (opera): *Overture; Acts I & II: Suites; Il pastor fido* (opera): *Suite; Terpsichore* (opera): *Suite* EBS, Gardiner
   ◇ Erato 2292-45378-2 [A] **M**

Oboe Concertos Nos. 1–3; Concerto Grosso in C (Alexander's Feast), HWV318; Sonata à cinque in B♭, HWV288 Reichenberg (ob), English Concert, Pinnock
   ◇ DG Archiv 415 291-2 [A] **F**

6 Organ Concerti, Op. 4; Organ Concerti: in F (Cuckoo and the Nightingale), HWV295; in A, HWV296 Hurford (org), Concertgebouw CO, Rifkin
Decca 430 569-2, 2CDs [A] **M**

6 Organ Concerti, Op. 7; Organ Concerti: in D min., HWV304; in F, HWV305a Hurford (org), Concertgebouw CO, Rifkin
Decca 433176-2, 2CDs [A] **M**

6 Organ Concerti, Op. 4; 6 Organ Concerti, Op. 7; Organ Concerto in A, HWV296 Preston (org), English Concert, Pinnock
   ◇ DG Archiv 413 465-2, 2CDs [D] **F**

6 Concerti Grossi, Op. 3; Alcina (opera): *Overture; Ariodante* (opera): *Overture* ASMF, Marriner
Decca 430 261-2 [A] **M**

Concerti Grossi, Op. 3 Brandenburg Consort, Goodman
   ◇ Hyperion CDA 66633 [D] **F**

Concerti Grossi, Op. 6 I Musici
Philips 422 370-2, 3 CDs **F**

12 Concerti Grossi, Op. 6 Nos. 1–4 English Concert, Pinnock
   ◇ DG Archiv 410 897-2 [D] **F**

12 Concerti Grossi, Op. 6 Nos. 5–8 English Concert, Pinnock
   ◇ DG Archiv 410 898-2 [D] **F**

12 Concerti Grossi, Op. 6 Nos. 9–12 English Concert, Pinnock
   ◇ DG Archiv 410 899-2 [D] **F**

Music for the Royal Fireworks, HWV351 Cleveland Symphonic Winds, Fennell
(+ Holst: *Suites for Military Band*)
Telarc CD 80038 [D] **F**

Music for the Royal Fireworks, HWV351; The Water Music, HWV348–50 Orpheus CO
DG 435 390-2 [D] **F**

Water Music (complete) EBS, Gardiner
   ◇ Philips 434 122-2 [D] **F**

Overtures: *Agrippina; Alceste; Il pastor fido; Samson; Saul (Acts I & II); Teseo* English Concert, Pinnock
   ◇ DG Archiv 419 219-2 [D] **F**

⊂ *The Complete Chamber Music* Various artists
   ◇ CRD 3373/8, 6 seperate CDs [A] **F**

Recorder Sonatas Nos. 1–6 Petri (rec), Jarrett (hpd)
   ◇ RCA RD 60441 [D] **F**

Trio Sonatas in G min., HWV393; in B min., HWV386b; B♭, HWV388; in D, HWV397; in G, HWV399; Violin Sonata in A, HWV361 English Concert, Pinnock
   ◇ DG Archiv 415 497-2 [D] **F**

S *Harpsichord Suites Nos. 1–8* Tilney (hpd)
DG Archiv 427 170-2, 2CDs [A] **M**

V *10 Duets* Fisher (sop), Bowman (alt), King's Consort, King
◇ Hyperion CDA 66440 [D] **F**

Aci, Galatea e Polifemo (dramatic cantata); **Recorder Sonatas
Nos. 3 & 5* Kirkby (sop), Watkinson (cont), Thomas (bs),
London Baroque, Medlam; *Piguet (rec), Toll (hpd),
Medlam (vcl)
◇ HM HMC90 1253/4, 2CDs [D] **F**

Acis and Galatea (oratorio), *HWV49b; Look down, harmonious
Saint* (cantata), *HWV124* McFadden (sop), Ainsley (ten),
Covey-Crump (ten), George (bs), Harre-Jones (alt), King's
Consort, King
◇ Hyperion CDA 66361/2, 2CDs [D] **F**

Alceste (incidental music), *HWV45; Comus* (incidental music)
Nelson (sop), Kirkby (sop), Kwella (sop), Cable (mez), Elliot
(ten), Thomas (bs), AAM, Hogwood
◇ L'Oiseau-Lyre 421 479-2 [A] **F**

Alexander's Feast (ode for St. Cecilia's day), *HWV75 (interpolates
Harp Concerto in Bb, H294; Organ Concerto in G, HWV289)*
Argenta (sop), Partridge (ten), George (bs), Lawrence-King
(hpd), Nicholson (org), Tragicomedia, The Sixteen O & Ch,
Christophers
◇ Collins 70162, 2CDs [D] **F**

L'Allegro, il penseroso ed il moderato (oratorio), *HWV55* Ginn
(tbl), Kwella (sop), McLaughlin (sop), Smith (sop), Davies
(ten), Hill (ten), Varcoe (bar), Monteverdi Ch, EBS,
Gardiner
◇ Erato 2292-45377-2, 2CDs [D] **F**

*Cantatas: Alpestre monte, HWV81; Mi palpita il cor, HWV132;
Tra le fiamme, HWV170; Tu fedel? Tu costante?, HWV171* Kirkby
(sop), AAM, Hogwood
◇ L'Oiseau-Lyre 414 473-2 [D] **F**

Aminta e Fillide Fisher (sop), Kwella (sop), London Handel O,
Darlow
◇ Hyperion CDA 66118 [A] **F**

Apollo e Dafne (cantata), *HWV83* Alexander (sop), Hampson
(bar), VCM, Harnoncourt
(+ Telemann: *Ino*)
◇ Teldec 2292-44633-2 [D] **F**

*As pants the hart (Chandos Anthem No. 6), HWV251; I will magnif
thee (Chandos Anthem No. 5b), HWV250b; O Sing unto the Lord
(Chandos Anthem No. 4a), HWV249a* Dawson (sop), Partridge
(ten), The Sixteen, Christophers
◇ Chandos CHAN 0504 [D] **F**

Athalia (oratorio), *HWV52* Sutherland (sop), Kirkby (sop),
Jones (trb), Bowman (alt), Rolfe Johnson (ten), Thomas (bs),
New College Ch, AAM, Hogwood
◇ L'Oiseau-Lyre 417 126-2, 2CDs [D] **F**

Belshazzar (oratorio), *HWV61* Augér (sop), Gooding (sop),
Robbin (mez), Bowman (alt), Short (alt), Rolfe Johnson (ten),
Robertson (ten), Wilson-Johnson (bar), Wistreich (bs), Englis
Concert O & Ch, Pinnock
◇ DG Archiv 431 793-2, 3CDs [D] **F**

Blessed are they that considereth the poor (Foundling Hospital Anthem), HWV268; Eternal source of light divine (Ode for the birthday of Queen Anne), HWV74 Nelson (sop), Kirkby (sop), Minty (mez), Bowman (alt), Hill (ten), Thomas (bs), Christ Church Cathedral Ch, AAM, Simon Preston
(+ Haydn: *Mass No. 2*)
✧ L'Oiseau-Lyre 421 654-2 [A] **F**

Brockes-Passion (oratorio), HWV48 Klietmann (ten), Gáti (bar), Zádori (sop), Minter (alt), Farkas (sop), de Mey (ten), Burzynski (bar), Halle Ch, Capella Savaria, McGegan
✧ Hungaroton HCD 12734/6, 3CDs [D] **F**

Cantatas: *Carco sempre di Gloria, HWV87; La Lucrezia; Mi palpita il cor, HWV132; Splenda l'alba in Oriente; Trio Sonata in G, HWV399* Lesne (alt), Seminario Musicale
✧ Virgin VC7 59059-2 [D] **F**

Cecilia vogi un sguardo (cantata); Silete venti (motet) Smith (sop), Elwes (ten), English Concert, Pinnock
✧ DG Archiv 419 736-2 [D] **F**

Chandos Anthems Nos. 1-11 (complete) Various soloists, The Sixteen Ch & O, Christophers
✧ Chandos CHAN 0554/7, 4CDs [D] **F**

Coronation Anthems: *The King shall rejoice, HWV260; Let Thy hand be strengthened, HWV259; My heart is inditing, HWV261; Zadok the Priest, HWV258* Westminster Abbey Ch, Pinnock (org), English Concert, Preston
✧ DG Archiv 410 030-2 [D] **F**

Deborah (oratorio) Kenny (sop), Gritton (sop), Denley (mez), Bowman (alt), George (bs), New College Ch, King's Consort, King
✧ Hyperion CDA 66841/2, 2 CDs [D] **F**

Dixit Dominus, HWV232; Nisi Dominus, HWV238; Salve Regina, HWV241 Westminster Abbey Ch, English Concert, Preston
✧ DG Archiv 423 594-2 [D] **F**

Esther (oratorio), HWV50 Kirkby (sop), Kwella (sop), Minter (alt), Rolfe Johnson (ten), Thomas (bs), Partridge (ten), Elliot (ten), King (ten), Westminster Cathedral Boys' Ch, AAM O & Ch, Hogwood
✧ L'Oiseau-Lyre 414 423-2, 2CDs [D] **F**

Have mercy upon me (Chandos Anthem No. 3), HWV248; In the Lord put I my trust (Chandos Anthem No. 2), HWV247; O be joyful in the Lord (Chandos Anthem No. 1), HWV246 Dawson (sop), Partridge (ten), The Sixteen O & Ch, Christophers
✧ Chandos CHAN 8600 [D] **F**

Hercules (oratorio), HWV60 Smith (sop), Walker (mez), Denley (mez), Rolfe Johnson (ten), Tomlinson (bs), Savidge (bar), Monteverdi Ch, EBS, Gardiner
✧ DG Archiv 423 137-2, 3CDs [D] **F**

Israel in Egypt (oratorio) Jenkin (sop), Dunkley (sop), Trevor (cont), MacKenzie (ten), Evans (bs), Birchall (bs), The Sixteen Ch & O, Christophers
✧ Collins 70352, 2CDs [D] **F**

Jephtha (oratorio), HWV70 Dawson (sop), Holton (sop), von Otter (mez), Chance (alt), Robson (ten), Varcoe (bar), Monteverdi Ch, EBS, Gardiner
✧ Philips 422 351-2, 3CDs [D] **F**

V *Joshua* (oratorio), *HWV64* Kirkby (sop), Bowman (alt), Ainsley (ten), George (bs), Oliver (trb), New College Ch, King's Consort, King
✧ Hyperion, CDA 66461/2, 2CDs [D] **F**

Judas Maccabeus, *HWV63* Kirkby (sop), Denley (mez), Bowman (alt), MacDougall (ten), George (bs), Birchall (bs), New College Ch, King's Consort, King
✧ Hyperion CDA 66641/2, 2CDs [D] **F**

The King shall Rejoice, HWV265; Te Deum in D (Dettingen), HWV283 Tipping (alt), Christophers (ten), Varcoe (bar), Pearce (bs), Westminster Abbey Ch, English Concert, Preston
✧ DG Archiv 410 647-2 [D] **F**

Let God arise (Chandos Anthem No. 11), HWV256; The Lord is my light (Chandos Anthem No. 10), HWV255 Dawson (sop), Partridge (ten), The Sixteen Ch & O, Christophers
✧ Chandos CHAN 0509 [D] **F**

Messiah (oratorio), *HWV56*
Rodgers (sop), Jones (mez), Robson (ten), Langridge (ten), Terfel (bs-bar), Collegium Musicum 90, Hickox
✧ Chandos CHAN 0522/3, 2CDs [D] **F**
Harwood (sop), Baker (mez), Esswood (alt), Tear (ten), Herincx (bs), Ambrosian Singers, ECO, Mackerras
EMI CZS7 62748-2, 2CDs **B**

My Song shall be alway (Chandos Anthem No. 7), HWV252; O come, let us sing (Chandos Anthem No. 8), HWV253; O praise the Lord with one consent (Chandos Anthem No. 9), HWV254 Kwella (sop), Bowman (alt), Partridge (ten), George (bs), The Sixteen Ch & O, Christophers
✧ Chandos CHAN 0505 [D] **F**

Ode for St. Cecilia's Day, HWV76 Lott (sop), Rolfe Johnson (ten), English Concert Ch & O, Pinnock
✧ DG Archiv 419 220-2 [D] **F**

La Resurrezione di Nostro Signor Gesú Cristo (oratorio) Argenta (sop), Schlick (sop), Laurens (mez), de Mey (ten), Mertens (bs), Amsterdam Baroque O, Koopman
✧ Erato 2292-45617-2, 2CDs [D] **F**

Samson (oratorio) Alexander (sop), Rolfe Johnson (ten), Prégardien (ten), Arnold Schoenberg Ch,VCM, Harnoncourt
✧ Teldec 9031 74871-2, 2 CDs [D] **F**

Saul, *HWV53* Dawson (sop), Brown (sop), Ragin (alt), Ainsley (ten), Mackie (ten), Miles (bar), Monteverdi Ch, EBS, Gardiner
✧ Philips 426 265-2, 3CDs [D] **F**

Solomon (oratorio), *HWV67* Watkinson (cont), Argenta (sop), Hendricks (sop), Rolfe Johnson (ten), Monteverdi Ch, EBS, Gardiner
✧ Philips 412 612-2 [D] **F**

Susanna (oratorio) Hunt (sop), Minter (alt), Feldman (sop), Parker (bar), J. Thomas (ten), D. Thomas (bs), U.C. Berkeley Chamber Ch, Philharmonia Baroque O, McGegan
✧ HM HMU 90 7030/2, 3CDs [D] **F**

Te Deum and Jubilate in D (Utrecht), HWV278-9 Kirkby (sop), Nelson (sop), Brett (alt), Elliot (ten), Covey-Crump (ten), Thomas (bs), Christ Church Cathedral Ch, AAM, Preston
✧ L'Oiseau-Lyre 414 413-2 [D] **F**

V *Theodora* (oratorio), *HWV68* Hunt (sop), Minter (alt), Lane (mez), Thomas (bs), U.C. Berkeley Chamber Ch, Philharmonia Baroque O, McGegan
◇ HM HMU90 7060/2, 3CDs [D] **F**

The Triumph of Time and Truth (oratorio), *HWV71* Fisher (sop), Kirkby (sop), Brett (alt), Partridge (ten), Varcoe (bar), London Handel O & Ch, Darlow
◇ Hyperion CDA 66071/2, 2CDs [D] **F**

HANSON, Howard (1896–1981) USA

O *Symphonies: No. 1 in E min. (Nordic); No. 2 (Romantic); *Song of Democracy* Eastman-Rochester O, *Eastman School of Music Ch, Hanson
Philips Mercury 432 008-2 [A] **M**

*Symphonies: No. 3; No. 6; *Fantasy-Variations on a Theme of Youth* *Rosenberger (pno), Seattle SO, Schwarz; New York Chamber SO, Schwarz
Delos DE 3092 [D] **F**

*Symphony No. 4; *Lament for Beowulf; Merry Mount: Suite; **Pastorale; **Serenade* Seattle SO & *Chorale, **New York Chamber SO, Schwarz
Delos DE 3105 [D] **F**

*Symphonis: No. 5 (Sinfonia sacra); *No. 7 (A Sea Symphony); Piano Concerto in G* Rosenberger (pno), Seattle SO & *Chorale, Schwarz
Delos DE 3130 [D] **F**

HARRIS, Roy (1898–1979) USA

O *Symphony No. 3* NYPO, Bernstein
(+ Schumann: *Symphony No. 3*)
DG 419 780-2 [D] **F**

HARTMANN, Karl Amadeus (1905–1963) GERMANY

O *Symphonies Nos. *1–8; **Gesangsszene* *Soffel (mez), **Fischer-Dieskau (bar), Bavarian RSO, Rieger (No. 1), Kubelik (Nos. 2, 4–6 & 8), Leitner (No. 3), Macal (No. 7)
Wergo WER 60187-50, 4CDs [A] **F**

*Symphony No. 2 (Adagio); *Gesangsszene; Sinfonia Tragica* *Nimsgern (bar), Bamberg SO, Rickenbacker
Koch 312952 [D] **F**

S *Jazz-Toccata and Fugue; 2 Kleine Suiten; Sonata: 27 April 1945; Sonatine* Mauser (pno)
Virgin VC7 59017-2 [D] **F**

HARTY, Sir Hamilton (1879–1941) IRELAND

O *A Comedy Overture; An Irish Symphony* Ulster O, Thomson
Chandos CHAN 8314 [D] **F**

*Piano Concerto in B min.; *In Ireland* (fantasy); *With the Wild Geese* (tone poem) Binns (pno), *Fleming (fl), Kelly (hp), Ulster O, Thomson
Chandos CHAN 8321 [D] **F**

Violin Concerto in D min.; Variations on a Dublin Air Holmes (vln), Ulster O, Thomson
Chandos CHAN 8386 [A] **F**

With the Wild Geese (tone poem) SNO, Gibson
(+ German: *Welsh Rhapsody*; MacCunn: *Land of Mountain and*

Flood; Smyth: *The Wreckers Overture*)
Classics for Pleasure CDCFP 4635 [A] B

V *The Children of Lir; Ode to a Nightingale* Harper (sop), Ulster O, Thomson
Chandos CHAN 8387 [D] F

HARVEY, Jonathan (born 1939) ENGLAND

V *Song Offerings* Walmsley-Clark (sop), London Sinfonietta, Benjamin
(+ Benjamin: *Antara;* Boulez: *Dérive; Mémoriale*)
Nimbus NI 5167 [D] F

HAYDN, Franz Joseph (1732–1809) AUSTRIA

O *Cello Concertos: No. 1 in C; No. 2 in D* Coin (vcl), AAM, Hogwood
◇ **L'Oiseau-Lyre 414 615-2 [D] F**

Horn Concertos: No. 1 in D; No. 2 in D; Trumpet Concerto in Eb; Divertimento a tre in Eb Thomson (hn), Wallace (tpt), Philharmonia O, Warren-Green
Nimbus NI 5010 [A] F

Keyboard Concertos Nos. 3, 4 & 11 Ax (pno/dir), Franz Liszt CO
Sony CD 48383 [D] F

Oboe Concerto in C Lencsés (ob), Stuttgart RSO, Marriner
(+ Hummel: *Introduction, Theme and Variations;* Martinů: *Oboe Concerto*)
Capriccio 10 308 [D] F

Trumpet Concerto in Eb Stringer (tpt), ASMF, Marriner
(+ Albinoni: *Trumpet Concerto in C;* Hummel: *Trumpet Concerto in Eb;* L. Mozart: *Trumpet Concerto in D;* Telemann: *2 Oboe and Trumpet Concerto No. 1*)
Decca 417 761-2 [A] M

Violin Concertos: No. 1 in C; No. 3 in A; No. 4 in G Tetzlaff (vln), Northern Sinfonia, Schiff
(+ Mozart: *Rondo in C*)
Virgin VC7 59065-2 [D] F

Symphonies Nos. 1–104; Symphonies A & B; *Sinfonia Concertante in Bb *Engl (vln), *Baranyi (vcl), *Ozim (ob), *Racz (bsn), Philharmonia Hungarica, Dorati
Decca 430 100-2, 32CDs [A] M

Symphonies Nos. 1–16 Philharmonia Hungarica, Dorati
Decca 425 900-2, 4CDs [A] M

Symphonies Nos. 1, 2, 4, 5, 10, 11, 18, 27, 32, 37 & 107 AAM, Hogwood
◇ **L'Oiseau-Lyre 436 428-2, 3 CDs [D] F**

Symphonies Nos. 3, 14, 15, 17, 19, 20, 25, 33, 36, 36 & 108 (Partita) AAM, Hogwood
◇ **L'Oiseau-Lyre 436 592-2, 3CDs [D] F**

Symphonies Nos. 6–8 English Concert, Pinnock
◇ **DG Archiv 423 098-2 [D] F**

Symphonies Nos. 9–12 Hanover Band, Goodman
◇ **Hyperion CDA 66529 [D] F**

Symphonies: No. 9 in C; No. 12 in E; No. 13 in D; No. 40 in F Austro-Hungarian Haydn O, Fischer
Nimbus NI 5321 [D] F

○ *Symphonies Nos. 13-16* Hanover Band, Goodman
◇ Hyperion CDA 66534 [D] **F**

Symphonies Nos. 17–33 Philharmonia Hungarica, Dorati
Decca 425 905-2, 4CDs [A] **M**

Symphonies Nos. 17-21 Hanover Band, Goodman
◇ Hyperion CDA 66533 [D] **F**

Symphonies Nos. 21–24, 28–31 & 34 AAM, Hogwood
◇ L'Oiseau-Lyre 430 082-2, 3CDs [D] **F**

*Symphonies: No. 22 in E♭ (Der Philosoph); No. 63 in C; No. 80 in
D min.* Orpheus CO
DG 427 337-2 [D] **F**

Symphonies Nos. 26, 35, 38–9, 41–2, 43, 52, 58–9 English
Concert, Pinnock
◇ DG Archiv 435 001-2, 6CDs [D] **M**

*Symphonies: No. 26 in D min. (Lamentatione); No. 52 in C min.;
No. 53 in D (L'Impériale)* La Petite Bande, Kuijken
◇ Virgin VC7 59148-2 [D] **F**

Symphonies Nos. 34–47 Philharmonia Hungarica, Dorati
Decca 425 910-2, 4CDs [A] **M**

Symphonies Nos. 35, 38–9, 41, 58–9 & 65 AAM, Hogwood
◇ L'Oiseau-Lyre 433 012-2, 3CDs [D] **F**

Symphonies Nos. 41–43 Tafelmusik, Weil
◇ Sony CD 48370 [D] **F**

*Symphonies: No. 44 in E min. (Trauersinfonie); No. 45 in F# min.
(Farewell); No. 49 in F min. (La Passione)* Amsterdam Baroque
O, Koopman
◇ Erato 2292-45243-2 [D] **F**

Symphonies Nos. 45 (Farewell) & 81 Orpheus CO
DG 423 376-2 [D] **F**

Symphonies Nos. 45–47 Hanover Band, Goodman
◇ Hyperion CDA 66522 [D] **F**

Symphonies Nos. 44, 51 & 52 Tafelmusik, Weil
◇ Sony CD 48371 [D] **F**

Symphonies Nos. 48–59 Philharmonia Hungarica, Dorati
Decca 425 915-2, 4CDs [A] **M**

Symphonies Nos. 48–50 Hanover Band, Goodman
◇ Hyperion CDA 66531 [D] **F**

Symphonies Nos. 60–71 Philharmonia Hungarica, Dorati
Decca 425 920-2, 4CDs [A] **M**

Symphonies: No. 60 in C (Il distratto); No. 70 in D; No. 90 in C
CBSO, Rattle
EMI CDC7 54297-2 [D] **F**

Symphonies Nos. 70–72 Hanover Band, Goodman
◇ Hyperion CDA 66526 [D] **F**

Symphonies Nos. 72–83 Philharmonia Hungarica, Dorati
Decca 425 925-2, 4CDs [A] **M**

Symphonies Nos. 73–75 Hanover Band, Goodman
◇ Hyperion CDA 66520 [D] **F**

Symphonies Nos. 76–78 Hanover Band, Goodman
◇ Hyperion CDA 66525 [D] **F**

O *Symphonies: No. 82 in C (Bear); No. 84 in Eb* Saint Paul CO, Wolff
Teldec 9031 74005-2 [D] **F**

Symphonies: No. 82 in C (L'Ours); No. 83 in G min. (La Poule); No. 84 in Eb Age of Enlightenment O, Kuijken
✧ Virgin VC7 59537-2 [D] **F**

Symphonies Nos. 84–95 Philharmonia Hungarica, Dorati
Decca 425 930-2, 4CDs [A] **M**

Symphonies: No. 85 in Bb (La Reine); No. 86 in D; No. 87 in A Age of Enlightenment O, Kuijken
✧ Virgin VC7 59557-2 [D] **F**

Symphonies: No. 88 in G; No. 90 in C; No. 92 in G (Oxford) Austro-Hungarian Haydn O, Fischer
Nimbus NI 5269 [D] **F**

Symphonies Nos. 90–92 Hanover Band, Goodman
✧ Hyperion CDA 66521 [D] **F**

Symphonies: No. 90 in C; No. 93 in D Eighteenth Century O, Brüggen
✧ Philips 422 022-2 [D] **F**

Symphonies: No. 92 in G (Oxford); No. 94 in G (Surprise); No. 96 (Miracle) Cleveland O, Szell
Sony CD 46332 [A] **B**

Symphonies Nos. 93–104 Concertgebouw O, C. Davis
Philips 432 286-2, 4CDs [A] **M**

Symphonies Nos. 93–98 RPO, Beecham
EMI CMS7 64389-2, 2CDs [A] **M**

Symphonies: No. 94 in G (Surprise); No. 101 in D (Clock) LPO, Jochum
DG 423 883-2 [A] **M**

Symphonies: No. 95 in C min.; No. 104 in D (London) LPO, Solti
Decca 417 330-2 [D] **F**

*Symphonies Nos. 96–104; Symphonies A & B; *Sinfonia Concertante* *Engl (vln), *Baranyi (vcl), *Ozim (ob), *Racz (bn), Philharmonia Hungarica, Dorati
Decca 425 935-2, 4CDs [A] **M**

Symphonies Nos. 99–104 RPO, Beecham
EMI CMS7 64066-2, 2CDs [A] **M**

Symphonies: No. 101 in D (Clock); No. 103 in Eb (Drum Roll) Eighteenth Century O, Bruggen
✧ Philips 422 249-2 [D] **F**

Symphonies: No. 103 in Eb (Drum Roll); No. 104 in D (London) Royal Concertgebouw O, Harnoncourt
Teldec 2292 435267-2 [D] **F**

C *Baryton Trios Nos. 71, 96, 113 & 126* Hsu (baryton), Miller (vla), Arico (vcl)
✧ ASV CDGAU 109 [D] **F**

Baryton Trios Nos. 87, 97, 101 & 111 Hsu (baryton), Miller (vla), Arico (vcl)
✧ ASV CDGAU 104 [D] **F**

C *4 Flute Trios (London); Divertimenti: in G; in D* Rampal (fl),
Stern (vln), Rostropovich (vcl)
Sony CD 37786 [D] **F**

6 Duos for Violin and Viola Kovacs (vln), Nemeth (vla)
Hungaroton HRC 071 [A] **B**

Piano Trios Nos. 1–41 (complete) Beaux Arts Trio
Philips 432 061-2, 9CDs [A] **M**

Piano Trios Nos. 24–26 London Fortepiano Trio
◇ Hyperion CDA 66297 [D] **F**

Piano Trios Nos. 27–30 Beths (vln), Bylsma (vcl) Levin (fnpo)
◇ Sony CD 53120 [D] **F**

Piano Trios Nos. 28–31 Beaux Arts Trio
Philips 420 790-2 [A] **F**

*The Seven Last Words of Christ on the Cross (String Quartets Nos.
50–56, Op. 71)* Lindsay Quartet
ASV CDDCA 853 [D] **F**

*String Quartet in E♭, Op. 1; 6 String Quartets, Op. 1 Nos. 1–4 and
6; 6 String Quartets, Op. 2 Nos. 1, 2, 4 & 6; String Quartet No. 43
in D, Op. 42; String Quartet, Op. 103* Tátrai Quartet
Hungaroton HCD 31089-91, 3CDs [D] **F**

6 String Quartets, Op. 9 Tátrai Quartet
Hungaroton HCD 31296/7, 2CDs [A] **F**

6 String Quartets, Op. 17 Tátrai Quartet
Hungaroton HCD 11382/3, 2CDs [D] **F**

6 String Quartets, Op. 20 Mosaiques Quartet
Astree Auvidis E8784, 2 CDs [D] **F**

*String Quartets: No. 32 in C, Op. 20/2; No. 44 in B♭, Op. 50/1; No.
76 in D min., Op. 76/2* Lindsay Quartet
ASV CDDCA 622 [D] **F**

*String Quartets: No. 34 in D, Op. 20/4; No. 47 in F♯ min., Op.
50/4; No. 77 in C (Emperor), Op. 76/3* Lindsay Quartet
ASV CDDCA 731 [D] **F**

*String Quartets: No. 35 in F min., Op. 20/5; No. 40 in D, Op. 33/4;
No. 70 in D, Op. 72/2* Lindsay Quartet
ASV CDDCA 674 [D] **F**

6 String Quartets, Op. 33 Weller Quartet
Nos. 1–3 (+ Op. 1/3):
Decca 433 691-2 [A] **M**
Nos. 4–6 (+ Op. 103):
Decca 433 692-2 [A] **M**

*String Quartet in D, Op. 42; String Quartet in D, Op. 64/5; String
Quartet in D, Op. 76/5* Lindsay Quartet
ASV CDDCA 637 [D] **F**

6 String Quartets, Op. 50 (Prussian) Salomon Quartet
◇ Hyperion CDA 66821/2, 2 separate CDs [D] **F**

3 String Quartets, Op. 54 Lindsay Quartet
ASV CDDCA 582 [D] **F**

*String Quartets: No. 58 in C, Op. 54/2; No. 67 in D (Lark),
Op. 64/5* Gabrieli Quartet
Chandos CHAN 8531 [D] **F**

C   *3 String Quartets, Op. 55* Kodály Quartet
Naxos 8.550397 [D] **B**

  6 String Quartets, Op. 64 Kodaly Quartet
Naxos 8.550673/4, 2 separate CDs [D] **B**

  3 String Quartets, Op. 71; 3 String Quartets, Op. 74 Salomon
Quartet
  ✧ Hyperion CDA 66065, 66098, 66124, 3 separate CDs [D] **F**

  6 String Quartets, Op. 76 Kodály Quartet
Naxos 8.550314/5, 2 separate CDs [D] **B**

  2 String Quartets, Op. 77 Tátrai Quartet
Hungaroton HCD 11776 [D] **F**

S   *Piano Sonatas: No. 11 in B; No. 31 in A♭; No. 39 in D; No. 47 in B
min.* Richter (pno)
Decca 436 455-2 [D] **F**

  Piano Sonatas: No. 18 in E♭; No. 59 in E♭ Brendel (pno)
Philips 426 815-2 [D] **F**

  *Piano Sonatas: No. 32 in G min.; No. 54 in G; No. 55 in B♭; No. 58
in C; No. 62 in E♭* Richter (pno)
Decca 436 454-2 [D] **F**

  *Piano Sonatas Nos. 33, 47, 50, 53, 54, 56 & 58–62; Adagio in F;
Fantasia in C; Variations in F min.* Brendel (pno)
Philips 416 643-2, 4CDs [D/A] **F**

  *Piano Sonatas: No. 33 in C min.; No. 60 in C; No. 62 in E♭;
Andante and Variations in F min.* Pletnev (pno)
Virgin VC7 59258-2 [D] **F**

  *Piano Sonatas: No. 47 in B min.; No. 53 in E min.; No. 56 in D;
Adagio in F; Fantasia in C* Brendel (pno)
Philips 412 228-2 [D] **F**

  Piano Sonatas Nos. 48–52 Staier (fpno)
  ✧ DHM RD 77160 [D] **F**

V   *14 Welsh Folksong Arrangements* Pearce (sop), Drake (hp)
Hyperion CDA 66104 [D] **F**

  Arianna a Naxos (cantata); *Berenice che fai* (cantata); *Miseri noi!*
(cantata); *Solo e pensoso* (aria); *Son pietosa, son bonina* (aria)
Augér (sop), Handel & Haydn Society, Hogwood
L'Oiseau-Lyre 425 496-2 [D] **F**

  Die Jahreszeiten (The Seasons – oratorio) Bonney (sop), Rolfe
Johnson (ten), Schmidt (bar), Monteverdi Ch, EBS, Gardiner
  ✧ DG Archiv 431 818-2, 2CDs [D] **F**

  *Mass No. 1a in G (Rorate coeli desuper); Mass No. 5 in E♭ (Missa
in honorem); Mass No. 6 in G (Missa Sancti Nikolai)* Nelson
(sop), Watkinson (cont), Minty (alt), Hill (ten), Covey-Crump
(ten), Thomas (bs), Christ Church Cathedral Ch, AAM,
Preston
  ✧ L'Oiseau-Lyre 421 478-2 [A] **F**

  Mass No. 2 in F (Missa brevis) Nelson (sop), Kirkby (sop),
Christ Church Cathedral Ch, AAM, Preston
(+ Handel: *Blessed are they that considereth the poor; Eternal source
of light divine*)
  ✧ L'Oiseau-Lyre 421 654-2 [A] **F**

  Mass No. 3 in C (Missa Cellensis in honorem) Nelson (sop),
Cable (mez), Hill (ten), Thomas (bs), Christ Church

Cathedral Ch, AAM, Preston
◇ L'Oiseau-Lyre 417 125-2 [D] **F**

Masses: No. 6 in G (Missa Sancti Nikolai); No. 12 in B♭
(Theresienmasse) Argenta (sop), Robbin (mez), Scade (ten),
Miles (bs), English Concert & Ch, Pinnock
◇ DG Archiv 437 807-2 [D] **F**

Masses: No. 7 in B♭ (Missa brevis Sancti Joannis de Deo); No. 8 in
*C; *Organ Concerto No. 1 in C* Smith (sop), Watts (cont), Tear
(ten), Luxon (bar), St. John's College Ch, ASMF, Guest;
*Preston (org), ASMF, Marriner
Decca 430 160-2 [A] **M**

Mass No. 9 in B♭ (Missa Sancti Bernardi von Offida) Cantelo
(sop), Minty (mez), Partridge (ten), Keyte (bs), St. John's
College Ch, ASMF, Guest
(+ Mozart: *Litaniae de venerabili*)
Decca 430 158-2 [A] **M**

Mass No. 10 in C (Mass in Time of War) Cantelo (sop), Watts
(cont), Tear (ten), McDaniel (bar), St. John's College Ch,
ASMF, Guest
(+ Mozart: *Vesperae solennes de confessore, K339*)
Decca 430 157-2 [A] **M**

Mass No. 11 in D min. (Nelson); Te Deum No. 2 in C Lott (sop),
Watkinson (cont), Davies (ten), Wilson-Johnson (bar), English
Concert O & Ch, Pinnock
◇ DG Archiv 423 097-2 [D] **F**

Mass No. 12 in B♭ (Theresienmasse) Spoorenberg (sop), Greevy
(mez), Mitchinson (ten), Krause (bar), St. John's College Ch,
ASMF, Guest
(+ M. Haydn: *Ave Regina;* Mozart: *Ave verum corpus*)
Decca 430 159-2 [A] **M**

Mass No. 13 in B♭ (Creation) Cantelo (sop), Watts (cont), Tear
(ten), Robinson (bs), St. John's College Ch, ASMF, Guest
(+ Mozart: *Mass No. 12*)
Decca 430 161-2 [A] **M**

Mass No. 14 in B♭ (Harmonienmasse) Spoorenberg (sop), Watts
(cont), Young (ten), Rouleau (bs), St. John's College Ch,
ASMF, Guest
(+ Mozart: *Vesperae de dominica*)
Decca 430 162-2 [A] **M**

Die Schöpfung (The Creation – oratorio*)* Janowitz (sop), Ludwig
(mez), Wunderlich (ten), Krenn (ten), Berry (bs), Vienna
Singverein, BPO, Karajan
DG 435 077-2, 2CDs [A] **M**

Stabat Mater Rozario (sop), Robbin (mez), Rolfe Johnson
(ten), Hauptmann (bs), English Concert & Ch, Pinnock
◇ DG Archiv 429 733-2 [D] **F**

AYDN, Michael (1737–1806) AUSTRIA

Horn Concerto in D; Organ & Viola Concerto in C; 6 Minuets;
**Divertimento in G* Tuckwell (hn), Preston (org), Shingles
(vla), ASMF, Marriner; *Vienna Octet
Decca 436 222-2 [A] **M**

Ave Regina St. John's College Ch, Guest
(+ J. Haydn: *Mass No. 12;* Mozart: *Ave verum corpus*)
Decca 430 159-2 [A] **M**

V *Missa Sancti Aloysii; Missa subtitulo St. Leopoldi; Vesperae pro fest*
Trinity College Ch, Marlow
Conifer CDCF 220 **[D] F**

HEADINGTON, Christopher (born 1930) ENGLAND

O *Violin Concerto* Wei (vln), LPO, Glover
(+ R. Strauss: *Violin Concerto*)
ASV CDDCA 780 **[D] F**

HEINICHEN, Johann David (1683–1729) GERMANY

O *Dresden Concerti* Koln Musica Antiqua, Goebel
DG Archiv 437 549-2, 2 CDs **[D] F**

HENZE, Hans Werner (born 1926) GERMANY

O *Symphonies Nos. 1–*6 BPO, *LSO, Henze
DG 429 854-2, 2CDs **[A] M**

EDITORS' CHOICE (see page 13): *Symphony No. 7; Barcorola*
CBSO, Rattle
EMI CDC7 54762-2 **[D] F**

C *String Quartets Nos. 1–5* Arditti Quartet
Wergo WER 60114/5, 2CDs **[D] F**

HÉROLD, Ferdinand (1791–1833) FRANCE

O *La Fille mal gardée* (ballet) ROHO, Lanchberry
(+ Lecocq: *Mam'zelle Angot*)
Decca 430 849-2, 2CDs **[A] M**

HERRMANN, Bernard (1911–1975) USA

O *North by Northwest* (film score) London Studio SO, Johnson
Unicorn-Kanchana UKCD 2040 **[D] M**

Psycho (film score) National PO, Herrmann
Unicorn-Kanchana UKCD 2021 **[A] M**

Symphony No. 1; The Fantasticks (song cycle) Rippon (bs),
Dickinson (cont), Amis (ten), Humphreys (sop), Thames
Chamber Ch, National PO, Herrmann
Unicorn-Kanchana UKCD 2063 **[A] M**

Vertigo (film score) Sinfonia of London, Mathieson
Philips Mercury 422 106-2 **[A] M**

V *Moby Dick* (cantata); *For the Fallen* Amis (ten), Kelly (bs), R.
Bowman (ten), Rippon (bs), Aeolian Singers, LPO, *National
PO, Herrmann
Unicorn-Kanchana UKCD 2061 **[A] M**

HILDEGARD OF BINGEN (1098–1179) GERMANY

V *Ave generosa; Columba aspexit; O ecclesia oculi tui; O euchari; O
ignis spiritus; O Jerusalem aure civitas; O presul vere; O viridissim
virga* Kirkby (sop), Gothic Voices, Muskett (symphony),
White (bagpipes), Page (hp)
Hyperion CDA 66039 **[A] F**

Ordo Virtutum (morality play) Sequentia
DHM GD 77051, 2CDs **[D] M**

Symphoniae; Spiritual Songs Sequentia
DHM GD 77020 **[A] M**

HINDEMITH, Paul (1895–1963) GERMANY

O *Concert Music, Op. 49* Kvapil (pno), Wallace (tpt), Wallace
Collection, Wright

(+ Janáček: *Capriccio;* Vackar: *Trumpet, Piano and Percussion Concerto*)
Nimbus NI 5103 [D] **F**

*Cello Concerto; **Theme and Variations 'The Four Temperaments'
*Wallfisch (vcl), **Shelley (pno), BBC PO, Tortelier
Chandos CHAN 9124 [D] **F**

Concerto for Orchestra CSO, Järvi
(+ Schmidt: *Symphony No. 3*)
Chandos CHAN 9000 [D] **F**

Violin Concerto; *Mathis der Maler (Symphony); **Symphonic Metamorphosis on Themes of Weber D. Oistrakh, LSO, Hindemith; *OSR, Kletzki; **LSO, Abbado
Decca 433 081-2 [A] **M**

Kammermusik Nos. 1–7; Kleine Kammermusik No. 1, Op. 24
Royal Concertgebouw O, Chailly
Decca 433 816-2, 2CDs [D] **F**

Mathis der Maler (Symphony); Symphonic Metamorphosis on Themes of Weber; *Trauermusik *Walther (vla), SFSO, Blomstedt
Decca 421 523-2 [D] **F**

Nobilissima visione: Suite; Konzertmusik, Op. 50; *Der Schwanendreher *Walther (vla), SFSO, Blomstedt
Decca 433 809-2 **F**

Symphony in Eb; Nobilissima visione; Neues vom Tage BBC PO, Tortelier
Chandos CHAN 9060 [D] **F**

Symphonia Serena; Symphony 'Die Harmonie der Welt' BBC PO, Tortelier
Chandos CHAN 9217 [D] **F**

A Frog he went a-courting; Kleine Sonata; 3 leichte Stücke; Sonata (1948) Berger (vcl), Mauser (pno)
Wergo WER 60145-50 [D] **F**

Sonatas: Bass Tuba; Horn; Horn in Eb; Trombone; Trumpet
Torchinsky (bs tuba), Jones (hn/Eb hn), Smith (tbn), Johnson (tpt), Gould (pno)
Sony CD 52671, 2CDs [A] **M**

Cello Sonata, Op. 11 No. 3; 3 Pieces, Op. 8 Berger (vcl), Mauser (pno)
Wergo WER 60144-50 [D] **F**

Organ Sonatas Nos. 1–3 Kee (org)
(+ Reger: *Organ works*)
Chandos CHAN 9097 [D] **F**

Solo Viola Sonatas Nos. 1–4 Imai (vla)
BIS BIS-CD 57 [D] **F**

In einer Nacht, Op. 15; Suite '1922', Op. 26 Mauser (pno)
Wergo WER 6181-2 [D] **F**

Piano Sonatas Nos. 1–3 Gould (pno)
Sony CD 52670 [A] **M**

20 Lieder Fischer-Dieskau (bar), Reimann (pno)
Orfeo C 15686 1A [D] **F**

When lilacs last in the door-yard bloom'd (Requiem for those we love) De Gaetani (mez), Stone (bar), Atlanta SO & Ch, Shaw
Telarc CD 80132 [D] **F**

HODDINOTT, Alun (born 1929) WALES

O *Doubles; The Heaventree of Stars; Passaggio; Star Children* BBC
Welsh SO, Otaka
Nimbus NI 5357 [D] **F**

Noctis Equi, Op. 132 Rostropovich (vcl), LSO, Nagano
(+ Honegger: *Cello Concerto;* Milhaud: *Cello Concerto*)
Erato 2292-45489-2 [D] **F**

S *Piano Sonatas Nos. 1–5* Jones (pno)
Nimbus NI 5369 [D] **F**

Piano Sonatas Nos. 6-10 Jones (pno)
Nimbus NI 5370 [D] **F**

HOLBROOKE, Joseph (1879–1958) ENGLAND

C *Eilen Shona* King (cl), Britten Quartet
(+ Cooke; Frankel; Maconchy: *Clarinet Quintets*)
Hyperion CDA 66428 [D] **F**

HOLLOWAY, Robin (born 1943) ENGLAND

V *Sea-Surface Full of Clouds, Op. 31; *Romanze, Op. 31* Walmsley
Clarke (sop), Cable (cont), Hill (ten), Brett (alt), *Gruenberg
(vln), R Hickox Singers., City of London Sinfonia, Hickox
Chandos CHAN 9228 [D] **F**

Since I Believe in God the Father Almighty Kendall (ten), Harvey
(bs), Gonville & Caius College Ch, Webber
(+ C. Wood: *St. Mark Passion*)
ASV CDDCA 854 [D] **F**

HOLMBOE, Vagn (born 1909) DENMARK

O *Symphony No. 4 (Sinfonia sacra), Op. 29; Symphony No. 5, Op. 35*
Aarhus SO, Hughes
BIS CD 572 [D] **F**

*Symphony No. 6, Op. 43; Symphony No. 7 (in one movement),
Op. 50* Aarhus SO, Hughes
BIS CD 573 [D] **F**

HOLST, Gustav (1874–1934) ENGLAND

O *Beni Mora (Oriental Suite); Brook Green Suite; Egdon Heath
(Homage to Hardy); The Perfect Fool (opera): Ballet Suite; St.
Paul's Suite; Short Festival Te Deum; Psalm 86* Various artists
EMI CDC7 49784-2 [A] **F**

*Beni Mora (Oriental Suite); Fugal Overture; Hammersmith;
Japanese Suite; Scherzo; Somerset Rhapsody* LPO, LSO, Boult
Lyrita SRCD 222 [A] **F**

*Brook Green Suite; St. Paul's Suite; Double Violin Concerto, Op. 49;
Fugal Concerto Op. 49/2; 2 Songs without Words, Op. 22; Lyric
Movement* Various artists, City of London Sinfonia, Hickox
Chandos CHAN 9270 [D] **F**

The Planets (suite) CSO & Ch, Levine
DG 429 730-2 [D] **F**

Suites for Military Band: No. 1 in E♭; No. 2 in F Cleveland
Symphonic Winds, Fennell
(+ Handel: *Music for the Royal Fireworks*)
Telarc CD 80038 [D] **F**

C *Air and Variations; 3 Pieces for Oboe and String Quartet* Francis
(ob), English Quartet

(+ Bax: *Oboe Quintet;* Jacob: *Oboe Quartet;* Moeran: *Fantasy Quartet*)
Chandos CHAN 8392 [D] **F**

*Piano and Wind Quintet; Wind Quintet in A♭ *Goldstone (pno), Elysian Wind Quintet
(+ Jacob: *Sextet in B♭, Op. 6*)
Chandos CHAN 9077 [D] **F**

A *Choral Fantasia, H177; Choral Symphony No. 1, H155*
Dawson (sop), Birch (org), Guildford Choral Society, RPO, Davan Wetton
Hyperion CDA 66660 [D] **F**

6 Choral Folk Songs; 2 Eastern Pictures; 13 Partsongs; Songs from 'The Princess' Theodore (ob), Truman (vcl), Williams (hp), Holst Singers, Layton
Hyperion CDA 66705 [D] **F**

The Cloud Messenger; The Hymn of Jesus Jones (mez), LSO & Ch, Hickox
Chandos CHAN 8901 [D] **F**

Dirge and Hymeneal; 2 Motets; 5 Partsongs CBS Ch, Markham (pno), Halsey
(+ Elgar: *Scenes from the Bavarian Highlands*)
Conifer CDCF 142 [D] **F**

*2 *Eastern Pictures; Hymn to Dionysus; Choral Hymns from the Rig Veda: Groups 1–4* *Ellis (hp), RCM Chamber Ch, RPO, Willcocks
Unicorn-Kanchana DKPCD 9046 [D] **F**

The Evening Watch; 6 Male Choruses; Nunc Dimittis; 7 Partsongs; Psalm 86; Psalm 148 Holst Singers & O, Davan Wetton
Hyperion CDA 66329 [D] **F**

HONEGGER, Arthur (1892–1955) FRANCE/SWITZERLAND

Cello Concerto Rostropovich (vcl), LSO, Nagano
(+ Hoddinott: *Noctis Equi;* Milhaud: *Cello Concerto*)
Erato 2292-45489-2 [D] **F**

3 Symphonic Movements: Pacific 231; Rugby; Horace victorieux; Pastorale d'été; La Tempête: Prélude; La Traversée des Andes: Suite; Le Vol sur l'Atlantique Toulouse Capitole O, Plasson
DG 435 438-2 [D] **F**

Symphony No. 1; Pastorale d'été; 3 Symphonic Movements: Pacific 231; Rugby; No. 3 Bavarian RSO, Dutoit
Erato 2292-45242-2 [D] **F**

Symphonies Nos. 2 & 3 (Liturgique) BPO, Karajan
DG 423 242-2 [A] **M**

Symphonies: No. 4 (Deliciae basiliensis); No. 5 (Di tre re); Pacific 231 Toulouse Capitole O, Plasson
EMI CDM7 64275-2 [A] **M**

Jeanne d'Arc au bûcher (stage oratorio) Keller (narr), Wilson (narr), Escourrou (narr), Pollet (sop), Command (sop), Stützman (cont), French Radio Ch, FNO, Ozawa
DG 429 412-2 [D] **F**

Le Roi David (dramatic psalm) Audel (narr), Danco (sop), De Montmollin (mez), Hamel (ten), Martin (pno), SRO & Ch, Ansermet
Decca 425 621-2 [A] **M**

HOVHANESS, Alan (born 1911) USA

O   *Mysterious Mountain (Symphony No. 2); Prayer of St. Gregory;*
Prelude and Quadruple Fugue; And God Created Whales; Alleluia
and Fugue; Celestial Fantasy Seattle SO, Hovhaness, Schwarz
Delos DE 3157 [D] F

Symphony No. 22 (City of Light); *Symphony No. 50 (Mount St.
Helens) Seattle SO, Hovhaness, *Schwarz
Delos DE 3137 [D] F

HOWELLS, Herbert (1892–1983) ENGLAND

O   *Piano Concerto No. 2; *Concerto for Strings; 3 Dances* Stott (pno)
*Stewart (vln), RLPO, Handley
Hyperion CDA 66610 [D] F

Concerto for Strings; Elegy; Serenade; Suite for Strings City of
London Sinfonia, Hickox
Chandos CHAN 9161 [D] F

C   *Clarinet Sonata* King (cl), Benson (pno)
(+ Bliss: *2 Pieces;* Cooke: *Clarinet Sonata;* Reizenstein:
Arabesques)
Hyperion CDA 66044 [D] F

String Quartet (In Gloucestershire) Divertimenti
(+ Dyson: *3 Rhapsodies*)
Hyperion CDA 66139 [D] F

Violin Sonatas: No. 1 in E, Op. 18; No. 2 in E♭, Op. 26; No. 3 in E
min., Op. 38; Cradle Song, Op. 9/1; 3 Pieces, Op. 28 Barritt (vln),
Edwards (pno)
Hyperion CDA 66665 [D] F

S   *Gadabout; Sarum Sketches, 3 Pieces; Slow Dance; Cobler's*
Hornpipe; Snapshots, Op, 30; The Chosen Tune; 4 Pieces from
Lambert's Clavichord; Musica Sine Nomine; Sonatina
Fingerhut (pno)
Chandos CHAN 9273 [D] F

Howells's Clavichord; Lambert's Clavichord McCabe (pno)
Hyperion CDA 66689 [D] F

Three Psalm Preludes – Sets 1 & 2; 3 Rhapsodies, Op. 17
Dearnley (org)
Hyperion CDA 66394 [D] F

Organ Sonata No. 1 in C min. Matthews (org)
(+ Parry: *Organ works*)
Herald HAVPCD 116 [D] F

V   **Flourish for a Bidding; *Howells's Clavichord: Walton's Toye;*
Jacob's Brawl; *Lambert's Clavichord: de la Mare's Pavane; *St.
Louis Comes to Clifton; House of the Mind; A Hymn for St. Cecilia;
King of Glory; New College Service; O Pray for the Peace of
Jerusalem; A Sequence for St. Michael *Higginbottom (org),
Burchell (org), New College Ch, Higginbottom
CRD 3454 [D] F

Behold, O God, Our Defender; Here is the Little Door (arr.); *Missa*
Aedis Christ; Sing Lullaby (arr.); *A Spotless Rose; Where wast*
Thou?; *6 Pieces: Nos. 1 & 6; *Psalm-Preludes Set 1: No. 1
Higginbottom (*org/dir), New College Ch
CRD 3455 [D] F

Behold, O God our Defender; Collegium Regale: Te deum; Jubilate;
Like as the Hart; St. Paul's Service; Take Him, Earth, for

Cherishing; *6 Pieces: No. 3; *Psalm-Preludes Set 2: No. 1
*Dearnley (org), Scott (org), St. Paul's Cathedral Ch, Dearnley
Hyperion CDA 66260 [D] **F**

✔ *Hymnus Paradisi; An English Mass* Kennard (sop), Ainsley
(ten), RLPO & Ch, Handley
Hyperion CDA 66488 [D] **F**

*Mass in the Dorian Mode; Come, my soul; Nunc dimittis; O salutaris
Hostia; Regina caeli; Salve Regina; Sweetest of Sweets* Finzi
Singers, Spicer
(+ Stevens: *Mass for Double Choir*)
Chandos CHAN 9021 [D] **F**

Requiem; The House of the Mind; A Sequence for St. Michael Finzi
Singers, Spicer
(+ Vaughan Williams: *Lord, Thou hast been our refuge, etc.*)
Chandos CHAN 9019 [D] **F**

Requiem Corydon Singers, Best
(+ Vaughan Williams: *Mass; Te Deum*)
Hyperion CDA 66076 [A] **F**

HUMMEL, Johann (1778–1837) AUSTRIA

○ *Bassoon Concerto in F* Thunemann (bsn), ASMF, Marriner
(+ Weber: *Andante e rondo ungarese; Bassoon Concerto*)
Philips 432 081-2 [D] **F**

Piano Concertos: in A min., Op. 85; in B min., Op. 89 Hough
(pno), ECO, Thomson
Chandos CHAN 8507 [D] **F**

Trumpet Concerto in E♭ Wilbraham (tpt), ASMF, Marriner
(+ Albinoni; *Trumpet Concerto in C;* Haydn: *Trumpet Concerto in
E♭;* L. Mozart: *Trumpet Concerto in D;* Telemann: *2 Oboe and
Trumpet Concerto No. 1*)
Decca 417 761-2 [A] **M**

Introduction, Theme and Variations in F, Op. 102 Lencsés (ob),
Stuttgart RSO, Marriner
(+ Haydn: *Oboe Concerto in C;* Martinů: *Oboe Concerto*)
Capriccio 10 308 [D] **F**

○ *Nocturne, Op. 99; Violin Sonatas in E♭, Op. 5/3, & D, Op. 50*
Holmes (vln), Burnett (fpno)
◇ Amon Ra CD-SAR 12 [A] **F**

Piano Quintet, Op. 87 Hausmusik
(+ Schubert: *Piano Quintet in A*)
◇ EMI CDC7 54264-2 [D] **F**

3 String Quartets, Op. 30 Delmé Quartet
Hyperion CDA 66568 [D] **F**

Septet in C (Septet Militaire), Op. 114 Nash Ensemble
(+ C. Kreutzer: *Septet in E♭, Op. 62*)
CRD 3390 [A] **F**

Septet in D min., Op. 74 Nash Ensemble
(+ Berwald: *Grand Septet in B♭*)
CRD 3344 [A] **F**

HUMPERDINCK, Engelbert (1854–1921) GERMANY

● *Hansel und Gretel: Overture; The Bluebird: Prelude & Star Dance;
Königskinder: Overture; Preludes to Acts II & III; The Sleeping
Beauty: Suite (Nos. 1-5)* Bamberg SO, Rickenbacher
Virgin VC7 91494-2 [D] **F**

HURLSTONE, William (1876–1906) ENGLAND

O *The Magic Mirror Suite; Variations on an Original Theme; Variations on an Hungarian Air* LPO, Braithwaite
Lyrita SRCD 208 [D] **F**

C *4 Characteristic Pieces* King (cl), Benson (pno)
(+ Finzi: *Five Bagatelles;* Ferguson: *4 Short Pieces, Op. 6;* Stanford: *Clarinet Sonata, Op. 129*)
Hyperion CDA 66014 [D] **F**

IBERT, Jacques (1890–1962) FRANCE

O *Bacchanale; Bostoniana; Escales; *Flute Concerto; Louisville Concerto; Suite symphonique (Paris); Hommage à Mozart*
*Hutchins (fl), Montreal SO, Dutoit
Decca 440 332-2 [D] **F**

Divertissement Ulster O, Tortelier
(+ Milhaud: *Le Boeuf sur le toit etc;* Poulenc: *Les Biches*)
Chandos CHAN 9023 [D] **F**

Flute Concerto Milan (fl), City of London Sinfonia, Hickox
Chandos CHAN 8840 [D] **F** (see collections)

Symphonie Concertante de Lancie (ob), LSO, Previn
(+ Françaix: *L'Horloge de flore;* Satie: *Gymnopédies Nos. 1 & 3;* R. Strauss: *Oboe Concerto*)
RCA GD 87989 [A] **M**

d'INDIA, Sigismondo (c.1582–1629) ITALY

V *Amico hai vint'io; Diana; Misera me; Piangono al pianger mio; Sfere fermate; Torna il sereno zefiro* Kirkby (sop), Rooley (chitarrone)
(+ Monteverdi: *Lamento d'Olympia, etc.*)
Hyperion CDA 66106 [D] **F**

D'INDY, Vincent (1851–1931) FRANCE

O *Jour d'été à la montagne, Op. 61; Tableaux de voyage, Op. 36* Loire PO, Dervaux
EMI CDM7 64364-2 [A] **M**

Symphonie sur un chant montagnard français, Op. 25; **Symphony No. 2 in Bb, Op. 57* *Ciccolini (pno), Paris O, Baudo; **Toulouse Capitole O, Plasson
EMI CDM7 63952-2 [A] **M**

Symphonie sur un chant montagnard français, Op. 25 Henriot-Schweitzer (pno), Boston SO, Monteux
(+ Berlioz: *Overture: Béatrice et Bénédict;* Franck: *Symphony in D min.*)
RCA GD 86805 [A] **M**

IRELAND, John (1879–1962) ENGLAND

O *Piano Concerto in Eb* Stott (pno), RPO, Handley
(+ Bridge: *Phantasm;* Walton: *Sinfonia Concertante*)
Conifer CDCF 175 [D] **F**

**Piano Concerto; *Legend; Mai-Dun* (symphonic rhapsody)
*Parkin (pno), LPO, Thomson
Chandos CHAN 8461 [D] **F**

A Downland Suite; The Holy Boy; Meditation on John Keble's Rogotation Hymn ECO, Garforth
(+ Bridge: *Suite for Strings*)
Chandos CHAN 8390 [D] **F**

O *Epic March; The Holy Boy; A London Overture; Greater Love Hath No Man* (motet); *These Things Shall Be; Vexila Regis (Hymn for Passion Sunday)* Terfel (bs-bar), LSO & Ch, Hickox
Chandos CHAN 8879 [D] **F**

The Forgotten Rite; The Overlanders (film score): *Suite; Satyricon* (overture); *Scherzo and Cortege on themes from Julius Caesar; Tritons* (symphonic prelude) LSO, Hickox
Chandos CHAN 8994 [D] **F**

C *Cello Sonata* Lloyd Webber (vcl), McCabe (pno)
(+ Bridge: *Elegy; Scherzetto;* Stanford: *Cello Sonata No. 2*)
ASV CDDCA 807 [D] **F**

Phantasie Trio in A min. Hartley Piano Trio
(+ Bridge: *Phantasie Trio in C min.;* Clarke: *Piano Trio*)
Gamut GAMCD 518 [D] **F**

S *Ballade; The Darkened Valley; Equinox; Greenways; In those Days; Leaves from a Child's Sketchbook; London Pieces; 2 Pieces; Prelude in E♭* Parkin (pno)
Chandos CHAN 9140 [D] **F**

Piano Sonata; The Almond Tree; Decorations; Merry Andrew; Preludes; Rhapsody; Summer Evening; The Towing-Path Parkin (pno)
Chandos CHAN 9056 [D] **F**

ISAAC, Heinrich (c.1450–1517) NETHERLANDS

Missa de apostolis; Optime...pastor; Regina caeli laetare; Resurrexi et adhuc tecum sum; Tota pulchra es; Virgo prudentissima Tallis Scholars, Phillips
Gimell CDGIM 023 [D] **F**

IVES, Charles (1874–1954) USA

O *Calcium Light Night; Country Band March; Largo Cantabile: Hymn* (from *A Set of 3 Short Pieces for String Quartet*); *Orchestral Set No. 1 (Three Places in New England); Postlude in F; 4 Ragtime Dances; Set for Theatre Orchestra; Yale-Princetown Football Game* New England O, Sinclair
Koch 37025-2 [D] **F**

Central Park in the Dark; Holidays Symphony; The Unanswered Question (original and revised versions) CSO & Ch, Tilson Thomas
Sony CD 42381 [D] **F**

Symphony No. 1 Detroit SO, Järvi
(+ Barber: *Essays for Orchestra Nos. 1–3*)
Chandos CHAN 9053 [D] **F**

Symphonies Nos. 1 & 4 CSO, Tilson Thomas
Sony CD 44939 [D] **F**

Symphony No. 2; Central Park in the Dark; The Gong on the Hook and Ladder; Tone Roads: No. 1; A Set of 3 Short Pieces; The Unanswered Question NYPO, Bernstein
DG 429 220-2 [D] **F**

Symphony No. 3; Three Places in New England Eastman-Rochester O, Hanson
(+ Mennin: *Symphony No. 5;* Schuman: *New England Triptych*)
Philips Mercury 432 755-2 [A] **M**

O *Symphony No. 3; Three Places in New England; Central Park in the Dark; The Unanswered Question; March III with the Air 'Old Kentucky Home'; Fugue in 4 keys (The Shining Shore)* St. Louis SO, Slatkin
RCA 09026-61222-2 [D] **F**

Variations on 'America' (arr. Schuman) St. Louis SO, Slatkin
(+ Schuman: *Symphony No. 10, etc.*)
RCA RD 61282 [D] **F**

C *String Quartets Nos. 1 & 2; Scherzo (Holding your own)* Emerson Quartet
(+ Barber: *String Quartet*)
DG 435 864-2 [D] **F**

S *Piano Sonata No. 1* Lawson (pno)
(+ Griffes: *Piano Sonata;* Sessions: *Piano Sonata No. 2*)
Virgin VC7 59316 [D] **F**

Piano Sonata No. 2 'Concord Mass' Hamelin (pno)
(+ Wright: *Piano Sonata*)
New World NW378-2 [D] **F**

Three-page Sonata Lawson (pno)
(+ Barber: *Piano Sonata;* Carter: *Piano Sonata;* Copland: *Piano Sonata*)
Virgin VC7 59008-2 [D] **F**

V *26 Songs* Alexander (sop), Crone (pno)
Etcetera KTC 1020 [D] **F**

JACOB, Gordon (1895–1984) ENGLAND

O *5 Pieces* Reilly (harmonica), ASMF, Marriner
(+ Moody: *Little Suite;* Tausky: *Concertino;* Vaughan Williams: *Romance*)
Chandos CHAN 8617 [D] **F**

C *Divertimento* Reilly (harmonica), Hindar Quartet
(+ Moody: *Harmonica Quintet; Suite dans le style français*)
Chandos CHAN 8802 [D] **F**

Oboe Quartet Francis (ob), Members of the English Quartet
(+ Bax: *Oboe Quintet;* Holst: *Air and Variations; 3 Pieces;* Moeran: *Fantasy Quartet*)
Chandos CHAN 8392 [D] **F**

Sextet in Bb, Op. 6 Goldstone (pno), Elysian Wind Quintet
(+ Holst: *Piano and Wind Quintet; Wind Quintet*)
Chandos CHAN 9077 [D] **F**

JANÁČEK, Leoš (1854–1928) MORAVIA

O *Complete orchestral works* Brno, Sate PO, Jilek
Supraphon 11 1834-2 033, 3 CDs [D] **F**

Capriccio; Concertino Firkušný (pno), Czech PO, Neumann
(Dvořák: *Piano Concerto*)
RCA RD 60781 [D] **F**

Capriccio Kvapil (pno), Wallace Collection, Wallace
(+ Hindemith: *Concert Music, Op. 49;* Vackar: *Trumpet, Piano and Percussion Concerto*)
Nimbus NI 5103 [D] **F**

Sinfonietta; Taras Bulba VPO, Mackerras
(+ Shostakovich: *Age of Gold: Suite*)
Decca 430 727-2 [D] **M**

O *Sinfonietta* Bavarian RSO, Kubelik
(+ Smetana: *Hakon Jarl; Prague Carnival; Richard III;*
Wallenstein's Camp)
DG 437 254-2 [A] **M**

Taras Bulba Cleveland O, Dohnanyi
(+ Dvořák: *Symphony No. 6*)
Decca 430 204-2 [D] **F**

C *Mládí (Youth)* Orpheus CO
(+ Bartók: *Divertimento; Romanian Dances*)
DG 415 668-2 [D] **F**

Violin Sonata Kremer (vln), Argerich (pno)
(+ Bartók: *Violin Sonata No. 1;* Messiaen: *Theme et Variations*)
DG 427 351-2 [D] **F**

EDITORS' CHOICE (see page 14): *String Quartets Nos. 1 & 2*
Vanburgh Quartet
(+ Dvořák: *String Quartet No. 10*)
Collins 13812 [D] **F**

S *Along an Overgrown Path; In the Mist; Reminiscence; Piano Sonata*
(1.X.1905); Theme and Variations (Zdenka) Firkušný (pno)
DG 429 857-2 [A] **M**

Amarus (cantata) Němečková (sop), Vodička (ten), Zítek
(ten), Czech PO & Ch, Mackerras
(+ Martinů: *Field Mass*)
Supraphon C37-7735 [D] **F**

Diary of One Who Disappeared (song cycle); Sinfonietta*
*Balleys (cont), *Langridge (ten), *Women of RIAS Chamber
Ch, BPO, Abbado
DG 427 313-2 [D] **F**

Glagolitic Mass Söderström (sop), Drobková (cont), Livora
(ten), Novák (bs), CPO & Ch, Mackerras
Supraphon C37-7448 [D] **F**

ANEQUIN, Clément (c.1485–1558) FRANCE

20 Chansons Clément Janequin Ensemble
HM HMC90 1099 [A] **F**

OACHIM, Joseph (1831–1907) AUSTRO-HUNGARY

D *Violin Concerto in the Hungarian Style, Op. 11; Hamlet* (overture),
Op. 4; Heinrich IV (overture), *Op. 7* Oliviera (vln), LPO,
Botstein
Pickwick MCD 27 [D] **M**

OPLIN, Scott (1868–1917) USA

Rags: *A Breeze from Alabama; The Cascades; The Crysanthemum;*
The Easy Winners; Elite Syncopations; The Entertainer; Maple leaf
Rag; Original Rags; Palm leaf Rag; Peacherine Rag; Something
Doing; The Strenuous Life; Sunflower Slow Drag; Swipesy; The
Sycamore; Weeping Willow Hyman (pno)
RCA GD 87993 [D] **F**

OSQUIN DESPREZ (c.1440–1521) FRANCE

Ave maria, virgo serena; Ave noblissima creatura; Miserere mei,
Deus; O bone et dulcissime Jesu; Salve regina; Stabat mater
dolorosa; Usquequo, Domine Paris Chapelle Royale Ch,
Herreweghe
HM HMC90 1243 [D] **F**

v   *Benedicta es* Tallis Scholars, Phillips
(+ Palestrina: *Missa Benedictus es*)
Gimell CDGIM 001 [D] **F**

Missa 'Ave maris stella'; 10 Motets & Chansons Taverner Consort
& Ch, Parrott
EMI CDC7 54659-2 [D] **F**

Missa La sol fa re mi; Missa Pange Lingua Tallis Scholars,
Phillips
Gimell CDGIM 009 [D] **F**

*Missa L'homme armé sexti toni; Missa L'homme armé super voces
musicales* Tallis Scholars, Phillips
Gimell CDGIM 019 [D] **F**

KABALEVSKY, Dmitri (1904–1987) RUSSIA

o   *Cello Concertos: No. 1 in G min., Op. 49; No. 2 in C min., Op. 77;
*Improvisato; *Rondo* Tarasova (vcl), Russian SO, Dudurova;
*Likhopol (vln), Kuritskaya (pno)
Olympia OCD 292 [D] **F**

Cello Concerto No. 2 in G, Op. 77 R. Wallfisch (vcl), LPO,
Thomson
(+ Glazunov: *Chant du ménestrel;* Khachaturian: *Cello Concerto*)
Chandos CHAN 8579 [D] **F**

Violin Concerto in C, Op. 48 Mordkovitch (vln), SNO, Järvi
(+ Khachaturian: *Violin Concerto*)
Chandos CHAN 8918 [D] **F**

Romeo and Juliet: Suite, Op. 55 Moscow SO, Kitaenko
(+ Glazunov: *Symphony No. 9* [unfinished]; Lvov: *Violin
Concerto*)
Olympia OCD 147 [A] **F**

Symphonies: No. 1 in C♯ min., Op. 18; No. 2 in C min., Op. 19
Szeged SO, Acel
Olympia OCD 268 [D] **F**

*Symphony No. 4, Op. 54; *Requiem, Op. 72* Leningrad
PO/Kabalevsky; *Soloists, Moscow SO & Ch, Kabalevsky
Olympia OCD 290, 2 CDs [A] **F**

c   *Cello Sonata in B♭, Op. 71; Scherzo, Op. 27/14; Novelette, Op.
27/25; Round-Dance Op. 60/2; Etude, Op. 27/3; Major-Minor
Studies for Solo Cello, Op. 68; In Memory of Sergei Prokoviev, Op.
79; *6 Preludes and Fugues, Op. 61* Tarasova (vcl), Polezhaev
(pno); *McLachlan (pno)
Olympia OCD 294 [D] **F**

String Quartets: No. 1, Op. 8; No. 2 in G min., Op. 44 Glazunov
Quartet
Olympia OCD 293 [D] **F**

s   *Piano Sonatas Nos. 1 & 2; Sonatina No. 2; 4 Preludes, Op. 5;
Rondo in A min., Op. 59* McLachlan (pno)
Olympia OCD 267 [D] **F**

*Piano Sonata No. 3 in F, Op. 46; 24 Preludes; Sonatina in C, Op.
13 No. 1* McLachlan (pno)
Olympia OCD 266 [D] **F**

KALINNIKOV, Vasily (1866–1901) RUSSIA

o   *Symphony No. 1 in G min.* SNO, Järvi
(+ Glazunov: *The Sea; Spring*)
Chandos CHAN 8611 [D] **F**

o *Symphony No. 2 in A; The Cedar and the Palm; Tsar Boris* (opera):
   Overture SNO, Järvi
   Chandos CHAN 8805 [D] **F**

KANCHELI, Giya (born 1935) GEORGIA

o *Symphonies Nos. 1 & 7; Liturgy for Viola and Orchestra*
   *Belonogov (vla), Moscow State SO, Glushchenko
   Olympia OCD 424 [D] **F**

   *Symphonies Nos. 3 & *6* Gonashvili (ten), *Kharadze (vla),
   *Chaduneli (vla), Georgia State SO, Kakhidze
   Olympia OCD 401 [A] **F**

   Symphonies Nos. 4 & 5 Georgia State SO, Kakhidze
   Olympia OCD 403 [A] **F**

KETELBEY, Albert (1875–1959) ENGLAND

o *Bank Holiday ('Appy 'Ampstead); Bells across the Meadows; The
   Clock and the Dresden Figures; Dance of the Merry Mascots; In a
   Chinese Temple Garden; In a Monastery Garden; In a Persian
   Market; In the Mystic Land of Egypt; Sanctuary of the Heart; With
   Honour crowned* London Promenade O, Faris
   Philips 400 011-2 [D] **F**

KHACHATURIAN, Aram (1903–1978) ARMENIA

o *Cello Concerto* R. Wallfisch (vcl), LPO, Thomson
   (+ Glazunov: *Chant du ménestrel*; Kabalevsky: *Cello Concerto
   No. 2*)
   Chandos CHAN 8579 [D] **F**

   Piano Concerto; Gayeneh (ballet): *Suite; Masquerade* (incidental
   music): *Suite* Orbelian (pno), SNO, Järvi
   Chandos CHAN 8542 [D] **F**

   Violin Concerto in D min.
   Szeryng (vln), LSO, Dorati
   (+ Brahms: *Violin Concerto*)
   Philips Mercury 434 318-2 [A] **M**
   Mordkovitch (vln), SNO, Järvi
   (+ Kabalevsky: *Violin Concerto in C*)
   Chandos CHAN 8918 [D] **F**

   Spartacus: Ballet Suites Nos. 1–3 SNO, Järvi
   Chandos CHAN 8927 [D] **F**

   Symphony No. 2; Gayeneh (ballet): *Suite* SNO, Järvi
   Chandos CHAN 8945 [D] **F**

s *10 Children's Pieces; Poem; Sonata; Sonatina; Toccata; Valse from
   Masquerade* McLachlan (pno)
   Olympia OCD 423 [D] **F**

KNIPPER, Lev (1898–1974) RUSSIA

o *Concert Poem; Sinfonietta No. 1* *Shakhovskaya (vcl), Moscow
   Conservatoire CO, Teryan
   (+ Miaskovsky: *Symphony No. 7*)
   Olympia OCD 163 [A] **F**

KNUSSEN, Oliver (born 1952) ENGLAND

o *Coursing, Op. 17;, Ophelia Dances, Book 1, Op. 13; Symphonies
   Nos. 2 & 3; Cantata, Op. 15; Trumpets, Op. 12* Various artists,
   Knussen
   Unicorn-Kanchana UKCD 2010 [D] **M**

V *Songs without Voices*, Op. 26; **Sonya's Lullaby*, Op. 16;
*Variations, Op. 24; ***Hums and Songs of Winnie-the-Pooh*, Op. 6;
**4 Late Poems and an Epigram of Rainer Maria Rilke, Op. 23;
***Ocean de terre, Op. 10; *****Whitman Settings*, Op. 25
Saffer (sop), */****Shelton (sop), Lincoln Centre
Chamber Music Society O, Knussen; */****Serkin (pno)
Virgin VC7 59308-2 [D] **F**

KODÁLY, Zoltán (1882–1967) HUNGARY

O *Dances from Galánta; Dances from Marosszék; *Háry János Suite*
*Philharmonia Hungarica, Minneapolis SO, Dorati
(+ Bartók: *Hungarian Sketches; Romanian Folkdances*)
Philips Mercury 432 005-2 [A] **M**

Háry János Suite Cleveland O, Szell
(+ Mussorgsky: *Pictures at an Exhibition;* Prokofiev: *Lieutenant
Kijé Suite*)
Sony CD 48162 [A] **B**

C **Duo*, Op. 7; *Solo Cello Sonata*, Op. 4 *Gingold (vln), Starker (vcl)
Delos DE 1015 [A] **F**

String Quartets Nos. 1 & 2 Kodály Quartet
Hungaroton HCD 12362-2 [D] **F**

V **Budavári Te Deum; Missa Brevis* *Andor (sop), Ekert (sop),
Makkay (sop), Mohácsi (sop), *Szirmay (cont), Réti (ten),
Gregor (bs), Hungarian Radio Ch, Budapest SO, Ferencsik
Hungaroton HCD 11397-2 [A] **F**

Hymn of Zrinyi; *Psalmus Hungaricus, Op. 13 Luxon (bar),
Brighton Festival Ch, Heltay; *Kozma (ten), Brighton Festival
Ch, Wandsworth School Boys' Ch, LSO, Kertész
(+ Dvořák: *Requiem*)
Decca 421 810-2, 2CDs [A] **M**

KOECHLIN, Charles (1867–1950) FRANCE

O *The Jungle Book* Berlin RSO, Zinman
RCA 09026 61955 2, 2CDs [D] **M**

*The Seven Stars Symphony, Op. 132; ***Ballade*, Op. 50 *Pellie
(ondes martenot), **Rigutto (pno), Monte-Carlo PO, Myrat
EMI CDM7 64369-2 [D] **M**

C *14 Chants*, Op. 157b; *Morceau de lecture pour la flûte*, Op. 218;
Flute Sonata, Op. 52; *Sonata for Two Flutes*, Op. 75; *Premier
album de Lilian* (from film score), Op. 139; *Deuxième album de
Lilian*, Op. 149 Smith (fl), Buyse (fl), West (sop), Amlin (pno)
Hyperion CDA 66414 [D] **F**

Morceau de lecture, Op. 218; **15 Pièces*, Op. 180; **Horn Sonata*,
Op. 70; *20 Sonneries*, Op. 123: Nos. 1, 3, 10, 13 & 20; 20
Sonneries, Op. 142: Nos. 2 & 5; 10 Sonneries, Op. 153/2: Nos. 2, 3,
5 & 11 Tuckwell (hn), *Blumenthal (pno)
ASV CDDCA 716 [D] **F**

V *7 Chansons pour Gladys*, Op. 151; *16 chansons and rondels*
Leblanc (sop), Sharon (pno)
Hyperion CDA 66243 [D] **F**

KOKKONEN, Joonas (born 1921) FINLAND

O *Cello Concerto; Symphonic Sketches; Symphony No. 4* Thedéen
(vcl), Lahti SO, Vänskä
BIS BIS-CD 468 [D] **F**

O *Symphony No. 1; Music for Strings; *The Hades of the Birds* (song cycle) *Groop (mez), Lahti SO, Söderblom
BIS BIS-CD 485 [D] **F**

Symphony No. 2; Inauguratio; *Erekhthion (cantata); *The Last Temptations* (opera): *Interludes* *Vihavainen (sop), Groenroos (bar), Lahti SO, Vänskä
BIS BIS-CD 498 [D] **F**

Symphony No. 3; *Opus Sonorum; **Requiem *Sivonen (pno), **Isokoski (sop), **Groenroos (bar), Savonlinna Opera Festival Ch, Lahti SO, Söderblom
BIS BIS-CD 508 [D] **F**

C *Piano Quintet; String Quartets Nos. 1–3* Valsta (pno), Sibelius Academy Quartet
BIS BIS-CD 458 [D] **F**

KORNGOLD, Erich (1897–1957) AUSTRO-HUNGARY/USA

O *Adventures of Robin Hood* (film score) Utah SO, Kojian
TER Classics CDTER 1066 [A]

Cello Concerto; Film Scores (excerpts): *Another Dawn; Anthony Adverse; Of Human Bondage; The Prince and the Pauper; The Private Lives of Elizabeth and Essex; The Sea Wolf* Gabarro (vcl), National PO, Gerhardt
RCA GD 80185 [A] **M**

Film Scores (excerpts): *Juarez; The Private Lives of Elizabeth and Essex* National PO, Gerhardt
(+ film scores by Newman, Steiner and Waxman)
RCA GD 80183 [A] **M**

Symphony in F♯, Op. 40; *Abschiedslieder *Finnie (sop), BBC PO, Downes
Chandos CHAN 9171 [D] **F**

C *Piano Trio in D, Op. 1* Beaux Arts Trio
(+ Zemlinsky: *Piano Trio*)
Philips 434 072-2 [D] **F**

String Sextet in D, Op. 10 Raphael Ensemble
(+ Schoenberg: *Verklärte Nacht*)
Hyperion CDA 66425 [D] **F**

KRAMÁŘ František (1759–1831) BOHEMIA

O *Clarinet Concerto in E♭, Op. 36; Clarinet Concerto in E min., Op. 86; *Double Clarinet Concerto in E♭, Op. 35* Friedli (cl), *Pay (cl), ECO, Pay
Claves CD-50 8602 [D] **F**

Flute Concerto No. 1 in G, Op. 30; Flute and Oboe Concertino, Op. 65; Oboe Concerto in F, Op. 52 Graf (fl/dir), Holliger (ob/dir), ECO
Claves CD 50-8203 [D] **F**

C *Octet Partitas in B♭, Op. 67 & E♭, Op. 79* Nash Ensemble
(+ Dvořák: *Serenade for Wind in D min., Op. 44*)
CRD 3410 [A] **F**

KRASA, Hans (1899–1944) CZECHOSLOVAKIA

String Quartet Hawthorne Quartet
(+ Haas: *String Quartets Nos. 1 & 2*)
Decca 440 853-2 [D] **F**

KREISLER, Fritz (1875–1962) AUSTRIA/USA

C *Allegretto in the style of Boccherini; Allegretto in the style of Porpora;*
   Caprice viennois; Cavatina; La Chasse in the style of Cartier; La
   Gitana; Grave in the style of W.F. Bach; Gypsy caprice; Liebesfreud;
   Liebesleid; Praeludium and Allegro in the style of Pugnani;
   Recitativo and scherzo-caprice; Schön Rosmarin; Shepherd's
   Madrigal; Sicilienne and Rigaudon in the style of Francoeur; Toy
   Soldiers' march; Viennese rhapsodic fantasia Shumsky (vln),
   Kaye (pno)
   ASV CDQS 6039 [A] B

   Caprice in E♭ (Wieniawski); Caprice viennois; Danse espagnole
   (Granados); La Gitana; Larghetto (Weber); Liebesfreud; Liebesleid;
   Polichinelle; La Précieuse; Recitativo and scherzo-caprice; Rondo on
   a theme of Beethoven; Serenade espagnole (Glazunov); Slavonic
   dance No. 10 in E min. (Dvořák); Syncopation; Tambourin chinois;
   Tango (Albéniz); Zigeuner Mintz (vln), Benson (pno)
   DG 423 876-2 [A] M

KREUTZER, Conradin (1780–1849) GERMANY

C *Septet in E♭, Op. 62* Nash Ensemble
   (+ Hummel: *Septet in C, Op. 114*)
   CRD 3390 [A] F

KUHLAU, Friedrich (1786–1832) GERMANY/DENMARK

O *Concertino for 2 Horns, Op. 45; Piano Concerto in C, Op. 7;*
   Elverhøj Overture Lansky-Otto (hn), Werke (hn), Ponti (pno),
   Odense SO, Maga
   Unicorn-Kanchana DKPCD 9110 [D] F

LALO, Edouard (1823–1892) FRANCE

O *Cello Concerto in D min.* Haimowitz (vcl), CSO, Levine
   (+ Bruch: *Kol Nidrei, Op. 47;* Saint-Saëns: *Cello Concerto No. 1*)
   DG 427 323-2 [D] F

   Symphonie espagnole, Op. 21
   Stern (vln), Philadelphia O, Ormandy
   (+ Bruch: *Violin Concerto No. 1*)
   Sony/CBS CD 45555 [A] M

LAMBERT, Constant (1905–1951) ENGLAND

O *Horoscope* (ballet): *Suite* English Northern PO, Lloyd-Jones
   (+ Bliss: *Checkmate;* Walton: *Façade*)
   Hyperion CDA 66436 [D] F

V **Rio Grande; **Summer's Last Will and Testament; Aubade*
   héroïque *Burgess (mez), *Gibbons (pno), **Shimell (bar),
   *Opera North Ch, **Leeds Festival Ch, English Northern
   PO, Lloyd-Jones
   Hyperion CDA 66565 [D] F

LANGGAARD, Rued (1893–1952) DENMARK

O *Symphonies No. 1 (Klippepastoraler); Fra Dybet* Danish
   National Radio Ch & SO, Segerstam
   Chandos CHAN 9249 [D] F

   Symphonies Nos. 4–6 Danish National RSO, Järvi
   Chandos CHAN 9064 [D] F

LANGLAIS, Jean (1907–1991) FRANCE

V *3 Paraphrases grégoriennes, Op. 5: Hymne d'actions de grâce (Te*
   Deum); 3 Poèmes évangéliques, Op. 2: L'Anonciation; Triptyque

grégorien: Rosa mystica; Messe solonelle; *Missa salve regina
O'Donnell (org), Lumsden (org), *ECO Brass Ensemble,
Westminster Cathedral Ch, Hill
Hyperion CDA 66270 [D] **F**

.ASSUS, Orlando de (1532–1594) NETHERLANDS/GERMANY

*Alma redemptoris mater; Ave Maria gratia plena; Magnificat
Praeter rerum seriem; Misa pro defunctis; O bone Jesu* Pro
Cantione Antiqua, Hamburg Early Music Wind Ensemble,
Collegium Aureum, Turner
DHM GD 77066 [A] **M**

*Alma redemptoris mater; Ave regina caelorum; Hodie completi
sunt; Missa Osculetur me; Osculetur me; Regina coeli; Salve regina
mater; Timor et tremor* Tallis Scholars, Phillips
Gimmell CDGIM 018 [D] **F**

*Exaltabo te Domine; Missa Qual donna attende; Missa Venatorum;
Psalmi Davidis poenitentales: De profundis; Tristis est anima mea*
Christ Church Cathedral Ch, Darlington
Nimbus NI 5150 [D] **F**

Lagrime di San Petro Huelgas Ensemble, van Nevel
Sony CD 53373 [D] **F**

9 Lamentationes Hieremiae; Motets: *Aurora lucis rutilat; Christus
resurgens; Magnificat Aurora lucis rutilat; Missa Pro defunctis;
Regina coeli; Surgens Jesu* Pro Cantione Antiqua, Turner
Hyperion CDA 66321/2, 2CDs [D] **F**

*Missa super Bell'Amfitrit'alterna; Psalmi Davidis penitentialis:
Domine exaudi;* Motets: *Alma redemptoris Mater; Omnes de Saba
venient; Salve regina; Tui sunt coeli* Christ Church Cathedral Ch,
Preston
Decca 433 679-2 [A] **M**

.AWES, Henry (1596–1662) ENGLAND

Songs: *Amintor's welladay; Come, sad turtle; Farewell, despairing
hopes; Hark, shepherd swains; I laid me down; I prithee send me; In
quel gelato core; The Lark; Man's life is but vain; My soul the great
God's praises sing; Orpheus's Hymn; Sing fair Clorinda; Sitting by
the streams; Slide soft you silver floods; Sweet, stay awhile; Thee and
thy wondrous deeds; This mossy bank* Consort of Musicke,
Rooley
◇ Hyperion CDA 66135 [D] **F**

.AWES, William (1602–1645) ENGLAND

Airs; Consort Setts: *a 5 in C min.; a 5 in F; a 6 in C min.; a 6 in F;
Divisions in G min.* Fretwork, Nicholson
◇ Virgin VC7 59021-2 [D] **F**

.ECLAIR, Jean-Marie (1697–1764) FRANCE

*Quatrième livre de sonates, Op. 9: Nos. 7 & 9; Troisième livre de
sonates, Op. 5: No. 6* Trio Sonnerie
◇ ASV CDGAU 106 [D] **F**

6 Ouvertures et Sonates, Op. 13 Purcell Quartet
◇ Chandos CHAN 0542 [D] **F**

6 Sonatas for Strings, Op. 4 Purcell Quartet
◇ Chandos CHAN 0536 [D] **F**

6 Sonatas, Op. 3 Holloway (vln), Banchini (vln)
◇ Erato 2292-45013-2 [D] **F**

C *6 Sonatas, Op. 12* Holloway (vln), Banchini (vln)
◇ Erato 2292-45519-2 [D] **F**

LECOCQ, Charles (1832–1918) FRANCE

O *Mam'zelle Angot* (ballet) National PO, Bonynge
(+ Hérold: *La Fille mal gardée*)
Decca 430 849-2, 2CDs [A] **M**

LEIGHTON, Kenneth (1929–1988) ENGLAND

O *Cello Concerto, Op. 31; *Symphony No. 3* R. Wallfisch (vcl),
*Mackie (ten), SNO, Thomson
Chandos CHAN 8741 [D] **F**

*Missa Brevis; Crucifixus pro nobis; An Evening Hymn; Let all the
World; Lully, Lulla (Coventry Carol); Magnificat and Nunc Dmitti
(Second Service); Te Deum* Mackie (ten), St. Paul's Cathedral
Ch, Scott
Hyperion CDA 66489 [D] **F**

Veris gratia, Op. 9 R. Wallfisch (vcl), Caird (ob), RLPO,
Handley
(+ Finzi: *Cello Concerto*)
Chandos CHAN 8471 [D] **F**

LHÉRITIER, Jean (c.1480–after 1552) FRANCE

V *Nigra sum* Tallis Scholars, Phillips
(+ De Silva: *Nigra sum;* Palestrina: *Missa Nigra sum;* Victoria:
Nigra sum)
Gimell CDGIM 003 [D] **F**

LIGETI, György (born 1923) HUNGARY/AUSTRIA

O *Chamber Concerto; Ramifications; Aventures; *String Quartet No. 2
**Lux aeterna* Ensemble Intercontemporain, Boulez; *LaSalle
Quartet; **North German Radio Ch, Franz
DG 423 244-2 [A/D] **M**

C *String Quartet No. 1* Hagen Quartet
(+ Lutoslawski: *String Quartet;* Schnittke: *Kanon in memorium
Stravinsky*)
DG 431 686-2 [D] **F**

LISZT, Franz (1811–1886) HUNGARY

O *Piano Concertos: No. 1 in E♭; No. 2 in A; Fantasia on Hungarian
Folk Themes; Fantasy on a Theme from Beethoven's 'Ruins of
Athens'; Grand Symphonic Fantasy on Themes from Berlioz's
'Lelio'; Malediction; Polonaise brillante; Totentanz;
Wandererfantasie (Schubert arr.)* Béroff (pno), LGO, Masur
EMI CZS7 67214-2, 2CDs [A] **B**

*Piano Concertos: No. 1 in E♭; No. 2 in A; Fantasia on Hungarian
Folk Themes; Totentanz* Thibaudet (pno), Montreal SO, Dutoit
Decca 433 075-2 [D] **F**

Piano Concerto No. 3 in E♭; De profundis; Totentanz (1853
version) Mayer (pno), LSO, Vásáry
ASV CDDCA 778 [D] **F**

A Dante Symphony Kincses (sop), Hungarian Radio Ch,
Budapest SO, Lehel
Hungaroton HCD 11918 [A] **F**

Fantasia on Hungarian Folk Themes
Bolet (pno), LSO, Fischer
(+ Addinsell: *Warsaw Concerto;* Gershwin: *Rhapsody in Blue;*

Gottschalk: *Grande fantaisie;* Litolff: *Concerto symphonique No. 4*)
Decca 430 726-2 [D] **M**

⊃ *A Faust Symphony* Riegel (ten), Tanglewood Festival Ch,
Boston SO, Bernstein
DG 431 470-2 [A] **M**

Hungarian Rhapsodies Nos. 1–6 LSO, Dorati
(+ Enescu: *Romanian Rhapsody No. 1*)
Philips Mercury 432 015-2 [A] **M**

The Complete Symphonic Poems LPO, Haitink
Volume 1
Philips 438 751-2, 2 CDs [A] **B**
Volume 2
Philips 438 754-2, 2 CDs [A] **B**

*Les Préludes; Mazeppa; Tasso, lamento e trionfo; Mephisto Waltz
No. 2; Hungarian Rhapsodies Nos. 2, 4 & 5; *Fantasia on
Hungarian Folk Themes* *Cherkassky (pno), BPO, Karajan
DG 415 967-2, 2CDs [A] **F**

*À la chapelle sixtine; Fantasia and Fugue in G min. (Bach arr.); 6
Preludes and Fugues (Bach arr.)* Howard (pno)
Hyperion CDA 66438 [D] **F**

*Abschied; Am Grabe Richard Wagners; Dem Andenken Petöfis; Der
Bilde Sänger; Carousel de Mme. Pelet-Narbonne; Epithalum zu
Edward Reményis Vermählungsfeier; 5 Kleine Klavierstücke;
Lugubre gondola; Mosonyis Grabgeleit; Nuages gris; Piano piece in
F♯; 2 Piano Pieces; R.W.– Venezia; Recueillement; Resignazione;
Romance oubliée; Schlafos, Frage und Antwort (two versions);
Toccata; Ungarische Königslied; Ungarns Gott; Unstern: sinistre,
disastro; Wiegenlied* Howard (pno)
Hyperion CDA 66445 [D] **F**

Transcriptions: Auber: *3 pièces;* Bellini: *Réminiscences de Norma;*
Berlioz: *Benvenuto Cellini: Bénédiction et serment;* Donizetti:
*Réminiscences de Lucia di Lammermoor; Lucia di Lammermoor
funeral march and cavatina;* Duke Ernst of Saxe-Coburg-Gotha:
Tony: Hunting Chorus; Glinka: *Ruslan and Ludmilla march;*
Gounod: *Faust: Waltz;* Handel: *Almira sarabande and chaconne;*
Meyerbeer: *Africaine illustrations;* Mozart: *Réminiscences de Don
Juan;* Tchaikovsky: *Eugene Onegin Polonaise;* Verdi: *Aida:
Danza sacra e duetto finale;* Wagner: *Tristan und Isolde: Liebestod;*
Weber: *Der Freischütz Overture* Howard (pno)
Hyperion CDA 66371/2, 2CDs [D] **F**

*Album d'un Voyageur; Chanson dur Bearn; Fantasie romantique sur
deux melodies suisses; Faribolo Pastour* Howard (pno)
Hyperion CDA 66601/2, 2 CDs [D] **F**

*Albumblatt in Walzerform; Bagatelle sans tonalité; 3 Caprices-
valses: Nos. 1 & 2; Ländler in A♭; Mephisto Waltzes Nos. 1–4;
Valse-impromptu; 4 Valses oubliées* Howard (pno)
Hyperion CDA 66201 [D] **F**

*Alleluja and Ave Maria (Arcadelt arr.); Ave Maria (Die Glocken
von Rom); Ave Maria (versions II–IV); Ave maris stella;
Harmonies poétiques et religieuses; L'hymne du Pape; 2 Hymnes; In
festo transfigurationis Domine nostri Jesu Christe; Invocation; O
Roma nobilis; 2 Pieces from the Hungarian Coronation Mass;
Sancta Dorothea; Slavimo slavno slaveni!; Stabat mater; Urbi et
orbi, bénédiction papale; Vexilla regis prodeunt; Zum Haus des
Herrn ziehen wir* Howard (pno)
Hyperion CDA 66421/2, 2CDs [D] **F**

S *Années de pèlerinage* (complete) Berman (pno)
DG 437 206-2, 3CDs [A] **M**

Années de pèlerinage (année 1): Suisse Bolet (pno)
Decca 410 160-2 [D] **F**

Années de pèlerinage (année 2): Italie Bolet (pno)
Decca 410 161-2 [D] **F**

*Années de pèlerinage (année 2) Supplément: Venezia e Napoli;
Années de pèlerinage (année 3)* Bolet (pno)
Decca 411 803-2 [D] **F**

Schubert transcriptions: *Auf dem Wasser zu singen; Aufenthalt;
Erlkönig; Die Forelle* (second version); *Horch, horch die Lerch;
Lebewohl; Der Lindenbaum; Lob der Tränen; Der Müller und der
Bach; Die Post; Das Wandern; Wohin?* Bolet (pno)
Decca 414 575-2 [D] **F**

*Ballades: No. 1 in Db; No. 2 in B min.; Berceuse; Impromptu in F♯;
Klavierstück in Ab; 2 Légendes; 2 Polonaises* Howard (pno)
Hyperion CDA 66301 [D] **F**

6 Chants polonais (Chopin arr.); Danse macabre (Saint-Saëns arr.)
Berlioz transcriptions: *Les Francs-juges Overture; Idée fixe
(Symphonie Fantastique); Marche des pèlerins (Harold en Italie); Le
Roi Lear Overture; Valses des Sylphes (Le Damnation de Faust)*
Howard (pno)
Hyperion CDA 66346 [D] **F**

*3 Concert Studies; 2 Concert Studies; 6 Consolations; Réminiscences
de Don Juan (Mozart arr.)* Bolet (pno)
Decca 417 523-2 [A] **F**

*11 Chorales: Crux ave benedicte; Jesus Christe; Meine Seele; Nun
danket alle Gott; Nun ruhen alle Wälder; O Haupt; O Lamm Gottes
O Traurigkeit; Vexilla Regis; Was Gott tut; Wer nur den Lieben; Via
crucis; Weihnachtsbaum* Howard (pno)
Hyperion CDA 66388 [D] **F**

*Deuxième fantaisie sur des motifs des Soirées musicales; Grande
fantaisie sur des motifs des Soirées musicales; Nuits d'été à
Pausilippe; Soirées italiennes; Soirées musicales; Tre Sonetti di
Petrarca; Venezia e Napoli* Howard (pno)
Hyperion CDA 66661/2, 2CDs [D] **F**

12 Études d'exécution transcendante (1838 version) Weber (pno)
Pickwick MCD 10 [D] **B**

12 Études d'exécution transcendante (1851 version) Arrau (pno)
Philips 416 458-2 [A] **F**

6 Études d'exécution transcendante d'après Paganini Petrov (pno)
(+ Chopin: *Souvenir de Paganini*; Schumann: *6 Studies on
Caprices by Paganini*)
Olympia OCD 144 [A] **F**

*Fantasia and Fugue on the Name B-A-C-H; Funeral odes; Grosses
Konzertsolo; Variations on 'Weinen, Klagen, Sorgen, Zagen';
Weinen, Klagen, Sorgen, Zagen (Prelude after Bach)* Howard (pno)
Hyperion CDA 66302 [D] **F**

Hungarian Rhapsodies Nos. 1–19
Szidon (pno)
DG 423 925-2, 2CDs [A] **M**
Cziffra (pno)
EMI C257 67888-2, 2CDs [A] **B**

3 Orchestral movements from 'Christus' 4 Pieces from 'Elisabeth'; 2 Polonaises from 'Stanislaus'; Salve Polonia Howard (pno)
Hyperion CDA 66466 [D] **F**

Polonaise brillante: Introduction Milne (pno)
(+ Weber: *Piano Sonatas Nos. 3 & 4; Polacca brillante*)
CRD 3486 [D] **F**

Piano Sonata in B min.; 2 Légendes; Scherzo and March Demidenko (pno)
Hyperion CDA 66616 [D] **F**

Piano Sonata in B min.; Funérailles; La lugubre gondola II; La Notte; Nuages gris Zimerman (pno)
DG 431 780-2 [D] **F**

Symphonies Nos. 1–9 (Beethoven arr.) Katsaris (pno)
Teldec 9031-71619-2, 6CDs [D] **M**

Transcriptions of songs by Beethoven, Mendelssohn, Franz, Dessauer, Schumann & Rubinstein Howard (pno)
Hyperion CDA 66481/2, 2 CDs [D] **F**

Transcriptions of theatre music by Beethoven, Mendelssohn, Liszt, Weber & Lassen Howard (pno)
Hyperion CDA 66575 [D] **F**

An Italian Recital (Aux cypres de la Villa d'Este; Les Jeux d'eau à la Villa d'Este; La lugubre gondola; 'Dante' Sonata, etc.) Hough (pno)
Virgin VC7 59222-2 [D] **F**

The Major Piano Works Arrau (pno)
Philips 432 305-2, 5 CDs [A] **M**

'The Young Liszt': The Complete Juvenilia Howard (pno)
Hyperion CDA 66771/2, 2 CDs [D] **F**

Organ music: Évocation à la Chapelle Sixtine; Fantasia and Fugue on 'Ad nos, ad salutarem undam'; Prelude and Fugue on the name B-A-C-H; Variations on 'Weinen, Klagen, Sorgen, Zagen' Kaunzinger (org)
Novalis 150 069-2 [D] **F**

18 Lieder Fassbaender (cont), Thibaudet (pno)
Decca 430 512-2 [D] **F**

Missa choralis Atkinson (trb), Tinkler (trb), Royall (alt), Kendall (ten), Suart (bs), St. John's College Ch, Cleobury (org), Guest
(+ Dvořák: *Mass in D*)
Decca 430 364-2 [A] **M**

ITOLFF, Henry (1818–1891) ENGLAND/FRANCE

Concerto symphonique No. 4 in D min., Op. 112: Scherzo Ortiz (pno), RPO, Atzmon
(+ Addinsell: *Warsaw Concerto;* Gershwin: *Rhapsody in Blue;* Gottschalk: *Grande fantaisie;* Liszt: *Fantasia on Hungarian Folk Themes*)
Decca 430 726-2 [D] **M**

LOYD, George (born 1913) ENGLAND

Piano Concertos Nos. 1 & 2 Roscoe (pno), BBC PO, Lloyd
Albany TROY 037-2 [D] **F**

Piano Concerto No. 3 Stott (pno), BBC PO, Lloyd
Albany TROY 019-2 [D] **F**

O *Piano Concerto No. 4; The Lily-leaf and the Grasshopper; The Transformation of the Naked Ape* Stott (pno), *LSO, *Lloyd
Albany AR 004 [D] **F**

Symphonies Nos. 1 & 12 Albany SO, Lloyd
Albany TROY 032-2 [D] **F**

Symphonies Nos. 2 & 9 BBC PO, Lloyd
Albany TROY 005-2 [D] **F**

Symphony No. 4 in B Albany SO, Lloyd
Albany AR 002 [D] **F**

Symphony No. 5 BBC PO, Lloyd
Albany TROY 022-2 [D] **F**

Symphonies Nos. 6 & *10 (Winter Journeys); John Socman (opera): Overture* BBC PO, *BBC PO Brass, Lloyd
Albany TROY 015-2 [D] **F**

Symphony No. 7 BBC PO, Lloyd
Albany TROY 057-2 [D] **F**

Symphony No. 11 Albany SO, Lloyd
Albany TROY 060-2 [D] **F**

C *Lament, Air and Dance; Violin Sonata* Little (vln), Roscoe (pno)
Albany TROY 029-2 [D] **F**

S *An African Shrine; The Aggressive Fishes; Intercom Baby; The Road to Samarkand; St. Anthony and the Bogside Beggar* Roscoe (pno)
Albany AR 003 [D] **F**

V *A Symphonic Mass* Brighton Festival Ch, Bournemouth SO, Lloyd
Albany TROY 100 [D] **F**

LLOYD WEBBER, Andrew (born 1948) ENGLAND

O *Variations* J. Lloyd Webber (vcl), LPO, Maazel
(+ W. Lloyd Webber: *Aurora*)
Philips 420 342-2 [D] **F**

V *Requiem* Brightman (sop), Domingo (ten), Miles-Kingston (trb), Drew (trb), Lancelot (org), Winchester Cathedral Ch, ECO, Maazel
EMI CDC7 47146-2 [D] **F**

LLOYD WEBBER, William (1914–1982) ENGLAND

O *Aurora* LPO, Maazel
(+ A. Lloyd Webber: *Variations*)
Philips 420 342-2 [D] **F**

C *Air varié; In the half-light; Arabesque; Badinage de Noël; Presto for Perseus; Romantic Evening; Scherzo in G min.; Song without words The Divine Compassion: Thou art the King; Over the bridge; The pretty washer-maiden; A Rent for love; The Saviour: The King of Love; So lovely the rose; Utopia, Missa Sanctae Mariae Magdalenae* J. Lloyd Webber (vcl), Lill (pno); Graham-Hall (ten), Ledger (pno); Richard Hickox Singers, Watson (hpd), Hickox
ASV CDDCA 584 [D] **F**

LOCATELLI, Pietro (1695–1764) ITALY

O *12 Violin Concertos, Op. 3 (L'Arte del Violino)* E. Wallfisch (vln), Raglan Baroque Players, Kraemer
◇ Hyperion CDA 66721/3, 3CDs [D] **F**

○ *12 Flute Sonatas, Op. 2* Stephen Preston (fl), Hogwood (hpd)
◇ L'Oiseau-Lyre 436 191-2, 2 CDs [A] **F**

12 Sonate da camera, Op. 6: Nos. 1, 6, 11 & 12 Locatelli Trio
◇ Hyperion CDA 66363 [D] **F**

LOCKE, Matthew (1621/2–1677) ENGLAND

♦ *Audi, Domine; Be Thou Exalted; Descende caelo cincta sororibus; How doth the city sit solitary; Jesu auctor clementie; Lord, let me know mine end; O be joyful; Super flumina Babylonis* New College Ch, Parley of Instruments, Higginbottom
◇ Hyperion CDA 66373 [D] **F**

LOURIE, Arthur (1892–1966) RUSSIA

○ *A Little Chamber Music; *Little Gidding (Four Intonations on T.S. Eliot); **Concerto da Camera* Klug (vln), *Riegel (ten), **Kremer (vln), Deutsche Kammerphilharmonie
DG 437 788-2 [D] **F**

LUDFORD, Nicholas (c.1485–c.1557) ENGLAND

♦ *Missa Benedicta; Magnificat Benedicta* Cardinall's Musick, Carwood
ASV CDGAU 132 [D] **F**

EDITORS' CHOICE (see page 12): *Missa Christi Virgo Dilectissima; Domina Ihesu Christe* The Cardinall's Musick, Carwood
ASV CDGAU 133 [D] **F**

Missa Videte miraculum; Ave cuius conceptio Cardinall's Musick, Carwood
ASV CDGAU 131 [D] **F**

LULLY, Jean-Baptiste (1632–1687) FRANCE

♦ *Anima Christe; Ave coeli; Dixit Dominus; Dimine salvum; Exaudi Deus; Laudate pueri; O dulcissime; O sapientia; Omnes gentes; Regina coeli; Salve regina* Les Arts Florissants Vocal & Instrumental Ensembles, Christie
◇ HM HMC90 1274 [D] **F**

Divertissements Nos. I–III (arr. Sempé) Laurens (mez), Capriccio Stravagante, Sempé
◇ DHM RD 77218 [D] **F**

LUMBYE, Hans Christian (1810–1874) DENMARK

○ *15 Galops, Polkas and Waltzes* Odense SO, Guth
Unicorn-Kanchana DKPCD 9089 [D] **F**

LUTOSLAWSKI, Witold (1913–1994) POLAND

○ *Chain 2; Partita* Mutter (vln), BBC SO, Lutoslawski
(+ Stravinsky: *Violin Concerto*)
DG 423 696-2 [D] **F**

Cello Concerto Rostropovich (vcl), Paris O, Lutoslawski
(+ Dutilleux: *Cello Concerto*)
EMI CDC7 49304-2 [A] **F**

Piano Concerto; Chain 3; Novelette Zimerman (pno), BBC SO, Lutoslawski
DG 431 664-2 [D] **F**

Concerto for Orchestra; Funeral Music for String Quartet; Venetian Games Warsaw National PO, Rowicki
Philips 426 663-2 [A] **M**

O *Dance Preludes* King (cl), ECO, Litton
(+ Blake: *Clarinet Concerto;* Seiber: *Clarinet Concertino*)
Hyperion CDA 66215 [D] **F**

Symphonies Nos. 1 & 2; Symphonic Variations; Music funèbre for Strings Polish National RSO, Lutoslawski
EMI CDM5 65076-2 [A] **M**

Symphony No. 3; Concerto for Orchestra CSO, Barenboim
Erato 4509 91711-2 [D] **F**

C *String Quartet* (1964)
LaSalle Quartet
(+ Cage: *String Quartet;* Mayuzumi: *Prelude;* Penderecki: *String Quartet*)
DG 423 245-2 [A] **M**
Varsovia Quartet
(+ Penderecki: *String Quartet No. 2;* Szymanowski: *String Quartets Nos. 1 & 2*)
Olympia OCD 328 [A] **F**
Hagen Quartet
(+ Ligeti: *String Quartet No. 1;* Schnittke: *Kanon in memorium I: Igor Stravinsky*)
DG 431 686-2 [D] **F**

LVOV, Alexey (1798–1870) RUSSIA

O *Violin Concerto in A min.* Stadler (vln), Leningrad PO, Charnushenko
(+ Glazunov: *Symphony No. 9* [unfinished]; Kabalevsky: *Romeo and Juliet: Suite*)
Olympia OCD 147 [A] **F**

LYADOV, Anatole (1855–1914) RUSSIA

O *About Olden Times* (ballad), *Op. 21b; Baba-Yaga, Op. 56; The Enchanted Lake, Op. 62; 3 Fanfares; Kikimora, Op. 63; A Musical Snuff-box, Op. 32; Polonaise (in memory of Pushkin), Op. 49; Polonaise in D (for the unveiling of the statue of Anton Rubinstein), Op. 55; 8 Russian Folksongs, Op. 58* Mexico City SO, Bátiz
ASV CDDCA 657 [D] **F**

LYAPUNOV, Sergey (1859–1924) RUSSIA

O *Hashish* (symphonic poem), *Op. 53; Polonaise, Op. 16; Solemn Overture on Russian Themes, Op. 7; Zhelyazova Volya* (symphonic poem), *Op. 37* USSR State Academy SO, Svetlanov
OCD 129 [A] **F**

Symphony No. 1; Ballade Moscow State SO, Glushchenko
Olympia OCD 519 [D] **F**

S *12 Transcendental Studies, Op. 11* Binns (pno)
Pearl SHE 9624 [D] **F**

McCARTNEY, Paul (born 1942) ENGLAND

V *Liverpool Oratorio* (orch. Davis) Te Kanawa (sop), Burgess (mez), Hadley (ten), White (bs), Budd (trb), Liverpool Anglican Cathedral Ch, RLPO & Ch, Davis
EMI CDS7 54371-2, 2CDs [D] **F**

MacCUNN, Hamish (1868–1916) SCOTLAND

O *Land of Mountain and Flood* (overture), *Op. 3* SNO, Gibson
(+ German: *Welsh Rhapsody;* Harty: *With the Wild Geese;* Smyth: *The Wreckers Overture*)
Classics for Pleasure CDCFP 4635 [A] **B**

MacDOWELL, Edward (1860–1908) USA

O *Piano Concertos: No. 1 in A min., Op. 15; No. 2 in D min., Op. 23*
Amato (pno), LPO, Freeman
Olympia OCD 353 [D] F

S *Piano Sonatas Nos. 1–3* Tocco (pno)
Kingdom KCLCD 2009 [D] F

Piano Sonata No. 4 in E min. (Keltic), Op. 59 Landes (pno)
(+ Griffes: *3 Fantasy Pieces; Piano Sonata; 3 Tone Pictures*)
Koch 37045-2 [D] F

MACHAUT, Guillaume de (c.1300–1377) FRANCE

♩ *Amours me fait désirer; Biaute que toutes autes père; Dame, à qui
m'ottri; Dame, à vous sans retollir; Dame, de qui toute ma joie vient;
Dame, je sui cilz; Dame, mon cuer en vous remaint; Douce dame
jolie, pour Dieu; Felix virgo; Foy porter; Je vivroie liement; Rose,
liz, printemps, verdure; Tuit mi penser sont* Kirkby (sop), Van
Evera (sop), Covey-Crump (ten), Gothic Voices, Page
Hyperion CDA 66087 [D] F

Messe de Nostre Dame; Je ne cesse de prier; Pas de tor en thies pais
Hilliard Ensemble, Hillier
Hyperion CDA 66358 [D] F

MACONCHY, Elizabeth (born 1907) ENGLAND

C *Clarinet Quintet* King (cl), Britten Quartet
(+ Cooke: *Clarinet Quintet*; Frankel: *Clarinet Quintet*;
Holbrooke: *Eilen Shona*)
Hyperion CDA 66428 [D] F

String Quartets Nos. 1–4 Hanson Quartet
Unicorn-Kanchana DKPCD 9080 [D] F

String Quartets Nos. 5–8 Bingham Quartet
Unicorn-Kanchana DKPCD 9081 [D] F

Quartets for Strings Nos. 9–13 Mistry Quartet
Unicorn-Kanchana DKPCD 9082 [D] F

MADERNA, Bruno (1920–1973) ITALY

♩ *Aura; Biogramma; Quadrivium* North German RSO, Sinopoli
DG 423 246-2 [A] M

MADETOJA, Leevi (1887–1947) FINLAND

♩ *Symphonies: No. 1, Op. 29; No. 2, Op. 35* Iceland SO, Sakari
Chandos CHAN 9115 [D] F

*Symphony No. 3 in A min.; The Ostrobothnians (opera): Suite, Op.
45; Huvonaytelmaalku (comedy overture), Op. 53; Okon Fuoco
(ballet): Suite No. 1, Op. 58* Iceland SO, Sakari
Chandos CHAN 9036 [D] F

MAHLER, Gustav (1860–1911) AUSTRIA

● *Symphonies Nos. 1–10* Various soloists, Bavarian RSO & Ch,
Kubelik
DG 429 042-2, 10CDs [A] M

Symphony No. 1 in D Concertgebouw, Bernstein
DG 427 303-2 [D] F

Symphony No. 2 in C min. (Resurrection)
Schwarzkopf (sop), Rössl-Majdan (mez), Philharmonia O &
Ch, Klemperer
EMI CDM7 69662-2 [A] M

o *Symphony No. 3 in D min.*
Van Nes (cont), Tölz Boys' Ch, Ernst-Senff Ch, BPO, Haitink
Philips 432 162-2, 2CDs [D] **F**

Symphony No. 4 in G
Mathis (sop), BPO, Karajan
DG 419 863-2 [A] **M**
Raskin (sop), Cleveland O, Szell; *von Stade (sop), LPO, Davis
(+ *Lieder eines fahrenden Gesellen*)
Sony CD 46535 [A] **B**

Symphony No. 5 in C♯ min.
NPO, Barbirolli
EMI CDM7 64749-2 [A] **M**
VPO, Bernstein
DG 423 608-2 [D] **F**

*Symphony No. 6 in A min.; *5 Rückert Lieder* *Ludwig (mez),
BPO, Karajan
DG 415 099-2, 2CDs [A] **F**

Symphony No. 7 CBSO, Rattle
EMI CDC7 54344-2 [D] **F**

Symphony No. 8 in E♭ Connell (sop), Wiens (sop), Lott (sop),
Schmidt (sop), Denize (sop), Versalle (ten), Hynninen (bar),
Sotin (bs), Tiffin Boys' Ch, LPO & Ch, Tennstedt
EMI CDS7 47625-8, 2CDs [D] **F**

Symphony No. 9 BPO, Karajan
DG 410 726-2, 2CDs [D] **F**

Symphony No. 10 (ed. Cooke) Bournemouth SO, Rattle
EMI CDC7 54406-2 [D] **F**

v *Im Lenz; Lieder eines fahrenden Gesellen; Lieder und Gesänge;
Winterlied* Baker (mez), Parsons (pno)
Hyperion CDA 66100 [D] **F**

*Kindertotenlieder; *Lieder eines fahrenden Gesellen; Rückert Lieder
Nos. 1 & 3–5* Fischer-Dieskau (bar), BPO, Böhm; *Bavarian
RSO, Kubelik
DG 415 191-2 [A] **F**

Das klagende Lied Dunn (sop), Fassbaender (mez), Hollweg
(ten), Baur (trb), Schmidt (bar), Bavarian RSO & Ch, Chailly
Decca 425 719-2 [D] **F**

Des knaben Wunderhorn Hampson (bar), Parsons (pno)
Teldec 9031 74726-2 [D] **F**

Das Lied von der Erde Baker (mez), King (ten),
Concertgebouw O, Haitink
Philips 432 279-2 [A] **M**

Lieder aus Des Knaben Wunderhorn Nos. 1–10, 13 & 14
Schwarzkopf (sop), Fischer-Dieskau (bar), LSO, Szell
EMI CDC7 47277-2 [A] **F**

*Lieder eines fahrenden Gesellen; 7 Early Lieder; *11 Early Lieder;*
(orch. Berio) Hampson (bar), Lutz (pno), *Philharmonia O,
Berio
Teldec 9031 74002-2 [D] **F**

*Lieder eines fahrenden Gesellen; Rückert Lieder; Lieder from Des
Knaben Wunderhorn; Lieder from Aus der Jugendzeit* Ludwig
(mez), Fischer-Dieskau (bar), Berry (bs), Bernstein (pno)
Sony CD 47170, 2CDs [A] **M**

♪ *Lieder selection* von Otter (mez), Gothoni (pno)
(+ Wolf: *9 Lieder*)
DG 423 666-2 [D] **F**

MALIPIERO, Gian Francesco (1882–1973) ITALY

▭ *String Quartets Nos. 1–8* Orpheus Quartet
ASV CDDCD 457, 2CDs [D] **F**

MARAIS, Marin (1656–1728) FRANCE

▭ *Pièces de viole: Livre 1, Part 1* (complete) Smithsonian
Chamber Players
✧ DHM RD 77146 [D] **F**

*Pièces de viole: Livre 2, Part 1: No. 20; Livre 3, Part 1: Nos. 40–2,
55 & 58; Pièces en trio: Nos. 1–4, 6, 7, 9, 58, 61–3, 66 & 67*
Purcell Quartet
✧ Hyperion CDA 66310 [D] **F**

MARCELLO, Alessandro (1684–1750) ITALY

▷ *6 Oboe Concertos (La Cetra)* Holliger (ob), Berne Camerata,
Füri
DG 427 137-2 [A] **M**

MARINI, Biagio (c.1587–1685) ITALY

▭ *E l'armi cinesi (balletto)* Consort of Musicke, Rooley
(+ Monteverdi: *Madrigals, Book 8 (Balletti): Il ballo della ingrate,
etc.*)
✧ Virgin VC7 59620-2 [D] **F**

MARTIN, Frank (1890–1974) SWITZERLAND

▷ *Trombone Ballade; Piano Ballade; Harpsichord Concerto* Rosin
(tbn), Benda (pno), Jaccotet (hpd), Lausanne CO, Martin
Jecklin-Disco JD 529-2 [A] **F**

*Cello Concerto; Les quatre éléments *Decross (vcl), Royal
Concertgebouw O, Haitink
Preludio PRL 2147 [A] **M**

*Concerto for 7 Wind Instruments, Timpani, Percussion and String
Orchestra; Études; *Polyptique* *Blankestijn (vln), COE,
Fischer
DG 435 383-2 [D] **F**

*Piano Quintet; String Quintet; String Trio; Trio sur des mélodies
populaires irlandaises* Schmid-Wyss (pno), Zurich Chamber
Ensemble
Jecklin-Disco JD 646-2 [A] **F**

Piano Trio on Popular Irish Folk Tunes Borodin Trio
(+ Debussy: *Piano Trio;* Turina: *Piano Trio No. 1*)
Chandos CHAN 9016 [D] **F**

Der Cornet Lipovšek (cont), Austrian RSO, Zagrosek
Orfeo C 164881A [D] **F**

Golgotha (oratorio); **Messe pour double choeur* Staempfli,
Montmollin, Tappy, Huttenlocher, Orchestre Symphonique,
Faller; *Midi Chamber Ch, Martin
Erato 2292-45779-2 [D] **F**

Requiem Speiser (sop), Bollen (cont), Tappy (ten), Lagger
(bs), Lausanne Women's Ch, Union Ch, OSR, Martin
Jecklin-Disco JD 631-2 [A] **F**

MARTINŮ, Bohuslav (1890–1959) BOHEMIA

o *Cello Concertos Nos. 1 & 2; Cello Concertino* R. Wallfisch (vcl), Czech PO, Bělohlávek
Chandos CHAN 9015 [D] **F**

Oboe Concerto Lencsés (ob), Stuttgart RSO, Marriner
(+ Haydn: *Oboe Concerto in C;* Hummel: *Introduction, Theme and Variations*)
Capriccio 10 308 [D] **F**

Violin Concertos Nos. 1 & 2 Suk (vln), Czech PO, Neumann
Supraphon 11 0702-2 [A] **F**

3 Estampes; Overture; The Parables; La Rhapsodie Czech PO, Bělohlávek
Supraphon 10 4140-2 [D] **F**

La Revue de Cuisine; Sinfonietta la Jolla; Tre Ricercari St. Paul CO, Hogwood
Decca 433 660-2 [D] **F**

Serenades Nos. 1–5 Prague CO
Supraphon 11 0098-2 [D] **F**

Symphonies Nos. 1–6 Czech PO, Neumann
Supraphon 11 0382-2, 3CDs [A] **M**

Symphonies Nos. 1 & 2 Berlin SO, Flor
RCA RD 60154 [D] **F**

Symphonies Nos. 3 & 4 Bamberg SO, Järvi
BIS BIS-CD 363 [D]

c *4 Madrigals for Oboe, Clarinet and Bassoon; 3 Madrigals for Violin and Viola; Madrigal Sonata for Piano, Flute and Violin; 5 Madrigal Stanzas for Violin and Piano* Dartington Ensemble
Hyperion CDA 66133 [D] **F**

Nonet; La Revue de cuisine; Trio in F Dartington Ensemble
Hyperion CDA 66084 [D] **F**

Piano Quartet (1942) Domus
(+ Dvořák: *Bagatelles;* Suk: *Piano Quartet*)
Virgin VC7 59245-2 [D] **F**

Cello Sonatas Nos. 1-3 Isserlis (vcl), Evans (pno)
Hyperion CDA 66296 [D] **F**

Flute Sonata Hall (fl), Jacobson (pno)
(+ Bartók: *15 Hungarian Peasant Songs;* Prokofiev: *Flute Sonata*
Pickwick MCD 26 [D] **B**

s *3 Czech Dances; 7 Czech Dances; 12 Esquisses; 4 Movements; Les Ritournelles; Window onto the Garden* Kvapil (pno)
Unicorn-Kanchana DKPCD 9140 [D] **F**

Études and Polkas; Fantasy and Toccata; Julietta (opera): Moderato (arr. Firkušný); *Les Ritournelles; Piano Sonata* Firkušný (pno)
RCA RD 87987 [D] **F**

v *The Epic of Gilgamesh* (oratorio) Depoltavá (sop), Margita (ten) Kusnjer (bar), Vele (bs), Karpíšek (narr), Slovak PO & Ch, Košler
Marco Polo 8.223316 [D] **F**

Field Mass Sítek (bar), Czech PO & Ch, Mackerras
(+ Janáček: *Amarus*)
Supraphon C37-7735 [D] **F**

MARTUCCI, Giuseppe (1856–1909) ITALY

o *Piano Concerto No. 1 in D min.; *Canzone dei ricordi (lyric poem)*
Caramiello (pno), *Yakar (sop), Philharmonia O, d'Avalos
ASV CDDCA 690 [D] **F**

*Piano Concerto No. 2 in B♭ min., Op. 66; Canzonetta, Op. 55/1;
Giga, Op. 61/3; Minuetto, Op. 57/2; Momento musicale, Op. 57/3;
Serenata, Op. 57/1; Tempo di gavotta, Op. 55/2 *Caramiello
(pno), Philharmonia O, d'Avalos
ASV CDDCA 691 [D] **F**

Giga, Op. 61/3; Notturno, Op. 70/1; Novelette, Op. 82/2 La Scala
PO, Muti
(+ Busoni: *Turandot Suite;* Casella: *Paganiniana*)
Sony CD 53280 [D] **F**

*Symphony No. 1 in D min., Op. 75; Notturno in G♭, Op. 70/1;
Noveletta, Op. 82/2; Tarantella, Op. 44/6* Philharmonia O,
d'Avalos
ASV CDDCA 675 [D] **F**

*Symphony No. 2 in F, Op. 81; *Andante, Op. 69/2; Colore
orientale, Op. 44/3 *Ives (vcl), Philharmonia O, d'Avalos
ASV CDDCA 689 [D] **F**

MASSENET, Jules (1842–1912) FRANCE

o *Piano Concerto in E♭; Solo Piano Works: Devant la Madonne; 2
Impromptus; Musique pour bercer les petits enfants; 2 Pièces; 10
Pièces de genre; Toccata in B♭; Valse folle; Valse très lente* Ciccolini
(pno), *Monte Carlo PO, *Cambreling
EMI CDM7 64277-2 [A] **M**

Le Cid (opera): Ballet music National PO, Bonynge
(+ Delibes: *Sylvia*)
Decca 425 475-2, 2CDs [A] **M**

Cigale (ballet) Hartle (sop), National PO, Bonynge
(+ Tchaikovsky: *Swan Lake*)
Decca 425 413-2, 3CDs [A] **M**

Scenes alsaciennes; Scenes pittoresques; Don Quichotte Monte-Carlo
Opera O, Gardiner
Erato 2292-45859-2 [D] **F**

Scenes dramatiques; Scenes de Feerie; Le dernier Someil de la Vierge
Monte-Carlo Opera O, Gardiner
Erato 2292-45858-2 [D] **F**

MATHIAS, William (1934–1992) WALES

o *Symphonies: No. 1, Op. 31; No. 2 (Summer Night), Op. 90* BBC
Welsh SO, Mathias
Nimbus NI 5260 [D] **F**

*Symphony No. 3; Helios; *Oboe Concerto; Requiescat* *Cowley
(ob), BBC Welsh SO, Llewellyn
Nimbus NI 5343 [D] **F**

s *Complete Organ Music* Scott (org)
Nimbus NI 5367 [D] **F**

v *As truly as God is our Father; Ave Rex, Op. 45; A Grace, Op. 89/3;
I will celebrate; Jesus College Service, Op. 53; Let the people praise
thee (royal wedding anthem), Op. 87; Missa Aedis Christi, Op. 92;
O how amiable, Op. 90/3; Rex gloriae, Op. 83* Christ Church
Cathedral Ch, Lawford (org), Darlington
Nimbus NI 5243 [D] **F**

V   *Lux aeterna* Lott (sop), Cable (mez), Walker (mez), Bach Ch,
St. George's Chapel Ch, LSO, Willcocks
Chandos CHAN 8695 [D] **F**

MATTHEWS, David (born 1942) ENGLAND

O   *Symphony No. 4, Op. 52* East of England O, Nabarro
Collins 20062 [D] **F**

MAW, Nicholas (born 1935) ENGLAND

O   *Odyssey* CBSO, Rattle
EMI CDS7 54277-2, 2CDs [D] **F**

MAXWELL DAVIES, Peter (born 1934) ENGLAND

O   Film scores: *The Boyfriend; The Devils: Suites; *Seven in nomine*
*Thomas (sop), Aquarius, N. Cleobury
Collins 10952 [D] **F**

Cello Concerto: Oboe Concerto Conway (vcl), Miller (ob),
Scottish CO, Maxwell Davies
Unicorn-Kanchana DKPCD 9085 [D] **F**

*Trumpet Concerto; *Symphony No. 4* Wallace (tpt), SNO,
*Scottish CO, Maxwell Davies
Collins 11812 [D] **F**

Violin Concerto Stern (vln), RPO, Previn
(+ Dutilleux: *Violin Concerto*)
Sony/CBS CD 42449 [D] **F**

*Jimmack the Postie; Kinlochie, his Fantasia; An Orkney wedding,
with Sunrise; Renaissance Scottish dances; *Farewell to Stromness;
*Yesnaby Ground; **Lullaby for Lucy; **Seven Songs Home*
Scottish CO, **St. Mary's Edinburgh Ch, Maxwell Davies;
*Maxwell Davies (pno)
Unicorn-Kanchana DKPCD 9070 [D] **F**

*Sinfonia; *Sinfonia Concertante* *Nicholson (fl), *Miller (ob),
*Morrison (cl), *Newman (bsn), *Cooke (hn), *Fry (perc)
Scottish CO, Maxwell Davies
Unicorn-Kanchana UKCD 2026 [D] **M**

*Sinfonietta Accademica; *Into the Labyrinth* (cantata) *Mackie
(ten), Scottish CO, Maxwell Davies
Unicorn-Kanchana UKCD 2022 [A] **M**

*Sir Charles: His Pavan; The Turn of the Tide; *Worldes Blis*
BBC PO, *RPO, Maxwell Davies
Collins 13902 [D] **F**

*Strathclyde Concertos Nos. *3 & **4* *Cook (ob), *Franks (tpt),
**Morrison (cl), Scottish CO, Maxwell Davies
Collins 12392 [D] **F**

*Strathclyde Concertos Nos. *5 & **6* *Clark (vln),*Marwood
(vla), **Nicholson (fl), Scottish CO, Maxwell Davies
Collins 13032 [D] **F**

*Strathclyde Concertos Nos. *7 & **8; A Spell for Green Corn: The
Macdonald Dances* *McTier (db), **Leveaux (bsn), Scottish
CO, Maxwell Davies
Collins 13862 [D] **F**

*Ave maris stella; Image, reflection, shadow; *Runes from a holy
island* Fires of London, *Maxwell Davies
Unicorn-Kanchana UKCD 2038 [A] **M**

V *Black Pentecost; Stone Litany* Jones (mez), Wilson-Johnson
(bar), BBC PO, Maxwell Davies
Collins 13662 [D] **F**

*Eight Songs for a Mad King; **Miss Donnithorne's Maggot
*Eastman (bar), **Thomas (sop), Fires of London, Maxwell
Davies
Unicorn-Kanchana DKPCD 9052 [D] **F**

MAYERL, Billy (1902–1959) ENGLAND

S *April's Fool; Evening Primrose; Four Aces –suite: Nos. 2 & 3;
From a Spanish lattice; The Harp of the Winds; 3 Japanese Pictures:
Almond Blossom; The Joker; The Legends of King Arthur: prelude;
Guinevere; Lady of the Lake; The Passing of Arthur; Marigold;
Nimble-fingered Gentleman; Railroad rhythm; Shallow waters; Song
of the Fir-Tree* Parkin (pno)
Chandos CHAN 8560 [D] **F**

*Aquarium Suite; Autumn Crocus; Bats in the Belfry; 3 Dances in
syncopation; Four Aces – suite: Nos. 1 & 4; Green tulips;
Hollyhock; Hop-'o-my-thumb; Jill all alone; Mistletoe; The Parade
of the Sandwich-board Men; Sweet William; White heather*
Parkin (pno)
Chandos CHAN 8848 [D] **F**

MAYUZAMI, Toshiro (born 1929) JAPAN

C *Prelude* LaSalle Quartet
(+ Cage: *String Quartet;* Lutoslawski: *String Quartet;*
Penderecki: *String Quartet*)
DG 423 245-2 [A] **M**

MEDTNER, Nikolay (1880–1951) RUSSIA

⊃ *Piano Concerto No. 1 in C min., Op. 33* Zhukov (pno), USSR
TV & Radio Large O, Rozhdestvensky
(+ Balakirev: *Piano Concerto No.1;* Rimsky-Korsakov: *Piano
Concerto*)
Mezhdunarodnaya Kniga MK 417087 [A] **F**

Piano Concertos: No. 2 in C min., Op. 50; No. 3 in E min., Op. 60
Demidenko (pno), BBC Scottish SO, Maksymiuk
Hyperion CDA 66580 [D] **F**

√ *Violin Sonatas: No. 1 in B min., Op. 21; No. 3 in E min. (Epic),
Op. 57; Nocturne No. 3 in C min., Op. 16/3* Labko (vln),
Svetlanov (pno)
Russian Disc RDCD 11017 [A] **F**

Violin Sonata No. 2 in G, Op. 44; Piano Quintet in C, Op. Posth.
Labko (vln), Svetlanov (pno), Borodin Quartet
Russian Disc RDCD 11019 [A] **F**

S *3 Dithyrambs, Op. 10/2; 2 Elegies, Op. 59/2; Fairy Tale in D min.;
3 Fairy Tales, Op. 9/3; 2 Fairy Tales, Op. 14; 4 Fairy Tales, Op.
26/2; 4 Fairy Tales, Op. 35/4; 5 Forgotten Melodies, Op. 39 (Set 2):
Nos. 1 & 3; 3 Hymns, Op. 49* Milne (pno)
CRD 3338 [A] **F**

Improvisation No. 2, Op. 47; Piano Sonata in F min. Milne (pno)
CRD 3461 [D] **F**

Piano Sonata in E min., Op. 25/2; Sonata Triad, Op. 11
Milne (pno)
CRD CRD 3339 [A] **F**

S *Improvisation No. 2, Op. 47; Sonate-idylle, Op. 56; Forgotten Melodies, Op. 39* Wild (pno)
Chesky AD1 [D] **F**

Piano Sonata in G min., Op. 22; Sonata Reminiscenza in A min., Op. 38/1; Dancing Fairy Tale, Op. 48/1; 5 Fairy Tales; Funeral March, Op. 31/2; The Organ Grinder, Op. 54/3; Russian Fairy Tale, Op. 42/1 Tozer (pno)
Chandos CHAN 9050 [D] **F**

Sonata Elegia, Op. 11/2; Sonata Reminiscenza, Op. 38/1; Sonata Tragica, Op. 39/5; Canzona Matinata, Op. 39/4; Canzona Serenata, Op. 38/6; Dithyrambe, Op. 10/2; Fairy Tale, Op. 20/1; Theme and Variations, Op. 55 Demidenko (pno)
Hyperion CDA 66636 [D] **F**

MÉHUL, Nicolas (1763–1817) FRANCE

O *Symphonies Nos. 1–4; La Chasse de jeune Henri (opera): Overture; Le trésor supposé (opera): Overture* Gulbenkian Foundation O, Swierczewski
Nimbus NI 5184/5, 2CDs [D] **F**

MENDELSSOHN, Fanny (1805–1847) GERMANY

C *3 Pieces for piano duet* Duo Tal & Groethuysen
(+ Felix Mendelssohn: *Piano duets*)
Sony CD 48494 [D] **F**

Piano Trio in D, Op. 11 Dartington Piano Trio
(+ C. Schumann: *Piano Trio in G min., Op. 17*)
Hyperion CDA 66331 [D] **F**

MENDELSSOHN, Felix (1809–1847) GERMANY

O Overtures: *Athalia, Op. 74; Calm Sea and Prosperous Voyage, Op. 27; The Hebrides, Op. 26; The Marriage of Camacho, Op. 10; A Midsummer Night's Dream, Op. 17; Ruy Blas, Op. 95* Bamberg SO, Flor
RCA 07863-57905-2 [D] **F**

EDITORS' CHOICE (see page 14): *Piano Concertos: No. 1 in G min., Op. 25; No. 2 in D min., Op. 40; Capriccio brillant, Op. 22* Shelley (pno/dir), LMP
Chandos CHAN 9215 [D] **F**

Double Piano Concertos: in A♭; in E Coombs (pno), Munro (pno), BBC Scottish SO, Maksymiuk
Hyperion CDA 66567 [D] **F**

*Violin Concerto in D min.; *Violin and Piano Concerto in D min.* Kremer (vln), *Argerich (pno), Orpheus CO
DG 427 338-2 [D] **F**

Violin Concerto in E min., Op. 64 Milstein (vln), VPO, Abbado
(+ Tchaikovsky: *Violin Concerto*)
DG 419 067-2 [A] **M**

A Midsummer Night's Dream (Overture and Incidental Music, Opp. 21 & 61) Wiens (sop), Walker (mez), LPO & Ch, Litton
Classics for Pleasure CD-CFP 4593 [D] **B**

String Symphonies Nos. 1–12 London Festival O, Pople
Hyperion CDA 66561/3, 3CDs [D] **F**

String Symphonies Nos. 8–10 Orpheus CO
DG 437 528-2 [D] **F**

Symphonies Nos. 1–5 Mathis (sop), Rebmann (sop), Hollweg (ten), German Opera Ch, BPO, Karajan
DG 429 664-2, 3CDs [A] **M**

Symphony No. 2 in Bb (Hymn of Praise) Mathis (sop), Rebmann (sop), Hollweg (ten), German Opera Ch, BPO, Karajan
DG 431 471-2 [A] **M**

Symphonies: No. 3 in A min. (Scottish), Op. 56; No. 4 in A (Italian), Op. 90
LCP, Norrington
◇ EMI CDC7 54000-2 [D] **F**
SFSO, Blomstedt
Decca 433 811-2 [D] **F**

Andante & Variations Op. 83a; Andante and Allegro brillant, Op. 92; Piano Trio, Op. 66 (arr.) Duo Tal & Groethuysen (pno duo)
(+ Fanny Mendelssohn: *Piano duets*)
Sony CD 48494 [D] **F**

Cello Sonatas: No. 1 in Bb, Op. 45; No. 2 in D, Op. 58; Songs without Words, Opp. 19/1, & 109; Variations concertantes, Op. 17 Harrell (vcl), Canino (pno)
Decca 430 198-2 [D] **F**

Piano Quartets Nos. 1–3 Domus
Virgin VC7 59628-2 [D] **F**

Piano Trios: No. 1 in D min., Op. 49; No. 2 in C min., Op. 66 Trio Fontenay
Teldec 2292-44947-2 [D] **F**

String Octet in Eb, Op. 20; String Quintet No. 1 in A, Op. 18 Hausmusik
EMI CDC7 49958-2 [D] **F**

String Quartets Nos. 1–6; String Quartet in Eb; 4 Movements, Op. 81 Melos Quartet
DG 415 883-2, 3CDs [A] **M**

Violin Sonata in F min., Op. 4; Violin Sonata in F Mintz (vln), Ostrovsky (pno)
DG 419 244-2 [D] **F**

Andante and rondo capriccioso, Op. 14; Andante cantabile and presto agitato in B; Capriccio, Op. 5; Capriccio, Op. 118; 3 Caprices, Op. 33; 2 Klavierstücke; Perpetuum mobile in C, Op. 119; Scherzo in B min.; Scherzo a capriccio in F# min. Jones (pno)
Nimbus NI 5069 [A] **F**

3 Fantasias, Op. 16; Fantasia on 'The Last Rose of Summer'; Fantasy in F# min., Op. 28; Variations in Bb, Op. 83; Variations in Eb, Op. 82; Variations sérieuses, Op. 54 Jones (pno)
Nimbus NI 5072 [A] **F**

Kinderstücke, Op. 72; Piano Sonata in E, Op. 6; Piano Sonata in G min., Op. 105; Piano Sonata in Bb, Op. 106 Jones (pno)
Nimbus NI 5070 [A] **F**

Prelude and Fugue in E min.; 3 Preludes, Op. 104a; 6 Preludes and Fugues, Op. 35; 3 Studies, Op. 104b; Study in F min. Jones (pno)
Nimbus NI 5071 [A] **F**

Songs without Words: Book 1, Op. 19; Book 2, Op. 30; Book 3, Op. 38; Book 4, Op. 53; Book 5, Op. 62; Book 6, Op. 67; Book 7,

Op. 85; Book 8, Op. 102; Albumblatt, Op. 117; Gondellied in A;
Kinderstücke, Op. 72; 2 Klavierstücke Barenboim (pno)
DG 423 931-2, 2CDs [A] **M**

S *Allegro maestoso in C; Allegro in B♭; Allegro, Chorale and Fugue in*
D; Andante in D; Andante in F; 2 Fugues; 3 Preludes and Fugues,
Op. 37; 6 Organ Sonatas, Op. 65 Scott (org)
Hyperion CDA 66491-2, 2CDs [D] **F**

V *6 Anthems, Op. 79; Ehre sei Gott in der Hohe; Hear my Prayer;*
Heilig heilig ist Gott, der Herr Zabaoth; Kyrie eleison in A; 3 Psalms,
Op. 78; 3 Sacred Pieces, Op. 23/2: Ave Maria; No. 3: Mitten wir im
Leben sind; Verleih uns frieden Corydon Singers, Best
Hyperion CDA 66359 [D] **F**

Elijah (oratorio) Ameling (sop), Burmeister (mez), Adam
(bs-bar), Leipzig Radio Ch, LGO, Sawallisch
Philips 438 368-2, 2CDs [A] **B**

27 Lieder Bonney (sop), Parsons (pno)
Teldec 2292-44946-2 [D] **F**

40 Lieder Fischer-Dieskau (bar), Sawallisch (pno)
EMI CMS7 64827-2, 2 CDs [A] **M**

Paulus (oratorio), *Op. 36* Janowitz (sop), Lang (cont),
Blochwitz (ten), Adam (bs), LGO & Radio Ch, Masur
Philips 420 212-2, 2CDs [A] **F**

MENNIN, Peter (1923–1983) USA

O *Symphony No. 5* Eastman-Rochester O, Hanson
(+ Ives: *Symphony No. 3; Three Places in New England;* Schuman:
New England Triptych)
Philips Mercury 432 755-2 [A] **M**

MENOTTI, Gian Carlo (born 1911) ITALY/USA

O *Amahl and the Night Visitors* (opera): *Suite; Sebastian* (ballet):
Suite New Zealand SO, Schenck
(+ Barber: *Souvenirs* [ballet]: *Suite*)
Koch 37005-2 [D] **F**

MERCADANTE, Saverio (1795–1870) ITALY

O *Flute Concertos: in D; in E; in E min.* Galway (fl), I Solisti
Veneti, Scimone
RCA 09026-61447-2 [D] **F**

MESSAGER, Andre (1853–1929) FRANCE

O *Les Deux Pigeons* Welsh National Opera O, Bonynge
Decca 433 700-2 [D] **F**

MESSIAEN, Olivier (1908–1992) FRANCE

O *Des Canyons aux étoiles; Couleurs de la cité céleste; Oiseaux exotiques*
Crossley (pno), London Sinfonietta, Salonen
Sony/CBS CD 44762 2CDs [D] **F**

Turangalîla Symphony Y. Loriod (pno), J. Loriod (ondes
martenot), Paris Bastille O, M-W. Chung
DG 431 781-2 [D] **F**

C *Quartet for the End of Time; *Le Merle noir* *Zoller (fl), Aloys
Kontarsky (pno); Gruenberg (vln), de Peyer (cl), Pleeth (vcl),
Beroff (pno)
EMI CDM7 63947-2 [A] **M**

Theme et Variations Kremer (vln), Argerich (pno)
(+ Bartók: *Sonata No. 1;* Janáček: *Sonata*)
DG 427 351-2 [D] **F**

Cantéjodoyâ; 4 Études de rhythme; Fantasie burlesque; Rondeau
Hill (pno)
Unicorn-Kanchana DKPCD 9051 [D] **F**

Catalogues d'oiseaux (complete) Ugorski (pno)
DG 439 214-2, 3 CDs [D] **F**

Catalogue d'oiseaux 1–6 Hill (pno)
Unicorn-Kanchana DKPCD 9062 [D] **F**

Catalogue d'oiseaux 7–10 Hill (pno)
Unicorn-Kanchana DKPCD 9075 [D] **F**

Catalogue d'oiseaux 11–13; La Fauvette des jardins Hill (pno)
Unicorn-Kanchana DKPCD 9090 [D] **F**

Pièce pour le tombeau de Paul Dukas; 8 Préludes Hill (pno)
Unicorn-Kanchana DKPCD 9078 [D] **F**

8 Préludes; Vingt regards sur l'enfant Jésus Beroff (pno)
EMI CMS7 69161-2, 2CDs [A] **M**

Vingt regards sur l'enfant Jésus Hill (pno)
Unicorn-Kanchana DKP 9122/3, 2CDs **F**

**Visions de l'Amen; Fantaisie Burlesque; Petites esquisses d'oiseaux;
Pièce pour le Tombeau de Paul Dukas; Rondeau* Hill (pno),
*Frith (pno)
Unicorn-Kanchana DKPCD 9144 [D] **F**

*Apparition de l'église éternelle; Livre d'orgue; Verset pour la fête de
la dédicace* Bate (org)
Unicorn-Kanchana DKPCD 9028 [D] **F**

*L'Ascension; 9 Méditations sur le mystère de la Sainte Trinité; Messe
de la Pentecôte* Bate (org)
Unicorn-Kanchana DKPCD 9024/5, 2CDs [D] **F**

Le Banquet céleste; La Nativité du Seigneur Bate (org)
Unicorn-Kanchana DKPCD 9005 [D] **F**

Les Corps glorieux; Diptyque Bate (org)
Unicorn-Kanchana DKPCD 9004 [D] **F**

Le Livre du Saint Sacrement Bate (org)
Unicorn-Kanchana DKPCD 9067/8, 2CDs [D] **F**

*O sacrum convivium; 3 Petites liturgies de la présence divine; 5
Rechants* London Sinfonietta Ch, London Sinfonietta,
Edwards
Virgin VC7 59051-2 [D] **F**

*La Transfiguration de Notre Seigneur Jesus Christ; *La Nativité du
Seigneur* Sylvester (ten), Aquino (bar), Westminster
Symphonic Ch, National SO, Dorati; *Preston (org)
Decca 425 616-2, 2CDs [A] **M**

MEYERBEER, Giacomo (1791–1864) GERMANY

Les Patineurs (ballet; arr. Lambert) National PO, Bonynge
(+ Tchaikovsky: *Sleeping Beauty*)
Decca 425 468-2, 3CDs [A] **M**

12 Songs Hampson (bar), Parsons (pno)
(+ Rossini: *7 Songs*)
EMI CDC7 54436-2 [D] **F**

MIASKOVSKY, Nikolay (1881–1950) RUSSIA

o *Cello Concerto in C min., Op. 66* J. Lloyd Webber (vcl), LSO, M. Shostakovich
(+ Shostakovich: *The Limpid Stream: Adagio;* Tchaikovsky: *Variations on a Rococo Theme; Nocturne*)
Philips 434 106-2 [D] **F**

*Violin Concerto in D min., Op. 44; *Symphony No. 22 in B min., Op. 54* Feighin (vln), USSR RSO, Dmitriev; *USSR SO, Svetlanov
Olympia OCD 134 [A] **F**

*Lyric Concertino in G, Op. 32/3; *Symphony No. 3 in A min., Op. 15* USSR SO, Verbitzky; *Svetlanov
Olympia OCD 177 [A] **F**

2 Pieces, Op. 46/1 Moscow SO, Dudarova
(+ Mosolov: *3 Children's Scenes; 4 Newspaper Announcements;* Popov: *Symphony No. 2*)
Olympia OCD 170 [A] **F**

Symphonies: No. 1 in C min., Op. 3; No. 19 in E♭, Op. 46 USSR Ministry of Culture SO, Rozhdestvensky
Russian Disc RDCD 11 007 [A] **F**

*Symphonies: No. 5 in D, Op. 18; *No. 11 in B♭ min., Op. 34* USSR SO, Ivanov; *Moscow SO, Dudarova
Olympia OCD 133 [A] **F**

Symphony No. 7 in B min., Op. 24 USSR RSO, Ginsburg
(+ Knipper: *Concert Poem; Sinfonietta*)
Olympia OCD 163 [A] **F**

Symphony No. 8 in A, Op. 26 Czech RSO, Stankowsky
Marco Polo 8.223297 [D] **F**

Symphony No. 12 in G min., Op. 35; Silence, Op. 9 Slovak RSO (Bratislava), Stankowsky
Marco Polo 8.223302 [D] **F**

**Symphony No. 27 in C min., Op. 85; Sinfonietta No. 2, Op. 68* USSR State Academy SO, Verbitzky; *Svetlanov
Olympia OCD 168 [A] **F**

c *String Quartets: No. 3 in D min., Op. 33/3; No 10 in F, Op. 67/1; No. 13 in A min., Op. 86* Leningrad Taneiev Quartet
Olympia OCD 148 [A] **F**

s *Piano Sonatas Nos. 1–3 & 6* McLachlan (pno)
Olympia OCD 214 [D] **F**

Piano Sonatas Nos. 4 & 5; Sonatina in E min., Op. 57; Prelude, Op. 58 McLachlan (pno)
Olympia OCD 217 [D] **F**

Piano Sonatas Nos. 7–9; Reminiscences, Op. 29; Rondo-Sonata in B♭ min.; Scherzo; Yellowed Leaves, Op. 31 McLachlan (pno)
Olympia OCD 252 [D] **F**

MILHAUD, Darius (1892–1974) FRANCE

o *Cello Concerto No. 1, Op. 136* Rostropovich (vcl), LSO, Nagano
(+ Hoddinott: *Noctis Equi;* Honegger: *Cello Concerto*)
Erato 2292-45489-2 [D] **F**

*Le Boeuf sur le toit (ballet), Op. 58; *Le Printemps, Op. 18* Kremer (vln), LSO, Chailly; *Kremer (vln), Bashkirova (pno)
(+ Chausson: *Poème;* Satie: *Choses vues à droite et à gauche;*

Vieuxtemps: *Fantasia appassionata*)
Philips 432 513-2 [A] **M**

o *Le Boeuf sur le toit, Op. 58; La Création du Monde* (ballet), *Op. 81*
Ulster O, Tortelier
(+ Ibert: *Divertissement;* Poulenc: *Les Biches*)
Chandos CHAN 9023 [D] **F**

Symphonies Nos. 1 & 2; Suite provençale Toulouse Capitole O,
Plasson
DG 435 437-2 [D] **F**

c *La Cheminée du roi René, Op. 205; Divertimento, Op. 229b;*
Pastorale, Op. 147; 2 Sketches, Op. 227b; Suite d'après Corrette,
Op. 161b Athena Ensemble
Chandos CHAN 6536 [A] **M**

Clarinet Sonatina, Op. 127; Flute Sonatina, Op. 76; Oboe
Sonatina, Op. 337; Sonata for Flute, Oboe, Clarinet and Piano,
Op. 47 Brunner (cl), Nicolet (fl), Holliger (ob),
Maisenberg (pno)
Orfeo CO 60831A [D] **F**

Scaramouche, Op. 165b K. & M. Labèque (pno duo)
(+ Poulenc: *Double Piano Concerto; Capriccio; Élégie;*
Embarquement pour Cythère; Sonata for 4 Hands)
Philips 426 284-2 [D] **F**

v *Alissa; L'amour chante; Poèmes juifs* Farley (sop),
Constable (pno)
ASV CDDCA 810 [D] **F**

MINKUS, Leon (1826–1917) RUSSIA

o *La Bayadère* (orch. Lanchbery) ECO, Bonynge
Decca 436 917-2, 2CDS [D] **F**

MOERAN, Ernest J. (1894–1950) ENGLAND

o *Cello Concerto; Sinfonietta* R. Wallfisch (vcl), Bournemouth
Sinfonietta, del Mar
Chandos CHAN 8456 [D] **F**

*Violin Concerto; Lonely Waters; Whythorne's Shadow
**Mordkovitch (vln), Ulster O, Handley
Chandos CHAN 8807 [D] **F**

In the Mountain Country; *Rhapsody in F♯; Rhapsodies Nos. 1 & 2
**Fingerhut (pno), Ulster O, Handley
Chandos CHAN 8639 [D] **F**

Serenade in G; *Nocturne *Mackey (bar), *Renaissance Singers,
Ulster O, Handley
(+ Warlock: *Capriol Suite; Serenade for Strings*)
Chandos CHAN 8808 [D] **F**

Symphony in G min.; Overture to a Masque Ulster O, Handley
Chandos CHAN 8577 [D] **F**

c *Fantasy Quartet* Francis (ob), Members of the English Quartet
(+ Bax: *Oboe Quintet;* Holst: *Air and Variations; 3 Pieces;* Jacob:
Oboe Quartet)
Chandos CHAN 8392 [D] **F**

String Quartet in A min.; *Violin Sonata in E min. Melbourne
Quartet; *Scotts (vln), Talbot (pno)
Chandos CHAN 8465 [D] **F**

MONTEVERDI, Claudio (1567–1643) ITALY

V   *Ab aeterno ordinata sum; Confitebor tibi, Domine I, II, and III;
Deus tuorum militum; Iste confessor; Laudate Dominum II; Nisi
Dominus aedificaverit domum; Su le penne de' venti* Kirkby (sop),
Partridge (ten), Thomas (bs), Parley of Instruments
✧ Hyperion CDA 66021 [D] **F**

*Adoramus te, Christe; Beatus vir; Chi vol che m'innamore;
Confitebor tibi, Domine II & V; E questa vita un lampo; Gloria in
excelsis Deo; Laudate Dominum, O omnes gentes I; O ciechi il tanto
affaticar* Les Arts Florissants Vocal & Instrumental
Ensembles, Christie
✧ HM HMC90 1250 [D] **F**

*Cantata domino; Domine, ne in furore; Missa de cappella a 4; Missa
in illo tempore* Phillips (org), The Sixteen, Christophers
✧ Hyperion CDA 66214 [D] **F**

*Chiome d'oro; Come dolci hoggi l'auretta; Con che saovita; Mentre
vaga Angioletta; Ogni amante e guerrier; Ohimè, dov'è il mio ben?;
Parlo miser' taccio; S'el vostro cor, Madonna; Tempro la cetra;
Vorrei baciarti o Filli* Kirkby (sop), Nelson (sop), Holden (sop),
Elliot (ten), King (ten), Thomas (bs), Consort of Musicke,
Rooley
✧ L'Oiseau-Lyre 421 480-2 [D] **F**

*Lamento d'Olympia; Maladetto sia l'aspetto; Ohimè ch'io cado; Quel
sguardo sdegnosetto; Voglio di vita uscia* Kirkby (sop), Rooley
(chitarrone)
(+ d'India: *Amico hai vint'io, etc.*)
✧ Hyperion CDA 66106 [D] **F**

Madrigals, Book 2 (complete) Consort of Musicke, Rooley
✧ Virgin VC7 59282-2 [D] **F**

Madrigals, Book 3 (complete) Consort of Musicke, Rooley
✧ Virgin VC7 59283-2 [D] **F**

Madrigals, Book 4 (complete) Consort of Musicke, Rooley
✧ L'Oiseau-Lyre 414 148-2 [D] **F**

Madrigals, Book 5 (complete) Consort of Musicke, Rooley
✧ L'Oiseau-Lyre 410 291-2 [D] **F**

Madrigals, Book 6 (complete) Consort of Musicke, Rooley
✧ Virgin VC7 59605-2 [D] **F**

Madrigals, Book 8: Madrigali amorosi Consort of Musicke,
Rooley
✧ Virgin VC7 59621-2 [D] **F**

*Madrigals, Book 8: (Balletti): Il ballo delle ingrate; Il
combattimento di Tancredi e Clorinda; Volgendo il ciel* Consort of
Musicke, Rooley
(+ Marini: *El l'armi cinesi*)
✧ Virgin VC7 59620-2 [D] **F**

Vespro della Beata Vergine (vespers) Monoyios (sop), Pennichi
(sop), Chance (alt), Tucker (ten), Robson (alt), Naglia (ten),
Terfel (bs-bar), Miles (bar), His Majesties Sackbutts &
Cornetts, Monteverdi Ch, London Oratory Ch, EBS, Gardiner
✧ DG Archiv 429 565-2, 2CDs [D] **F**

MOODY, James (born 1907) ENGLAND

O   *Little Suite* Reilly (harmonica), ASMF, Marriner
(+ Jacob: *5 Pieces;* Tausky: *Concertino;*

Vaughan Williams: *Romance*)
Chandos CHAN 8617 [D] **F**

*Harmonica Quintet; *Suite dans le style français* Reilly
(harmonica), *Kanga (hp), Hindar Quartet
(+ Jacob: *Divertimento*)
Chandos CHAN 8802 [D] **F**

MORLEY, Thomas (1557/8–1602) ENGLAND

12 Ayres/Canzonets & 2 Madrigals Consort of Musicke, Rooley
◇ L'Oiseau-Lyre 436 862-2 [D] **F**

MOSOLOV, Alexandr (1910–1973) RUSSIA

*Piano Concerto No. 1, Op. 14; Suite on Soldiers' Songs; Zavod (The
Iron Foundry); Collective Farm Meadows; Front Roads*
Khuntsaria (pno), USSR SO, Kozhukar; Osipov Russian Folk
O, Gnutov; USSR SO, Svetlanov; USSR Radio & TV Ch,
Kutuzov
Olympia OCD 176 [A] **F**

3 Children's Scenes, Op. 18; 4 Newspaper Announcements, Op. 21
Lee (sop), Bolshoi Theatre Ensemble Soloists, Lazarev
(+ Miaskovsky: *2 Pieces;* Popov: *Symphony No. 2*)
Olympia OCD 170 [A] **F**

MOSZKOWSKI, Moritz (1854–1925) POLAND/GERMANY

Piano Concerto in E, Op. 59 Lane (pno), BBC Scottish SO,
Maksymiuk
(+ Paderewski: *Piano Concerto in A min.*)
Hyperion CDA 66452 [D] **F**

MOZART, Leopold (1719–1787) GERMANY/AUSTRIA

Trumpet Concerto in D
Wilbraham (tpt), ASMF, Marriner
(+ Albinoni: *Trumpet Concerto in C;* Haydn: *Trumpet Concerto in
Eb;* Hummel: *Trumpet Concerto in Eb;* Telemann: *2 Oboe and
Trumpet Concerto No. 1*)
Decca 417 761-2 [A] **M**

MOZART, Wolfgang Amadeus (1756–1791) AUSTRIA

*Bassoon Concerto in Bb, K191; Clarinet Concerto in A, K622; Flute
Concerto No. 1 in G, K313; Flute and Harp Concerto in C, K299;
Horn Concertos Nos. 1–4; Oboe Concerto in C, K314; Sinfonia
Concertante in Eb, K297b; Andante for Flute and Orchestra in C,
K315* Various artists, Orpheus CO
DG 431 665-2, 3CDs [D] **B**

Clarinet Concerto in A, K622; Horn Concertos Nos. 1 & 4 Neidich
(cl), Jolley (hn), Orpheus CO
DG 423 377-2 [D] **F**

*Flute Concertos: No. 1 in G, K313; No. 2 in C, K314; Flute and
Harp Concerto in C, K299; Andante in C, K315; Rondo, K373;
Eine kleine Nachtmusik, K525* Galway (fl), Robles (hp), COE
RCA RD 87861, 2CDs [D] **F**

Horn Concertos Nos. 1–4
Civil (hn), ASMF, Marriner
(+ *Rondo in Eb, K371*)
Philips 420 709-2 [A] **M**

Horn Concertos Nos. 1–4 Brown (hn), Age of Enlightenment O,
Kuijken
◇ Virgin VC7 59558-2 [D] **F**

O *Piano Concertos (after J.C. Bach), K103 Nos. 1–3* Perahia
(pno/dir), ECO
(+ Schröter: *Piano Concerto in C, Op. 3 No. 3*)
Sony CD 39222 [D] **F**

Piano Concertos Nos. 1–6, 9, & 11–27 Anda (pno), Salzburg
Mozarteum Camerata Academica
DG 429 001-2, 10 CDs [A] **M**

*Piano Concertos Nos. 5, 6, 8, 9 & 11–27; *Double Piano Concerto
in Eb, K365; **Triple Piano Concerto in F, K242*
Bilson (fpno), */**Levin (fpno), **Tan (fpno), EBS,
Gardiner
◇ DG Archiv 431 211-2, 9CDs [D] **M**

Piano Concertos Nos. 1–4 Perahia (pno/dir), ECO
Sony CD 39225 [D] **F**

*Piano Concertos: No. 5 in D, K175; No. 6 in Bb, K238; Rondo in D
K382* Schiff (pno), Salzburg Camerata Academica, Végh
Decca 430 517-2 [D] **F**

Piano Concertos: No. 6 in Bb, K238; No. 13 in C, K415 Perahia
(pno/dir), ECO
Sony CD 39223 [A] **F**

*Piano Concertos: No. 8 in C, K246; No. 11 in F, K413; Concert
Rondo in A* Schiff (pno), Salzburg Mozarteum, Végh
Decca 433 042-2 [D] **F**

Piano Concertos: No. 9 in Eb, K271; No. 17 in G, K453 Shelley
(pno/dir), London Mozart Players
Chandos CHAN 9068 [D] **F**

Piano Concertos: No. 12 in A, K414; No. 19 in F, K459 Shelley
(pno/dir), London Mozart Players
Chandos CHAN 9256 [D] **F**

Piano Concertos: No. 12 in A, K414; No. 13 in C, K415
Ashkenazy (pno/dir), Philharmonia O
Decca 410 214-2 [D] **F**

Piano Concertos Nos. 14–16 Barenboim (pno/dir), ECO
EMI CDM7 69124-2 [A] **M**

Piano Concertos: No. 15 in Bb, K450; No. 16 in D, K451 Perahia
(pno/dir), ECO
Sony CD 37824 [D] **F**

Piano Concertos: No. 17 in G, K453; No. 18 in Bb, K456 Perahia
(pno/dir), ECO
Sony CD 36686 [D] **F**

Piano Concertos: No. 19 in F, K459; No. 23 in A, K488 Pollini
(pno), VPO, Böhm
DG 413 793-2 [A] **F**

Piano Concertos: No. 19 in F, K459; No. 27 in Bb, K595 Schiff
(pno), Salzburg Camerata Academica, Vegh
Decca 421 259-2 [D] **F**

Piano Concertos: No. 20 in D min., K466; No. 23 in A, K488
Tan (fpno), LCP, Norrington
◇ EMI CDC7 54366-2 [D] **F**
Shelley (pno/dir), London Mozart Players
Chandos CHAN 8992 [D] **F**

Piano Concertos: No. 20 in D min., K466; No. 21 in C, K467
Schiff (pno), Salzburg Mozarteum Camerata Academica, Végh
Decca 430 510-2 [D] **F**

Piano Concertos: No. 21 in C, K467; No. 25 in C, K503
Kovacevich (pno), LSO, C. Davis
Philips 426 077-2 [A] **B**

Piano Concertos: No. 22 in E♭, K482; No. 23 in A, K488
Barenboim (pno/dir), ECO
EMI CDM7 69122-2 [A] **M**

Piano Concertos: No. 23 in A, K488; No. 24 in C min., K491
Kempff (pno), Bamberg SO, Leitner
DG 423 885-2 [A] **M**

Piano Concertos: No. 23 in A, K488; No. 26 in D (Coronation), K537 Casadesus (pno), Cleveland O, Szell
Sony/CBS CD 45884 [A] **M**

Piano Concertos: No. 24 in C min., K491; No. 25 in C, K503 Tan (fpno), LCP, Norrington
✧ EMI CDC7 54295-2 [D] **F**

Piano Concertos: No. 25 in C, K503; No. 26 in D (Coronation), K537 Ashkenazy (pno/dir), Philharmonia O
Decca 411 810-2 [D] **F**

Piano Concerto No. 27 in B♭, K595; *Double Piano Concerto in E♭, K365 Emil Gilels (pno), *Elena Gilels (pno), VPO, Böhm
DG 419 059-2 [A] **M**

Double Piano Concerto in E♭, K365; Triple Piano Concerto in F, K242 (2-piano version); Andante & 5 Variations in G, K501; Fantasia in F min., K608 Perahia (pno/dir), Lupu (pno), ECO
Sony CD 44915 [D] **F**

Violin Concertos Nos. 1–5 & 7; Adagio in E, K261; Violin and Piano Concerto in D, K315f; Concertone in C, K190; Rondo in B♭, K269; Rondo in C, K373; Sinfonia Concertante in A, K320e; Sinfonia Concertante in E♭, K364 Szeryng (vln), Poulet (vln), Giurrana (vla) etc., ASMF, Marriner, NPO, Gibson
Philips 422 508-2, 4CDs [D/A] **M**

Violin Concertos: No. 1 in B♭, K207; No. 2 in D, K211; No. 5 in A K219 (Turkish) Huggett (vln/dir), Age of Enlightenment O
✧ Virgin VC5 45010 2 [D] **F**

Violin Concerto No. 2 in D, K211; Violin Concerto in D, K271a (spurious); Rondo in C, K373 Lin (vln), ECO, Leppard
Sony CD 44913 [D] **F**

Violin Concertos: No. 3 in G, K216; No. 5 in A (Turkish), K219 Mutter (vln), BPO, Karajan
DG 415 327-2 [D] **F**

Violin Concertos: No. 4 in D, K218; No. 5 in A (Turkish), K219 Shumsky (vln), Scottish CO, Tortelier
Nimbus NI 5009 [A] **F**

Complete Dance Music Vienna Mozart Ensemble, Boskovsky
Philips 422 506-2, 6CDs [A] **M**

Divertimenti for Strings Nos. 1–3, K136–8; Divertimenti: No. 1 in E♭, K113; No. 7 in D, K205; No. 10 in F, K247; No. 11 in D, K251; No. 15 in B♭, K287; No. 17 in D, K334; March in D, K290;

March in F, K248; March in D, K445; Ein Musikalischer Spass (A Musical Joke), K522; Serenade No. 13 in G (Eine kleine Nachtmusik), K525 ASMF Chamber Ensemble
Philips 422 504-2, 5CDs [D] **M**

○ *Divertimenti: No. 10 in F, K247; No. 17 in D, K334*
L'Archibudelli
◇ Sony CD 46494 [D] **F**

Complete Divertimenti and Serenades for Wind Holliger Wind Ensemble; Netherlands Wind Ensemble, de Waart; ASMF, Marriner
Philips 422 505-2, 6CDs [D/A] **M**

6 German Dances, K509; 6 German Dances, K536; 6 German Dances, K567; 6 German Dances, K571; 12 German Dances, K586 Tafelmusik, Weil
◇ Sony CD 46696 [D] **F**

Organ (Epistle) Sonatas Nos. 1–17 Watson (org), King's Consort Classical O, King
◇ Hyperion CDA 66377 [D] **F**

Overtures: *La Clemenza di Tito; Cosí fan Tutte; Don Giovanni; Die Entführung aus dem Serail; Idomeneo; Le Nozze di Figaro; Der Schauspieldirektor; Die Zauberflöte; Serenade No. 13 in G (Eine kleine Nachtmusik), K525* Tafelmusik, Weil
◇ Sony CD 46695 [D] **F**

Rondo in C, K373 Tetzlaff (vln), Northern Sinfonia, Schiff
(+ Haydn: *Violin Concertos: No. 1 in C; No. 3 in A; No. 4 in G*)
Virgin VC7 59065-2 [D] **F**

Serenades: No. 1 in D, K100; No. 3 in D, K185; No. 4 in D (Colloredo), K203; No. 5 in D, K204; No. 6 in D (Serenata notturna), K239; No. 7 in D (Haffner), K250; No. 8 in D (Notturno for 4 Orchestras), K286; No. 9 in D (Posthorn), K320; No. 13 in G (Eine kleine Nachtmusik), K525; Cassations: No. 1 in G (Final-Musik), K63; No. 2 in Bb, K99; Divertimento No. 2 in D, K131; Gallimathias musicum, K32; Marches: in D, K62; in D, K189; in D, K237; in D, K215; in D, K249; in D, K335 Nos. 1 & 2 ASMF, Marriner
Philips 422 503-2, 7CDs [D] **M**

Serenades: No. 6 in D (Serenata notturna), K239; No. 13 in G (Eine kleine Nachtmusik), K525; Symphony in F, K76; March in D K290 Amsterdam Baroque O, Koopman
◇ Erato 2292-45713-2 [D] **F**

Serenade No. 7 in D (Haffner), K250; March in D, K249 Amsterdam Baroque O, Koopman
◇ Erato 2292-45436-2 [D] **F**

Serenade No. 10 (for 13 wind instruments) in Bb, K361; Serenade No. 11 (for wind) in Eb, K375 Netherlands Wind Ensemble, de Waart
Philips 420 711-2 [A] **M**

Serenades (for wind): No. 11 in Eb, K375; No. 12 in C min., K388 Orpheus CO
DG 431 683-2 [D] **F**

Serenade No. 13 in G (Eine kleine Nachtmusik), K525 Academy of London, Stamp
(+ Prokofiev: *Peter and the Wolf*; Saint-Saëns: *Carnival of the Animals*)
Virgin VC7 59533-2 [D] **F**

Moscow Virtuosi, Spivakov
(+ *Divertimenti for Strings Nos. 1–3, K136–8*)
RCA RD 60066 [D] **F**

*Sinfonia concertante in Eb, K364; *Concertone in C, K190*
Perlman (vln), Zukerman (vla/*vln), Israel PO, Mehta
DG 415 486-2 [D] **F**

Complete Symphonies AAM, Hogwood
Volume 1
◇ L'Oiseau-Lyre 417 140-2, 2CDs [A] **F**
Volume 2
◇ L'Oiseau-Lyre 417 518-2, 2CDs [A] **F**
Volume 3
◇ L'Oiseau-Lyre 417 592-2, 3CDs [A] **F**
Volume 4
◇ L'Oiseau-Lyre 417 841-2, 3CDs [A] **F**
Volume 5
◇ L'Oiseau-Lyre 421 104-2, 3CDs [A] **F**
Volume 6
◇ L'Oiseau-Lyre 421 085-2, 3CDs [D] **F**
Volume 7
◇ L'Oiseau-Lyre 421 135-2, 3CDs [D/A] **F**

Symphonies: Nos. 1–41; in Bb, K55b; in F, K75; in D, K81; in C, K96; in D, K97; in A, KAnh223 Prague CO, Mackerras
Telarc CD 80300, 10CDs [D] **M**

23 Early Symphonies, K16-214 English Concert, Pinnock
◇ DG 437 792-2, 4 CDs [D] **F**

Symphonies Nos. 17–19, 22 & 32 Amsterdam Baroque O, Koopman
◇ Erato 2292-45714-2 [D] **F**

Symphonies: No. 21 in A, K134; No. 23 in D, K181; No. 24 in Bb, K182, No. 27 in G, K199 Amsterdam Baroque O, Koopman
◇ Erato 2292-45544-2 [D] **F**

Symphonies: No. 25 in G min., K183; No. 26 in Eb, K184; No. 29 in A, K201 English Concert, Pinnock
◇ DG Archiv 431 679-2 [D] **F**

*Symphonies Nos. 28, 33, 35 (Haffner), 39, 40 & 41 (Jupiter); Serenade No. 13 in G (Eine kleine Nachtmusik), K525; Serenade No. 9 in D (Posthorn) K320; *Exsultate jubilate, K165; Marriage of Figaro: Overture* *Raskin (sop), Cleveland O, Szell
Sony CD 46515, 3 CDs [A] **F**

Symphonies: No. 29 in A, K201; No. 33 in Bb, K319 EBS, Gardiner
◇ Philips 412 736-2 [D] **F**

Symphonies: Nos. 31, 34, 35, 36, 38 & 41 Amsterdam Baroque O, Koopman
◇ Erato 2292-45857-2, 2CDs [D] **F**

Symphonies: No. 31 in D (Paris), K297 (first version); No. 34 in C, K338 EBS, Gardiner
◇ Philips 420 937-2 [D] **F**

Symphonies: No. 35 in D (Haffner), K385; No. 38 in D (Prague), K504; No. 39 in Eb, K543 ECO, Barenboim
EMI Eminence CD-EMX 2097 [A] **M**

Symphonies: No. 35 in D (Haffner), K385; No. 40 in G min., K550; No. 41 in C (Jupiter), K551 Cleveland O, Szell
Sony CD 46333 [A] **B**

o *Symphonies: No. 36 in C (Linz), K425; No. 28 in C, K200*
Eighteenth Century O, Brüggen
◇ Philips 432 177-2 [D] **F**

Symphonies: No. 38 in D (Prague), K504; No. 39 in Eb, K543
COE, Harnoncourt
Teldec 4509 90866-2 [D] **F**

Symphonies: No. 38 in D (Prague), K504; No. 40 in G min., K550
LCP, Norrington
◇ EMI CDC7 54336-2 [D] **F**

Symphonies: No. 39 in Eb, K543; No. 41 in C (Jupiter), K551
LCP, Norrington
◇ EMI CDC7 54090-2 [D] **F**

6 Symphonies after Serenades: in D, K100; in D, K185; in D, K203; in D, K204; in D, K250; in D, K320 Tafelmusik, Weil
◇ Sony CD 47260, 2CDs [D] **F**

c *Clarinet Quintet in A, K581; Flute Quartets Nos. 1–4; Oboe Quartet in F, K370; Horn Quintet in Eb, K407; Bassoon and Cello Duo, K292; various completed fragments* Pay (cl), Bennett (fl), Grumiaux Trio, Brown (hn), Black (ob), Thunemann (bsn), Orton (vcl), ASMF Chamber Ensemble
Philips 422 510-2, 3CDs [A/D] **M**

Clarinet Quintet in A, K581 de Peyer (cl), Melos Ensemble
(+ Brahms: *Clarinet Quintet*)
EMI CDM7 63116-2 [A] **M**

*Divertimento in Eb for String Trio, K563; *Duos Nos. 1 & 2 for Violin and Viola, K423–4; **6 Preludes and Fugues for String Trio, K404a; String Trio in Bb, K266* Grumiaux Trio;
*Grumiaux (vln), Pellicia (vla); **ASMF Chamber Ensemble
Philips 422 513-2, 2CDs [A/D] **M**

Divertimento in Eb for String Trio, K563; 6 Preludes and Fugues, K404a L'Archibudelli
◇ Sony 46497 [D] **F**

Flute Quartets Nos. 1–4 Bennett (fl), Grumiaux Trio
Philips 422 835-2 [A] **M**

*Grande Sestetto Concertante (after the Sinfonia Concertante, K364); *Duos Nos. 1, K423 & 2, K424* L'Archibudelli; *V. Beths (vln), Kussmaul (vla)
◇ Sony CD 46631 [D] **F**

Piano Trios Nos. 1–6; Piano Trio in D min., K442; Piano Quartets Nos. 1, K478, & 2, K493; Piano and Wind Quintet in Eb, K452; Adagio and Rondo in C min., K617; Divertimento in Bb for Piano Trio, K254 Beaux Arts Trio, Giurrana (vla), Hoffman (glass harmonica), Nicolet (fl), Schouten (vla), Decross (vcl), Brendel (pno), Holliger (ob)
Philips 422 514-2, 5CDs [A/D] **M**

Piano Trios Nos. 1–6 Trio Fonteney
Teldec 2292 46439-2, 2 CDs [D] **F**

Piano Quartets Nos. 1, K478, & 2, K493 Beaux Arts Trio, Giurrana (vla)
Philips 410 391-2 [D] **F**

Piano and Wind Quintet, K452 Perahia (pno), Black (ob), King (cl), Halstead (hn), Sheen (bsn)
(+ Beethoven: *Piano and Wind Quintet*)
Sony/CBS CD 42099 [D] **F**

C *Piano Trios Nos. 1–6* London Fortepiano Trio
✧ Hyperion CDS 44021/3, 3CDs [D] **F**

String Quartets Nos. 1–23 Italian Quartet
Philips 422 512-2, 8CDs [A] **M**

String Quartets: No. 14 in G, K387; No. 23 in F, K590 Brandis
Quartet
Orfeo C0 41831A [D] **F**

String Quartets: No. 16 in E♭, K428; No. 17 in B♭ (Hunt), K458
Italian Quartet
Philips 422 832-2 [A] **M**

*String Quartets: No. 17 in B♭, K458 (Hunt); No. 19 in C, K465
(Dissonance); No. 23 in F, K590* Musikverein Quartet
Decca 433 694-2 [A] **M**

String Quintets Nos. 1–6 Grumiaux Ensemble
Philips 422 511-2, 3CDs [A] **M**

String Quintets: No. 3 in C, K515; No. 4 in G min., K516
Hausmusik
✧ CDC7 54482-2 [D] **F**

String Quintets: No. 5 in D, K593; No. 6 in E♭, K614
Hausmusik
✧ CDC7 54876-2 [D] **F**

*Violin Sonatas Nos. 1–36; Adagio in C min., K396; Allegro in B♭,
K372; Andante and Allegretto in C, K404; Andante and Fugue,
K402; Sonatina in C, K46d; Sonatina in F, K46e; 6 Variations on
'Hélas, j'ai perdu mon amant'; 12 Variations on 'La bergère
Célimène'* Poulet (vln), Verlet (fpno); Grumiaux (vln), Klien
(pno); van Keulen (vln), Brautigam (pno)
Philips 422 515-2, 7CDs [A/D] **M**

Violin Sonatas Nos. 17–28 & 32–36 Perlman (vln),
Barenboim (pno)
DG 431 784-2, 4CDs [D] **M**

*Violin Sonatas: No. 26 in B♭, K378; No. 28 in E♭, K380; No. 32 in
E♭, K454; Sonatina in F, K547* I. Oistrakh (vln),
Zersalova (pno)
Olympia OCD 125 [A] **F**

*Sonatas: in C for Piano Duet, K19d; in B♭ for Piano Duet, K358; in
D for Piano Duet, K381; in F for Piano Duet, K497; in C for Piano
Duet, K521; in D for Two Pianos, K448; Adagio and Allegro in F
min., K594; Andante with 5 Variations in G, K501; Fantasia in F
min., K608* Eschenbach (pno), Frantz (pno)
DG 435 042-2, 2CDs [A] **M**

S *Complete solo keyboard works* (excluding sonatas) Uchida (pno),
Haebler (pno), Koopman (hpd), Mathot (hpd)
Philips 422 518-2, 5CDs [D/A] **M**

Piano Sonatas Nos. 1–18 Eschenbach (pno)
DG 419 445-2, 5 CDs [A] **M**

*Piano Sonatas: No. 8 in A min., K310; No. 18 in D, K576;
Fantasia in C min., K475; Fantasia in D min., K397; 12
Variations on 'Je suis Lindor', K354* Tan (fpno)
EMI CDC7 54021-2 [D] **F**

V *Complete Religious Works* (excluding Masses) Various artists
and orchestras conducted by C. Davis, Kegel, Winkler
Philips 422 520-2, 5CDs [A/D] **M**

V *Complete Concert Arias* Various artists and orchestras conducted
by Hager, C. Davis, Schreier, Marriner, Harrer
Philips 422 523-2, 8CDs [D/A] **M**

Complete Shorter Vocal Works Various artists and orchestras
conducted by Marriner, Hager, Schreier
Philips 422 522-2, 6CDs [A/D] **M**

Complete Lieder Ameling (sop), Baldwin (pno), etc.
Philips 422 524-2, 2CDs [D] **M**

Lieder (selection) Schreier (ten), Schiff (pno)
Decca 430 514-2 [D] **F**

Ave verum corpus St. John's College Ch, Guest
(+ M. Haydn: *Ave Regina;* J. Haydn: *Mass No. 12*)
Decca 430 159-2 [A] **M**

Litaniae de venerabili Marshall (sop), Cable (mez), Evans (ten),
Roberts (bs), St. John's College Ch, Wren O, Guest
(+ Haydn: *Mass No. 9*)
Decca 430 158-2 [A] **M**

Masses Nos. 1–19 Various artists and orchestras conducted by
C. Davis, Kegel, Harrer, Gardiner and Schreier
Philips 422 519-2, 9CDs [A/D] **M**

*Masses: No. 11 in C (Credo), K257; No. 12 in C (Spauermesse),
K258; No. 13 in C (Organ Solo), K259* Monoyios (sop), Schlick
(sop), Graf (cont), Groenewald (cont), Pfaff (ten), Schafer
(ten), Mertens (bs), Selig (bs), Köln Chamber Ch, Collegium
Cartusianum, Neumann
✧ EMI CDC7 54037-2 [D] **F**

Mass No. 12 in C, K258 Palmer (sop), Cable (mez), Langridge
(ten), Roberts (bs), St. John's College Ch, Wren O, Guest
(+ Haydn: *Mass No. 13 in B♭*)
Decca 430 161-2 [A] **M**

Mass No. 16 in C (Coronation), K317 Tomova-Sintow (sop),
Baltsa (mez), Krenn (ten), van Dam (bs), Vienna Singverein,
BPO, Karajan
(+ Beethoven: *Missa Solemnis*)
DG 423 913-2, 2CDs [A] **M**

Mass No. 18 in C min. (Great), K421 Hendricks (sop), Perry
(sop), Schreier (ten), Luxon (bar), Vienna Singverein, BPO,
Karajan
DG 439 012-2 [D] **M**

Mass No. 19 in D min. (Requiem), K626 Schlick (sop),
Watkinson (cont), Prégardien (ten), van der Kamp (bs),
Netherlands Bach Society Ch, Amsterdam Baroque O,
Koopman
✧ Erato 2292-45472-2 [D] **F**

Vesperae de Dominica, K321 Marshall (sop), Cable (mez), Evans
(ten), Roberts (bs), St. John's College Ch, Wren O, Guest
(+ Haydn: *Mass No. 14 in B♭*)
Decca 430 162-2 [A] **M**

Vesperae solennes de confessore, K339 Palmer (sop), Cable (mez),
Langridge (ten), Roberts (bar), St. John's College Ch, Wren
O, Guest
(+ Haydn: *Mass No. 10 in C*)
Decca 430 157-2 [A] **M**

MUNDY, William (c.1529–1591) ENGLAND

V *Adolescentulus sum ego; Ah, helpless wretch; Beatus et sanctus; Evening service; Kyrie; O Lord, the maker of all things; O Lord, the world's saviour; The secret sins; Sive vigilem; Videte miraculum; Vox patris caelestis* The Sixteen, Christophers
Hyperion CDA 66319 [A] **F**

Vox patris caelestis Tallis Scholars, Phillips
(+ Allegri: *Miserere mei*; Palestrina: *Missa Papae Marcelli*)
Gimell CDGIM 339 [A] **F**

MUSSORGSKY, Modest (1839–1881) RUSSIA

O *Chorus of Priestesses (Salammbo); The Destruction of Sennacherib; Calitis's Journey; Joshua; Night on a Bare Mountain* (original version); *Oedipus in Athens; Prelude (Khovanshchina); Scherzo in Bb; Triumphal March* LSO, Abbado
RCA 09026 61354-2 [A] **M**

Night on a Bare Mountain (original version) LPO, Lloyd-Jones
(+ Rimsky-Korsakov: *Scheherazade*)
Philips 420 898-2 [A] **M**

Night on a Bare Mountain (arr. Rimsky-Korsakov); *Pictures at an Exhibition* (orch. Ravel) Atlanta SO, Levi
Telarc CD 80296 [D] **F**

Pictures at an Exhibition (orch. Ravel)
CSO/Reiner
(+ Respighi: *Pines of Rome; Fountains of Rome*)
RCA 09026 61401-2 [A] **M**
Cleveland O, Szell
(+ Kodály: *Háry János Suite*; Prokofiev: *Lieutenant Kijé Suite*)
Sony CD 48162 [A] **B**

S *Pictures at an Exhibition* Pletnev (pno)
(+ Tchaikovsky: *Sleeping Beauty: Suite* [arr. Pletnev])
Virgin VC7 59611-2 [D] **F**

NEWMAN, Alfred (1900–1970) USA

O Film score excerpts: *Airport; Anastasia; Best of Everything; The Bravados; Captain from Castile; Conquest; Down to the Sea in Ships; How to Marry a Millionaire; The Robe; The Song of Bernadette; Twentieth Century Fox Fanfare; Wuthering Heights* Band of the Grenadier Guards, Ambrosian Singers, National PO, Gerhardt
RCA GD 80184 [A] **M**

All About Eve: Main Title National PO, Gerhardt
(+ film scores by Korngold, Steiner, Waxman)
RCA GD 80183 [A] **M**

NIELSEN, Carl (1865–1931) DENMARK

O *Aladdin* (complete) Ejsing (cont), Paevatalu (bar), Danish National Radio SO & Ch, Rozhdestvensky
Chandos CHAN 9135 [D] **F**

*Aladdin (suite); *Springtime in Fünen* *Nielsen (sop), *von Binzer (ten), *Klint (bs), *Muko University Ch, *St. Klemens Children's Ch, Odense SO, Veto
Unicorn-Kanchana DKPCD 9054 [D] **F**

Clarinet Concerto; Flute Concerto; Violin Concerto Thomsen (cl), Christiansen (fl), Sjøgren (vln), Danish RSO, Schønwandt
Chandos CHAN 8894 [D] **F**

O   *Violin Concerto* Lin (vln), Swedish RSO, Salonen
(+ Sibelius: *Violin Concerto*)
Sony/CBS CD44548 [D] **F**

Helios Overture; Symphony No. 5 SNO, Gibson
(+ Sibelius: *Nightride and Sunrise; Spring Song*)
Chandos CHAN 6533 [A] **M**

Symphonies Nos. 1–6 Bott (sop), Roberts (bar), SNO, Thomson
Chandos CHAN 9163/5, 3CDs [D] **F**

Symphonies: No. 1 in G min.; No. 6 (Sinfonia Semplice) SFSO,
Blomstedt
Decca 425 607-2 [D] **F**

*Symphonies: No. 2 (The Four Temperaments); No. 3 (Sinfonia
espansiva)* SFSO, Blomstedt
Decca 430 280-2 [D] **F**

Symphonies: No. 4 (Inextinguishable); No. 5 SFSO, Blomstedt
Decca 421 524-2 [D] **F**

Symphony No. 4 (Inextinguishable) BPO, Karajan
DG 413 313-2 [D] **F**

C   *Allegretto in F for 2 Recorders; Canto serioso for Horn and
Piano; Fantasy Piece in G min. for Clarinet and Piano; 2 Fantasy
Pieces for Oboe and Piano; Serenata in vano; Suite for Flute, Viola
and Harp* (arr.): *The Fog is Lifting; The Children are Playing;
Faith and Hope are Playing; Wind Quintet* Sandvik (rec), P.
Hannevold (rec); Olsen (hn), Brynildsen (cl), S. Hannevold
(ob), Andsnes (pno); Sandvik (fl), Tomter (vla), Bergen Wind
Quintet
BIS BIS-CD 428 [D] **F**

Violin Sonatas: No. 1 in A; No. 2 Mordkovitch (vln), Benson
(pno)
Chandos CHAN 8598 [D] **F**

Wind Quintet Ensemble Wien-Berlin
(+ Taffanel: *Wind Quintet in G min.*)
Sony CD 45996 [D] **F**

S   *Complete Solo Piano Music* Westenholz (pno)
BIS BIS-CD 167/8 [A] **F**

Commotio; 29 Little Preludes; 2 Preludes; *3 Motets Westenholz
(org); *Camarata Chamber Ch, Enewold
BIS BIS-CD 131 [A] **F**

NONO, Luigi (1924–1990) ITALY

O   *La Lontananza nostalgica utopica futura; 'Hay que caminar'
sognando* Kremer (vln), Grindenko (vln), Tonband
DG 435 870-2 [D] **F**

*...sofferte ondo serene... for piano and magnetic tape; *Como una ola
de fuerza y luz for soprano, piano, orchestra and magnetic tape;
**Contrappunto dialettico alla mente for voices through magnetic
tape* Pollini (pno); *Taskova (sop), Pollini (pno), Bavarian
RSO, Abbado; **Various artists, RAI Chamber Ch,
Antonellini
DG 423 248-2 [A] **M**

NOSKOWSKI, Zygmunt (1846–1909) POLAND

C   *Piano Quartet in D min., Op. 8* Polish Piano Quartet
(+ Zelinski: Piano Quartet)
Olympia OCD 381 [D] **F**

NOVAK, Vítězslav (1870–1949) CZECHOSLOVAKIA

O *Pan* (symphonic poem), *Op. 43* Slovak PO, Bílek
Marco Polo 8.223325 [D] **F**

Slovak Suite, Op. 32; South Bohemian Suite, Op. 64 Czech PO,
Vajner
Supraphon CO-1743 [D] **F**

NYMAN, Michael (born 1948) ENGLAND

O *Prospero's Books* (film score) Michael Nyman Band, Nyman
Argo 425 224-2 [D] **F**

C *String Quartets Nos. 1–3* Balanescu Quartet
Argo 433 093-2 [D] **F**

V *Songbook* Lemper (sop), Michael Nyman Band, Nyman
Decca 425 227-2 [D] **F**

*Time Will Pronounce; Self-Laudatory Hymn of Inanna & her
Omnipotence; The Convertibility of Lute Strings; For John Cage*
Various artists
Argo 440 282-2 [D] **F**

OFFENBACH, Jacques (1819–1880) GERMANY/FRANCE

O Overtures: *Barbe-Bleue; La belle Hélène; La Grande-duchesse de
Gérolstein; Orpheus in the Underworld; Vert-Vert; Barcarolle (Tales
of Hoffmann)* BPO, Karajan
DG 400 044-2 [D] **F**

ONSLOW, Georges (1784-1853) ENGLAND/FRANCE

C *String Quartets: in C min., Op. 56; in F# min., Op. 46/1; Variations
on 'God Save the Queen', Op. 9/1* Coull Quartet
ASV CDDCA 808 [D] **F**

ORFF, Carl (1895–1982) GERMANY

V *Carmina Burana* (cantata) Janowitz (sop), Stolze (ten),
Fischer-Dieskau (bar), Schöneberg Boys Ch, Berlin German
Opera O & Ch, Jochum
DG 423 886-2 [A] **M**

De temporum fine comoedia (symbolic drama) Tomowa-Sintow
(sop), Ludwig (mez), Schreier (ten), Greindl (bs), Boysen
(spkr), RIAS Chamber Ch, etc., Köln RSO, Karajan
DG 429 859-2 [A] **M**

PACHELBEL, Johann (1653–1706) GERMANY

● *Canon and Gigue in D* Orpheus CO
DG 492 390-2 [D] **F** (see collections – *Popular Baroque*)

*Praeludium, Fugue and Chaconne in D min.; Chaconne in F min.;
Prelude and Fugue in C min.; Toccata in F; Toccata and Ricercare
in C min.; 10 Chorale Preludes* Jacob (org)
Virgin VC7 59197-2 [D]

PADEREWSKI, Jan (1860–1941) POLAND

● *Piano Concerto in A min., Op. 17* Lane (pno), BBC Scottish SO,
Maksymiuk
(+ Moszkowski: *Piano Concerto in E, Op. 59*)
Hyperion CDA 66452 [D] **F**

PAGANINI, Niccolò (1782–1840) ITALY

● *Violin Concertos Nos. 1–6* Accardo (vln), LPO, Dutoit
DG 437 210-2, 3CDs [A] **B**

O *Violin Concertos Nos. 1 & 2* Accardo (vln), LPO, Dutoit
DG 415 378-2 [A] **F**

Violin Concerto No. 2 in B min. (trans. Hall) Hall (gtr), London
Mozart Players, Litton
(+ Castelnuovo-Tedesco: *Guitar Concerto No. 1*; Sarasate:
Ziguenerweisen)
Decca 440 293-2 [D] **F**

C *Complete Music for Violin and Guitar* Shaham (vln),
Sollscher (gtr)
DG 437 837-2 [D] **F**

S *24 Caprices, Op. 1* Perlman (vln)
EMI CDC7 47171-2 [A] **F**

PAINE, John Knowles (1839–1906) USA

O *Symphony No. 1 in C min., Op. 23; As You Like It (overture),
Op. 28* NYPO, Mehta
New World NW 374-2 [D] **F**

Symphony No. 2 in A (In the Spring), Op. 34 NYPO, Mehta
New World NW 350-2 [D] **F**

PAISIELLO, Giovanni (1740–1816) ITALY

O *Piano Concertos: No. 1 in C; No. 5 in D; No. 7 in A; No. 8 in C*
Monetti (pno), ECO, Gonley
ASV CDDCA 873 [D] **F**

*Piano Concertos: No. 2 in F; No. 3 in A; No. 4 in G min.; No. 6
in Bb* Monetti (pno), ECO, Gonley
ASV CDDCA 872 [D] **F**

PALESTRINA, Giovanni da (1525/6–1594) ITALY

V *Assumpta est Maria; Missa Assumpta est Maria; Missa Sicut
lilium inter spinas; Sicut lilium inter spinas I* Tallis Scholars,
Phillips
Gimell CDGIM 020 [D] **F**

*Ave Maria (offertory); Canite tuba; Hodie Christus natus est;
Jubilate Deo omnis terra; Missa Hodie Christus natus est; O
magnum mysterium; Tui sunt caeli* King's College Ch,
Ledger
EMI Eminence CD-EMX 2098 [A] **M**

*Duo ubera tua; Magnificat Primi Toni; Missa Aeterna Christi
munera; Nigra sum, sed formosa; Quae est ista; Sicut cervus; Super
flumina Babylonis; Surge, amica mea; Vidi turbam magnam*
Westminster Cathedral Ch, O'Donnell
Hyperion CDA 66490 [D] **F**

Missa Ave Maria; Missa De beata Virgine Westminster Cathedral
Ch, O'Donnell
Hyperion CDA 66364 [D] **F**

Missa Benedicta es Tallis Scholars, Phillips
(+ Josquin: *Benedicta es*)
Gimell CDGIM 001 [D] **F**

Missa brevis; Missa Nasce la gioia mia Tallis Scholars, Phillips
(+ Primavera: *Nasce la gioia mia*)
Gimell CDGIM 008 [D] **F**

Missa Dum complerentur; 5 Motets Christ Church Cathedral Ch
Dartington
Nimbus NI 5100 [D] **F**

Missa Nigra sum Tallis Scholars, Phillips
(+ De Silva: *Nigra sum;* Lhéritier: *Nigra sum;* Victoria: *Nigra sum*)
Gimell CDGIM 003 [D] **F**

Missa O Rex gloriae; Missa Viri Galilaei; O Rex gloriae; Viri Galilaei Westminster Cathedral Ch, O'Donnell
Hyperion CDA 66316 [D] **F**

Missa Papae Marcelli Tallis Scholars, Phillips
(+ Allegri: *Miserere mei;* Mundy: *Vox Patris caelestis*)
Gimell CDGIM 339 [A] **F**

PANUFNIK, Andrzej (1914–1991) POLAND/BRITAIN

*Autumn Music; Heroic Overture; Nocturne; *Sinfonia Rustica; Tragic Overture* Peebles (pno), LSO, Horenstein; *Monte Carlo Opera O, Panufnik
Unicorn-Kanchana UKCD 2016 [A] **M**

*Concerto festivo; Concerto for Timpani, Percussion and Strings; Katyń Epitaph; Landscape; **Sinfonia sacra* Goedicke (timpani), Frye (perc), LSO, **Monte Carlo Opera O, Panufnik
Unicorn-Kanchana UKCD 2020 [A] **M**

*Bassoon Concerto; Violin Concerto; *Hommage à Chopin* Thompson (bsn), Smietana (vln), *Jones (fl), London Musici, Stephenson
Conifer CDCF 182 [D] **F**

Sinfonia Concertante for Flute, Harp & Strings; Concertino for Timpani, Percussion & Strings; Harmony Jones (fl), Masters (hp), Benjafield (perc), Cole (timp), London Musici, Stephenson
Conifer CDCF 217 [D] **F**

*Sinfonia sacra; *Arbor cosmica* Royal Concertgebouw O, *NY Chamber Symphony, Panufnik
Elektra-Nonesuch 7559-79228-2 [D] **F**

Symphony No. 8 Boston SO, Ozawa
(+ Sessions: *Concerto for Orchestra*)
Hyperion CDA 66050 [D] **F**

Symphony No. 9; Piano Concerto Poblocka (pno), LSO, Panufnik
Conifer CDCF 206 [D] **F**

String Quartets Nos. 1–3; String Sextet; Song to the Virgin Mary Chilingirian String Quartet, Chase (vla), Orton (vcl)
Conifer CDCF 218 [D] **F**

PARRY, Hubert (1848–1918) ENGLAND

The Birds: Bridal March; An English Suite; Overture to an Unwritten Tragedy; Lady Radnor's Suite; Symphonic Variations LSO, LPO, Boult
Lyrita SRCD 220 [A] **F**

Lady Radnor's Suite English String O, Boughton
(+ Bridge: *Suite;* Butterworth: *The Banks of Green Willow, etc.*)
Nimbus NI 5068 [D] **F**

Symphonies Nos. 1–5; Symphonic Variations LPO, Bamert
Chandos CHAN 9120/2, 3CDs [D] **F**

Symphony No. 1 in G min.; From Death to Life (symphonic poem) English SO, Boughton
Nimbus NI 5296 [D] **F**

o *Symphony No. 1 in G min.; Concertstück in G min.* LPO, Bamert
Chandos CHAN 9062 [D] **F**

Symphony No. 2 in F (Cambridge); Symphonic Variations LPO,
Bamert
Chandos CHAN 8961 [D] **F**

Symphonies: No. 3 in C (English); No. 4 in E min. LPO, Bamert
Chandos CHAN 8896 [D] **F**

Symphony No. 5 in B min. (symphonic fantasia); *Elegy for
Brahms; From Death to Life* (symphonic poem) LPO, Bamert
Chandos CHAN 8955 [D] **F**

C *Violin Sonata in D, Op. 103; Fantasie-Sonata in B min., Op. 78;
12 Short Pieces* Gruenberg (vln), Vignoles (pno)
Hyperion CDA 66157 [D] **F**

Nonet in B♭ Capricorn
(+ Stanford: *Serenade*)
Hyperion CDA 66291 [D] **F**

*Piano Trio in E min.; *Piano Quartet in A♭* *Inoue (vla), Deakin
Piano Trio
Meridian CDE84248 [D] **F**

S *Chorale Preludes on: Dundee; Martyrdom; Rockingham; St. Ann's;
the Old 104th; Elegy in A♭; Fantasia and Fugue in G*
Matthews (org)
(+ Howells: *Organ Sonata No. 1 in C min.*)
Herald HAVPCD 116 [D] **F**

V *Evening Service in D; Hear my words, ye people; I was glad;
Jerusalem; 6 Songs of Farewell* Judd (org), St. George's Chapel
Ch, Windsor, Robinson
Hyperion CDA 66273 [D] **F**

Invocation to Music Dawson (sop), Davies (ten), Rayner Cook
(bar), LPO & Ch, Bamert
Chandos CHAN 9025 [D] **F**

*The Soul's Ransom; Choric Song from Tennyson's 'The Lotus
Eaters'* Jones (sop), Wilson-Johnson (bar), LPO & Ch, Bamer
Chandos CHAN 8990 [D] **F**

PÄRT, Arvo (born 1935) ESTONIA/AUSTRIA

o *Arbos; Pari intervalli; An den Wassern zu Babel; De Profundis; Es
sang vor langen Jahren; Stabat Mater; Summa* Stuttgart State O
Brass Ensemble, Davies; Bowers-Broadbent (org); Hilliard
Ensemble; Bickley (sop), Kremer (vln), Mendelssohn (vla);
Dawson (sop), Covey-Crump (ten)
ECM 831 959-2 [D] **F**

*Cantus in Memory of Benjamin Britten; Festina Lente; Fratres;
Spiegel im Spiegel; Summa; Tabula Rasa* Little (vln), Roscoe
(pno), Bournemouth Sinfonietta, Studt
EMI Eminence CD-EMX 2221 [D] **M**

Cello Concerto; Perpetuum mobile; Symphonies Nos. 1–3
Helmerson (vcl), Bamberg SO, Järvi
BIS BIS-CD 434 [D] **F**

*Symphony No. 2; Collage; *Credo; Festina lente; Fratres; Summa;
Wenn Bach Bienen gesuchet hatte* *Berman (pno), Philharmonia
O & Ch, Järvi
Chandos CHAN 9134

Festina lente; *Miserere; ***Sarah was ninety years old* Bonn
Beethovenhalle O, Davies; *Western Wind Chamber Ch,
Hilliard Ensemble, Hillier
ECM 847 539-2 [D] F

Fratres for 12 cellos; *Tabula rasa; **Fratres for violin and piano
12 Cellos of the BPO, *Kremer (vln), Grindenko (vln);
Schnittke (prepared pno), Lithuanian CO, Sondeckis;
**Kremer (vln), Jarrett (pno)
ECM 817 764-2 [D] F

Passio Domini nostri Jesu Christe secundum Johannem George
(bs), Potter (ten), Dawson (sop), Covey-Crump (ten), Layton
(vln), Maxwell (ob), Wilson (vcl), Ducket (bsn), Bowers-
Broadbent (org), Western Wind Chamber Ch, Hillier
ECM 837 109-2 [D] F

PENDERECKI, Krzysztof (born 1933) POLAND

Anaklasis; Canticum Canticorum Salomonis; *Capriccio; De Natura
*Sonoris Nos. 1 & 2; The Dream of Jacob; Fonogrammi; Threnody
for the Victims of Hiroshima* Wilkomirska (vln), Polish National
RSO, LSO, Penderecki
EMI CDM5 65077-2 [A] F

*Cello Concerto No. 2; Viola Concerto; Dream of Jacob; Paradise
Lost* (opera): *Adagietto* Monighetti (vcl), Kamasa (vla), Polish
NRO, Wit
Polski Nagrania PNCD 020 [A] F

Violin Concerto; *Symphony No. 2 Kulka (vln), Polish NRO,
Penderecki; *Polish NRO, Kaspszyk
Polski Nagrania PNCD 019 [A] F

String Quartet No. 1 LaSalle Quartet
(+ Cage: *String Quartet;* Lutoslawski: *String Quartet;* Mayuzumi:
Prelude)
DG 423 245-2 [A] M

String Quartet No. 2 Varsovia Quartet
(+ Lutoslawski: *String Quartet;* Szymanowski: *String Quartets
Nos. 1 & 2*)
Olympia OCD 328 [A] F

Polish Requiem Haubold (sop), Wingrodska (mez), Terzakis
(ten), Smith (bs), North German & Bavarian Radio Chs, North
German RSO, Penderecki
DG 429 720-2, 2CDs [D] F

St. Luke Passion von Osten (sop), Roberts (bar), Rydl (bs),
Lubaszenko (narr), Crakow Boys' Ch, Polish National PO &
Ch, Penderecki
Argo 430 328-2 [D] F

Utrenya Woytowicz (sop), Ambroziak (sop), Szczepańska
(mez), Pustelak (ten), Ladysz (bs), Denysenko (bs), Carmeli
(bs), Lagger (bs), Pioneer Ch, Warsaw National PO & Ch,
Markowski
Polski Nagrania PNCD 018 [A] F

PERGOLESI, Giovanni (1710–1736) ITALY

Magnificat Vaughan (sop), Baker (mez), Partridge (ten), Keyte
(bs), King's College Ch, ASMF, Willcocks
(+ Vivaldi: *Gloria, RV 589; Magnificat, RV611*)
Decca 425 724-2 [A] M

V *Stabat Mater; *In coelestibus regnis; Salve regina in A min.* Fisher (sop), *Chance (bs), King's Consort, King
Hyperion CDA 66294 [D] **F**

PFITZNER, Hans (1869–1949) GERMANY

O *Das Käthchen von Heilbronn* (incidental music), *Op. 17: Overture;*
Palestrina (opera): *Preludes to Acts I–III; Die Rose vom*
Liebesgarten (opera): *Miracle of the Blossoms; Funeral March*
Bavarian RSO, Sawallisch
Orfeo C 168881 A [D] **F**

C *Piano Quintet in C, Op. 23; Clarinet and Piano Sextet in G min.,*
Op. 55 Consortium Classicum
Orfeo C281 931 [D] **F**

V *18 Lieder* Fischer-Dieskau (bar), Höll (pno)
Orfeo C 036821 A [D] **F**

Von deutscher Seele (cantata) Giebel (sop), Topper (mez),
Wunderlich (ten), Wiener (bs), Bavarian RSO & Ch, Keilberth
(+ Schoeck: *Lebendig begraben*)
DG 437 033-2 [A] **M**

PHILIPS, Peter (1560/1–1628) ENGLAND

S *Almand (Tregian); Aria a 5; Aria del Gran Duca Ferdinando;*
Balla d'amore; Galliard (Coranto); Galliard a 5; Pavan
(Passamezzo); Pavan a 2; Pavan and Galliard; Pavan and
Galliard (Dolorosa); Pavan and Galliard (after Morley); Pavan
and Galliard (Paget); Pavan and Galliard (1580); Pavan and
Galliard in F Parley of Instruments
Hyperion CDA 66240 [D] **F**

16 Motets Winchester Cathedral Ch, Parley of Instruments, Hill
Hyperion CDA 66643 [D] **F**

PIERNÉ, Gabriel (1863–1937) FRANCE

O *Piano Concerto in C min., Op. 42; Ramuntcho* (ballet): *Suites Nos.*
1 & 2 Aschatz (pno), Lorraine PO, Houtmann
BIS BIS-CD 381 [D] **F**

Cydalise et le Chèvre-pied; Ramuntcho (complete) Paris National
Opéra O, Mari
EMI CDM7 64278-2 [A] **M**

C *Piano Quintet; *Flute Sonata, Op. 36* Hubeau (pno), Viotti
Quartet; *Charlier (fl), *Hubeau (pno)
Erato 2292 45525-2 [A] **F**

V *Les Enfants à Bethléem* (mystery play) Chamonin (mez), Schae
(mez), Orliac (ten), Frémeau (bar), Deiber (narr), FNR
Maîtrise, de Rozel
Erato 2292-45008-2 [D] **F**

PISTON, Walter (1894–1976) USA

O *The Incredible Flutist* (ballet) Louisville O, Mester
(+ Gottschalk arr.: *Cakewalk*)
Albany TROY 016-2 [A] **F**

*Symphony No. 4; *Capriccio for Harp and Strings; Three New*
*England Sketches; **Serenata* *Wunrow (hp), Seattle SO,
**New York Chamber SO, Schwarz
Delos DE 3106 [D] **F**

*Symphonies Nos. *5, 7 & 8* Louisville O, *Whitney, Mester
Albany AR 011 [A] **F**

O *Symphony No. 6; The Incredible Flutist* (ballet): *Suite; Three New England Sketches* St. Louis SO, Slatkin
RCA RD 60798 [D] **F**

PIZZETTI, Ildebrando (1880–1968) ITALY

V *Messe di requiem; 3 Composizione corali; 2 Composizione corali*
Danish National Radio Chamber Ch, Parkman
Chandos CHAN 8964 [D] **F**

PONCE, Manuel (1882–1948) MEXICO

S *Mazurkas Nos. 1–7 & 19; 9 Piano Pieces* Osorio (pno)
ASV CDDCA 874 [D] **F**

POPOV, Gavriil (1904–1972) RUSSIA

O *Symphony No. 2 in C (The Homeland)* Bolshoi Theatre
Ensemble Soloists, Lazarev
(+ Miaskovsky: *2 Pieces;* Mossolov: *3 Children's Scenes, etc.*)
Olympia OCD 170 [A] **F**

POTTER, Cipriani (1792–1871) ENGLAND

O *Symphonies: No. 8 in E♭; No. 10 in G min.* Milton Keynes CO,
Wetton
Unicorn-Kanchana DKPCD 9091 [D] **F**

POULENC, Francis (1899–1963) FRANCE

O *Les animaux modèles* (ballet music); *Les Biches* (ballet); *Concert
champêtre; Double Piano Concerto; 2 Marches et un intermède; Les
mariés de la tour Eiffel* (ballet): *La baigneuse de Trouville;
Discourse du Génal; Matelote provençale; Pastourelle; Sinfonietta;
Suite français* Various artists, Paris Conservatoire O, Paris
Philharmonia O, Paris O, Cluytens
EMI CZS7 62690-2, 2CDs [D/A] **B**

Aubade; Sinfonietta Evans (pno), New London O, Corp
(+ Hahn: *Le bal de Béatrice d'Este: Suite*)
Hyperion CDA 66347 [D] **F**

Les Biches (ballet) Ulster O, Tortelier
(+ Milhaud: *Le Boeuf sur le toit, etc.;* Ibert: *Divertissement*)
Chandos CHAN 9023 [D] **M**

*Concert champêtre; Organ Concerto *Koopman (hpd), Alain
(org), Rotterdam PO, Conlon
Erato 2292-45233-2 [D] **F**

Organ Concerto; Piano Concerto; Double Piano Concerto Hurford
(org), Rogé (pno), Deferne (pno), Philharmonia O, Dutoit
Decca 436 546-2 [D] **F**

*Double Piano Concerto; Capriccio; Élégie; Embarquement pour
Cythère; Sonata for 4 hands* K. & M. Labèque (pno duo/2 pnos)
(+ Milhaud: *Scaramouche*)
Philips 426 284-2 [D] **F**

: *Élégie for Horn and Piano; Sextet for Piano and Wind Quintet;
Cello Sonata; Clarinet Sonata; Clarinet and Bassoon Sonata;
*Double Clarinet Sonata; Flute Sonata; Horn, Trumpet and
Trombone Sonata; Oboe Sonata; Violin Sonata; **Trio for Oboe,
Bassoon and Piano* Various artists
EMI CZS7 62736-2, 2CDs [A] **B**

Sextuor; Trio; Clarinet Sonata; Flute Sonata; Oboe Sonata
Various artists, Rogé (pno)
Decca 421 581-2 [D] **F**

S *Humoresque; Improvisations Nos. 4, 5, 9–11 & 14; 3 Intermezzi; 8 Nocturnes; Presto in B♭; Suite in C; Thème varié; Villageoises* Rogé (pno)
Decca 425 862-2 [D] **F**

Improvisations Nos. 1–3, 6–8, 12, 13 & 15; 3 Mouvements perpétuels; 2 Novelettes; Novelette sur un thème de Falla in E min.; Pastourelle; 3 Pièces; Les soirées de Nazelles; Valse Rogé (pno)
Decca 417 438-2 [D] **F**

V *Ave verum corpus; Exultate deo; Laudes de Saint Antoine de Padoue; Mass in G; 4 Motets pour le temps de Noël; 4 Motets pour un temps de pénitence; 4 Petites prières de Saint François d'Assise; Salve regina* Trinity College Ch, Marlow
Conifer CDCF 151 [D] **F**

Gloria; Litanies à la Vierge; Stabat mater Dubosc (sop), Westminster Singers, City of London Sinfonia, Hickox
Virgin VC7 59286-2 [D] **F**

15 Melodies Lott (sop), Johnson (pno), Songmakers' Almanac
Hyperion CDA 66147 [D] **F**

PRAETORIUS, Michael (c.1571–1621) GERMANY

V *Magnificat; Aus tiefer Not; Peccavi fateor; Psalms of David: CXVI; Der Tag vertreibt die finster Nacht; Venite exultemus Domino* Huelgas Ensemble, van Nevel
Sony CD 48039 [D] **F**

Terpsichore (excerpts); *Allein Gott in der Höh; Aus tiefer Not; Christus, der uns selig macht; Erhalt uns, Herr; Gott der Vater; Resonet in laudibus* Boys of the Cathedral & Abbey Church, St. Albans, Early Music Consort of London, Munrow
EMI CDM7 69024-2 [A] **M**

V *Terpsichore: Nos. 1, 283–5 & 310; Musae Sioniae VI, No. 53: Es ist ein Ros' entsprungen; Polyhymnia caduceatrix et panegyrica Nos. 9–11, 12 & 17; Puericinium Nos. 2, 4 & 5* Westminster Cathedral Ch, Parley of Instruments, Hill
Hyperion CDA 66200 [D] **F**

PREVIN, André (born 1929) GERMANY/USA/ENGLAND

O *Guitar Concerto; Piano Concerto* Fernández (gtr), Ashkenazy (pno), RPO, Previn
Decca 425 107-2 [D] **F**

PRIMAVERA, Giovanni (c.1540/45–after 1585) ITALY

V *Nasce la gioia mia* Tallis Scholars, Phillips
(+ Palestrina: *Missa brevis; Missa Nasce la gioia mia*)
Gimell CDGIM 008 [D] **F**

PROKOFIEV, Sergey (1891–1953) RUSSIA

O *Boris Godunov* (incidental music), *Op. 70b: Fountain Scene; Polonaise; Dreams* (symphonic tableau), *Op. 6; Eugene Onegin* (incidental music), *Op. 71: Minuet; Polka; Mazurka; 2 Pushkin Waltzes, Op. 120; Romeo and Juliet* (ballet): *Suite No. 2, Op. 64c* SNO, Järvi
Chandos CHAN 8472 [D] **F**

Chout (The Tale of The Buffoon), Op. 21 (ballet) USSR Ministry of Culture SO, Rozhdestvensky
Olympia OCD 126 [D] **F**

Cinderella (ballet), *Op. 87* Cleveland O, Ashkenazy
Decca 410 162-2, 2CDs [D] **F**

Piano Concertos Nos. 1–5; Overture on Hebrew Themes, Op. 34;
Visions fugitives, Op. 22 Beroff (pno), LGO, Masur
EMI CMS7 62542-2, 2CDs [A] **M**

Piano Concerto No. 1 in Dь, Op. 10; Suggestion diabolique Op. 4/4
Gavrilov (pno), LSO, Rattle
(+ Balakirev: *Islamey;* Tchaikovsky: *Piano Concerto No.1, etc.*)
EMI CDM7 64329-2 [A] **F**

Piano Concertos: No. 2 in G min., Op. 16; No. 3 in C, Op. 26
Gutierrez (pno), Royal Concertgebouw O, Järvi
Chandos CHAN 8889 [D] **F**

Piano Concerto No. 4, Op. 53 Fleisher (pno), Boston SO, Ozawa
(+ Britten: *Diversions;* Ravel: *Piano Concerto for the Left Hand*)
Sony CD 47188 [D] **F**

Piano Concerto No. 5 in G min., Op. 55 Richter (pno), Warsaw
National PO, Wislocki
(+ Rachmaninov: *Piano Concerto No. 2*)
DG 415 119-2 [A] **F**

Violin Concertos: No. 1 in D, Op. 19; No. 2 in G min., Op. 63
Mintz (vln), Chicago SO, Abbado
DG 410 524-2 [D] **F**

Violin Concerto No. 2 in G min., Op. 63 Heifetz (vln), Boston
SO, Munch
(+ Glazunov: *Violin Concerto;* Sibelius: *Violin Concerto*)
RCA RD 87019 [A] **F**

Festive Poem for the 30th Anniversary of October 1917, Op. 113
USSR Ministry of Culture SO, Rozhdestvensky
(+ Eshpay: *Lenin is With Us;* Shostakovich: *October, Op. 131, etc.*)
Olympia OCD 201 [D] **F**

The Gambler (opera), Op. 49: 4 Portraits and Dénouement; Semyon
Kotko (symphonic suite), Op. 81b SNO, Järvi
Chandos CHAN 8803 [D] **F**

Lieutenant Kijé Suite, Op. 60 Cleveland O, Szell
(+ Kodály: *Háry János Suite;* Mussorgsky: *Pictures at an*
Exhibition)
Sony CD 48162 [A] **B**

Lieutenant Kijé Suite, Op. 60; **Alexander Nevsky (cantata), Op. 78*
*Elias (mez), CSO & *Ch, Reiner
(+ Glinka: *Ruslan and Lyudmila Overture*)
RCA GD60176 [A] **M**

On the Dnieper (ballet), Op. 51; Le Pas d'acier (ballet), Op. 41
USSR Ministry of Culture SO, Rozhdestvensky
Olympia OCD 103 [D] **F**

Peter and the Wolf, Op. 67 Gielgud (narr), Academy of London,
Stamp
(+ Mozart: *Serenade No. 13;* Saint-Saëns: *Carnival of the*
Animals)
Virgin VC7 59533-2 [D] **F**

Prodigal Son (ballet), Op. 46; Andante, Op. 29b; Divertissement,
Op. 43; Symphonic Song, Op. 57 SNO, Järvi
Chandos CHAN 8728 [D] **F**

Romeo and Juliet (ballet), Op. 64 Cleveland O, Maazel
Decca 417 510-2, 2CDs [A] **F**

O *Scythian Suite, Op. 20* LSO, Abbado
(+ Bartók: *The Miraculous Mandarin; Two Portraits*)
DG 410 598-2 [D] **F**

*Symphonies Nos. 1–7; Russian Overture, Op. 72; Scythian Suite,
Op. 20* LSO, LPO, Weller
Decca 430 782-2, 4CDs [A] **M**

*Symphonies: No. 1 in D, Op. 25 (Classical); No. 7 in C♯ min., Op.
131; Love for Three Oranges (opera): Suite* Philharmonia O,
Malko
Classics for Pleasure CD-CFP 4523 [A] **B**

Symphony No. 1 in D, Op. 25 (Classical) ASMF, Marriner
(+ Bizet: *Symphony in C*; Stravinsky: *Pulcinella Suite*)
Decca 417 734-2 [A] **M**

*Symphony No. 2 in D min., Op. 40; Romeo and Juliet (ballet):
Suite No. 1, Op. 64b* SNO, Järvi
Chandos CHAN 8368 [D] **F**

*Symphonies: No. 3 in C min., Op. 44; No. 4 in C, Op. 112 (revised
version)* Moscow SO, Kitaenko
Olympia OCD 260 [D] **F**

Symphonies: No. 5 in B♭, Op. 100; No. 1 in D, Op. 25 (Classical)
BPO, Karajan
DG 437 253-2 [A] **M**

*Symphony No. 6 in E♭, Op. 111; Waltz Suite, Op. 110: Nos. 1, 5 &
6* SNO, Järvi
Chandos CHAN 8359 [D] **F**

C *Overture on Hebrew Themes, Op. 34* Borodin Trio, E. Turovsky
(vln), Golani (vla), Campbell (pno)
(+ Arensky: *Piano Trio No. 2*; Shostakovich: *Romances on Verses
by Alexander Blok*)
Chandos CHAN 8924 [D] **F**

Cello Sonata in C, Op. 119 Harrell (vcl), Ashkenazy (pno)
(+ Shostakovich: *Moderato; Cello Sonata*)
Decca 421 774-2 [D] **F**

Flute Sonata, Op. 94 Hall (fl), Jacobson (pno)
(+ Bartók: *15 Hungarian Peasant Songs*; Martinů: *Flute Sonata*)
Pickwick MCD 26 [D] **B**

String Quartets: No. 1 in B min., Op. 50; No. 2 in F, Op. 92
American Quartet
Olympia OCD 340 [D] **F**

Violin Sonatas: No. 1 in F min., Op. 80; No. 2 in D, Op. 94a
Mintz (vln), Bronfman (pno)
DG 423 575-2 [D] **F**

S *Piano Sonatas Nos. 1–9; 3 Pieces, Op. 59 Nos. 2 & 3; 2 Sonatinas,
Op. 54; Visions fugitives, Op. 22* Lill (pno)
ASV CDDCS 314, 3CDs [D] **F**

Piano Sonatas Nos. 1, 4, 5 & 10 McLachlan (pno)
Olympia OCD 255 [D] **F**

*Piano Sonata No. 3 in A min., Op. 28; 10 Pieces, Op. 12; 3 Pieces
from 'Cinderella', Op. 95; Thoughts, Op. 62* Berman (pno)
Chandos CHAN 9069 [D] **F**

*Piano Sonata No. 4 in C min., Op. 29; Music for Children, Op. 65
6 Pieces, Op. 52* Berman (pno)
Chandos CHAN 8926 [D] **F**

Piano Sonata No. 5 in C, Op. 38 (rev. Op. 135); 10 Pieces from 'Romeo and Juliet', Op. 75; 4 Pieces, Op. 32; Love for Three Oranges (opera): March and Scherzo (arr.) Berman (pno)
Chandos CHAN 8851 [D] **F**

Piano Sonatas Nos. 6–8 Donohoe (pno)
EMI CDC7 54281-2 [D] **F**

Piano Sonata No. 7 in B♭, Op. 83 Pollini (pno)
(+ Boulez: *Piano Sonata No. 2;* Stravinsky: *3 Movements from Petrushka;* Webern: *Variations*)
DG 419 202-2 [A] **F**

Piano Sonata No. 9 in C, Op. 103; Chose en soi, Op. 45 (A & B); Divertissement, Op. 43b; Studies, Op. 2 Berman (pno)
Chandos CHAN 9211 [D] **F**

Visions fugitives, Op. 22 Demidenko (pno)
(+ Scriabin: *Piano works*)
Conifer CDCF 204 [D] **F**

5 Akhmatova Poems, Op. 27; 2 Poems, Op. 9; 5 Poems, Op. 36; 3 Romances, Op. 73 Farley (sop), Aronov (pno)
Chandos CHAN 8509 [D] **F**

Alexander Nevsky (cantata), Op. 78 Reynolds (mez), LSO & Ch, Previn
(+ Rachmaninov: *The Bells*)
EMI CDM7 63114-2 [A] **M**

Ballad of an Unknown Boy (cantata), Op. 93; *On Guard of Peace (oratorio), Op. 124 Poliakova (sop), Makhov (ten), *Arkhipova (mez), *Mironov (trb), *Maksakova (speaker), *Myshkin (narr), USSR Radio Ch & SO, Rozhdestvensky
Olympia OCD 206 [A] **F**

Cantata for the 20th Anniversary of the October Revolution; The Stone Flower: Excerpts Rozhdestvensky (narr), Philharmonia O & Ch, Järvi
Chandos CHAN 9095 [D] **F**

3 Children's Songs, Op. 68; 5 Poems, Op. 23; 12 Russian Folksongs, Op. 104: Nos. 1 & 2; 5 Songs without Words, Op. 35; The Ugly Duckling, Op. 18 Farley (sop), Vignoles (pno)
ASV CDDCA 669 [D] **F**

Ivan the Terrible (ed. Palmer) Finnie (cont), Storojev (bs-bar), Philharmonia O & Chorus, Järvi
Chandos CHAN 8977 [D] **F**

UCCINI, Giacomo (1858–1924) ITALY

Crisantemi; 3 Minuets; Scherzo in A min.; String Quartet in D; *Foglio d'album; *Piccolo tango; **Avanti! Urania!; **E l'uccellino; **Inno a Diana; **Menti all'avviso; **Morire?; **Salve del ciel regina; **Sole e amore; **Storiella d'amore; **Terra e mare Raphael Quartet, *Crone (pno), **Alexander (sop), Crone (pno)
Etcetera KTC 1050 [D] **F**

Messa di Gloria Carreras (ten), Prey (bar), Ambrosian Singers, Philharmonia O, Scimone
Erato 2292-45197-2 [D] **F**

URCELL, Henry (1659–1695) ENGLAND

Excerpts from 45 stage works; Chaconne in G min.; Overture in D min.; Overture in G min.; Pavan in G min.; 4 Pavans; Trio sonata

in G min. Various artists, Taverner Ch, AAM, Hogwood
✧ L'Oiseau-Lyre 425 893-2, 6CDs [A] **M**

C *Chaconne in G min.; Fantasia upon a Ground; 4 Pavans: Nos. 1 &
4; 10 Sonatas: Nos. 1 & 2; 12 Sonatas: Nos. 8–12* Purcell
Quartet
✧ Chandos CHAN 8663 [D] **F**

*Fantasia in F (on one note); 3 Fantasias; 9 Fantasias; In nomine in
G min.; In Nomine in G min. (Dorian)* VCM
✧ Amadeo 423 419-2 [A] **F**

Pavan in G min.; 4 Pavans: Nos. 2 & 3; 12 Sonatas: Nos. 1–7
Purcell Quartet
✧ Chandos CHAN 8591 [D] **F**

*10 Sonatas in 4 Parts: Nos. 3–10; *Prelude in G min.; **4
Voluntaries: Nos. 2 & 4* Purcell Quartet; *Mackintosh (vln);
**Wooley (org)
✧ Chandos CHAN 8763 [D] **F**

V *March and Canzona in C min.; Come ye sons of art, away; Funeral
Music for Queen Mary* Lott (sop), Brett (alt), Williams (alt),
Allen (bar), Equale Brass, Monteverdi O & Ch, Gardiner
✧ Erato 2292-45123-2 [A] **F**

Complete Odes and Welcome Songs Various artists, Ch of New
College Oxford, King's Consort, King
✧ Hyperion CDS 44031/8, 8CDs [D] **M**

*Arise, my muse (Ode for the birthday of Queen Mary); Now does the
glorious day appear (Ode for the birthday of Queen Mary); Welcome
to all the pleasures (Ode for St. Cecilia's Day)* Fisher (sop),
Bonner (sop), Bowman (alt), Chance (alt), Daniels (ten),
Ainsley (ten), George (bs), Pott (bs), King's Consort, King
✧ Hyperion CDA 66314 [D] **F**

The Complete Anthems & Services Various artists, King's Consort,
King
✧ CDA 66585, 66609, 66623, 66644, 66656, 66663, 66677, 7
separate CDs [D] **F**

Anthems: *Blow up the trumpet in Sion; Hear my prayer, O Lord; I
will sing unto the Lord; Jubilate in D; Lord, how long wilt thou be
angry; O God, Thou art my God; O God, Thou hast cast us out; O
Lord God of Hosts; Remember not, Lord, our offences; Save me, O
God; Morning Service; Coronation Music for King James II;
Funeral Music for Queen Mary* Jackson (org), Trinity College
Ch, Marlow
Conifer CDCF 152 [D] **F**

*Celebrate this Festival (Ode for the birthday of Queen Mary); Fly,
bold rebellion (Welcome ode for King Charles II); Sound the Trumpet
(Welcome ode for King James II)* Fisher (sop), Bonner (sop),
Bowman (alt), Kenny (alt), Covey-Crump (ten), Muller (ten),
George (bs), Pott (bs), King's Consort, King
✧ Hyperion CDA 66412 [D] **F**

*Celestial music did the gods inspire (ode); From hardy climes and
desperate toils of war (Welcome song); Ye Tuneful Muses (Welcome
ode for King James II)* Fisher (sop), Bonner (sop), Bowman
(alt), Daniels (alt), Covey-Crump (ten), George (bs), Pott (bs)
King's Consort, King
✧ Hyperion CDA 66456 [D] **F**

*Great Parent Hail (Welcome song); Summer's Abscence unconcerned
we bear (Welcome song for King Charles II); Welcome, welcome,*

glorious morn (Welcome song for the birthday of Queen Mary)
Fisher (sop), Tubb (sop), Bowman (alt), Short (alt), Covey-Crump (ten), Ainsley (ten), George (bs), Pott (bs), King's Consort, King
◇ Hyperion CDA 66476 [D] **F**

V *Hail Bright Cecilia (Ode for St. Cecilia's Day); Who can from Joy refrain? (Ode for the birthday of the Duke of Gloucester)* Fisher (sop), Bowman (alt), Covey-Crump (ten), Ainsley (ten), George (bs), Keenlyside (trb), New College Ch, King's Consort, King
◇ Hyperion CDA 66349 [D] **F**

My heart is inditing (verse anthem), *Z30; O Sing Unto the Lord* (verse anthem) *Praise the Lord, O Jerusalem* (verse anthem), *Z46; They that go down to the sea in Ships* (verse anthem), *Z57; Te Deum and Jubilate Deo in D* Christ Church Cathedral Ch, English Concert, Pinnock
◇ DG Archiv 427 124-2 [A] **M**

QUILTER, Roger (1877–1953) ENGLAND

V *Arab love song; At close of day; 7 Elizabethan Lyrics; Go, lovely rose; I arise from dreams of thee; In the bud of the morning-o; Love's philosophy; Music when soft voices die; Now sleeps the crimson petal; 3 Shakespeare Songs, Op. 6; 4 Songs, Op. 14; 3 Songs of William Blake, Op. 20; To Julia: 6 Songs, Op. 8* Luxon (bar), Willison (pno)
Chandos CHAN 8782 [D] **F**

RACHMANINOV, Sergey (1873–1943) RUSSIA/USA

O *Concerto Élégiaque (orch. of Piano Trio No. 2); Corelli Variations (orch.); Vocalise* Detroit SO, Järvi
Chandos CHAN 9261 [D] **F**

Piano Concertos Nos. 1–4
Collard (pno), Toulouse Capitole O, Plasson
EMI CZS7 67419-2, 2CDs [A] **B**

Piano Concertos: No. 1 in F♯ min., Op. 1; No. 4 in G min., Op. 40; Rhapsody on a Theme of Paganini, Op. 43 Wild (pno), RPO, Horenstein
Chesky CD 41 [A] **F**

Piano Concerto No. 1 in F♯ min., Op. 1; Rhapsody on a Theme of Paganini, Op. 43 Pletnev (pno), Philharmonia O, Pesek
Virgin VC7 59506-2 [D] **F**

Piano Concerto No. 2 in C min., Op. 18 Richter (pno), Warsaw National PO, Wislocki
(+ Prokofiev: *Piano Concerto No. 5*)
DG 415 119-2 [A] **F**

*Piano Concertos: No. 2 in C min., Op. 18; *No. 3 in D min., Op. 30; Preludes: Op. 3/2 in C♯ min.; Op. 23/6 in E♭* Janis (pno), Minneapolis SO, *LSO, Dorati
Philips Mercury 432 759-2 [A] **M**

Piano Concerto No. 3 in D min., Op. 30 Horowitz (pno), NYPO, Ormandy
RCA 09026 61564-2 [A] **F**

Piano Concerto No. 4 in G min., Op. 40 Michelangeli (pno), Philharmonia O, Gracis
(+ Ravel: *Piano Concerto in G*)
EMI CDC7 49326-2 [A] **F**

O *Piano Concerto No. 4 in G min., Op. 40* (original version);
Monna Vanna (opera) *Black (pno), Walker (sop), McCoy
(ten), Thorsteinsson (ten), Milnes (bar), Karousatos (bar),
Iceland, Opera Ch, Iceland SO, Buketoff
Chandos CHAN 8987 [D] **F**

The Rock (fantasy), *Op. 7* LSO, Previn
(+ Shostakovich: *Symphony No. 5*)
RCA GD 86801 [A] **M**

Symphonies Nos. 1–3
Philadelphia O, Ormandy
(+ *Vocalise, Op. 34/11*)
Sony/CBS CD 45678, 2CDs [A] **M**
LSO, Previn
(+ *Isle of the dead; Symphonic Dances; Aleko: excerpts; Vocalise*)
EMI CMS7 64530-2, 3CDs [A] **M**

Symphony No. 1 in D min., Op. 13; 4 Etudes-Tableaux (orch.
Respighi) BBC Welsh SO, Otaka
Nimbus NI 5311 [D] **F**

Symphony No. 2 in E min., Op. 27; Isle of the Dead (symphonic
poem), *Op. 29* BPO, Maazel
DG 429 490-2 [D] **M**

Symphony No. 3 in A min., Op. 44; Symphonic Dances, Op. 45
BPO, Maazel
DG 429 981-2 [D] **M**

Symphony No. 3 in A min., Op. 44 LSO, Previn
(+ Shostakovich: *Symphony No. 6*)
EMI CDM7 69564-2 [A] **M**

C *6 Morceaux, Op. 11; 2 Pieces; Polka italienne; Romance in G;
Russian Rhapsody; Suites Nos. 1 & 2; Symphonic Dances* Engerer
(pno), Maisenberg (pno)
HM HMC90 1301/2, 2CDs [D] **F**

Cello Sonata in G minor Op. 19 Hoffman (vcl), Collard (pno)
(+ Chopin: *Cello Sonata*)
EMI CDC7 54819-2 [D] **F**

*Suites for 2 Pianos: *No. 1, Op. 5; *No. 2, Op. 17; Études-
Tableaux, Op. 33* Ashkenazy (pno), *Previn (pno)
Decca 425 029-2 [A] **M**

Trios élégiaques: No. 1 in G min.; No.2 in D min., Borodin Trio
Chandos CHAN 8341 [D] **F**

S *Complete transcriptions* Shelley (pno)
Hyperion CDA 66486 [D] **F**

Complete Solo Piano Music Shelley (pno)
Hyperion CDS 44041/8, 8CDs [D/A] **M**

Études-Tableaux, Opp. 33 & 39 Fergus-Thompson (pno)
ASV CDDCA 789 [D] **F**

9 Études-Tableaux from Opp. 33/39; 13 Preludes from Opp. 23/32
Richter (pno)
Olympia OCD 337 [A/D] **F**

*Fragments in A♭; Fughetta in F; 4 Pieces; Morceaux de Fantaisie in
G min.; 3 Nocturnes; Oriental Sketch in B♭; Piece in D min.; Piano
Sonata No. 2 (original version); Song without Words in D min.*
Shelley (pno)
Hyperion CDA 66198 [D] **F**

6 Moments Musicaux, Op. 16; 7 Morceaux de Salon, Op. 10
Shelley (pno)
Hyperion CDA 66184 [D] **F**

24 Preludes, Opp. 23 & 32; Piano Sonata No. 2 in Bb min., Op. 36
Ashkenazy (pno)
Decca 414 417-2, 2CDs [A/D] **F**

*24 Preludes, Opp. 23 & 32; Prelude in F; Prelude in D min.;
5 Morceaux de Fantaisie, Op. 3* Shelley (pno)
Hyperion CDA 66081/2, 2 separateCDs [D] **F**

*Piano Sonatas: No. 1 in D min., Op. 28; No. 2 in Bb min. (original
version), Op. 36* Fergus-Thompson (pno)
Kingdom KCLCD 2007 [D] **F**

*Variations on a Theme of Chopin, Op. 22; Variations on a Theme of
Corelli, Op. 42; Mélodie in E, Op. 3/3 (revised version); Scherzo
from 'A Midsummer Night's Dream' (Mendelssohn)* Shelley (pno)
Hyperion CDA 66009 [A] **F**

Piano Recital Rachmaninov (pno rolls)
Decca 440 066-2 [A] **M**

The Bells (choral symphony), *Op. 35* Armstrong (sop), Tear
(ten), Shirley-Quirk (bar), LSO & Ch, Previn
(+ Prokofiev: *Alexander Nevsky*)
EMI CDM7 63114-2 [A] **M**

The Complete Songs Söderström (sop), Ashkenazy (pno)
Decca 436 920-2, 3 CDs [A] **M**

Songs: *Op. 4 Nos. 1, 3 & 4; Op. 8 No. 5; Op. 14 No. 9; Op. 21 No. 6;
Op. 26 Nos. 2, 6 & 13* Hvorostovsky (bar), Boshniakovich (pno)
(+ Tchaikovsky: *Songs*)
Philips 432 119-2 [D] **F**

Vespers (All-night Vigil), Op. 37 Corydon Singers, Best
Hyperion CDA 66460 [D] **F**

RAFF, Joachim (1822–1882) GERMANY

◗ *Symphony No. 5 in E (Leonore), Op. 177* LPO, Herrmann
Unicorn-Kanchana UKCD 2031 [A] **M**

RAMEAU, Jean-Philippe (1683–1764) FRANCE

◗ *Abaris (Les Boréades – tragédie lyrique): Suite; Dardanus (tragédie
en musique): Suite* Eighteenth Century O, Brüggen
✧ Philips 420 240-2 [D] **F**

Hippolyte et Aricie (tragédie en musique): Suite La Petite Bande,
Kuijken
✧ DHM GD77009 [A] **M**

Complete Harpsichord Music
Gilbert (hpd)
DG Archiv 427 176-2, 2CDs [A] **M**
Rousset (hpd)
L'Oiseau-Lyre 425 886-2, 2CDs [D] **F**

Les Indes Galantes (trans. Rameau) Gilbert (hpd)
HM HMC 90 1028 [A] **F**

In convertendo; Laboravi; Quam dilecta Gari (sop), Monbaliu
(sop), Ledroit (alto), de Mey (ten), Kooy (bs), Varcoe (bar),
Jansen (org), Ghent Collegium Vocale, Paris Chapelle Royale
O & Ch, Herreweghe
✧ HM HMC 90 1078 [A] **F**

RAVEL, Maurice (1875–1937) FRANCE

O   *Complete Orchestral Music* Various artists, Ulster O, Tortelier
Chandos CHAN 9206, 4 CDs [D] **M**

*Alborada del gracioso; Une barque sur l'ocean; Boléro; Ma mère
l'oye; Rapsodie espagnole* BPO, Boulez
DG 439 859-2 [D] **F**

*Alborada del gracioso; L'éventail de Jeanne: Fanfare; Ma mère
l'oye; *Shéhérazade; La valle des cloches; La valse* *Ewing (sop),
CBSO, Rattle
EMI CDC7 54204-2 [D] **M**

*Alborada del gracioso; Pavane pour une infante defunte; Rapsodie
espagnole* CSO, Reiner
(+ Debussy: *Images: Iberia*)
RCA GD 60179 [A] **M**

Boléro; Daphnis et Chloé: Suite No. 2 BPO, Karajan
(+ Debussy: *La Mer; Prélude à l'après-midi d'un faune*)
DG 427 250-2 [A] **M**

*Boléro; L'éventail de Jeanne: Fanfare; Ma mère l'oye; Pièce en forme
de habañera; Rapsodie espagnole* LSO, Tilson Thomas
Sony CD 44800 [D] **F**

Piano Concerto in G Michelangeli (pno), Philharmonia O, Gracis
(+ Rachmaninov: *Piano Concerto No. 4*)
EMI CDC7 49326-2 [A] **F**

*Piano Concerto in G; Piano Concerto for the left hand; Une Barque
sur l'ocean; L'Éventail de Jeanne: Fanfare; Menuet antique* Rogé
(pno), Montreal SO, Dutoit
Decca 410 230-2 [D] **F**

Piano Concerto for the left hand Fleisher (pno), Boston SO,
Ozawa
(+ Britten: *Diversions;* Prokofiev: *Piano Concerto No. 4*)
Sony CD 47188 [D] **F**

Daphnis et Chloé (ballet) Montreal SO, Dutoit
Decca 400 055-2 [D] **F**

Ma mère l'oye Ulster O, Tortelier
(+ Debussy: *La Boite a Joujoux*)
Chandos CHAN 8711 [D] **F**

Le Tombeau de Couperin; Valses nobles et sentimentales Ulster O,
Tortelier
(+ Debussy: *Petite Suite, etc.*)
Chandos CHAN 8756 [D] **F**

Tzigane Perlman (vln), NYPO, Mehta
(+ Chausson: *Poème;* Saint-Saëns: *Havanaise; Introduction and
rondo capriccioso;* Sarasate: *Carmen Fantasy*)
DG 423 063-2 [D] **F**

C   *Berceuse sur le nom de Fauré; Piano Trio; Violin Sonata (1928);
Violin and Cello Sonata* Kantorow (vln), Muller (vcl),
Rouvier (pno)
Erato 2292-45920-2 [A] **F**

*Boléro; Introduction and Allegro; Ma mère l'oye; Rapsodie
espagnole; La Valse* Lortie (pno), Mercier (pno)
Chandos CHAN 8905 [D] **F**

Entre cloches; Frontispiece; Ma mère l'oye; Rapsodie espagnole
Alfons & Aloys Kontarsky (pno)

(+ Debussy: *Piano duet works*)
DG 427 259-2, 2CDs [A] **M**

C *Frontispiece; Introduction and Allegro; Rapsodie espagnole; Shéhérazade (Ouverture de féerie); Sites auriculaires: Entre cloches; La valse* Coombs (pno), Scott (pno)
Gamut GAMCD 517 [D] **F**

Piano Trio in A min. Rembrandt Trio
(+ Chaminade: *Piano Trio No. 1*; Sant-Saëns: *Piano Trio No. 1*)
Dorian DOR 90187 [D] **F**

String Quartet in F
Britten Quartet
(+ Vaughan Williams: *String Quartet No. 1; On Wenlock Edge*)
EMI CDC7 54346-2 [D] **F**

String Quartet in F Carmina Quartet
(+ Debussy: *String Quartet*)
Denon CO-75164 [D] **F**

Violin Sonata (1827) Takezawa (vln), de Silva (pno)
(+ Debussy: *Violin Sonata;* Saint-Saëns: *Violin Sonata No. 1*)
RCA 09026 61386-2 [D] **F**

S *Complete Solo Piano Works* Thibaudet (pno)
Decca 433 515-2, 2CDs [D] **F**

À la manière de Borodine; À la manière de Chabrier; Menuet antique; Menuet sur le nom de Haydn; Prélude; Sonatine; Le Tombeau de Couperin Perlemuter (pno)
Nimbus NI 5011 [A] **F**

À la manière de Borodine; À la manière de Chabrier; Menuet antique; Menuet sur le nom de Haydn; Pavane pour une infante défunte; Prelude; Sérénade grotesque; Sonatine
Fergus-Thompson (pno)
ASV CDDCA 809 [D] **F**

Gaspard de la nuit; Jeux d'eau; Le Tombeau de Couperin; Valses nobles et sentimentales Fergus-Thompson (pno)
ASV CDDCA 805 [D] **F**

V *Histoires naturelles* Stutzmann (cont), C. Collard (pno)
(+ Debussy: *Ariettes oubliées, etc.*)
RCA RD 60899 [D] **F**

RAVENSCROFT, Thomas (c.1582– c.1635) ENGLAND

V *19 Songs* Consort of Musicke, Rooley (lte/dir)
Virgin VC7 59035-2 [D] **F**

RAWSTHORNE, Alan (1905–1971) ENGLAND

O *Piano Concertos Nos. 1 & 2; *Concerto for 2 Pianos* Tozer (pno), *Cislowski (pno), LPO, Bamert
Chandos CHAN 9125 [D] **F**

REGER, Max (1873–1916) GERMANY

O **2 Romanzen, Op. 50; Symphonische Prolog, Op. 108* *Maile (vln), Berlin RSO, Albrecht
Schwann 311076 [A] **F**

4 Symphonic Poems after Böcklin, Op. 128; Variations and Fugue on a Theme of Hiller, Op. 100 Concertgebouw O, Järvi
Chandos CHAN 8794 [D] **F**

Variations and Fugue on a Theme of Beethoven, Op. 86; Eine Ballettsuite, Op. 130; 4 Tone Pictures after Böcklin, Op. 128

Norrkoping SO, Segerstam
BIS CD-601 [D] **F**

S *6 Burlesques, Op. 58; Introduction and Passacaglia; 12 Walzer-Capricen, Op. 9; Variations and Fugue, Op. 132a* Tal (pno), Groethuysen (pno)
Sony CD 47671 [D] **F**

V *Aus Tiefer Not, Op. 67/3; Herr, wie du willst; Introduction, Passacaglia and Fugue in E min., Op. 127; Nun freut euch lieben Christen, Op. 67/28; Straf mich nicht in deinem Zorn, Op. 40/2; Von Himmel hoch, Op. 67/40; Wer weiss, wie nahe, Op. 6/48* Barber (org)
Hyperion CDA 66223 [D] **F**

Aus Tiefer Not, Op. 67/3; Intermezzo in F min., Op. 129/7; Introduction and Passacaglia in D min., Op. Posth.; Prelude in D min., Op. 65/7 Kee (org)
(+ Hindemith: *Organ Sonatas Nos. 1–3*)
Chandos CHAN 9097 [D] **F**

REICH, Steve (born 1936) USA

O *Variations* SFSO, De Waart
(+ Adams: *Shaker Loops*)
Philips 412 214-2 [A] **F**

C *Music for a Large Ensemble; Octet; *Violin Phase* Ensemble, Reich; *Guibbory (vln)
ECM 827 287-2 [A] **F**

Music for 18 Musicians Ensemble, Reich
ECM 821 417-2 [A] **F**

*Clapping Music; *Piano Phase; **Come out; **It's gonna Rain* Hartenberger, Reich; *Tiles (pno), *Nieman (pno); **Reich (pno)
Elektra-Nonesuch 7559-79169-2 [D] **F**

*Different Trains; *Electric Counterpoint* Kronos Quartet; *Metheny (gtr)
Elektra-Nonesuch 7559-79176-2 [D] **F**

6 Marimbas; Sextet Steve Reich & Musicians
Elektra-Nonesuch 7559-79138-2 [D] **F**

Drumming Steve Reich & Musicians
Elektra-Nonesuch 7559-79170-2 [D] **F**

Music for Mallet Instruments, Voices and Organ; Four Sections Steve Reich & Musicians
Elektra-Nonesuch 7559-79220-2 [D] **F**

V *The Desert Music* Brooklyn PO & Ch, Tilson Thomas
Elektra-Nonesuch 7559-79101-2 [D] **F**

Tehillim Vocal & Instrumental Ensembles, Manahan
ECM 827 411-2 [A] **F**

REICHA, Antonín (1770–1836) CZECHOSLOVAKIA/FRANCE

C *String Quintets Nos. 1–3* L'Archibudelli
✧ Sony CD 53118 [D] **F**

Wind Quintet in B♭, Op. 88/5; Wind Quintet in A, Op. 91/5 Prague Academic Wind Quintet
Hyperion CDA 66379 [D] **F**

REIZENSTEIN, Franz (1911–1968) GERMANY/ENGLAND

○ *Arabesques, Op. 47* King (cl), Benson (pno)
(+ Bliss: *2 Pieces;* Cooke: *Clarinet Sonata;* Howells: *Clarinet Sonata*)
Hyperion CDA 66044 [D] **F**

RESPIGHI, Ottorino (1879–1936) ITALY

○ *Ancient Airs and Dances: Suites Nos. 1–3* Boston SO, Ozawa
DG 419 868-2 [A] **M**

Belkis, Queen of Sheba (ballet): *Suite; Metamorphosen modi XII*
Philharmonia O, Simon
Chandos CHAN 8405 [D] **F**

*The Birds; 3 Botticelli Pictures; *Il Tramonto; **Adagio con variazioni* *Finnie (sop), **R. Wallfisch (vcl), Bournemouth Sinfonietta, Vasary
Chandos CHAN 8913 [D] **F**

La Boutique fantasque (ballet) National PO, Bonynge
(+ Chopin: *Les Sylphides*)
Decca 430 723-2 [D] **M**

Brazilian Impressions; Church Windows Philharmonia O, Simon
Chandos CHAN 8317 [D] **F**

Brazilian Impressions; Church Windows; Roman Festivals
Cincinnati SO, Lopez-Cobos
Telarc CD-80356 [D] **F**

*Concerto gregoriano; Poema autunnale; Ballata delle Gnomidi
*Mordkovitch (vln), BBC PO, Downes
Chandos CHAN 9232 [D] **F**

Fountains of Rome; Pines of Rome; Roman Festivals Philadelphia O, Muti
EMI CDC7 47316-2 [D] **F**

Fountains of Rome; Pines of Rome; Ancient Airs and Dances: Suite No. 3 BPO, Karajan
DG 413 822-2 [A] **F**

Piano Concerto; Concerto in modo misolidio Tozer (pno)
BBC PO, Downes
Chandos CHAN 9285 [d] **F**

Pines of Rome; Fountains of Rome CSO, Reiner
(+ Mussorgsky: *Pictures at an Exhibition*)
RCA 09026 61401-2 [A] **M**

Sinfonia dramatica BBC PO, Downes
Chandos CHAN 9213 [D] **F**

Violin Sonata in B min. Chung (vln), Zimerman (pno)
(+ R. Strauss: *Violin Sonata*)
DG 427 617-2 [D] **F**

**Aretusa; *Il Tramonto; Lauda per la Natività del Signore; 3 Botticelli Pictures* *Baker (mez), City of London Sinfonia, Hickox
Collins 13492 [D] **F**

REUBKE, Julius (1834–1858) GERMANY

Sonata in B♭ min.; Sonata on the 94th Psalm Bowyer (org)
(+ Schumann; *6 Fugues)*
Nimbus NI 5361 [D] **F**

REVUELTAS, Silvestre (1899–1940) MEXICO

O *Caminos; Música para Charlar; Ventanas* RPO, Bátiz
   (+ Chavez: *Symphonies Nos. 1 & 4*)
   ASV CDDCA 653 [D] **F**

RHEINBERGER, Joseph (1839–1901) GERMANY

O *Organ Concerto No. 1 in F, Op. 137* Murray (org), RPO, Ling
   (+ Dupré: *Organ Symphony, Op. 25*)
   Telarc CD 80136 [D] **F**

RILEY, Terry (born 1935) USA

C *Salome Dances for Peace* Kronos Quartet
   Elektra-Nonesuch 7559-79217-2, 2CDs [D] **F**

RIMSKY-KORSAKOV, Nikolay (1844–1908) RUSSIA

O *Capriccio espagnol, Op. 34; Golden Cockerel* (opera): *Suite; Russian Easter Festival Overture, Op. 36* LSO, Dorati
   (+ Borodin: *Prince Igor: Polovtsian Dances*)
   Philips Mercury 434 308-2 [A] **M**

   Piano Concerto No. 1 in C♯ min., Op. 30 Binns (pno), English Northern PO, Lloyd-Jones
   (+ Balakirev: *Piano Concerto Nos. 1 & 2*)
   Hyperion CDA 66640 [D] **F**

   Piano Concerto No. 1 in C♯ min., Op. 30 Zhukov (pno), USSR TV & Radio Large O, Dmitriev
   (+ Balakirev: *Piano Concerto No. 1;* Medtner: *Piano Concerto No. 1*)
   Mezhdunarodnaya Kniga MK 417087 [A] **F**

   Opera excerpts: *Christmas Eve; Le Coq d'or; Legend of the Invisible City of Kitezh; May Night; Mlada; The Snow Maiden; The Tale of Tsar Saltan* SNO, Järvi
   Chandos CHAN 8327/9, 3CDs [D] **F**

   Fantasia on Serbian Themes, Op. 6; On the Tomb, Op. 61; Overture on Russian Themes, Op. 20; Russian Easter Festival Overture, Op. 36; Sadko (musical picture): *Op. 5; Sinfonietta on Russian Themes, Op. 31* USSR State Academy SO, Svetlanov
   Olympia OCD 211 [A] **F**

   Sheherazade (symphonic suite), *Op. 35*
   LPO, Haitink
   (+ Mussorgsky: *Night on a Bare Mountain – original version*)
   Philips 420 898-2 [A] **M**
   CSO, Reiner
   (+ Debussy: *La Mer*)
   RCA GD 60875 [A] **M**

   Symphonies Nos. 1–3; Capriccio espagnol, Op. 34; Russian Easter Festival Overture, Op. 36 Gothenburg SO, Järvi
   DG 423 604-2, 2CDs [D] **F**

   Symphonies: No. 1 in E, Op. 1; No. 2 (Antar), Op. 9 USSR State Academy SO, Svetlanov
   Olympia OCD 158 [A] **F**

C *Capriccio espagnol, Op. 34; Neopolitan song, Op. 63; Scheherazade* (symphonic suite), *Op. 35* Goldstone, Clemmow (pno duo)
   Gamut GAMCD 521 [D] **F**

   Piano and Wind Quintet in B♭ Capricorn
   (+ Glinka: *Grand Sextet in E♭*)
   Hyperion CDA 66163 [A] **F**

C *Piano Trio in C min.* Moscow Piano Trio
(+ Shchedrin: *Echo Sonata*)
Olympia OCD 140 [A] **F**

RODRIGO, Joaquín (born 1902) SPAIN

O *Concierto Andaluz for 4 guitars; Concierto de Aranjuez; Concierto madrigal; Concierto para una fiesta; Fantasia para un gentilhombre; Bajanda de la Meseta; En los trigales; Junto al Generalife; 3 Piezas españolas; Romance de Durandarte; Sonata a la española; Tiento antiguo; 3 Petites Pièces* P. Romero (gtr) Los Romeros (gtrs), ASMF, Marriner
Philips 432 581-2, 3CDs [A] **M**

Concierto de Aranjuez; *Fanatasia para um gentilhombre; Invocation & Dance; Tres piezas españolas Bream (gtr), COE, Gardiner; *RCA Victor CO, Brouwer
RCA 09026 61611-2 [A] **M**

ROMBERG, Andreas (1767–1821) GERMANY

C *Clarinet Quintet in Eb, Op. 57* King (cl), Britten Quartet
(+ Fuchs: *Clarinet Quintet;* Stanford: *Fantasy Pieces*)
Hyperion CDA 66479 [D] **F**

ROPARTZ, Joseph Guy (1864–1955) FRANCE

O *Symphony No. 3* Pollet (sop), Stutzmann (cont), Dran (ten), Vassar (bs-bar), Toulouse Capitole O, Plasson
EMI CDM7 64689-2 [A] **M**

V *16 Melodies* Le Texier (bar), Biros (pno)
Auvidis Valois V4701 [D] **F**

ROSETTI, Antonio (1746–1792) BOHEMIA

O *Horn Concerto in E, K3:42; Horn Concerto in E, K3:44; Horn Concerto in Eb, K3:39* Tuckwell (hn/dir) ECO
Classics for Pleasure CD-CFP 4578 [D] **B**

ROSLAVETS, Nikolay (1881–1944) RUSSIA

C *Viola Sonata No. 1* Bashmet (vla), Muntian (pno)
(+ Glinka: *Viola Sonata;* Shostakovich: *Viola Sonata*)
RCA 09026 61273-2 [D] **F**

ROSSINI, Gioachino (1792–1868) ITALY

O *Introduction, Theme and Variations* Neidich (cl), Orpheus CO
(+ Weber: *Clarinet Concertino; Clarinet Concertos Nos. 1 & 2*)
DG 435 875-2 [D] **F**

Complete Overtures ASMF, Marriner
Philips 434 016-2, 3CDs [A] **M**

Overtures: *Il barbiere di Siviglia; La gazza ladra; Guillaume Tell; L'italiana in Algeri; La scala di seta; Il signor Bruschino; Semiramide* LCP, Norrington
◇ EMI CDC7 54091-2 [D] **F**

Overtures: *Il barbiere di Siviglia; La Cenerentola; La gazza ladra; Guillaume Tell; L'italiana in Algeri; La scala di seta; Il signor Bruschino* CSO, Reiner
RCA GD 60387 [A] **M**

String Sonatas Nos. 1–6 ASMF, Marriner
(+ Bellini: *Oboe Concerto;* Donizetti: *String Quartet;* Cherubini: *Horn Sonata*)
Decca 430 563-2, 2CDs [A] **M**

V   *L'âme délaissée; Ariette à l'ancienne; Beltà crudele; Canzonetta spagnuola; Giovanna d'Arco; Mi lagnerò tacendo (6 settings); Nizza; L'Orpheline du Tyrol; La Pastorella; Pompadour, la grande coquette; La regata veneziana; Il Trovatore* Bartoli (mez), Spencer (pno)
Decca 430 518-2 [D] **F**

Petite messe solennelle Field (sop), Owens (mez), Barham (ten), Tomlinson (bs), Nettle (pno), Markham (pno), CBSO Ch, Halsey
Conifer CDCF 184 [D] **F**

7 Songs Hampson (bar), Parsons (pno)
(+ Meyerbeer: *12 Songs*)
EMI CDC7 54436-2 [D] **F**

Stabat Mater Field (sop), Jones (mez), Davies (ten), Earle (bs), LSO Ch, City of London Sinfonia, Hickox
Chandos CHAN 8780 [D] **F**

ROTA, Nino (1911–1979) ITALY

S   *Complete Solo Piano Works* Laval (pno)
Auvidis Valois V4698 [D] **F**

ROUSSEL, Albert (1869–1937) FRANCE

O   *Bacchus et Ariane* (ballet), *Op. 43: Suite No. 2; Suite in F, Op. 33* Paris O, Dutoit
Erato 2292-45278-2 [D] **F**

Suite in F, Op. 33 Detroit SO, Paray
(+ Chabrier: *Orchestral works*)
Philips Mercury 434 303-2 [A] **M**

Symphonies: No. 1 (Le poème de la forêt), Op. 7; No. 3 in G min., Op. 42 FNO, Dutoit
Erato 2292-45253-2 [D] **F**

Symphonies: No. 2 in B♭, Op. 23; No. 4 in F, Op. 53 FNO, Dutoit
Erato 2292-45254-2 [D] **F**

C   *Serenade, Op. 30; Trio, Op. 40; Trio, Op. 58* Gallois (fl), Cambreling (hp), Michalakakos (vla), Grout (vcl), Paris String Trio
Erato 2292-45009-2 [D] **F**

S   *Doute; 3 Pieces, Op. 5; Prelude and Fugue, Op. 29; Rustiques, Op. 16; Segovia, Op. 49; Sonatine, Op. 46; Suite in F♯ min., Op. 14* Parkin (pno)
Chandos CHAN 8887 [D] **F**

Psalm 80 Mitchinson (ten), Paris O, Baudo
(+ Schmitt: *Psalm 47*)
EMI CDM7 64368-2 [A] **F**

RUBBRA, Edmund (1901–1986) ENGLAND

O   *Improvisations on Virginal Pieces by Giles Farnaby, Op. 50; Symphony No. 10 (Sinfonia da camera), Op. 145; A Tribute (for RVW on his 70th birthday), Op. 56* Bournemouth Sinfonietta, Schönzeler
Chandos CHAN 6599 [A] **M**

Resurgam Overture, Op. 149; Symphonies Nos. 3, Op. 49 & 4, Op. 53; A Tribute (for RVW on his 70th birthday), Op. 56 Philharmonia O, Del Mar
Lyrita SRCD 202 [D] **F**

○ *Symphonies Nos. 2 & *7; Festive Overture* NPO, Handley;
*LPO, Boult
Lyrita SRCD 235 [A] **F**

Symphonies Nos. 3 & 4; Resurgam; A Tribute Philharmonia O,
Del Mar
Lyrita SRCD 202 [D] **F**

*Symphonies Nos. 6 & 8; *Soliloquy* Philharmonia O, Del Mar;
*de Saram (vcl), LSO, Handley
Lyrita SRCD 234 [A] **F**

✓ *Missa in honorem sancti domini, Op. 66; 3 Hymn Tunes, Op. 114;
Magnificat and Nunc Dimittis, Op. 65; 3 Motets, Op. 76* Gonville
& Caius College Ch, Webber
(+ Hadley: *Choral works*)
ASV CDDCA 881 [D] **F**

RUBINSTEIN, Anton (1829–1894) RUSSIA

§ *Piano Sonatas No. 1 in E min., Op. 12; No. 3 in F, Op. 41*
Howard (pno)
Hyperion CDA 66017 [D] **F**

Piano Sonatas: No. 2 in C min., Op. 20; No. 4 in A min., Op. 100
Howard (pno)
Hyperion CDA 66105 [D] **F**

RUTTER, John (born 1945) ENGLAND

✓ *All things bright and beautiful; For the beauty of the earth; A Gaelic
blessing; Gloria; God be in my head; The Lord bless you and keep
you; The Lord is my shepherd; O clap your hands; Open thou mine
eyes; Praise ye the Lord; A prayer of St. Patrick* Cambridge
Singers, Philips Jones Brass Ensemble, City of London
Sinfonia, Rutter
Collegium COLCD 100 [D] **F**

*Brother Heinrich's Christmas; The Reluctant Dragon; The Wind in
the Willows* Various artists, City of London Sinfonia, Hickox,
*Rutter
Collegium COLCD 115 [D] **F**

Requiem; I will lift up mine eyes Ashton (sop), Dean (sop),
Cambridge Singers, City of London Sinfonia, Rutter
Collegium COLCD 103 [D] **F**

SAINT-SAËNS, Camille (1835–1921) FRANCE

○ *Carnival of the Animals* Nel (pno), Snell (pno), Academy of
London, Stamp
(+ Mozart: *Serenade No. 13;* Prokofiev: *Peter and the Wolf*)
Virgin VC7 59533-2 [D] **F**

*Cello Concerto No. 1 in A min., Op. 33; *Allegro appassionato,
Op. 43; *Chant saphique, Op. 91; *Gavotte, Op. posth.; ***Prière,
Op. 158; *Romances Nos. 1 & 2, Opp. 36/51; *Cello Sonata No. 1
in C min., Op. 32; **The Swan* Isserlis (vcl), LSO, Tilson
Thomas; *Devoyon (pno); **Tilson Thomas, Moore (pnos);
***Grier (org)
RCA 09026 61678-2 [D] **F**

Cello Concerto No. 1 in A min., Op. 33 Haimowitz (vcl), CSO,
Levine
(+ Bruch: *Kol Nidrei, Op. 47;* Lalo: *Cello Concerto*)
DG 427 323-2 [D] **F**

O *Piano Concertos Nos. 1–5* Ciccolini (pno), Paris O, Baudo
EMI CMS7 69443-2, 2CDs [A] **B**

Piano Concertos: No. 2 in G min., Op. 22; No. 4 Collard (pno),
RPO, Previn
EMI CDC7 47816-2 [D] **F**

*Violin Concertos Nos. 1–3; Caprice andalous, Op. 122; Le Deluge:
Prelude; Étude, Op. 52/6: Étude en forme de valse; Havanaise,
Op. 83; Introduction & rondo capriccioso, Op. 28; Morceau de
concert, Op. 62; *La Muse et le poète, Op. 132; Romance in Db,
Op. 37; Romance in C, Op. 48* Hoelscher (vln), *Kirschbaum
(vcl), NPO, Dervaux
EMI CMS7 64790-2, 2 CDs [A] **M**

Violin Concerto No. 3 in B min., Op. 61 Perlman (vln), Paris O,
Barenboim
(+ Wieniawski: *Violin Concerto No. 2*)
DG 410 526-2 [D] **F**

*Danse macabre, Op. 40; *Le Déluge* (oratorio), Op. 45: Prélude;
Samson et Dalila (opera): Bacchanale; *Symphony No. 3 in C
min., Op. 78* Litaize (org), CSO, *Paris O, Barenboim
DG 415 847-2 [A] **M**

Havanaise, Op. 83; Introduction & rondo capriccioso, Op. 28
Perlman (vln), NYPO, Mehta
(+ Chausson: *Poème;* Ravel: *Tzigane;* Sarasate: *Carmen Fantasy*)
DG 423 063-2 [D] **F**

Introduction & rondo capriccioso, Op. 28
Oistrakh (vln), Boston SO, Munch
(+ Chausson: *Symphony in Bb; Poème*)
RCA GD 60683 [A] **M**

Le rouet d'Omphale Op. 31 Boston SO, Munch
(+ Berlioz: *Orchestral works*)
RCA 09026 61400-2 [A] **M**

*Symphonies: Nos. 1–*3; in A; in F* *Gavoty (org), FNRO,
Martinon
EMI CZS7 62643-2, 2CDs [A] **B**

Symphony No. 3 in C min. (Organ), Op. 78 Preston (org), BPO,
Levine
(+ Dukas: *L'apprenti sorcier*)
DG 419 617-2 [D] **F**

C *Berceuse, Op. 38; Élégie, Op. 120; Élégie, Op. 143; Romance in Db,
Op. 37; Violin Sonatas: No. 1 in D min., Op. 75; No. 2 in Eb, Op.
102* Charlier (vln), Hubeau (pno)
Erato 2292-45017-2 [A] **F**

*Carnival of the Animals; Piano Trio No. 1 in F, Op. 18; Septet in
Eb, Op. 65* Nash Ensemble
Virgin VC7 59514-2 [D] **F**

Piano Trio No. 1 in F, Op. 18 Rembrandt Trio
(+ Chaminade: *Piano Trio No.1;* Ravel: *Piano Trio*)
Dorian DOR 90187 [D] **F**

Romance, Op. 67 Tuckwell (hn), Ashkenazy (pno)
(+ Brahms: *Horn Trio;* Franck: *Violin Sonata;* Schumann:
Adagio and Allegro)
Decca 433 695-2 [A] **F**

Violin Sonata No. 1 in D min., Op. 75 Takezawa (vln),
de Silva (pno)

(+ Debussy: *Violin Sonata;* Ravel: *Violin Sonata [1927]*)
RCA 09026 61386-2 [D] **F**

SALLINEN, Aulis (born 1935) FINLAND

○ *Cello Concerto; Shadows; Symphony No. 4* Noras (vcl), Helsinki PO, Kamu
Finlandia FACD 346 [D] **F**

SAMMARTINI, Giovanni-Battista (1700–1775) ITALY

○ *Symphony in D, JC14; Symphony in G, JC39; String Quintet No. 3 in G* Ensemble 415, Banchini
(+ Giuseppe Sammartini: *Concerti grossi Nos. 6 & 8; Recorder Concerto in F*)
◇ HM HMA90 1245 [A] **M**

SAMMARTINI, Giuseppe (1695–1750) ITALY

○ *Concerti grossi Nos. 6 & 8; Recorder Concerto in F* Ensemble 415, Banchini
(+ Giovanni Sammartini: *Symphony in D, JC14; Symphony in G, JC39; String Quintet No. 3 in G*)
◇ HM HMA90 1245 [A] **M**

SARASATE, Pablo (1844–1908) SPAIN

○ *Carmen Fantasy, Op. 25* Perlman (vln), NYPO, Mehta
(+ Chausson: *Poème;* Ravel: *Tzigane;* Saint-Saëns: *Havanaise; Introduction and rondo capriccioso*)
DG 423 063-2 [D] **F**

Zigeunerweisen, Op. 20 Shaham (vln), LSO, Foster
(+ Wieniawski: *Violin Concertos Nos. 1 & 2; Légende*)
DG 431 815-2 [D] **F**

Zigeunerweisen (trans. Hall) Hall (gtr), LMP, Litton
(+ Castelnuovo-Tedesco: *Guitar Concerto No. 1;* Paganini: *Violin Concerto No. 2*)
Decca 440 293-2 [D] **F**

SATIE, Erik (1866–1925) FRANCE

○ *Les Aventures de Mercure; La belle excentrique; 5 Grimaces for 'A Midsummer Night's Dream'; Gymnopédies Nos. 1 & 3* (orch. Debussy); *Jack-in-the-box* (orch. Milhaud); *Morceaux en forme de poire; Parade; Relâche* Utah SO, Abravanel
Vanguard 08.4030.71 [A] **M**

Choses vues à droite et à gauche Kremer (vln), LSO, Chailly
(+ Chausson: *Poème;* Milhaud: *Le Boeuf sur le toit; Le printemps;* Vieuxtemps: *Fantasia appassionata*)
Philips 432 513-2 [A] **M**

Gymnopédies Nos. 1 & 3 de Lancie (ob), LSO, Previn
(+ Ibert: *Symphonie Concertante;* Françaix: *L'horloge de flore;* R. Strauss: *Oboe Concerto*)
RCA GD 87989 [A] **M**

Avant-dernières pensées; Embryons desséchés; 6 Gnossiennes; 3 Gymnopédies; Heures séculaires et instantanées; Je te veux; Parade (excerpt); *Pièces froides; Prélude de la porte héroïque du ciel; Sports et divertissements; Valses du précieux degoûté; Véritables préludes flasques; Vieux séquins et vieilles cuirasses* MacGregor (pno)
Collins 10532 [D] **F**

Avant-dernières pensées; Chapitres tournés en tous sens; Croquis et agaceries d'un gros bonhomme en bois; Descriptions automatiques; 2 rêveries nocturnes; Heures séculaires et instantanées; Nocturnes

Nos. 1–3 & 5; Nouvelles pièces froides; Pièces froides; Prélude de la porte héroïque du ciel; Les trois valses distinguées d'un précieux dégoût; Véritables préludes flasques Rogé (pno)
Decca 421 713-2 [D] **F**

S *Embryons desséchés; 6 Gnossiennes; 3 Gymnopédies; Je te veux; Nocturne No. 4; Le Picadilly; 4 préludes flasques; Prélude en tapisserie; Sonatine bureaucratique; Vieux séquins et vieilles cuirasses* Rogé (pno)
Decca 410 220-2 [D] **F**

SAXTON, Robert (born 1953) ENGLAND

O *Violin Concerto; In the Beginning; *I will Awake the Dawn* Little (vln), BBC SO, Bamert; *BBC Singers, Poole
Collins 12832 [D] **F**

SCARLATTI, Alessandro (1660–1725) ITALY

V *Dixit Dominus II* Argenta (sop), Attrot (sop), Denley (mez), Stafford (ten), Varcoe (bar), English Concert O & Ch, Pinnock
(+ Vivaldi: *Gloria in D, RV 589*)
◈ DG Archiv 423 386-2 [D] **F**

Cantatas: *Correa nel seno amato; *Già lusingato appieno; Variations on 'La Folia' *Dawson (sop), Purcell Quartet
◈ Hyperion CDA 66254 [D] **F**

SCARLATTI, Domenico (1685–1757) ITALY

S *Keyboard Sonatas Nos. 1–555* Ross (hpd)
Erato 2292-45309-2, 34CDs [A] **M**

Keyboard Sonatas Nos. 1, 9, 30, 69, 113, 127, 132, 133, 141, 144, 159, 175, 215, 380, 430, 481, 492 & 502 MacGregor (pno)
Collins 13222 [D] **F**

Keyboard Sonatas Nos. 3, 52, 184, 185, 191–3, 208, 209, 227, 238, 239, 252 & 253 Leonhardt (hpd)
RCA GD71955 [A] **M**

Keyboard Sonatas Nos. 8, 11, 52, 87, 159, 169, 202, 206, 208, 209, 215, 377, 380, 415, 430, 446 Van Asperen (hpd)
EMI CDC7 54483-2 [D] **F**

Keyboard Sonatas Nos. 33, 39, 54, 55, 96, 146, 162, 198, 322, 380, 455, 466, 474, 481, 491, 525 & 531 Horowitz (pno)
Sony CD 53460 [A] **M**

Keyboard Sonatas Nos. 46, 87, 95, 99, 124, 201, 204, 490–2, 513, 520 & 521 Pinnock (hpd)
CRD 3368 [A] **F**

Keyboard Sonatas Nos. 113, 119, 120, 146, 213, 318, 319, 380, 381, 466, 501 & 502 Black (hpd)
CRD 3442 [D] **F**

SCHARWENKA, Xaver (1850–1924) POLAND

S *Piano Sonata No. 1, Op. 6; Eglantine Waltz, Op. 84; Impromptu, Op. 17; Polish Dances, Op. 3; Polonaise, Op. 12; Polonaise, Op. 4. Valse-caprice, Op. 31* Tanyel (pno)
Collins 13252 [D] **F**

Piano Sonata No. 2 in E♭, Op. 36; 2 Dances Polonaises, Op. 29; Romanzero, Op. 33; Sonatina, Op. 52/1 Tanyel (pno)
Collins 13522 [D] **F**

S *Theme & Variations, Op. 48, Barcarolle, Op. 14; Novellete &*
Melodie, Op. 22; 4 Polish Dances, Op. 58; Scherzo, Op. 4
Tanyel (pno)
Collins 13652 [D] **F**

SCHMELZER, Johann (c.1620–1680) AUSTRIA

C *Balletto di centauri; Balletto di spiritelli; Sonata a 7 flauti; Sonata*
con arie; Sonata I a 8 New London Consort, Pickett
(+ Biber: *7 Sonatas for Instrumental Ensemble*)
◊ L'Oiseau-Lyre 425 834-2 [D] **F**

SCHMIDT, Franz (1874–1939) AUSTRIA

O *Symphony No. 2 in E♭* CSO, Järvi
Chandos CHAN 8779 [D] **F**

Symphony No. 3 in A CSO, Järvi
(+ Hindemith: *Concerto for Orchestra*)
Chandos CHAN 9000 [D] **F**

C *Piano Quintet in G* Weiss (pno), VPO Quintet
(+ Bruckner: *String Quintet in F*)
Decca 430 296-2 [A] **M**

SCHMITT, Florent (1870–1958) FRANCE

O *La tragédie de Salomé; *Psalm 47* *Sweet (sop), *Gil (org),
*French Radio Ch, French Radio New PO, Janowski
Erato 2292-45029-2 [D] **F**

V *Psalm 47* Gulot (sop), Litaize (org), ORTF Ch, FRNO,
Martinon
(+ Roussel: *Psalm 80*)
EMI CDM7 64368-2 [A] **M**

SCHNITTKE, Alfred (born 1934) RUSSIA

O *Cello Concerto No. 1; *4 Hymns; Klingende Buchstaben (solo cello)*
Thedéen (vcl), Danish National RSO, Segerstam; *Radoukanov,
Davidsson, Fredlund, Kamata, Holdar, Loguin (vcls)
BIS BIS-CD 507 [D] **F**

*Cello Concerto No. 2; *In memoriam...* Rostropovich (vcl), LSO,
Ozawa; *LSO, Rostropovich
Sony CD 48241 [D] **F**

*Oboe and Harp Concerto; Piano Concerto No. 3; *Concerto grosso*
No. 1 Jahren (ob), Lier (hp), Pöntinen (pno), *Bergqvist (vln),
*Swedrup (vln), *Pöntinen (hpd), New Stockholm CO,
Markiz
BIS BIS-CD 377 [D] **F**

Concerti grossi: No. 3; No. 4 (Symphony No. 5) Royal
Concertgebouw O, Chailly
Decca 430 698-2 [D] **F**

Concerto grosso No. 5 Kremer (vln), VPO, von Dohnányi
(+ Glass: *Violin Concerto*)
DG 437 091-2 [D] **F**

*Viola Concerto; *Trio Sonata (arr. Bashmet)* Bashmet (vla),
LSO, Rostropovich; *Moscow Soloists, Bashmet
RCA RD 60446 [D] **F**

Violin Concertos Nos. 1 & 2 Lubotsky (vln), Malmö SO, Klas
BIS BIS-CD 487 [D] **F**

Violin Concertos Nos. 3 & 4 Krysa (vln), Malmö SO, Klas
BIS BIS-CD 517 [D] **F**

O *Klein Sommernachtstraum; Passacaglia; Ritual; *Seid nüchtern und wachet (Faust Cantata)* Malmö SO, Segerstam; *Blom (cont), Bellini (alt), Devos (ten), Cold (bs), Malmö SO & Ch, De Priest
BIS BIS-CD 437 [D] **F**

Symphony No. 1 Dominique (pno), Kallenberg (vln), Lannerholm (trb), Royal Stockholm PO, Segerstam
BIS CD 577 [D] **F**

Quasi una Sonata; Piano Trio; Piano Sonata No. 2 Rostropovitch (vcl/cond), Lubotsky (vln), I. Schnittke (pno), ECO
Sony CD 53271 [D] **F**

Symphony No. 3 Stockholm PO, Klee
BIS BIS-CD 477 [D] **F**

Symphony No. 4; *Requiem Bellini (alt), Parkman (ten), Uppsala Academic Chamber Ch, Stockholm Sinfonietta, Kamu; *Salomonsson (sop), Sjöberg (sop), Lindholm (sop), Eker (cont), Högman (ten), Uppsala Academic Chamber Ch, Stockholm Sinfonietta, Parkman
BIS BIS-CD 497 [D] **F**

C *Kanon in memorium I: Igor Stravinsky* Hagen Quartet
(+ Ligeti: *String Quartet No. 1*; Lutoslawski: *String Quartet*)
DG 431 686-2 [D] **F**

Piano Quintet; Canon for Solo Violin and Strings; Gratulationsrondo; Sonata No. 1 for Violin & Chamber Orchestra Various artists
Sony 53357 [D] **F**

Sonata in the Olden Style; Violin Sonata No. 1 Dubinsky (vln), Edlina (pno)
(+ Shostakovich: *Violin Sonata, Op. 134*)
Chandos CHAN 8343 [D] **F**

String Quartets Nos. 1–3 Tale Quartet
BIS BIS-CD 467 [D] **F**

V *Minnesang; Choir Concerto* Danish National Radio Ch, Parkman
Chandos CHAN 9126 [D] **F**

SCHOECK, Othmar (1886–1957) SWITZERLAND

O *Cello Concerto No. 1 in A, Op. 61; Sommernacht, Op. 58* Goritzki (vcl/dir), Neusse German Chamber Academy
Claves CD50-8502 [D] **F**

*Concerto quasi una fantasia in Bb, Op. 21; Serenade, Op. 1; Suite in Ab, Op. 59 *Hoelscher (vln), ECO, Griffiths
Novalis 150 070-2 [D] **F**

C *Cello Sonata* Goritzki (vcl), Levine (pno)
(+ Weill: *Cello Sonata*)
Claves CD50-8908 [D] **F**

V *Lebendig begraben* (song cycle), *Op. 40* Fischer-Dieskau (bar), Berlin RSO, Rieger
(+ Pfitzner: *Von deutscher Seele*)
DG 437 033-2 [A] **M**

Das Stille Leuchten (song cycle), *Op. 60* Fischer-Dieskau (bar), Höll (pno)
Claves CD50-8910 [D] **F**

V *Unter Sternen* (song cycle), *Op. 55* Fischer-Dieskau (bar), Höll (pno)
Claves CD50-8606 [D] **F**

SCHOENBERG, Arnold (1874–1951) AUSTRIA/USA

O *Chamber Symphonies Nos. 1, Op. 9 & 2, Op. 38; Verklärte Nacht* Orpheus CO
DG 429 233-2 [D] **F**

Piano Concerto, Op. 42; Violin Concerto, Op. 36 Brendel (pno), Zeitlin (vln), Bavarian RSO, Kubelik
(+ Berg: *Violin Concerto*)
DG 431 740-2 [A] **M**

Pelleas und Melisande (symphonic poem), *Op. 5; Variations for Orchestra, Op. 31; Verklärte Nacht, Op. 4* BPO, Karajan
(+ Berg: *Lyric Suite, etc.*; Webern: *5 Movements, etc.*)
DG 427 424-2, 3CDs [A] **M**

5 Orchestral Pieces, Op. 16 LSO, Dorati
(+ Berg: *3 Orchestral Pieces; Lulu: Symphonic Suite;* Webern: *5 Pieces*)
Philips Mercury 432 006-2 [A] **M**

C *String Quartet in D; String Quartets Nos. 1–4* LaSalle Quartet
(+ Berg: *Lyric Suite; String Quartet, Op. 3;* Webern: *6 Bagatelles, etc.*)
DG 419 994-2, 4CDs [A] **M**

String Trio, Op. 45; Verklärte Nacht, Op. 4 LaSalle Quartet, McInnes (vla), Pegis (vcl)
DG 423 250-2 [A] **M**

Suite, Op. 29; Wind Quintet, Op. 26 London Sinfonietta, Atherton
Decca 433 083-2 [A] **M**

Verklärte Nacht, Op. 4 Raphael Ensemble
(+ Korngold: *String Sextet*)
Hyperion CDA 66425 [D] **F**

Piano Pieces, Opp. 33a & b; 3 Piano Pieces, Op. 11; 6 Piano Pieces, Op. 19; 5 Piano Pieces, Op. 23; Suite, Op. 25 Pollini (pno)
DG 423 249-2 [A] **M**

V *Das Buch der hängenden Gärten* (song cycle), *Op. 15;* *Pierrot Lunaire* (song cycle), *Op. 21* *DeGaetani (mez), Kalish (pno), Contemporary Chamber Ensemble, Weisberg
Elektra-Nonesuch 7559-79327-2 [A] **F**

3 Deutsche Volkslieder; Dreimal Tausend Jahre, Op. 50a; Friede auf Erden, Op.13; Kol Nidre, Op. 39; Moderner Psalm, Op. 50c; O daß der Sinnen doch so viele sind; Psalm 130, Op. 50b; 3 Satiren, Op. 28; 4 Stücke, Op. 27; 6 Stücke, Op. 35; A Survivor from Warsaw, Op. 46; 3 Volkslieder, Op. 49; Wenn der schwer Gedrückte klagt Shirley-Quirk (bar), Reich (narr), BBC SO & Singers, Boulez
Sony CD 44571, 2CDs [A/D] **M**

Pierrot Lunaire, Op. 21; Erwartung, Op. 17; Lied der Waldtaube Various artists, Boulez
Sony CD 48466 [A] **M**

Gurrelieder; *8 Lieder* Borkh (sop), Topper (mezzo), Engen (bs), Bavarian RSO & Ch, Kubelik; *Fischer-Dieskau (bar), Reimann (pno)
(+ Berg: *4 Lieder, Op. 2;* Webern: *Lieder*)
DG 431 744-2, 2 CDs [A] **M**

V *Ode to Napoleon Bonaparte, Op. 41* Griffiths (spkr), Litwin (pno), LaSalle Quartet
(+ Webern: *String Trio, etc.*)
DG 437 036-2 [A] **M**

SCHRÖTER, Johann (c1752–1788) GERMANY

O *Piano Concerto in C, Op. 3/3* Perahia (pno/dir), ECO
(+ Mozart: *Piano Concertos, K103 Nos. 1–3*)
Sony/CBS CD 39222 [D] **F**

SCHUBERT, Franz (1797–1828) AUSTRIA

O *Konzertstück in D, D345; Polonaise in B♭, D580; Rondo in A, D438* Kantorow (vln), Netherlands PO, Krivine
(+ Schumann: *Violin Concerto*)
Denon CO-1666 [D] **F**

Rosamunde (Die Zauberharfe): Overture, D644, and Incidental Music, D797 (complete) von Otter (mez), Ernst-Senff Ch, COE, Abbado
DG 431 655-2 [D] **F**

Symphonies Nos. 1–6 & 8–9; Grand Duo in C, D812 (orch. Joachim); Rosamunde (Die Zauberharfe) Overture, D644 COE, Abbado
DG 423 651-2, 5CDs [D] **F**

Symphonies: No. 1 in D, D82; No. 2 in B♭, D125 COE, Abbado
DG 423 652-2 [D] **F**

Symphonies: No. 3 in D, D200; No. 5 in B♭, D485; No. 6 in C, D589 RPO, Beecham
EMI CDM7 69750-2 [A] **M**

Symphonies: No. 3 in D, D200; No. 8 in B min. (Unfinished), D759 VPO, Kleiber
DG 415 601-2 [A] **F**

Symphonies: No. 4 in C min. (Tragic), D417; No. 6 in C, D589 LCP, Norrington
◇ EMI CDC7 54210-2 [D] **F**

Symphonies: No. 5 in B♭, D485; No. 6 in C, D589 Classical Band, Weil
◇ Sony CD 46697 [D] **F**

Symphonies: No. 5 in B♭, D485; No. 8 in B min. (Unfinished), D759 LCP, Norrington
◇ EMI CDC7 49968-2 [D] **F**

Symphonies: No. 8 in B min. (Unfinished), D759; No. 9 in C (Great), D944
Classical Band, Weil
◇ Sony CD 48132 [D] **F**
Cleveland O, Szell
Sony CD 48268 [A] **B**

Symphony No. 9 in C (Great), D944 LCP, Norrington
◇ EMI CDC7 49949-2 [D] **F**

C *Divertissement à la Hongroise, D818; German Dance in G, D618; Marches héroïques, D602; 4 Polonaises, D599* Crommelynck Duo (pno duo)
Claves CD50-8802 [D] **F**

C *Fantaisie in F min., D940; Rondo in A, D951; Rondo in D, D608;
Sonata in B♭, D617* Eden, Tamir (pno duo)
CRD 3465 [D] **F**

Fantasy in C, D934; Sonata (Duo) in A, D574; Sonatinas Nos. 1–3
Stern (vln), Barenboim (pno)
Sony CD 44504, 2CDs [D] **F**

*Fantasy in C, D934; Rondo brillant in B min., D895; Sonata
(Duo) in A, D574* Kremer (vln), Afanassiev (pno)
DG 431 654-2 [D] **F**

Octet in F, D803
AAM Chamber Ensemble
✧ L'Oiseau-Lyre 425 519-2 [D] **F**
Berlin Philharmonia Ensemble
Denon CO-75671 [D] **F**

Piano Quintet in A, D667 (Trout) Hausmusik
(+ Hummel: *Piano Quintet, Op. 87*)
✧ EMI CDC7 54264-2 [D] **F**

*Piano Quintet in A, D667 (Trout); *String Quartet No. 14 in D
min. (Death and the Maiden), D810* Curzon (pno), Vienna Octet;
*VPO Quartet
Decca 417 459-2 [A] **M**

**Piano Quintet in A, D667 (Trout); String Trios: in B♭, D581; in
B♭, D28* *Haebler (pno), *Cazauran (db), Grumiaux Trio
Philips 422 838-2 [A] **M**

*Piano Trio No. 1 in B♭, D898; Notturno in E♭, D897; Trio
Movement in B♭, D28* Collard (pno), Dumay (vln),
Lodéon (vcl)
EMI CDC7 49165-2 [D] **F**

Piano Trio No. 2 in E♭, D929; Sonata in B♭, D28 Beaux Arts
Trio
Philips 426 096-2 [A] **M**

Piano Trio No. 2 in E♭, D929; Sonatensatz, D28 Castle Trio
Virgin VC7 59303-2 [D] **F**

Sonata in A min. (Arpeggione), D821 Rostropovich (vcl),
Britten (pno)
(+ Debussy: *Cello Sonata;* Schumann: *5 Stücke in Volkston*)
Decca 417 833-2 [A] **M**

String Quartets Nos. 1–15 Melos Quartet
DG 419 879-2, 6CDs [A] **M**

String Quartets: No. 8 in B♭, D112; No. 13 in A min., D804
Lindsay Quartet
ASV CDDCA 593 [D] **F**

*String Quartets: No. 10 in E♭, D87; No. 14 in D min. (Death and
the Maiden), D810* Britten Quartet
EMI CDC7 54345-2 [D] **F**

*String Quartets: No. 12 in C min. (Quartettsatz), D703; No. 14 in
D min. (Death and the Maiden), D810* Lindsay Quartet
ASV CDDCA 560 [D] **F**

*String Quartets: No. 13 in A min., D804; No. 14 in D min. (Death
and the Maiden), D810* Italian Quartet
Philips 426 383-2 [A] **M**

C *String Quartet No. 14 in D min. (Death and the Maiden), D810*
(arr. Mahler) Moscow Soloists, Bashmet
(+ Beethoven: *String Quartet No. 11, Op. 95*, arr. Mahler)
RCA RD 60988 [D] **F**

String Quartet No. 15 in G, D887 Lindsay Quartet
ASV CDDCA 661 [D] **F**

String Quintet in C, D956 Lindsay Quartet, Cummings (vcl)
ASV CDDCA 537 [D] **F**

*String Quintet in C, D956; *Rondo, D438* *Beths (vln),
L'Archibudelli
◇ Sony CD 46669 [D] **F**

S *Fantasy in C (Wanderer), D760; Piano Sonata No. 16 in A min.,
D845* Pollini (pno)
DG 419 672-2 [A] **F**

8 Impromptus, D899 & 935; 12 Waltzes D145 O'Conor
Telarc CD80337 [D] **F**

6 Moments musicaux, D780; Piano Sonata No. 19 in C min., D958
Lupu (pno)
Decca 417 785-2 [A] **M**

Piano Sonatas Nos. 1–21 Kempff (pno)
DG 423 496-2, 7CDs [A] **M**

*Piano Sonatas: No. 1 in E, D157; No. 14 in A min., D784; No. 20
in A, D959* Lupu (pno)
Decca 425 033-2 [A] **M**

Piano Sonata No. 4 in A min., D537 Michelangeli (pno)
(+ Brahms: *4 Ballades, Op. 10*)
DG 400 043-2 [D] **F**

*Piano Sonatas: No. 6 in E min., D566; No. 14 in A min., D784;
No. 17 in D, D850* Schiff (pno)
Decca 440 306-2 [D] **F**

*Piano Sonatas: No. 8 in F# min., D571; No. 15 in C (Relique),
D840; No. 16 in A min., D845* Schiff (pno)
Decca 440 305-2 [D] **F**

*Piano Sonatas: No. 9 in B, D575; No. 11 in F min., D625; 6
Moments musicaux, D780* Richter (pno)
Olympia OCD 286 [A] **F**

*Piano Sonatas: No. 13 in A, D664; No. 14 in A min., D784;
Impromptus, D899/2&4* Richter (pno)
Olympia OCD 288 [D] **F**

Piano Sonatas: No. 14 in A min., D784; No. 17 in D, D850
Brendel (pno)
Philips 422 063-2 [D] **F**

*Piano Sonatas: No. 14 in A min., D784; No. 18 in G, D894;
Waltzes, D145* Ashkenazy (pno)
Decca 425 017-2 [A] **M**

Piano Sonatas: No. 16 in A min., D845; No. 18 in G, D894
Lupu (pno)
Decca 417 640-2 [A] **F**

Piano Sonatas: No. 19 in C min., D958; No. 20 in A, D959
Pollini (pno)
DG 427 327-2 [D] **F**

Piano Sonatas: No. 19 in C min., D958; No. 21 in B♭, D960
Richter (pno)
Olympia OCD 335 [D] F

Vocal Duets, Trios and Quartets Ameling (sop), Baker (mez),
Schreier (ten), Laubenthal (ten), Fischer-Dieskau (bar),
Moore (pno)
DG 435 596-2, 2CDs [A] M

Lieder (near-complete) Fischer-Dieskau (bar), Moore (pno)
DG 437 214-2, 21CDs [A] B

Lieder: Volume 1 (1811–17) Fischer-Dieskau (bar),
Moore (pno)
DG 437 215-2, 9CDs [A] B

Lieder: Volume 2 (1817–28) Fischer-Dieskau (bar),
Moore (pno)
DG 437 225-2, 9CDs [A] B

*Lieder Edition Volume 1: Der Alpenjäger, D588; Amalia, D195;
An den Frühling (second version), D587; An den Mond (second
version), D296; Erster Verlust, D226; Die Erwartung, D159; Der
Fischer, D225; Der Flüchtling, D402; Das Geheimnis (first version),
D250; Der Jüngling am Bache, D30; Lied, D284; Meeres Stille
(second version), D216; Nähe des Geliebten, D162; Der Pilgrim,
D794; Schäfers Klagelied D121; Sehnsucht (second version), D636;
Thekla (first version), D73; Wanderers Nachtlied I, D224; Wonne
der Wehmut, D260* Baker (mez), Johnson (pno)
Hyperion CDJ 33001 [D] F

*Lieder Edition Volume 2: Am Bach im Frühling, D361; Am Flusse
(second version), D766; Auf der Donau, D553; Fahrt zum Hades,
D526; Fischerlied (I & II), D351/562; Fischerweise, D881; Der
Schiffer, D536; Selige Welt, D743; Der Strom, D565; Der Taucher,
D77; Widerschein (first version), D639; Wie Ulfru fischt, D525*
Varcoe (bar), Johnson (pno)
Hyperion CDJ 33002 [D] F

*Lieder Edition Volume 3: Abschied, D475; An die Freunde, D654;
Augenlied, D297; Iphigenia, D573; Der Jüngling und der Tod,
D545; Lieb Minna, D222; Liedesend, D473; Nacht und Träume,
D827; Namenstagslied, D695; Pax vobiscum, D551; Rückweg,
D476; Trost im Liede, D546; Viola, D786; Der Zwerg, D771*
Murray (mez), Johnson (pno)
Hyperion CDJ 33003 [D] F

*Lieder Edition Volume 4: Alte Liebe rostet nie, D477; Am See, D124;
Am Strome, D539; An Herrn Josef von Spaun (Epistel), D749; Auf
der Riesenkoppe, D611; Das war ich, D174; Das gestörte Glück,
D309; Liebeslauschen, D698; Liebesrausch, D179; Liebeständelei,
D206; Der Liedler, D209; Nachtstück, D672; Sängers Morgenlied
(I & II), D163/ 165; Sehnsucht der Liebe, D180* Langridge (ten),
Johnson (pno)
Hyperion CDJ 33004 [D] F

*Lieder Edition Volume 5: Die Allmacht, D852; An die Natur, D372;
Die Erde, D989; Ganymed, D544; Klage der Ceres, D323; Das Lied
im Grünen, D917; Morgenlied, D381; Die Mutter Erde, D788; Die
Sternenwelten, D307; Täglich zu singen, D533; Wehmut, D772*
Connell (sop), Johnson (pno)
Hyperion CDJ 33005 [D] F

*Lieder Edition Volume 6: Abendlied für die Entfernte, D856; Abends
unter der Linde (I & II), D235/237; Abendstern, D806; Alinde,
D904; An die Laute, D905; Des Fischers Liebesglück, D933;*

Jagdlied, D521; Der Knabe in der Wieg (Wiegenlied), D529; Die Nacht, D534; Die Sterne, D939; Der Vater mit dem Kind, D906; Vor meiner Wiege, D927; Wilkommen und Abschied, D767; Zur guten Nacht, D903 Rolfe Johnson (ten), Johnson (pno)
Hyperion CDJ 33006 [D] **F**

V *Lieder Edition Volume 7: An den Frühling (first version), D283; An die Nachtigall, D196; An den Mond, D193; Idens Nachtgesang, D227; Idens Schwanenlied, D317; Der Jüngling am Bache (second version), D192; Kennst du das Land?, D321; Liane, D298; Die Liebe, D210; Luisens Antwort, D319; Das Mädchens Klage (second version), D191; Meeres Stille (first version), D215a; Mein Grüss an den Mai, D305; Minona oder die Kunde der Dogge, D152; Naturgenuss, D188; Das Rosenband, D280; Das Sehen, D231; Sehnsucht, D879; Die Spinnerin, D247; Die Sterbende, D186; Stimme der Liebe, D187; Von Ida, D228; Wer kauft Liebesgötter?, D261* Ameling (sop), Johnson (pno)
Hyperion CDJ 33007 [D] **F**

Lieder Edition Volume 8: Abendlied der Fürstin, D495; An den Mond in einer Herbstnacht, D614; Berthas Lied in der Nacht, D653; Erlkönig, D328; Die frühen Gräber, D290; Hochzeitlied, D463; In der Mitternacht, D464; Die Mondnacht, D238; Die Nonne (first version), D208; Romanze, D114; Die Sommernacht, D289; Ständchen, D920; Stimme der Liebe (second version), D418; Trauer der Liebe, D465; Wiegenlied, D498 Walker (mez), Johnson (pno)
Hyperion CDJ 33008 [D] **F**

*Lieder Edition Volume 9: Blanka, D631; 4 Canzonen, D688; Daphne am Bach, D411; Didone abbandonata, D510; Der gute Hirt, D449; *Der Hirt auf dem Felsen, D965; Lambertine, D301; Liebe schwärmt auf allen Wegen; Lilla an die Morgenröte, D273; Misero pargoletto, D42; La pastorella al prato, D513; Der Sänger am Felsen, D482; Thekla (second version), D595; Der Vollmond strahlt (Romanze), D797* Augér (sop), *King (cl), Johnson (pno)
Hyperion CDJ 33009 [D] **F**

Lieder Edition Volume 10: Adelwold und Emma, D211; Am Flusse (first version), D160; An die Apfelbäume, D197; An die Geliebte, D303; An Mignon, D161; Auf den Tod einer Nachtigall, D201; Auf einen Kirchhof, D151; Harfenspieler (I); Labetrank der Liebe, D302; Die Laube, D214; Die Liebende, D207; Der Sänger, D149; Seufzer, D198; Der Traum, D213; Vergebliche Liebe, D177; Der Weiberfreund, D271 Hill (ten), Johnson (pno)
Hyperion CDJ 33010 [D] **F**

Lieder Edition Volume 11: An den Tod, D518; Auf dem Wasser zu singen, D774; Auflösung, D807; Aus 'Heliopolis' (I & II), D753/754; Dithyrambe, D801; Elysium, D584; Der Geistertanz, D116; Der König in Thule, D367; Lied des Orpheus, D474; Nachtstück, D672; Schwanengesang, D744; Seligkeit, D433; So lass mich scheinen (first version), D727; Der Tod und das Mädchen, D531; Verklärung, D59; Vollendung, D989; Das Zügenglöcklein, D871 Fassbaender (mez), Johnson (pno)
Hyperion CDJ 33011 [D] **F**

Lieder Edition Volume 12: Adelaide, D95; Advokaten, D37; Andenken, D99; Lied aus der Ferne, D107; Ballade, D134; Betena, D102; Don Gayseros, D93; Geistertanz, D50; Jugendlicher Maienschwung, D61; An Laura, D115; Lied der Liebe, D109; Nachtgesang, D119; Schatten, D50; Sehnsucht, D123; Trost, An Elisa, D97; Trost in Tränen, D120; Vatermörder, D10;

Verschwunden sind die Schmerzen, D88 Thompson (ten), Argenta (sop), Ainsley (ten), Jackson (bs), Johnson (pno)
Hyperion CDJ 33012 [D] **F**

Lieder Edition Volume 13: Altoschottische Ballade, D923; Ave Maria, D839; Gesang der Norna, D831; Gretchen am Spinnrade, D118; Gretchens Bitte, D564; Jäger, ruhe vor der Jagd, D838; Lied der Anne Lyle, D830; Marie, D658; Marienbild, D623; Normans Gesang, D846; Raste Kreiger!, D837; Refrainlieder, D866 Nos. 1 & 3; Shilrik und Vinvela, D293; Szene aus Faust, D126 McLaughlin (sop), Johnson (pno)
Hyperion CDJ 33013 [D] **F**

Lieder Edition Volume 14: Amphiaraos, D166; An die Leier, D737; Antigone und Oedipe, D542; Entsühnte Orest, D699; Fragment auf dem Aeschylus, D450; Freiwilliges Versinken, D700; Die Götter Griechenlands, D677; Gruppe aus dem Tartarus, D583; Hektors Abschied, D312; Hippolits Lied, D890; Lied eines Schiffers an die Dioskuren, D360; Memnon, D541; Orest auf Taurus, D548; Philioktet, D540; Uraniens Flucht, D554; Zurnenden Diana, D707 Hampson (bar), Johnson (pno)
Hyperion CDJ 33014 [D] **F**

Lieder Edition Volume 15: An di untergehende Sonne, D457; Am Fenster, D878; Binde Knabe, D833; Im Freien, D880; Junge Nonne, D828; Klage an den Mond, D436; Kolmas Klage, D217; Lied, D403; Mainacht, D194; Mondabend, D141; Morgenkuss, D264; Unglückliche, D713; Wanderer an den Mond, D870; Winterabend, D938 Price (sop), Johnson (pno)
Hyperion CDJ 33015 [D] **F**

Lieder Edition Volume 16: An Emma, D113; An die Freude, D654; Die Bürgschaft, D246; Die Entzuckung an Laura I & II, D390 & D577; Das Geheimnis, D793; Der Jüngling am Bache, D638; Laura am Clavier, D388; Leichenfantasie, D7; Das Mädchen aus der Fremde, D252; Der Pilgrim, D794; Sehnsucht, D52; Die vier Weltalter, D391 Allen (bar), Johnson (pno)
Hyperion CDJ 33016 [D] **F**

Lieder Edition Volume 17: Am Grabe Anselmos, D504; An den Mond, D468; An die Nachtigall, D497; An meinen Klavier, D342; Aus 'Diego Manazares' (Ilmerine), D458; Der Einsiedelei, D393; Frühlinglied, D938; Geheimnis, D491; Der Herbstabend, D405; Herbstlied, D501; Der Herbstnacht, D404; Klage, D371; Klage um Ali Bey, D496a; Lebenslied, D508; Leiden der Trennung, D509; Lied, D373; Lied in der Abwesenheit, D416; Litanei, D343; Lodas Gespenst, D150; Lorma, D376; Minnelied, D429; Pflicht und Liebe, D467; Phidile, D500; Winterlied, D401 Popp (sop), Johnson (pno)
Hyperion CDJ 33017 [D] **F**

Lieder Edition Volume 18: Abendlied, D499; An den Schlaf, D447; An die Entfernte, D765; An die Harmonie, D394; An mein Herz, D860; Auf den Tod eine Nachtigall, D399; Auf der Brucke, D853; Das Blume und der Quell, D874; Blumenlied, D431; Drang in die Ferne, D770; Emtelied, D399; Das Finden, D219; Das Heimweh, D456 & 851; Im Frühling, D882; Im Walde, D834; Lebensmut, D883; Der Liebliche Stern, D861; Die Nacht, D358; Tiefes Leid, D876; Über Wildermann, D884; Um Mitternacht, D862 Schreier (ten), Johnson (pno)
Hyperion CDJ 33018 [D] **F**

Lieder Edition Volume 19: Abendlied, D276; Auf dem See, D543; Auf dem Wasser zu singen, D774; Bein Winde, D669; Der Blumen Schmerz, D731; Die Blumensprache, D519; Gott im Frühling,

*D448; Im Heine, D738; Im See, D476; Der liebliche Stern, D861;
Nach einem Gewitter, D561; Nachtviolen, D752; Die Rose, D745;
Die Sterne, D176; Die Sternennachte, D670; Suleika I & II, D720
& 717; Vergissmeinnicht, D792* Lott (sop), Johnson (pno)
Hyperion CDJ 33019 [D] **F**

V *Lieder Edition, Volume 20: 'An 1815 Schubertiad'* (32 Lieder)
Rozario (sop), Ainsley (ten), Bostridge (ten), George, (bs),
Johnson (pno)
Hyperion CDJ 33020 [D] **F**

38 Lieder Fischer-Dieskau (bar), Moore (pno)
EMI CMS7 63566-2, 2CDs [A] **M**

74 Lieder Ameling (sop), Baldwin (pno), Jansen (pno)
Philips 438 528-2, 4 CDs [A] **M**

21 Lieder Bär (bar), Parsons (pno)
EMI CDC7 54773-2 [D] **F**

24 Goethe Settings Fassbaender (mez), Garben (pno)
Sony CD 53104 [D] **F**

Complete Sacred Music, Vol. 1 (incl. the complete Masses)
Donath (sop), Popp (sop), Fischer-Dieskau (bar), Fassbaender
(mez), Schreier (ten), Araiza (ten), Protschka (ten), Dallapozza
(ten), Bavarian RSO & Ch, Sawallisch
EMI CMS7 64778-2, 3 CDs [A/D] **M**

Complete Sacred Music, Vol. 2 (shorter choral works) Donath
(sop), Popp (sop), Fischer-Dieskau (bar), Fassbaender (mez),
Protschka (ten), Dallapozza (ten), Tear (ten), Bavarian RSO &
Ch, Sawallisch
EMI CMS7 64783-2, 3 CDs [A/D] **M**

Mass No. 6 in E♭, D950 Mattila (sop), Lipovšek (cont), Hadley
(ten), Pita (ten), Höll (bs), Vienna State O Ch, VPO, Abbado
DG 423 088-2 [D] **F**

Die schöne Müllerin (song cycle), *D795; Schwanengesang* (Lieder
collection), *D957; Die Winterreise* (song cycle), *D911*
Fischer-Dieskau (bar), Moore (pno)
DG 437 235-2, 3CDs [A] **B**

Die schöne Müllerin (song cycle), *D795*
Bär (bar), Parsons (pno)
EMI CDC7 47947-2 [D] **F**
Prégardien (ten), Staier (fpno)
◇ DHM 05472 77273-2 [D] **F**

Schwanengesang (Lieder collection), *D957; An die Musik, D547;
An Sylvia, D891; Die Forelle, D550; Heidenröslein, D257; Im
Abendrot, D799; Der Musensohn, D764; Der Tod und das Mädchen,
D531* Fischer-Dieskau (bar), Moore (pno)
DG 415 188-2 [A] **F**

Schwanengesang (Lieder collection), *D957; Am Fenster, D878;
Herbst, D945; Sehnsucht, D879; Der Wanderer an den Mond,
D870; Wiegenlied, D867* Fassbaender (mez), Reimann (pno)
DG 429 766-2 [D] **F**

Die Winterreise (song cycle), *D911*
Fischer-Dieskau (bar), Moore (pno)
DG 415 187-2 [A] **F**
EDITORS' CHOICE (see page 12): Schreier (ten), Schiff (pno)
Decca 436 122-2 [D] **F**

Fassbaender (mez), Reimann (pno)
EMI CDC7 49846-2 [D] **F**

SCHUMAN, William (born 1910) USA

○ *Judith* (ballet); *New England Triptych; Symphony for Strings; Variations on 'America'* Seattle SO, Schwarz
Delos DE 3115 [D] **F**

New England Triptych Eastman-Rochester O, Hanson
(+ Ives: *Symphony No. 3; Three Places in New England;* Mennin: *Symphony No. 5*)
Philips Mercury 432 755-2 [A] **M**

Symphony No. 3 NYPO, Bernstein
(+ Harris: *Symphony No. 3*)
DG 419 780-2 [D] **F**

Symphony No. 10 (American Muse); American Festival Overture; New England Triptych St. Louis SO, Slatkin
(+ Ives: *Variations on 'America'*)
RCA RD 61282 [D] **F**

SCHUMANN, Clara (1819–1896) GERMANY

○ *Piano Trio in G min., Op. 17* Dartington Piano Trio
(+ F. Mendelssohn: *Piano Trio in D, Op. 11*)
Hyperion CDA 66331 [D] **F**

SCHUMANN, Robert (1810–1856) GERMANY

○ *Cello Concerto in A min., Op. 129;* **Adagio and Allegro, Op. 70;* **5 Stücke im Volkston, Op. 102;* **Fantasiestücke, Op. 73* Ma (vcl), Bavarian RSO, C. Davis; **Ax (pno)
Sony CD 42663 [D] **F**

Piano Concerto in A min., Op. 54 Kovacevich (pno), BBC SO, C. Davis
(+ Grieg: *Piano Concerto*)
Philips 412 923-2 [A] **M**

Violin Concerto in D min., Op. posth. Kantorow (vln), Netherlands PO, Krivine
(+ Schubert: *Konzertstück in D, D345; Polonaise in Bb, D580; Rondo in A, D438*)
Denon CO-1666 [D] **F**

Overtures: *Genoveva, Op. 81; Julius Caesar, Op. 128; Manfred, Op. 115; Overture, Scherzo & Finale, Op. 52* LSO, Järvi
Chandos CHAN 6548 [D] **M**

Symphonies Nos. 1–4 BPO, Karajan
DG 429 672-2, 2CDs [A] **M**

Symphonies: No. 1 in Bb, Op. 38 (Spring); No. 4 in D min., Op. 120; Overture, Scherzo and Finale, Op. 52 Dresden State O, Sawallisch
EMI CDM7 69471-2 [A] **M**

Symphonies: No. 2 in C, Op. 61; No. 3 in Eb (Rhenish), Op. 97 Dresden State O, Sawallisch
EMI CDM7 69472-2 [A] **M**

Symphonies: No. 3 in Eb (Rhenish), Op. 97; No. 4 in D min., Op. 120 LCP, Norrington
◇ EMI CDC7 54025-2 [D] **F**

C *Adagio and Allegro, Op. 70* Tuckwell (hn), Ashkenazy (pno)
(+ Brahms: *Horn Trio;* Franck: *Violin Sonata;* Saint-Saëns:
Romance, Op. 67)
Decca 433 695-2 [A] **F**

Adagio and Allegro, Op. 70; Fantasiestück, Op. 73; Romanzen, Op. 94; 5 Stücke in Volkston, Op. 102 Holliger (ob), Brendel (pno)
Philips 426 386-2 [A] **M**

Piano Quartet in E♭, Op. 47 Ax (pno), Stern (vln), Laredo (vla), Ma (vcl)
(+ Beethoven: *Piano Quartet*)
Sony CD 53339 [D] **M**

*Piano Quartet in E♭, Op. 47; *Piano Quintet in E♭, Op. 44* Gould (pno), *Bernstein (pno), Juilliard Quartet
Sony/CBS CD44848 [A] **M**

Piano Trios Nos. 1–3; Fantasiestück, Op. 88 Beaux Arts Trio
Philips 432 165-2, 2CDs [D] **F**

Piano Trio No. 1 in D min., Op. 63 Trio Fonteney
(+ Brahms: *Piano Trio, Op. posth.*)
Teldec 2292-44927-2 [D] **F**

Piano Trios: No. 2 in F, Op. 80; No. 3 in G min., Op. 110; Fantasiestücke, Op. 88 Israel Piano Trio
CRD 3458 [A] **F**

String Quartets Nos. 1–3 Melos Quartet
(+ Brahms: *String Quartets Nos. 1–3*)
DG 423 670-2, 3CDs [D] **F**

Violin Sonatas: No. 1 in A min., Op. 105; No. 2 in D min., Op. 121 Kremer (vln), Argerich (pno)
DG 419 235-2 [D] **F**

5 Stücke in Volkston, Op. 102 Rostropovich (vcl), Britten (pno)
(+ Debussy: *Cello Sonata;* Schubert: *Arpeggione Sonata*)
Decca 417 833-2 [A] **M**

S *Album für die Jugend, Op. 68* Brownridge (pno)
Hyperion CDH 88039 [D] **M**

Arabeske, Op. 18; Blumenstück, Op. 19; Carnaval, Op. 9; Davidsbündlertänze, Op. 6; Fantasie in C, Op. 17; 8 Fantasiestücke, Op. 12; 3 Fantasiestücke, Op. 111; Faschingsschwank aus Wien, Op. 26; Humoreske, Op. 20; Kinderszenen, Op. 15; Kreisleriana, Op. 16; 4 Nachtstücke, Op. 23; 8 Noveletten, Op. 21; Papillons, Op. 2; 3 Romances, Op. 28; Piano Sonatas: No. 1 in F♯ min., Op. 11; No. 2 in G min., Op. 22; Waldszenen, Op. 82 Arrau (pno)
Philips 432 308-2, 7CDs [A] **M**

Blumenstück, Op. 19; 4 Fugues, Op. 72; March in G min., Op. 76/2; Nachtstücke, Op. 23; Toccata, Op. 7 Richter (pno)
Decca 436 456-2 [D] **F**

Carnaval, Op. 9; Papillons, Op. 2; Toccata, Op. 7 Licad (pno)
Sony CD 45742 [D] **F**

Davidsbündlertänze, Op. 6; Fantasiestücke, Op. 12; Blumenstück, Op. 19 Ashkenazy (pno)
Decca 425 109-2 [D] **F**

Études symphoniques, Op. 13; Arabeske, Op. 18 Pollini (pno)
DG 410 916-2 [D] **F**

S *Fantasie in C, Op. 17; Faschingsschwank aus Wien, Op. 26;*
Papillons, Op. 2 Richter (pno)
EMI CDM7 64625-2 [A] **M**

Fantasie in C, Op. 17; Piano Sonata No. 1 in F♯ min., Op. 11
Pollini (pno)
DG 423 134-2 [A] **F**

Kreisleriana, Op. 16; Kinderszenen, Op. 15 Argerich (pno)
DG 410 653-2 [D] **F**

8 Noveletten, Op. 21; Allegro, Op. 8; 3 Fantasiestücke, Op. 111;
Gesange der Fruhe, Op. 133 Brautigam (pno)
Olympia OCD 436 [D] **F**

Piano Sonata No. 2 in G min., Op. 22; Intermezzi, Op. 4;
Symphonic Studies, Op. 13; Toccata, Op. 7 Kazakevich (pno)
Conifer CDCF 227 [D] **F**

Piano Sonata No. 3, Op. 14; Humoreske, Op. 20; Fantasiestücke,
Op. 12 Horowitz (pno)
RCA GD 86680 [A] **M**

6 Studies on Caprices by Paganini, Op. 3 Petrov (pno)
(+ Chopin: *Souvenir de Paganini*; Liszt: *6 Études d'exécution*
transcendante d'après Paganini)
Olympia OCD 144 [A] **F**

Complete Organ Music Latry (org)
Sony CD 57490 [D] **F**

6 Fugues on B-A-C-H, Op. 60 Bowyer (org)
(+ Reubke; *Sonata in B♭ min., etc.*)
Nimbus NI 5361 [D] **F**

V *Dichterliebe* (song cycle), *Op. 48; Liederkreis* (song cycle), *Op. 39;*
Myrthen Lieder, Op. 25 Nos. 1, 2, 3, 7, 8, 13 & 24 Fischer-
Dieskau (bar), Moore (pno)
DG 415 190-2 [A] **F**

Dichterliebe, Op. 48; Liederkreis, Op. 39 I. Partridge (ten),
J. Partridge (pno)
Classics for Pleasure CD-CFP 4651 [A] **F**

Frauenliebe und Leben (song cycle), *Op. 42; Liederkreis, Op. 24*
(song collection); *Abends am Strand, Op. 45/3; Lehn deine Wang,*
Op. 142/2; Mein Wagen rollet langsam, Op. 142/4 Fassbaender
(mez), Gage (pno)
DG 415 519-2 [D] **F**

12 Kerner Lieder, Op. 35; Liederkreis (song collection), *Op. 24*
Bär (bar), Parsons (pno)
EMI CDC7 54027-2 [D] **F**

12 Kerner Lieder, Op. 35; Liederkreis, Op. 39 Price (sop),
Johnson (pno)
Hyperion CDA 66596 [D] **F**

5 Andersen Lieder, Op. 40; 12 Kerner Lieder, Op. 35; 5 Lieder, Op.
posth.; Sängers Trost, Op. 127/1; Trost im Gesang, Op. 142/1
Hampson (bar), Parsons (pno)
Teldec 2292-44935-2 [D] **F**

Lieder Recital Walker (mez), Vignoles (pno)
CRD 3401 [A] **F**

Das Paradies und die Peri, Op. 50 Wiens (sop), Herman (sop),
Gjevang (mez), Gambill, Prégardien (tens), OSR & Ch, Jordan
Erato 2292-45456-2, 2CDs [D] **F**

V *Manfred, Op. 115* Sieber (sop), Schreckenbach (cont), Ramirez (ten), Stamm (bs), Various speakers, RIAS Chamber Ch, Berlin RSO, Albrecht
Koch Schwann 3-1089-2 [D] **F**

Requiem, Op. 148; Requiem für Mignon, Op. 98b Donath (sop), Kaufmann (sop), Lipovšek (cont), Calm (mez), Rootering (bs), Bavarian RSO & Ch, Sawallisch
Eurodisc RD 69001 [D] **F**

Szenen aus Goethes Faust, Op. 53 Vyvyan (sop), Palmer (sop), Harwood (sop), Pears (ten), Jenkins (ten), Fischer-Dieskau (bar), Shirley-Quirk (bar), Aldeburgh Festival Singers, ECO, Britten
Decca 425 705-2, 2CDs [A] **M**

SCHÜTZ, Heinrich (1585–1672) GERMANY

V *Ach Herr, du Schöpfer aller Ding; Erbarm dich; Magnificat; Meine Seele erhebt; Quemadmodum desiderat cervus; Die Sieben Worte; Symphoniae sacrae: Anima mea; Adjuro vos* Clément Janequin Ensemble, Saqueboutiers de Toulouse, Junghänel (lte), Cable (gmba), Jansen
◇ HM HMC 90 1255 [D] **F**

Ach Herr, straf mich nicht; Cantate Domino; Christmas Story; Deutsches Magnificat; Herr, unser Herrscher; Ich freu mich des; Unser Herr Christus Heinrich Schütz Ch, Symphoniae Sacrae Chamber Ensemble, Norrington
◇ Decca 430 632-2 [A] **M**

Auf dem Gebirge; Freue dich des Weibes deiner Jugend; List nicht Ephraim mein teurer Sohn; Musicalische Exequien; Saul, Saul, was verfolgst du mich Monteverdi Ch, EBS, His Majesties Sagbutts & Cornets, Gardiner
◇ DG Archiv 423 405-2 [D] **F**

Bone Jesu; Bringt her dem Hernn; Eile, mich Gott; Habe deine Lust; Herzlich lieb hab ich dich; Ihr Heiligen; O Jesu, nomen dulce; O süsser; Was betrübst; Was hast du verwirket; Wie ein Rubin; Wohl dem, der nicht wandelt Concerto Vocale
◇ HM HMC 90 1097 [D] **F**

Christmas Oratorio; Easter Oratorio Stuttgart Chamber Ch, Musica Fiata Köln, Stuttgart Baroque O, Bernius
◇ Sony CD 45943 [D] **F**

Psalms of David (complete) Stuttgart Chamber Ch, Musica Fiata Köln, Bernius
◇ Sony CD 48042, 2CDs [D] **F**

SCOTT, Francis (1880–1958) SCOTLAND

S *Scottish Lyrics: Vol. 1 Nos. 1 & 2; Vol. 2/1; Vol. 3/1; Vol. 5 Nos. 1–3; There's News* McLachlan (pno)
(+ works by Center, Stevenson)
Olympia OCD 264 [D] **F**

SCRIABIN, Alexander (1872–1915) RUSSIA

O *Piano Concerto in F♯ min., Op. 20; *Poem of Ecstasy, Op. 54; Prometheus (Poem of Fire), Op..60* Ashkenazy (pno), LPO, *Cleveland O, Maazel
Decca 417 252-2 [A] **F**

*Poem of Ecstasy, Op. 54; *Prometheus (Poem of Fire), Op. 60; Symphonies Nos. **1–3* *Alexeev (pno), **Toczyska (mez),

**Myers (ten), Philadelphia O, Muti
EMI CDS7 54251-2, 3CDs [D] **F**

○ *Symphony No. 1 in E min., Op. 26* Gorokhovskaya (sop),
Pluzhnikov (ten), Leningrad Glinka State Academy Ch,
USSR RSO, Fedoseyev
Olympia OCD 159 [D] **F**

Symphony No. 2 in C min., Op. 29 SNO, Järvi
Chandos CHAN 8642 [D] **F**

Symphony No. 3 in C min. (Divine Poem), Op. 43 Danish
National RSO, Järvi
(+ Arensky: *Silhouettes*)
Chandos CHAN 8898 [D] **F**

○ *Piano Sonatas Nos. 1–10* Ashkenazy (pno)
Decca 425 579-2, 2CDs [A] **M**

*Piano Sonatas: No. 2 in G♯ min., Op. 19 (Sonata-fantasy); No. 9 in
F, Op. 68 (Black Mass); Études, Op. 8 Nos. 2, 4 & 5; Études, Op.
42 Nos. 3, 4 & 7; 4 Pieces, Op. 51; Vers la flamme, Op. 72*
Demidenko (pno)
(+ Prokofiev: *Visions fugitives*)
Conifer CDCF 204 [D] **F**

*Piano Sonata No. 3 in F♯ min., Op. 23; 2 Poems, Op. 32; Vers la
flamme, Op. 72* Fergus-Thompson (pno)
(+ Balakirev: *The Lark; Piano Sonata*)
Kingdom KCLCD 2001 [D] **F**

*Piano Sonatas: No. 3 in F♯ min., Op. 23; No. 5, Op. 53; Preludes:
Op. 11 Nos. 1, 3, 9, 10, 13, 14 & 16; Op. 15/2; Op. 16 Nos. 1 & 4;
Études: Op. 8 Nos. 7 & 12; Op. 42/5* Horowitz (pno)
RCA GD 86215 [A] mono/stereo **M**

*Piano Sonatas Nos. 4, 5, 9 & 10; 8 Études, Op. 42; 3 Pieces, Op.
2/1 (Étude in C♯ min.)* Fergus-Thompson (pno)
ASV CDDCA 776 [D] **F**

EIBER, Matyas (1905–1960) HUNGARY/ENGLAND

○ *Clarinet Concertino* King (cl), ECO, Litton
(+ Blake: *Clarinet Concerto*; Lutoslawski: *Dance Preludes*)
Hyperion CDA 66215 [D] **F**

EREBRIER, José (born 1938) URUGUAY

○ *Momento psicologico; Poema elegiaca* RPO, Serebrier
(+ Bloch: *Violin Concerto; Baal Shem*)
ASV CDDCA 785 [D] **F**

ESSIONS, Roger (1896–1985) USA

○ *Concerto for Orchestra* Boston SO, Ozawa
(+ Panufnik: *Symphony No. 8*)
Hyperion CDA 66050 [D] **F**

Rhapsody for Orchestra; Symphonies Nos. 4 & 5 Columbus SO,
Badea
New World NW 345-2 [D] **F**

Piano Sonata No. 2 Lawson (pno)
(+ Griffes: *Piano Sonata*; Ives: *Piano Sonata No. 1*)
Virgin VC7 59316 [D] **F**

When Lilacs last in the dooryard bloom'd Hinds (sop), Quivar
(mez), Cossa (bar), Tanglewood Festival Ch, Boston SO, Ozawa
New World NW 296-2 [D] **F**

SHAPERO, Harold (born 1920) USA

O   *Nine-minute Overture; Symphony for Classical Orchestra* LAPO, Previn
New World NW 373-2 [D] **F**

SHCHEDRIN, Rodion (born 1932) RUSSIA

O   *Carmen Ballet; *The Frescoes of Dionysus* (tone-poem) Moscow Virtuosi CO, Armenian State Chamber & Percussion Ensembles, Spivakov; *Bolshoi Theatre Soloists Ensemble, Lazarev
Olympia OCD 108 [A] **F**

*Chamber Suite; *The Humpbacked Horse* (ballet) Bolshoi Theatre Violin Ensemble, Reyontovich; *Moscow Stanislawsky Theatre O, Zhemchuzhin
Olympia OCD 219, 2CDs [A] **F**

Piano Concerto No. 1 in D; Humoresque; Imitating Albéniz; Piano Sonata in C; 2 Polyphonic Pieces; Prelude and Fugue in A min.; Prelude and Fugue in C; Prelude in G; Troika; The Humpbacked Horse (ballet): *Maidens' Round Dance; Scherzino; Ivan and his Elder Brothers* Shchedrin (pno), *Leningrad PO, Dimitriev
Olympia OCD 259 [A] **F**

S   *Echo Sonata* Stadler (vln)
(+ Rimsky-Korsakov: *Piano Trio in C min.*)
Olympia OCD 140 [A] **F**

SHEPPARD, John (c.1515–c.1559) ENGLAND

V   *Christe Redemptor omnium; In manus tuas I–III; Media vita; Rege. Tharsis; Sacris solemniis; Verbum caro* Tallis Scholars, Phillips
Gimell CDGIM 016 [D] **F**

Filiae Hierusalem venite; Haec dies; In manus tuas I; In pace in idipsum; Justi in perpetuum vivent; Lauden dicite Deo; Libera nos, salva nos I; Paschal Kyrie; Reges Tharsis et insulae; Spiritus sanctu procedens I; Verbo caro factum est The Sixteen, Christophers
Hyperion CDA 66259 [D] **F**

Gaude, gaude, gaude Maria; In manus tuas I; In pace; Laudem decite Deo; Verbo caro Clerkes of Oxenford, Wulstan
(+ Tallis: *Spem in alium, etc.*)
Classics for Pleasure CD-CFP 4638 [A] **B**

Gaude virgo Christophera; In manus tuas II; Libera nos, salva nos & II; Reges Tharsis Clerkes of Oxenford, Wulstan
(+ Tye: *Mass Euge bone*)
Proudsound PROUDCD 126 [D] **F**

Mass 'The Western Wynde'; Aeterne Rex altissime; Christe virgo dilectissima; Dum transisset sabbatum II; Hostes Herodes impie; In manus tuas III; Te deum The Sixteen, Christophers
Hyperion CDA 66603 [D] **F**

Missa Cantate; Ave maris stella; Deus tuorum militum II; Jesu salvator saeculi I & II; Salvator mundi Domine The Sixteen, Christophers
Hyperion CDA 66418 [D] **F**

SHOSTAKOVICH, Dmitry (1906–1975) RUSSIA

O   *The Adventures of Korzinkina: Suite, Op. 59; Alone: Suite, Op. 26; La Comédie Humaine, Op. 37; Scherzo in F♯ min., Op. 1; Scherzo E♭, Op. 7; Theme and Variations in B♭, Op. 3; Spanish Songs, Op. 100* Various artists
Olympia OCD 194 [A] **F**

○ *Age of Gold* (ballet): *Suite, Op. 22a* LPO, Haitink
(+ Janáček: *Sinfonietta; Taras Bulba*)
Decca 430 727-2 [D] **M**

Ballet Suites Nos. 1–3 SNO, Järvi
Chandos CHAN 8730 [D] **F**

Chamber Symphony, Op. 110a (arr. Barshai); *Symphony for
Strings, Op. 118a* (arr. Barshai) COE, Barshai
DG 429 229-2 [D] **F**

*Cello Concerto No. 1 in E♭, Op. 107; Piano Concertos: *No. 1 in C
min., Op. 35; **No. 2 in F, Op. 102* Rostropovich (vcl),
Philadelphia O, Ormandy; *Previn (pno), *Tachinno (tpt),
NYPO, Bernstein; **Bernstein (pno/dir), NYPO
Sony/CBS CD44850 [A] **M**

Cello Concertos: No. 1 in E♭, Op. 107; No. 2 in G, Op. 126 Schiff
(vcl), Bavarian RSO, M. Shostakovich
Philips 412 526-2 [D] **F**

*Piano Concertos: *No. 1 in C min., Op. 35; No. 2 in F, Op. 102;
The Unforgettable Year 1919* (film score), Op. 89: *The Assault on
Beautiful Gorky* Alexeev (pno), *Jones (tpt), ECO, Maksymiuk
Classics for Pleasure CD-CFP 4547 [D] **B**

Violin Concertos: No. 1 in A min., Op. 99; No. 2 in C♯ min., Op. 129
Sitkovetsky (vln), BBC SO, A. Davis
Virgin VC7 59601-2 [D] **F**

The Gadfly (film score): *Suite, Op. 97a* USSR Cinema SO,
Khachaturian
Classics for Pleasure CD-CFP4463 [A] **B**

The Golden Age Royal Stockholm PO, Rozhdestvensky
Chandos CHAN 9251/2, 2CDs [A] **F**

*Jazz Suites Nos. 1 & 2; Piano Concerto No. 1 in E♭, Op. 107; Tahiti
Trot., Op. 16* Brautigan (pno), Royal Concertgebouw O,
Chailly
Decca 433 702-2 [D] **F**

October (symphonic poem), Op. 131: *The Young Guard* (film
score): *Suite, Op. 75a* Moscow SO, Dudarova; *USSR Cinema
SO, Gamburg
(+ Eshpay: *Lenin is With Us;* Prokofiev: *Festive Poem for the 30th
Anniversary of October 1917*)
Olympia OCD 201 [D] **F**

*Symphonies: No. 1 in F min., Op. 10; No. 3 in E♭ (First of May),
Op. 20* USSR Ministry of Culture SO, Rozhdestvensky
Olympia OCD 161 [D] **F**

*Symphonies: No. 1 in F min., Op. 10; No. 7 in C (Leningrad),
Op. 60* CSO, Bernstein
DG 427 632-2, 2CDs [D] **F**

*Symphonies: No. 2 in B (To October), Op. 14; No. 15 in A, Op. 151;
The Flea* (incidental music), Op. 19: *Suite* Academic
Republican Ch, USSR Ministry of Culture SO,
Rozhdestvensky
Olympia OCD 258 [D] **F**

Symphony No. 4 in C min., Op. 43 SNO, Järvi
Chandos CHAN 8640 [D] **F**

O   *Symphonies: No. 5 in D min., Op. 47; No. 9 in E♭, Op. 70* USSR
Ministry of Culture SO, Rozhdestvensky
Olympia OCD 113 [D] M

  Symphony No. 5 in D min., Op. 47 LSO, Previn
(+ Rachmaninov: *The Rock*)
RCA GD 86801 [A] M

  *Symphonies: No. 6 in B min., Op. 54; No. 12 in D min. (The Year
1917), Op. 112* USSR Ministry of Culture SO,
Rozhdestvensky
Olympia OCD 111 [D] F

  Symphony No. 6 in B min., Op. 54 LSO, Previn
(+ Rachmaninov: *Symphony No. 3*)
EMI CDM7 69564-2 [A] M

  Symphony No. 7 in C (Leningrad), Op. 60 USSR Ministry of
Culture SO, Rozhdestvensky
Olympia OCD 118 [D] F

  Symphony No. 8 in C min., Op. 65 Washington National SO,
Rostropovich
Teldec 9031-74719-2 [D] F

  Symphony No. 10 in E min., Op. 93 BPO, Karajan
DG 429 716-2 [A] M

  Symphony No. 11 in G min. (The Year 1905) USSR Ministry of
Culture SO, Rozhdestvensky
Olympia OCD 152 [D] F

  Symphony No. 13 in B♭ min. (Babiy Yar), Op. 113 Safiulin (bs),
Yurlov Russian Ch, USSR Ministry of Culture SO,
Rozhdestvensky
Olympia OCD 132 [D] F

  *Symphony No. 14, Op. 135; *King Lear (incidental music), Op.
58: Suite* Kasrashubili (sop), Safiulin (bs), USSR Ministry of
Culture SO, Rozhdestvensky; *Romanova (mez), Leningrad
CO, Serov
Olympia OCD 182 [D] F

C   *Cello Sonata in D min., Op. 40; Moderato* Harrell (vcl),
Ashkenazy (pno)
(+ Prokofiev: *Cello Sonata*)
Decca 421 774-2 [D] F

  **Piano Quintet in G min., Op. 67; Piano Trio No. 2 in E min.,
Op. 67* Beaux Arts Trio, *Drucker (vln), *Dutton (vla)
Philips 432 079-2 [D] F

  String Quartets Nos. 1–15 Fitzwilliam Quartet
Decca 433 078-2, 6CDs [A] M

  String Quartets Nos. 1–14; *Piano Quintet *Richter (pno),
Borodin Quartet
EMI CMS5 65032-2, 6 CDs [A] M

  String Quartets: Nos. 1, 3 & 4; 2 Pieces, Op. 36 Shostakovich
Quartet
Olympia OCD 531 [A] F

  String Quartets Nos. 2, 5 & 7 Shostakovich Quartet
Olympia OCD 532 [A] F

  String Quartets Nos. 6, 8 & 9 Shostakovich Quartet
Olympia OCD 533 [A] F

C *String Quartets Nos. 10, 11 & 15* Shostakovich Quartet
Olympia OCD 534 [A] **F**

 String Quartets Nos. 12–14 Shostakovich Quartet
Olympia OCD 535 [A] **F**

 Viola Sonata Bashmet (vla), Muntian (pno)
(+ Glinka: *Viola Sonata;* Roslavets: *Viola Sonata No. 1*)
RCA 09026 61273-2 [D] **F**

 Violin Sonata, Op. 134 Dubinsky (vln), Edlina (pno)
(+ Schnittke: *Sonata in the Olden Style; Violin Sonata No. 1*)
Chandos CHAN 8343 [D] **F**

S *24 Preludes and Fugues, Op. 87* Nikolayeva (pno)
Hyperion CDA 66441/3, 3CDs [D] **F**

 24 Preludes, Op. 34
Nikolayeva (pno)
(+ *3 Fantastic Dances, Op. 5; Piano Sonata No. 1, Op. 12*)
Hyperion CDA 66620 [D] **F**
Mustonen (pno)
(+ Alkan: *25 Preludes*)
Decca 433 055-2 [D] **F**

V *From Jewish Poetry, Op. 79a; 2 Fables of Krylov, Op.4;*
3 Romances on Poems by Pushkin, Op. 46a; 6 Romances on Verses
by Raleigh, Burns & Shakespeare, Op. 62/140 Orgonasova (sop),
Dyadkova (mez), Stutzmann (cont), Langridge (ten),
Leiferkus (bs), Gothenburg SO, Järvi
DG 439 860-2 [D] **F**

 Hypothetically Murdered; Jazz Suite No. 1; 5 Fragments, Op. 42;
4 Songs, Op. 46 Kharitinov (bs), CBSO, Elder
United 88001-2 [D] **F**

 7 Romances on Verses by Alexander Blok, Op. 127 Pelle (sop),
Borodin Trio
(+ Arensky: *Piano Trio No. 2;* Prokofiev: *Overture on Hebrew*
Themes, Op. 35)
Chandos CHAN 8924 (D) **F**

 Suite on Verses of Michelangelo, Op. 145; 4 Verses of Captain
Lebyadkin, Op. 146 Fischer-Dieskau (bar), Berlin RSO,
Ashkenazy
Decca 433 319-2 [D] **F**

SIBELIUS, Jean (1865–1957) FINLAND

O *Autrefois, Op. 96/2; The Bard* (tone poem), *Op. 64; Presto in D;*
Spring Song (tone poem), *Op. 16; Suite caractéristique, Op. 100;*
Suite champêtre, Op. 98b; Valse chevaleresque, Op. 96/3; Valse
lyrique, Op. 96/1 Gothenburg SO, Järvi
BIS BIS-CD 384 [D] **F**

 Belshazzar's Feast (incidental music), *Op. 51: Alla marcia; The*
Dryad (tone poem), *Op. 45/1; Pan and Echo* (dance
intermezzo), *Op. 53; Swanwhite* (incidental music), *Op. 54: The*
Peacock Gothenburg SO, Järvi
BIS BIS-CD 359 [D] **F**

 Cassazione, Op. 6; Preludio; The Tempest (incidental music), *Op.*
109; Tiera (tone poem) Gothenburg SO, Järvi
BIS BIS-CD 448 [D] **F**

 Violin Concerto in D min. (1903/4 version); Violin Concerto in D
min., Op. 47 Kovakos (vln), Lahti SO, Vanska
BIS BIS-CD 500 [D] **F**

○ *Violin Concerto in D min., Op. 47; Serenade in G min., Op. 69/2;*
En Saga, Op. 9 Rachlin (vln), Pittsburgh SO, Maazel
Sony CD 53272 [D] **F**

Violin Concerto in D min., Op. 47
Heifetz (vln), CSO, Hendl
(+ Glazunov: *Violin Concerto;* Prokofiev: *Violin Concerto No. 2*)
RCA RD 87019 [A] **F**
Lin (vln), Swedish RSO, Salonen
(+ Nielsen: *Violin Concerto*)
Sony CD44548 [D] **F**
Little (vln), RLPO, Handley
(+ Brahms: *Violin Concerto*)
EMI Eminence CD-EMX 2203 [D] **M**

En Saga, Op. 9; Scènes historiques: Suites Nos. 1, Op. 25, & 2, Op.
66 Gothenburg SO, Järvi
BIS BIS-CD 295 [D] **F**

Finlandia, Op. 26; Legends, Op. 22: The Swan of Tuonela;
Tapiola (tone poem), Op. 112; Valse Triste, Op. 44/1 BPO,
Karajan
DG 413 755-2 [D] **F**

4 Legends (Lemminkäinen Suite), Op. 22 Gothenburg SO, Järvi
BIS BIS-CD 294 [D] **F**

Nightride and Sunrise, Op. 55; Spring Song (tone poem), Op. 16
SNO, Gibson
(+ Nielsen: *Helios Overture; Symphony No. 5*)
Chandos CHAN 6533 [A] **M**

Pelléas et Mélisande BPO, Karajan
(+ Grieg: *Peer Gynt: Suites Nos. 1 & 2*)
DG 410 026-2 [D] **F**

Pohjola's Daughter (symphonic fantasia), Op. 49; Rakastava, Op.
14; Tapiola (tone poem), Op. 112; Andante lirico Gothenburg
SO, Järvi
BIS BIS-CD 312 [D] **F**

Scaramouche (incidental music), Op. 71; The Language of the
Birds (Wedding march) Gothenburg SO, Järvi
BIS BIS-CD 502 [D] **F**

Scènes historiques: Suites Nos. 1, Op. 25, & 2, Op. 66 Gothenburg
SO, Järvi
BIS BIS-CD 295 [D] **F**

Symphonies Nos. 1–7 VPO, Maazel
Decca 430 778-2, 3CDs [A] **M**

Symphony No. 1 in E min., Op. 39; Finlandia, Op. 26; Karelia
Suite, Op. 11 Oslo PO, Jansons
EMI CDC7 54273-2 [D] **F**

Symphony No. 2 in D, Op. 43; Finlandia, Op. 26; Karelia Suite,
Op. 11 Philharmonia O, Ashkenazy
Decca 430 737-2 [D] **M**

Symphonies: No. 3 in C, Op. 52; No. 6 in D min., Op. 104
Philharmonia O, Ashkenazy
Decca 436 478-2 [D] **M**

Symphonies: No. 4 in A min., Op. 63; No. 6 in D min., Op. 104
BPO, Karajan
DG 415 108-2 [A] **F**

O *Symphonies: No. 4 in A min., Op. 63; No. 7 in C, Op. 105; Valse triste, Op. 44* BPO, Karajan
DG 439 527-2 [A] **M**

Symphony No. 5 in E♭, Op. 82; Finlandia, Op. 36; Tapiola, Op.112; Valse triste, Op. 44 BPO, Karajan
DG 439 418-2 [A] **B**

Symphonies: No. 5 in E♭, Op. 82; No. 7 in C, Op. 105 BPO, Karajan
DG 415 107-2 [A] **F**

Symphony No. 7 in C, Op. 105; Oceanides (tone poem), Op. 73; Pelléas et Mélisande (incidental music), Op. 46; Tapiola (tone poem), Op. 112 RPO, Beecham
EMI CDM7 63400-2 [A] **M**

C *Piano Quintet in G min.; String Quartet in D min., Op. 56 (Voces intimae)* Goldstone (pno), Gabrieli Quartet
Chandos CHAN 8742 [D] **F**

String Quartet in A min.; String Quartet in B♭, Op. 4 Sibelius Academy Quartet
Finlandia FACD 345 [D] **F**

S *6 Bagatelles, Op. 97; Longing; Mandolinato; 5 Pieces, Op. 75; 5 Pieces, Op. 85; 6 Pieces, Op. 94; Spagnuolo* Tawastsjerna (pno)
BIS BIS-CD 230 [D] **F**

The Cavalier; 5 Esquisses, Op. 114; Morceau romantique; 8 Pieces, Op. 99; 5 Pieces, Op. 101; 5 Pieces, Op. 103 Tawastsjerna (pno)
BIS BIS-CD 278 [D] **F**

6 Finnish Folksongs; 6 Impromptus, Op. 5; 4 Lyric Pieces, Op. 74; Piano Sonata in F, Op. 12 Tawastsjerna (pno)
BIS BIS-CD 153 [D] **F**

3 Lyric Pieces, Op. 41; Sonatines Nos. 1–3, Op. 67 Gould (pno)
(+ Bizet: *Nocturne No. 1; Variations chromatiques, Op. 3;* Grieg: *Piano Sonata)*
Sony CD 52654, 2CDs [A] **M**

4 Lyric Pieces, Op. 74; Pieces, Op. 76; 2 Rondinos, Op. 68; 3 Sonatinas, Op. 67 Tawastsjerna (pno)
BIS BIS-CD 196 [D] **F**

10 Pensées lyriques, Op. 40; 10 Pieces, Op. 58 Tawastsjerna (pno)
BIS BIS-CD 195 [D] **F**

10 Pieces, Op. 24; 10 Pieces, Op. 34 Tawastsjerna (pno)
BIS BIS-CD 169 [D] **F**

V *Arioso, Op. 3; Narcissus; Pelléas et Mélisande (incidental music), Op. 46: Three blind sisters; Row, row duck; 7 Songs, Op. 17; 6 Songs, Op. 36; 5 Songs, Op. 37; 6 Songs, Op. 88* von Otter (mez), Forsberg (pno)
BIS BIS-CD 457 [D] **F**

Luonnotar, Op. 70; 13 songs Hynninen (bar), Häggander (sop), Gothenburg SO, Panula
BIS BIS-CD 270 [D] **F**

Finlandia; Frodolin's folly; In the moonlight; Jonah's voyage; *The Lover; **March of the Finnish Jaeger battalion; Natus in curas; One hears the storm outside; 9 Partsongs, Op. 18 Nos. 1–3 & 5–9; 5 Partsongs, Op. 84; 2 Partsongs, Op. 108; Resemblance; The Roaring of a wave *Lindroos (ten), **Helsinki Garrison Band, Helsinki University Male Voice Ch, Hyokki, **Juuri
Finlandia FACD 205 [D] **F**

V *Kullervo Symphony, Op. 7* Mattila (sop), Hynninen (bar),
Laulun Ystävät Male Ch, Gothenburg SO, Järvi
BIS CD 313 [D] **F**

SIMPSON, Robert (born 1921) ENGLAND

O *Energy; The Four Temperaments; Introduction and Allegro on a
Bass by Max Reger; Volcano; Vortex* Desford Colliery Caterpillar
Band, Watson
Hyperion CDA 66449 [D] **F**

Symphonies Nos. 2 & 4 Bournemouth SO, Handley
Hyperion CDA 66505 [D] **F**

*Symphony No. 3; *Clarinet Quintet* LSO, Horenstein; *Walton
(cl), Aeolian Quartet
Unicorn-Kanchana UKCD 2028 [D] **M**

Symphony No. 6; Symphony No. 7 RLPO, Handley
Hyperion CDA 66280 [D] **F**

Symphony No. 9 (including talk by the composer)
Bournemouth SO, Handley
Hyperion CDA 66299 [D] **F**

Symphony No. 10 RLPO, Handley
Hyperion CDA 66510 [D] **F**

C *String Quartet No. 1; String Quartet No. 4* Delmé Quartet
Hyperion 66419 [D] **F**

String Quartet No. 2; String Quartet No. 5 Delmé Quartet
Hyperion 66386 [D] **F**

*String Quartet No. 3; String Quartet No. 6; String Trio (Prelude,
Adagio and Fugue)* Delmé Quartet
Hyperion 66376 [D] **F**

String Quartet No. 7; String Quartet No. 8 Delmé Quartet
Hyperion 66117 [D] **F**

*String Quartet No. 9 (32 Variations and a Fugue on a Theme of
Haydn)* Delmé Quartet
Hyperion 66127 [D] **F**

String Quartet No. 10; String Quartet No. 11 Coull Quartet
Hyperion CDA 66225 [D] **F**

String Quartet No. 12; String Quintet Coull Quartet, Bigley (vla)
Hyperion CDA 66503 [D] **F**

String Quartets Nos. 14 & 15; 2-Clarinet Quintet Vanburgh
Quartet, Farral (cl), Cross (bs cl)
Hyperion CDA 66626 [D] **F**

SMETANA, Bedřich (1824–1884) BOHEMIA

O *Hakon Jarl, Op. 16; Prague Carnival; Richard III, Op. 11;
Wallenstein's Camp, Op. 14* Bavarian RSO, Kubelik
(+ Janáček: *Sinfonietta*)
DG 437 254-2 [A] **M**

Má Vlast (complete) Czech PO, Kubelik
Supraphon 11 1208-2 [D] **F**

C *Piano Trio in G min. B104* Fontenay Trio
(+ Chopin: *Piano Trio*)
Teldec 2292-43715-2 [D] **F**

String Quartets: No. 1 in E min. (From my Life); No. 2 in D min.
Lindsay Quartet

(+ Dvořák: *Romance; Waltzes*)
ASV CDDCA 777 [D] **F**

SMYTH, Ethel (1858–1944) ENGLAND

○ *The Wreckers* (opera): *Overture* SNO, Gibson
(+ German: *Welsh Rhapsody;* Harty: *With the Wild Geese;*
MacCunn: *Land of Mountain and Flood*)
Classics for Pleasure CDCFP 4635 [A] **B**

✓ *Mass in D; The Boatswain's Mate* (opera): *Mrs Water's Aria;*
March of the Women Harrhy (sop), Hardy (mez), Dressen (ten),
Bohn (bar), Plymouth Music Series O & Ch, Brunelle
Virgin VC7 59022-2 [D] **F**

SOMERVELL, Arthur (1863–1937) ENGLAND

✓ *Maud* (song cycle); *A Shropshire Lad* (song cycle) Wilson-
Johnson (bar), Norris (pno)
Hyperion CDA 66187 [D] **F**

SOR, Fernando (1778–1839) SPAIN

⬡ *Études, Op. 6 Nos. 4, 6, 8; Études, Op. 29/23; Étude, Op. 35 Nos.*
16, 17; Fantasia, Op. 21; Fantaisie élégiaque, Op. 59; Grand Solo,
Op. 14; Sonata in C, Op. 154; Sonata in C, Op. 25
Fernández (gtr)
Decca 425 821-2 [D] **F**

SORABJI, Kaikhosru (1892–1988) ENGLAND

⬡ *Le jardin parfumé* (poem); *Nocturne; Pastiche on Chopin's Waltz;*
Pastiche on Rimsky-Korsakov's Hindu Song from 'Sadko'; Prelude,
Interlude and Fugue Habermann (pno)
ASV CDAMM 159 [D] **F**

Opus clavicembalisticum Ogdon (pno)
Altarus AIR-CD-9075, 4CDs [D] **F**

Piano Sonata No. 1 Hamelin (pno)
Altarus AIR-CD-9050 [D] **F**

Organ Symphony No. 1 Bowyer (org)
Continuum CCD 1001/2, 2CDs [D] **F**

SOUSA, John Philip (1854–1932) USA

◗ *Famous Marches* Philip Jones Ensemble, Howarth
Decca 410 290-2 [D] **F**

SOWERBY, Leo (1895–1968) USA

Trio (1953); *Trio in C♯ min.* Musica Gioiosa Trio
New World NW 365-2 [D] **F**

Fantasy for Flute Stops; Requiescat in pace; Symphony in G
Crozier (org)
Delos DE3075 [D] **F**

Passacaglia; Piano Sonata; Suite for Piano Quillman (pno)
New World NW 376-2 [D] **F**

SPOHR, Louis (1784–1859) GERMANY

Clarinet Concertos: No. 1 in C min., Op. 26; No. 4 in E min.
Leister (cl), Stuttgart RSO, de Burgos
Orfeo CO88101A [A] **F**

Clarinet Concertos: No. 2 in E♭, Op. 57; No. 3 in F min. Leister
(cl), Stuttgart RSO, de Burgos
Orfeo CO88201A [A] **F**

O *Symphonies: No. 6 in G (Historical), Op. 116; No. 9 in B min. (Seasons), Op. 143* Bavarian RSO, Rickenbacher
Orfeo CO94841A [D] **F**

C *Double Quartets: No. 1 in D min., Op. 65; No. 2 in E♭, Op. 77* ASMF Chamber Ensemble
Hyperion CDA66141 [D] **F**

Double Quartets: No. 3 in E min., Op. 87; No. 4 in G min., Op. 136 ASMF Chamber Ensemble
Hyperion CDA 66142 [D] **F**

Nonet in F, Op. 31; Octet in E, Op. 32 Nash Ensemble
CRD 3354 [A] **F**

Piano and Wind Quintet in C min., Op. 52; Septet in A min., Op. 147 Brown (pno), Nash Ensemble
CRD 3399 [A] **F**

String Quartet in A, Op. 93; String Quartet in B min., Op. 84/3 New Budapest Quartet
Marco Polo 8.223252 [D] **F**

String Quartets: in D min., Op. 11; in G min., Op. 27; in E♭, Op. 15/2 New Budapest Quartet
Marco Polo 8.223254 [D] **F**

2 String Quartets, Op. 4; String Quartet in D, Op. 15/4 New Budapest Quartet
Marco Polo 8.223253 [D] **F**

String Quartets, Op. 29 Nos. 1 & 2 New Budapest Quartet
Marco Polo 8.223255 [D] **F**

String Quartets, Op. 84 Nos. 1 & 2 New Budapest Quartet
Marco Polo 8.223251 [D] **F**

V *German Songs, Op. 25 Nos. 2 & 5: Scottische Lied; Zigeunerlied; 6 German Songs, Op. 37 No. 5: Lied beim Rudetanz; 6 German Songs, Op. 41 Nos. 3 & 6: An Mignon & Vanitas!; 6 German Songs Op. 72 No. 6: Schlaflied; 6 German Songs, Op. 103; 6 Songs, Op. 154* Fischer-Dieskau (bar), Varady (sop), Sitkovetsky (vln), Schoneberger (cl), Höll (pno)
Orfeo C103841A [D] **F**

STAINER, John (1840–1901) ENGLAND

V *The Crucifixion* (oratorio) Davies (ten), Wilson-Johnson (bar), St. Paul's Cathedral Ch, Scott (org), Lucas
Conifer CDCF 193 [D] **F**

STAMITZ, Carl (1745–1801) GERMANY

O *Cello Concertos: in A; in C; in G* Starck (vcl), South West German CO, Angerer
Claves CD50-8105 [A] **F**

STANFORD, Charles Villiers (1852–1924) IRELAND/ENGLAND

O *Piano Concerto No. 2 in C min., Op. 126; Concert Variations on 'Down around the Dead Men', Op. 71* Fingerhut (pno), Ulster O, Handley
Chandos CHAN 8736 [D] **F**

*Piano Concerto No. 2; Irish Rhapsody No. 4; Becket: Funeral March *Binns (pno), *LSO, *Braithwaite; LPO, Boult
Lyrita SRCD219 [A] **F**

Symphonies Nos. 1–7 Ulster O, Handley
Chandos CHAN 9279-82, 4CDs [D] **F**

○ *Symphony No. 1 in B♭; Irish Rhapsody No. 2* Ulster O, Handley
Chandos CHAN 9049 [D] **F**

Symphony No. 2 in D min. (Elegiac); *Clarinet Concerto in A min., Op. 80 *Hilton (cl), Ulster O, Handley
Chandos CHAN 8991 [D] **F**

Symphony No. 3 in F min. (Irish), Op. 28; Irish Rhapsody No. 5 in G min., Op. 147 Ulster O, Handley
Chandos CHAN 8545 [D] **F**

Symphony No. 4 in F, Op. 31; *Irish Rhapsody No. 6; Oedipus Tyrannus (incidental music), *Op. 29: Prelude* *Mordkovitch (vln), Ulster O, Handley
Chandos CHAN 8884 [D] **F**

Symphony No. 5 in D (L'Allegro ed il penseroso), Op. 56; Irish Rhapsody No. 4 in F, Op. 31 Ulster O, Handley
Chandos CHAN 8581 [D] **F**

Symphony No. 6 in E♭ (In memoriam G.F. Watts), Op. 94; Irish Rhapsody No. 1 in D min., Op. 78 Ulster O, Handley
Chandos CHAN 8627 [D] **F**

Symphony No. 7 in D min., Op. 124; *Concert Piece, Op. 181; **Irish Rhapsody No. 3, Op. 137 *Weir (org), **R. Wallfisch (vcl), Ulster O, Handley
Chandos CHAN 8861 [D] **F**

2 Fantasy Pieces King (cl), Britten Quartet
(+ Fuchs: *Clarinet Quintet;* Romberg: *Clarinet Quintet*)
Hyperion CDA 66479 [D] **F**

Serenade (nonet) in F Capricorn
(+ Parry: *Nonet in B♭*)
Hyperion CDA 66291 [D] **F**

Cello Sonata No. 2 Lloyd Webber (vcl), McCabe (pno)
(+ Bridge: *Elegy; Scherzetto;* Ireland: *Cello Sonata*)
ASV CDDCA 807 [D] **F**

Clarinet Sonata, Op. 129 King (cl), Benson (pno)
(+ Ferguson: *4 Short Pieces, Op. 6;* Finzi: *5 Bagatelles;* Hurlstone: *4 Characteristic Pieces*)
Hyperion CDA 66014 [D] **F**

Evening Service in A (Magnificat and Nunc dimittis), Op. 12; For lo, I rise up; The Lord is My Shepherd; 3 Latin Motets, Op. 38; 3 Motets, Op. 135 Nos. 1 & 3: Ye Holy Angels; Powerful God; O living Will; Ye Choirs of Jerusalem Worcester Cathedral Ch, Hunt
Hyperion CDA 66030 [D] **F**

TANLEY, John (1712–1786) ENGLAND

6 Organ Concerti, Op. 10 Gifford (org/dir), Northern Sinfonia
CRD 3365 [A] **F**

6 String Concerti, Op. 2 Parley of Instruments, Goodman
Hyperion CDA 66338 [D] **F**

TEINER, Max (1888–1971) AUSTRIA/USA

Film score excerpts: *All This and Heaven Too; Beyond the Forest; In This Our Life; Jezebel; The Letter; Now Voyager; A Stolen Life; Warner Brothers Fanfare* National PO, Gerhardt
(+ film scores by Korngold, Newman, Waxman)
RCA GD 80183 [A] **M**

O Film score excerpts: *The Big Sleep; The Charge of the Light Brigade; The Fountainhead; *Four Wives; **The Informer; Johnny Belinda; King Kong; Saratoga Trunk; Since You Went Away; Warner Brothers Fanfare* *Wild (pno), **Ambrosian Singers, National PO, Gerhardt
RCA GD 80136 [A] **M**

Gone With The Wind (film score) National PO, Gerhardt
RCA GD 80452 [A] **M**

STENHAMMER, Wilhelm (1871–1927) SWEDEN

O *Piano Concerto No. 1 in Bb min., Op. 1; Symphony No. 3: fragment* Widlund (pno), Stockholm PO, Rozhdestvensky
Chandos CHAN 9074 [D] **F**

Piano Concerto No. 2 in D min., Op. 23; Chitra (incidental music), *Op. 43* Ortiz (pno), Gothenburg SO, Järvi
BIS BIS-CD 476 [D] **F**

Excelsior! (symphonic overture), *Op. 13; Symphony No. 2 in G min., Op. 34* Gothenburg SO, Järvi
BIS BIS-CD 251 [D] **F**

Lodelezzi sings (incidental music), *Op. 39: Suite; *Midwinter, Op. 24; **Snöfrid, Op. 5; The Song, Op. 44: Interlude* */**Gothenburg Concert Hall Ch; **Åhlén (sop), Nilsson (mez), Zackrisson (ten), Enoksson (bs); Gothenburg SO, Järvi
BIS BIS-CD 438 [D] **F**

Serenade in F, Op. 31 (includes *Reverenza movement*)
Gothenburg SO, Järvi
BIS BIS-CD 310 [D] **F**

Symphony No. 1 in F Gothenburg SO, Järvi
BIS BIS-CD 219 [D] **F**

C *String Quartet No. 1 in C, Op. 2; *String Quartet No. 2 in C min., Op. 14* Fresk Quartet; *Copenhagen Quartet
Caprice CAP 21337 [A] **F**

String Quartet No. 3 in F, Op. 18; String Quartet No. 4 in A min., Op. 25 Gotland Quartet
Caprice CAP 21338 [A] **F**

*String Quartet No. 5 in C (Serenade), Op. 29; *String Quartet No. in D min., Op. 35* Gotland Quartet; *Copenhagen Quartet
Caprice CAP 21339 [A] **F**

V *30 Songs* von Otter (mez), Hagegård (bar), Forsberg (pno), Schuback (pno)
Musica Sveciae MSCD 623 [A] **F**

STERNDALE BENNETT, William (1816–1875) ENGLAND

O *Piano Concertos: No. 1 in D min., Op. 1; No. 3 in C min., Op. 9; Caprice in E, Op. 22* Binns (pno), LPO, Braithwaite
Lyrita SRCD 204 [D] **F**

Piano Concertos: No. 2 in Eb, Op. 4; No. 5 in F min.; Adagio for Piano and Orchestra Binns (pno), LPO, Braithwaite
Lyrita SRCD 205 [D] **F**

Piano Concerto No. 4 in F min.; Symphony in G min.; Fantasia in A, Op. 16 Binns (pno), Milton Keynes CO, Wetton
Unicorn-Kanchana UKCD 2032 [D] **M**

STEVENS, Bernard (1916–1983) ENGLAND

○ *Cello Concerto, Op. 18; A Symphony of Liberation* Baillie (vcl),
BBC PO, Downes
Meridian CDE 84124 [D] **F**

*Violin Concerto, Op. 4; Symphony No. 2, Op. 35 *Kovacic (vln),
BBC PO, Downes
Meridian CDE 84174 [D] **F**

≡ *Lyric Suite, Op. 30; String Quartet No. 2, Op. 34; Theme and
Variations, Op. 11* Delmé Quartet
Unicorn-Kanchana DKPCD 9097 [D] **F**

✦ *Mass for Double Choir* Finzi Singers, Spicer
(+ Howells: *Mass in the Dorian Mode, etc.*)
Chandos CHAN 9021 [D] **F**

STEVENSON, Ronald (born 1928) ENGLAND/SCOTLAND

○ *Piano Concertos Nos. 1 & 2* McLachlan (pno), Chethams SO,
Clayton
Olympia OCD 429 [D] **F**

Beltane Bonfire; Scottish Ballads Nos. 2 & 3 McLachlan (pno)
(+ piano works by Center, Scott)
Olympia OCD 264 [D] **F**

*Passacaglia on DSCH; Recitative and Air; Prelude and Fugue on
Themes from Busoni's 'Doktor Faust'* Stevenson (pno)
Altarus AIR-CD-9091 [D] **F**

TILL, William Grant (1895–1978) USA

◑ *Symphony No. 1 ('Afro-American')* Detroit SO, Järvi
(+ Ellington: *The River: Suite*)
Chandos CHAN 9154 [D] **F**

Symphony No. 2 (Song of a New Race) Detroit SO, Järvi
(+ Dawson: *Negro Folk Symphony;* Ellington: *Harlem*)
Chandos CHAN 9226 [D] **F**

TOCKHAUSEN, Karlheinz (born 1928) GERMANY

Klavierstücke XII–XIV Wambach (pno)
Schwann 310015 [D] **F**

9 Klavierstücke: I–IV, IX & X Wambach (pno)
Schwann 310016 [D] **F**

Stimmung Songcircle, Rose
Hyperion CDA 66115 [D] **F**

TRADELLA, Alessandro (1644–1682) ITALY

San Giovanni Battista (oratorio) Monoyios (sop), Bach (sop),
Cordier (alt), Prégardien (ten), Schopper (bs), Stagione,
Schneider
✧ DHM RD 77034 [D] **F**

TRAUSS FAMILY

● *Viennese New Year's Day Concerts*
1987: Battle (sop), VPO, Karajan
DG 419 616-2 [D] **F**
1988: VPO, Abbado
DG 423 662-2 [D] **F**
1989: VPO, C. Kleiber
Sony CD 45938 [D] **F**

1990: VPO, Mehta
Sony CD 45808 [D] **F**
1991: VPO, Abbado
DG 431 628-2 [D] **F**
1992: VPO, C. Kleiber
Sony CD 48376 [D] **F**
1993: VPO, Muti
Philips 438 493-2 [D] **F**

STRAUSS, Eduard (1835–1916) AUSTRIA

O *Bahn frei* VPO, Boskovsky
(+ orchestral works by Johann Strauss I, Johann Strauss II &
Josef Strauss)
Decca 425 426-2 [A] **M**

Fesche Geister VPO, Boskovsky
(+ orchestral works by Johann Strauss I, Johann Strauss II &
Josef Strauss)
Decca 425 425-2 [A] **M**

Mit Extrapost VPO, Boskovsky
(+ orchestral works by Johann Strauss I, Johann Strauss II &
Josef Strauss)
Decca 425 429-2 [A] **M**

STRAUSS, Johann I (1804–1849) AUSTRIA

O *Beliebte Speri-Polka* VPO, Boskovsky
(+ orchestral works by Johann Strauss II & Josef Strauss)
Decca 425 427-2 [A] **M**

Loreley-Rhein-Klänge VPO, Boskovsky
(+ orchestral works by Eduard Strauss, Johann Strauss II &
Josef Strauss)
Decca 425 429-2 [A] **M**

Piefke und Pufke; Radetzky March VPO, Boskovsky
(+ orchestral works by Eduard Strauss, Johann Strauss II &
Josef Strauss)
Decca 425 426-2 [A] **M**

Wettrennen VPO, Boskovsky
(+ orchestral works by Eduard Strauss, Johann Strauss II &
Josef Strauss)
Decca 425 425-2 [A] **M**

STRAUSS, Johann II (1825–1899) AUSTRIA

O *Accelerationen; Bitte schön!; Kaiser (Emperor) Waltz; Leichtes Blut;
Persischer Marsch; Rosen aus dem Süden; 's gibt nur a Kaiserstadt;
Schneeglöckchen; Tik-Tak; Vergnügungszug* VPO, Boskovsky
(+ orchestral works by Eduard Strauss, Johann Strauss I &
Josef Strauss)
Decca 425 429-2 [A] **M**

*Annen Polka; Auf der Jagd; An der schönen, blauen Donau (Blue
Danube); Carnevals-Botschafter; Egyptischer Marsch; Pizzicato
Polka; Tritsch-Tratsch; Frühlingsstimmen* VPO, Boskovsky
(+ orchestral works by Eduard Strauss, Johann Strauss I &
Josef Strauss)
Decca 425 425-2 [A] **M**

Cinderella (ballet); *Ritter Pasman; Le Beau Danube* (ballet)
National PO, Bonynge
Decca 430 852-2, 2 CDs [D/A] **M**

○ *Künstlerleben; Banditen-Galop; Champagne; Eljen a Magyar!; Jubel Marsch; Liebeslieder; Morgenblätter; Neue Pizzicato; Russischer Marsch; Unter Donner und Blitz; Wiener Blut; Wiener Bonbons* VPO, Boskovsky
(+ Josef Strauss: *Auf Ferienreisen; Dorfschwalben aus Österreich*)
Decca 425 428-2 [A] **M**

Demolirer; Du und Du; Freuet euch des Lebens; Lagunen Walzer; Perpetuum Mobile; Spanischer March; Stürmisch in Lieb' und Tanz; Geschichten aus dem Wienerwald VPO, Boskovsky
(+ orchestral works by Eduard Strauss, Johann Strauss I & Josef Strauss)
Decca 425 426-2 [A] **M**

Explosionen; Im Krapfenwald'; Lob der Frauen; Napoleon Marsch; Seid umschlungen Millionen; So ängstlich sind wir nicht; 1001 Nacht; Wein, Weib und Gesang; Wo die Zitronen blüh'n VPO, Boskovsky
(+ Johann Strauss I: *Beliebte Speri-Polka;* Josef Strauss: *Heiterer Muth; Libelle; Moulinet; Transaktionen*)
Decca 425 427-2 [A] **M**

STRAUSS, Josef (1827–1870) AUSTRIA

○ *Aquarellen; Brennende Liebe; Eingesendet; Frauenherz* VPO, Boskovsky
(+ orchestral works by Eduard Strauss, Johann Strauss I & Johann Strauss II)
Decca 425 426-2 [A] **M**

Auf Ferienreisen; Dorfschwalben aus Österreich VPO, Boskovsky
(+ Johann Strauss II: *Orchestral works*)
Decca 425 428-2 [A] **M**

Delirien; Die Emanzipierte VPO, Boskovsky
(+ orchestral works by Eduard Strauss, Johann Strauss I & Johann Strauss II)
Decca 425 429-2 [A] **M**

Dynamiden; Feuerfest!; Jockey; Schwätzerin; Sphärenklänge VPO, Boskovsky
(+ orchestral works by Eduard Strauss, Johann Strauss I & Johann Strauss II)
Decca 425 425-2 [A] **M**

Heiterer Muth; Libelle; Moulinet; Transaktionen VPO, Boskovsky
(+ orchestral works by Johann Strauss I & Johann Strauss II)
Decca 425 427-2 [A] **M**

STRAUSS, Richard (1864–1949) GERMANY

○ *Eine Alpensinfonie, Op. 64; Aus Italien, Op. 16; Divertimento; *Don Quixote, Op. 35; Macbeth, Op. 23; Metamorphosen* *P. Tortelier (vcl), *Rostal (vla), Dresden Staatskapelle, Kempe
EMI CMS7 64350-2, 3CDs [A] **M**

An Alpine Symphony; Die Frau ohne Schatten: Symphonic Fantasy CSO, Barenboim
Erato 2292 45997-2 [D] **F**

Also sprach Zarathustra, Op. 30; Le bourgeois gentilhomme: Suite, Op. 60; Der Rosenkavalier (opera): Waltzes CSO, Reiner
RCA 09026-60930-2 [A] **M**

Horn Concertos Nos. 1 & 2 Baumann (hn), LGO, Masur
(+ Weber: *Horn Concertino*)
Philips 412 237-2 [D] **F**

O *Also sprach Zarathustra, Op. 30; Der Burger als Edelmann: Suite;*
   *Violin Concerto in D min., Op. 8; Josephslegende (ballet), Op. 63:
   Symphonic Fragment; Der Rosenkavalier (opera): Waltzes; Salome
   (opera): Dance of the 7 Veils; Schlagobers (ballet): Waltz; Sinfonia
   Domestica, Op. 53; Tod und Verklärung, Op. 24 *Hoelscher (vln),
   Dresden Staatskapelle, Kempe
   EMI CMS7 64346-2, 3CDs [A] **M**

   Also sprach Zarathustra, Op. 30; Till Eulenspiegels lustige
   Streiche, Op. 28; Salome (opera): Dance of the 7 Veils BPO,
   Karajan
   DG 415 853-2 [A] **M**

   Le bourgeois gentilhomme: Suite, Op. 60; Divertimento, Op. 86
   Orpheus CO
   DG 435 871-2 [D] **F**

   *Burleske in D min.; Horn Concertos: No. 1 in E♭, Op. 11; No. 2 in
   E♭; Oboe Concerto; Don Juan, Op. 20; **Duet-Concertino; Ein
   Heldenleben, Op. 40; Panathenaenzug; ***Parergon, Op. 73; Till
   Eulenspiegels lustige Streiche, Op. 28 *Frager (pno), Damm (hn),
   Clement (ob), **Weise (cl), **Liebscher (bsn), ***Rosl (pno),
   Dresden Staatskapelle, Kempe
   EMI CMS7 64342-2, 3CDs [A] **M**

   Oboe Concerto de Lancie (ob), LSO, Previn
   (+ Ibert: *Symphonie Concertante;* Françaix: *L'horloge de flore;*
   Satie: *Gymnopédies Nos. 1 & 3*)
   RCA GD 87989 [A] **M**

   Violin Concerto in D min., Op. 8 Wei (vln), LPO, Glover
   (+ Headington: *Violin Concerto*)
   ASV CDDCA 780 [D] **F**

   Don Juan, Op. 20; Ein Heldenleben, Op. 40 BPO, Karajan
   DG 429 717-2 [A] **M**

   *Don Quixote, Op. 35; Tod und Verklärung, Op. 24 *Fournier
   (vcl), *Cappone (vla), BPO, Karajan
   DG 429 184-2 [A] **M**

   Metamorphosen; *Four Last Songs; **Oboe Concerto *Janowitz
   (sop),**Koch (ob), BPO, Karajan
   DG 423 888-2 [A] **M**

   Metamorphosen; Tod und Verklärung, Op. 24 BPO, Karajan
   DG 410 892-2 [D] **F**

   Sinfonia Domestica, Op. 53; Tod und Verklärung, Op. 24 CSO,
   Reiner
   RCA GD 60388 [A] **M**

   Symphony in F min., Op. 12; 6 Songs, Op. 68 Hulse (sop), SNO,
   Järvi
   Chandos CHAN 9166 [D] **F**

   Complete Music for Wind Ensemble London Winds
   Hyperion CDA 66731/2, 2 CDs [D] **F**

C *Piano Quartet in C min., Op. 13* Ames Piano Quartet
   (+ Widor: *Piano Quartet*)
   Dorian DOR 90176 [D] **F**

   String Quartet in A, Op. 2 Delmé Quartet
   (+ Verdi: *String Quartet in E min.*)
   Hyperion CDA 66317 [D] **F**

C *Violin Sonata in E♭, Op. 18* Chung (vln), Zimerman (pno)
(+ Respighi: *Violin Sonata in B min.*)
DG 427 617-2 [D] **F**

S *Piano Sonata, Op. 5; 5 Piano Pieces, Op. 3; *Ophelia Lieder,*
Op. 67; **Enoch Arden, Op. 38 *Schwarzkopf (sop), **Rains
(narr), Gould (pno)
Sony CD 52657, 2CDs [A] **M**

V *23 Lieder* Popp (sop), Sawallisch (pno)
EMI CDC7 49318-2 [D] **F**

140 Lieder Fischer-Dieskau (bar), Moore (pno)
EMI CMS7 63995-2, 6CDs [A] **M**

Der Abend, Op. 34/1; An den Baum Daphne; Deutsche Motette,
Op. 62; Die Göttin im Putzzimmer; Hymne, Op. 34/2 Soloists,
Copenhagen Boys' Ch, Danish National Ch & Chamber Ch,
Parkman
Chandos CHAN 9223 [D] **F**

Four Last Songs; Das Bächlein; Freundliche Vision; Die heiligen drei
Könige; Meinem Kinde; Morgen; Muttertändelei; Das Rosenband;
Ruhe, meine Seele; Waldseligkeit; Wiegenlied; Winterweihe;
Zueignung Schwarzkopf (sop), Berlin RSO, LSO, Szell
EMI CDC7 47276-2 [A] **F**

STRAVINSKY, Igor (1882–1971) RUSSIA/FRANCE/USA

○ *The Stravinsky Edition* (near-complete works under the
composer's direction or supervision) Various artists and
orchestras, Stravinsky, Craft
Sony CD46290, 22CDs [A] **M**

Ballets: *Agon; Apollo; Le Baiser de la fée; Bluebird pas-de-deux*
(arr.); *Jeu de cartes; Orpheus; Pulcinella; Scènes de ballet* LA
Festival SO, Columbia SO, Cleveland O, Chicago SO, CBC
SO, Stravinsky
Sony CD 46292, 3CDs [A] **M**

Circus Polka; Concerto for Chamber Orchestra; Concerto in D for
String Orchestra; 4 Études; Greeting Prelude; 8 Instrumental
Miniatures; 4 Norwegian Moods; Suites Nos. 1 & 2 for Small
Orchestra CBC SO, Stravinsky
Sony CD 46296 [A] **F**

Violin Concerto in D Mutter (vln), BBC SO, Lutoslawski
(+ Lutoslawski: *Chain II; Partita*)
DG 423 696-2 [D] **F**

Divertimento from 'Le Baiser de la fée' (symphonic suite); *Octet; 2*
Suites for small orchestra; L'Histoire du soldat: Concert Suite
London Sinfonietta, Chailly
Decca 433 079-2 [D] **F**

Ebony Concerto Stolzman (cl), Woody Herman's Thundering
Herd
(+ Bernstein: *Prelude, Fugue & Riffs;* Copland: *Clarinet Concerto;*
Corigliano: *Clarinet Concerto*)
RCA 09026 61360-2 [D] **F**

The Firebird (ballet); *Fireworks* (fantasy), *Op. 4; L'Histoire du*
soldat: Concert Suite; Les Noces (4 choreographic scenes); Petrushka
(ballet); *Renard* (burlesque); *The Rite of Spring* (ballet); *Scherzo*
à la Russe; *Scherzo fantastique, Op. 3 Various artists, *CBC SO,
Columbia SO, Stravinsky
Sony CD 46291, 3CDs [A] **M**

O *Firebird; Petrushka; Rite of Spring; *Apollon musagete* LPO, Haitink; *LSO, Markevitch
Philips 438 350-2, 2CDs [A] M

The Firebird (ballet); *Chant du rossignol; Fireworks; Scherzo à la Russe; Tango* LSO, Dorati
Philips Mercury 432 012-2 [A] M

Ballets: *Orpheus; Jeu de cartes* Royal Concertgebouw O, Järvi
Chandos CHAN 9014 [D] F

Petrushka (ballet); *Symphony in Three Movements* *Donohoe (pno), CBSO, Rattle
EMI CDC7 49053-2 [D] F

Ballets: *Pulcinella; Jeu de cartes* *Berganza (mez), *Davies (ten), *Shirley-Quirk (bar), LSO, Abbado
DG 423 889-2 [A] M

Pulcinella (ballet): *Suite* ASMF, Marriner
(Bizet: *Symphony in C;* Prokofiev: *Symphony No. 1*)
Decca 417 734-2 [A] M

The Rite of Spring (ballet); *Persephone* *Rolfe Johnson (ten), *Fournet (narr), *Tiffin Boys' Ch, LPO & *Ch, Nagano
Virgin VCK7 59077-2, 2CDs [D] M

*Symphony in C; Symphony in E♭, Op. 1; Symphony in Three Movements; *Symphony of Psalms* *CBC SO, Columbia SO, Stravinsky
(+ rehearsal sequences)
Sony CD 46294, 2CDs [A] M

C *Ballad; Berceuse; Chanson russe; Duo concertant; L'Histoire du soldat: Suite; Pastorale; Prélude et Ronde des princesses; Scherzo* American Chamber Players
Koch 37078-2 [D] F

Concerto for 2 Pianos; Sonata for 2 Pianos; Scherzo à la Russe; Le Sacre du printemps Ashkenazy (pno), Gavrilov (pno)
Decca 433 829-2 [D] F

Concerto for 2 Pianos; Sonata for 2 Pianos Alfons & Aloys Kontarsky (pnos)
(+ Bartók: *Sonata for 2 Pianos and Percussion*)
DG 437 027-2 [A] M

S *3 Movements from Petrushka* Pollini (pno)
(+ Boulez: *Piano Sonata No. 2;* Prokofiev: *Piano Sonata No. 7;* Webern: *Variations*)
DG 419 202-2 [A] F

V *Anthem ('The Dove Descending Breaks the Air'); Ave Maria; Babel; Cantata; Canticum Sacrum; Chorale-Variations on 'Von Himmel Hoch'; Credo; Introitus 'T.S. Eliot in memoriam'; Mass; Pater Noster; A Sermon, a Narrative and a Prayer; Threni* Various artists, Stravinsky
Sony CFD 46301, 2 CDs [A] M

Mass; Les Noces (4 choreographic scenes) Various artists, English Bach Festival O & Ch, Bernstein
DG 423 251-2 [A] M

*Mass; Symphony of Psalms; Ave Maria; *Canticum sacrum ad honorem Sancti Marci nominus; Credo; Pater Noster* *Ainsley (ten), *Roberts (bar), Westminster Cathedral Ch, O'Donnell
Hyperion CDA 66437 [D] F

SUK, Josef (1874–1935) BOHEMIA

○ *Asrael* (symphony), *Op. 27* RLPO, Pešek
Virgin VC7 59638-2 [D] **F**

Ripening (symphonic poem), *Op. 34; Praga* (symphonic poem), *Op. 26* RLPO, Pešek
Virgin VC7 59318-2 [D] **F**

C *Piano Quartet in A min., Op. 1* Domus
(+ Dvořák: *Bagatelles;* Martinů: *Piano Quartet*)
Virgin VC7 59245-2 [D] **F**

S *Piano Pieces, Op. 7; About Mother, Op. 28; Lullabies, Op. 33; Spring, Op. 22a; Summer, Op. 22b; Things lived and dreamt, Op. 30* Fingerhut (pno)
Chandos CHAN 9026/7, 2CDs [D] **F**

SULLIVAN, Sir Arthur (1842–1900) ENGLAND

○ *Cello Concerto in D; *Symphony in E (Irish); *Overture di ballo* Lloyd Webber (vcl), LSO, Mackerras; *RLPO, Groves
EMI CDM7 64726-2 [A] **M**

Overtures: *Di Ballo; The Gondoliers; HMS Pinafore; Iolanthe; Patience; The Pirates of Penzance; Princess Ida; Ruddigore; The Sorcerer; The Yeoman of the Guard* Scottish CO, Faris
Nimbus NI 5066 [D] **F**

Pineapple Poll (ballet – arr. Mackerras) RPO, Mackerras
Arabesque Z.8016 [D] **F**

✔ *16 Songs* Ommerlé (sop), Sylvan (bar), Wedow (pno)
Conifer CDCF 156 [D] **F**

SUPPÉ, Franz von (1819–1895) AUSTRIA

○ Overtures: *The Beautiful Galatea; Boccaccio; Light Cavalry; Morning, Noon and Night in Vienna; Pique Dame; Poet and Peasant* Detroit SO, Paray
(+ Auber: *Overtures: The Bronze Horse; Fra Diavolo; La Muette de Portici*)
Philips Mercury 434 309-2 [A] **M**

VENDSEN, Johan (1840–1911) NORWAY

○ *Symphonies: No. 1 in D, Op. 4; No. 2 in B♭, Op. 15; Swedish Folk Tunes* Gothenburg SO, Järvi
BIS BIS-CD 347 [D] **F**

ZYMANOWSKI, Karol (1882–1937) POLAND

○ *Violin Concertos Nos. 1, Op. 35 & 2, Op. 61; *Violin Sonata in D min., Op. 9; *King Roger* (opera): Roxana's Song* Wilkomirska (vln), Warsaw National PO, Rowicki; *Chmielewski (pno)
Polski Nagrania PNCD 064 [A] **F**

*Symphonies: No. 2 in B♭, Op. 19; *No. 3 (Song of the Night), Op. 27; Concert Overture in E, Op. 12* Polish National RSO, Kasprzyk, *Semkow
EMI CDM5 65082-2 [A] **M**

String Quartets: No. 1 in C, Op. 37; No. 2, Op. 56
Varsovia Quartet
(+ Lutoslawski: *String Quartet;* Penderecki: *String Quartet No. 2*)
Olympia OCD 328 [A] **F**
Carmina Quartet
(+ Webern: *Langsamer Satz*)
Denon CO-79462 [D] **F**

s *Études, Op. 4; Fantasy, Op. 14; Masques, Op. 34; Métopes, Op. 29*
Lee (pno)
Hyperion CDA 66409 [D] **F**

TAFFANEL, Paul (1844–1908) FRANCE

c *Wind Quintet in G min.* Ensemble Wien-Berlin
(+ Nielsen: *Wind Quintet, Op. 43*)
Sony CD 45996 [D] **F**

TAKEMITSU, Toru (born 1930) JAPAN

o *A Flock Descends into the Pentagonal Garden; Quatrain; Ring;*
Sacrifice; Stanza I; Valeria Various artists, Boston SO, Ozawa
DG 423 253-2 [A] **M**

   Rain Coming; Rain Spell; Riverrun; Tree Line London
Sinfonietta, Knussen
Virgin VC7 59020-2 [D] **F**

s *Corona; The Crossing; Far Away; Litany; Pause Uninterrupted;*
Piano Distance; Rain Tree Sketch; Les yeux clos Woodward (pno)
Etcetera KTC 1103 [D] **F**

TALLIS, Thomas (c.1505–1585) ENGLAND

v Responds: *Audivi vocem; Candidi facti; Dum transisset; Hodie*
nobis; Homo quidam; Honor, virtus; In pace; Loquebantur; Spem in
alium; Videte miraculum Taverner Ch & Consort, Parrott
EMI CDC7 49555-2 [D] **F**

   Gaude gloriosa; In jejunio; Lamentations of Jeremiah I & II;
Miserere nostri; O nata lux; O sacrum convivium; Salvatore mundi,
salva nos I & II; Suscipe quaeso Dominus; Te lucis I Taverner
Ch & Consort, Parrott
EMI CDC7 49563-2 [D] **F**

   Gaude gloriosa; Loquebantur variis linguis; Miserere nostri;
Salvator mundi, salve nos I & II; Sancte Deus; Spem in alium
Tallis Scholars, Phillips
Gimell CDGIM 006 [D] **F**

   Spem in alium; Ecce tempus idoneum; Gaude gloriosa; Loquebantur
variis linguis; O nata lux de lumine Clerkes of Oxenford,
Wulstan
(+ Sheppard: *Gaude Maria, etc.*)
Classics for Pleasure CD-CFP 4638 [A] **B**

TANEYEV, Sergey (1856–1915) RUSSIA

o *Symphony No. 4; The Oresteia* (opera): *Overture* Philharmonia O,
Järvi
Chandos CHAN 8953 [D] **F**

c *Piano Quintet in G min., Op. 30* Lowenthal (pno), Rosenthal
(vln), Kamei (vln), Thompson (vla), Kates (vcl)
Arabesque Z6539 [D] **F**

   Piano Trio in D, Op. 22 Borodin Trio
Chandos CHAN 8592 [D] **F**

   String Quartets Nos. 8 in C & 9 in A Leningrad Taneyev
Quartet
Olympia OCD 128 [A] **F**

TARTINI, Giuseppe (1692–1770) ITALY

o *Violin Concerto E min., D56; Violin Concerto in A, D96; Violin*
Concerto in A min., D113 Ughi (vln), Solisti Veneti, Scimone
Erato 2292 45380-2 [A] **M**

c *Violin Sonata in G min. (Devil's Trill); 12 Violin Sonatas and
   Pastorale, Op. 1 Nos. 2, 8, 10, 12 & 13* Locatelli Trio
   ✧ Hyperion CDA 66430 [D] **F**

   *Violin Sonatas: in A, BA4; in B♭, BB5 (Op. 5/6); in B♭, BD1; in D,
   BD19 E.* Wallfisch (vln), Locatelli Trio
   ✧ Hyperion CDA 66485 [D] **F**

TAUSKY, Vilem (born 1910) CZECHOSLOVAKIA/ENGLAND

o *Concertino* Reilly (harmonica), ASMF, Marriner
   (+Jacob: *5 Pieces;* Moody: *Little Suite;* Vaughan Williams:
   Romance)
   Chandos CHAN 8617 [D] **F**

TAVENER, John (born 1944) ENGLAND

o *The Protecting Veil; Thrinos (solo cello)* Isserlis (vcl), LSO,
   Rozhdestvensky
   (+Britten: *Cello Suite No. 3*)
   Virgin VC7 59052-2 [D] **F**

   The Repentant Thief A. Marriner (cl), LSO, Tilson Thomas
   Collins 20052 [D] **M**

   We Shall See Him As He Is BBC Welsh SO, Hickox
   Chandos CHAN 9128 [D] **F**

✔ **Ikon of Light; 2 Hymns to the Mother of God; The Lamb; The Tiger*
   *Duke Quartet members, The Sixteen, Christophers
   Collins 14052 [D] **F**

   Funeral Ikos; *Ikon of Light; Little Lamb, who made thee? Tallis
   Scholars, *Chilingirian Quartet, Phillips
   Gimell CDGIM 005 [D] **F**

   *Eonia; God is with us; Hymn for the Dormition; Hymn to the mother
   of God; Little Lamb; Love bade me welcome; Magnificat; Nunc
   Dimittis; Ode of St. Andrew; The Tiger; Today the Virgin; The
   Uncreated Eros* St. George's Chapel Ch, Robinson
   Hyperion CDA 66464 [D] **F**

TAVERNER, John (c.1490–1545) ENGLAND

✔ *Audivi vocem; Missa Gloria tibi Trinitas* The Sixteen, Christophers
   Hyperion CDA 66134 [D] **F**

   *Dum transisset Sabbatum; Ex eius tumba; Missa Sancti Wilhelmi; O
   Wilhelme* The Sixteen, Christophers
   Hyperion CDA 66427 [D] **F**

   Gaude plurimum; In pace in idipsum; Missa Corona Spinia The
   Sixteen, Christophers
   Hyperion CDA 66360 [D] **F**

   Kyrie; Missa O Michael The Sixteen, Christophers
   Hyperion CDA 66325 [D] **F**

   Mater Christi; Missa Mater Christi; O Wilhelme Christ Church
   Cathedral Ch, Darlington
   Nimbus NI 5218 [D] **F**

   *Mass 'The Western Wynde'; Alleluia, veni electa mea; O splendor
   gloriae; Te deum* The Sixteen, Christophers
   Hyperion CDA 66507 [D] **F**

TCHAIKOVSKY, Pyotr (1840–1893) RUSSIA

O *Piano Concerto No. 1; Theme and Variations, Op. 19/6* Gavrilov
(pno), Philharmonia O, Muti
(+ Balakirev: *Islamey;* Prokoviev: *Piano Concerto No. 1, etc.*)
EMI CDM7 64329-2 [A] **M**

Piano Concerto No. 1 in B♭ min., Op. 23 Wild (pno), RPO,
Fistoulari
(+ Dohnányi: *Variations on a Nursery Tune, Op. 25, etc.*)
Chesky CD 13 [A] **F**

Piano Concertos: No. 2 in G, Op. 44; No. 3 in E♭, Op. 73
Donohoe (pno), Bournemouth SO, Barshai
EMI CDC7 49940-2 [D] **F**

Piano Concerto No. 2 (arr. Siloti); **Concert Fantasia in G, Op. 56*
Gilels (pno), USSR Academic SO, Svetlanov; *Zhukov (pno),
USSR Academic SO, Kitaenko
Olympia OCD 229 [A] **F**

Violin Concerto in D, Op. 35 Milstein (vln), VPO, Abbado
(+ Mendelssohn: *Violin Concerto in E min.*)
DG 419 067-2 [A] **M**

1812 Overture, Op. 49; Francesca da Rimini (symphonic
fantasia), *Op. 32; Marche Slave, Op. 31; Romeo and Juliet* (fantasy
overture) RLPO, Edwards
EMI Eminence CD-EMX 2152 [D] **M**

*Festival Overture on the Danish National Hymn in D, Op. 15;
Hamlet: Incidental Music, Op. 67a; Mazeppa (opera): *Battle of
Poltava, Cossack Dance; Romeo and Juliet* (fantasy overture –
1869 version); *Serenade for Nikolas Rubinstein's Name Day*
*Kelly (sop), *Hammond-Stroud (bar), LSO, Simon
Chandos CHAN 8310/1, 2CDs [D] **F**

Francesca da Rimini (symphonic fantasia), *Op. 32; Hamlet*
(fantasy overture), *Op. 67* New York Stadium SO,
Stokowski
Dell'Arte CDDA9006 [A] **M**

Manfred Symphony, Op. 58 Philharmonia O, Muti
EMI CDM7 64872-2 [D] **M**

The Nutcracker (ballet), *Op. 71* LSO, Previn
Classics for Pleasure CFPD 4706, 2 CDs [A] **B**

The Nutcracker (ballet), *Op. 71; Serenade for Strings* LSO,
Dorati
Philips Mercury 432 750-2, 2CDs [A] **M**

Extended extracts from: *The Nutcracker; Sleeping Beauty; Swan
Lake* LSO, Previn
EMI CZS7 62816-2, 2CDs [A] **B**

Suites from: *The Nutcracker; Sleeping Beauty; Swan Lake* BPO,
Rostropovich
DG 429 097-2 [A] **M**

Serenade for Strings in C, Op. 48
BPO, Karajan
(+ Dvořák: *Serenade for Strings*)
DG 400 038-2 [D] **F**
Moscow Soloists, Bashmet
(+ Grieg: *Holberg Suite, Op. 40; 2 Norwegian Melodies, Op. 63*)
RCA RD 60368 [D] **F**

Sleeping Beauty (ballet), *Op. 66* National PO, Bonynge
(+ Meyerbeer: *Les Patineurs*)
Decca 425 468-2, 3CDs [A] M

Swan Lake (ballet), *Op. 20* National PO, Bonynge
(+ Massenet: *Le Cigale*)
Decca 425 413-2, 3CDs [A] F

Suites Nos. 1–4 USSR State Academy SO, Svetlanov
Olympia OCD 110, 2CDs [A] F

Suite No. 3 in G, Op. 55 USSR State Academy SO, Svetlanov
(+ Arensky: *Violin Concerto in A min.*)
Olympia OCD 106 [A] F

Symphonies Nos. 1–6 BPO, Karajan
DG 429 675-2, 4CDs [A] M

Symphony No. 2 in C min., Op. 17 (Little Russian) (original
version)*; Serenade for Nikolas Rubinstein's Name Day; Mazeppa*
(opera)*: Battle of Poltara & Cossack Dance; Festival Overture on
the Danish National Anthem in D, Op. 15* LSO, Simon
Chandos CHAN 9190 [D] F

Symphony No. 3 in D (Polish), Op. 29; Capriccio italien, Op. 45
BPO, Karajan
DG 419 178-2 [A] F

Symphonies Nos. 4–6 Leningrad PO, Mravinsky
DG 419 745-2, 2CDs [A] F

Symphony No. 4 in F min., Op. 36; Capriccio italien, Op. 45
BPO, Karajan
DG 419 872-2 [A] M

*Symphony No. 5 in E min., Op. 64; *Marche Slave, Op. 31;
Eugene Onegin (opera)*: Polonaise & Waltz* LSO, *Minneapolis
SO, Dorati
Philips Mercury 434 305-2 [A] M

Symphony No. 6 in B min. (Pathétique), Op. 74 BPO, Karajan
DG 419 486-2 [A] M

Variations on a Rococo Theme, Op. 33 Rostropovich (vcl), BPO,
Karajan
(+ Dvořák: *Cello Concerto*)
DG 415 819-2 [A] F

Variations on a Rococo Theme (original version); *Andante
Cantabile, Op. 11; Nocturne, Op. 19/4; Pezzo Capriccioso, Op. 62*
Isserlis (vcl), COE, Gardiner
Virgin VC7 59595-2 [D] F (see collections)

*String Quartets Nos. 1–3; String Quartet in Bb; *Souvenir de
Florence, Op. 70* Borodin Quartet, *Yurov (vla), *Milman (vcl)
Teldec 4509 90422-2, 2 CDs [D] F

String Quartets: No. 1 in D, Op. 11; No. 2 in F, Op. 22 Keller
Quartet
Erato 2292-45965-2 [D] F

String Quartet No. 3 in Eb, Op. 30; Adagio Molto in Bb
Shostakovich Quartet
(+ Grechaninov: *String Quartet No. 1*)
Olympia OCD 522 [A] F

Souvenir de Florence, Op. 70 Raphael Ensemble
(+ Arensky: *Quartet in A min.*)
Hyperion CDA 66648 [D] F

S *Complete Piano Works* Postnikova (pno)
Erato 2292-45969-2, 7CDs [D] **F**

*Album for the Young, Op. 39; *Album for the Young, Op. 39* (arr.
Dubinsky) Edlina (pno), *Dubinsky (vln), Zweig (vln),
Horner (vla), Turovsky (vcl)
Chandos CHAN 8365 [D] **F**

Piano Sonata in G, Op. 37; The Seasons, Op. 37b Katin (pno)
Olympia OCD 192 [D] **F**

Sleeping Beauty: Suite (arr. Pletnev) Pletnev (pno)
(+ Mussorgsky: *Pictures at an Exhibition*)
Virgin VC7 59611-2 [D] **F**

Piano Recital Richter (pno)
Olympia OCD 334 [D] **F**

V *22 Songs* Rodgers (sop), Vignoles (pno
Hyperion CDA 66617 [D] **F**

28 Songs Söderström (sop), Ashkenazy (pno)
Decca 436 204-2 [A/D] **M**

Songs: *Op. 6/4 & 6; Op. 25/1; Op. 28/6; Op. 38/1; Op. 60/4 & 11;
Op. 63/1; Op. 73/6* Hvorostovsky (bar), Boshniakovich (pno)
(+ Rachmaninov: *Songs*)
Philips 432 119-2 [D] **F**

TCHEREPNIN, Nikolay (1873–1945) RUSSIA

O *Piano Concertos Nos. 2, 3 & 5* McLachlan (pno), Chethams SO,
Clayton
Olympia OCD 439 [D] **F**

Le Pavillon d'Armide (ballet), *Op. 29: Suite* Leningrad PO,
Fedotov
(+ Conus: *Violin Concerto;* Glière: *Solemn Overture*)
Olympia OCD 151 [A] **F**

TELEMANN, Georg Philipp (1681–1767) GERMANY

O *Chandos Telemann Edition* Various artists, Collegium Musicum
90, Standage (vln/dir)
Volume 1: La Changeante
◇ CHAN 0519 [D] **F**
Volume 2: Ouverture burlesque
◇ CHAN 0512 [D] **F**
Volume 3: Domestic Music
◇ CHAN 0525 [D] **F**
Volume 4: Orchestral Music
◇ CHAN 0547 [D] **F**
Volume 5: Sonates Corellisantes, etc.
◇ CHAN 0549 [D] **F**

*Flute Concerto No. 4 in D; Recorder and Flute Concerto in E min.;
Trumpet Concerto in D; Violin, Cello and Trumpet Concerto in D;
Concerto No. 1 in D min. for 2 Chalumeaux; Concerto for 3 Oboes
and 3 Violins in B♭* Soloists, Cologne Musica Antiqua, Goebel
◇ DG Archiv 419 633-2 [D] **F**

*Flute, Oboe d'amore and Viola d'amore Concerto in E; Recorder
and Flute Concerto in E min.; Concerto for Strings in G (Polonois);
Concerto No. 1 in D for 3 Trumpets; Quartet in B♭* Soloists, AAM,
Hogwood
◇ L'Oiseau-Lyre 411 949-2 [D] **F**

o *Horn Concerto in D; Concerto for 2 Horns in E♭; Concerto No. 1 for 2 Horns and 2 Oboes in D; Concerto for 3 Horns and Violin in D; Overture-suite in F for 2 Horns* Baumann (hn), T. Brown (hn), Hill (hn), ASMF, I. Brown
Philips 412 226-2 [D] **F**

Double Horn Concerto; Triple Violin and Oboe Concerto; Recorder and Bassoon Concerto; Quadruple Violin Concerto Soloists, VCM, Harnoncourt
✧ Teldec 2292-43543-2 [A] **M**

Oboe Concertos: No. 2 in C min.; No. 3 in D; No. 4 in D min.; No. 6 in E min.; No. 8 in F min. Holliger (ob), ASMF, Brown
Philips 412 879-2 [D] **F**

Recorder and Bassoon Concerto in F; Recorder and Flute Concerto in E min.; Overture-suite in A min. Petri (rec), Bennett (fl), Thunemann (bsn), ASMF, Brown
Philips 410 041-2 [D] **F**

Violin Concertos: No. 2 in D; No. 3 in E; No. 9 in G; No. 10 in G min.; No. 14 in B♭ Brown (vln/dir), ASMF
Philips 411 125-2 [D] **F**

2 Oboe and Trumpet Concerto No. 1 Wilbraham (tpt), ASMF, Marriner
(+ Albinoni: *Trumpet Concerto in C;* Haydn: *Trumpet Concerto in E♭;* Hummel: *Trumpet Concerto in E♭;* L. Mozart: *Trumpet Concerto in D*)
Decca 417 761-2 [A] **M**

Darmstadt Overtures; Tafelmusik (excerpts) Concerto Amsterdam, Brüggen; VCM, Harnoncourt
✧ Teldec 2292-42723-2, 3CDs [A] **M**

Tafelmusik (Productions 1–3) VCM, Harnoncourt
✧ Teldec 2292 445688-2, 4CDs [D] **F**

Tafelmusik: Overtures Concerto Amsterdam, Brüggen
✧ Teldec 2292-43546-2 [A] **M**

c *Concerto da camera in A min.; Quartet in F; Quartet in G min.; Trio sonatas in D min.; in F; in G min.* Chandos Baroque Players
✧ Hyperion CDA 66195 [D] **F**

6 Paris Quartets Nos. 1 & 3; 6 'Nouveaux' Paris Quartets Nos. 2 & 6 Hazelzet (fl), Trio Sonnerie
✧ Virgin VC7 59049-2 [D] **F**

6 'Nouveaux' Paris Quartets Nos. 3 & 4; Quadri: Concerto secondo & Première Suite Hazelzet (fl), Trio Sonnerie
✧ Virgin VC5 45020-2 [D] **F**

Recorder Sonatas in A; in C; in C; in D min.; in F; in F min.; in F min. Schneider (rec), Zipperling (gmba), Hoeran (hpd)
✧ DHM GD 77153 [A] **M**

12 Sonate Melodische (nos. 3–7 & 10) Brüggen (rec), de Vries (ob), Bylsma (vcl), Moller (vcl), Leonhardt (hpd), van Asperen (hpd), Boston Museum Trio
✧ RCA GD 71957 [A] **M**

6 Sonates sans basses for 2 recorders Petri (rec), Selin (rec)
RCA RD 87903 [D] **F**

C   *Trio Sonatas in A min.; in C min.; in C min.; in E min.; in F; in F*
Cologne Camerata
DHM GD 77017 [A] **M**

S   *12 Fantasias for Solo Flute* Rampal (fl)
Denon CO-1790 [D] **F**

V   *Der für die Sünden der Welt (Brockes Passion)* Blatmann (sop),
Farkas (sop), Zádori (sop), Markert (cont), Popken (alt),
Klietmann (ten), Capella Savaria, McGegan
✧ Hungaroton HCD 31130-2, 3CDs [D] **F**

    Die Donner Ode (cantata); *Deus judicum tuum* (motet) Kwella
(sop), Denley (alt), Tucker (ten), Roberts (bs), George (bs),
Collegium Musicum 90, Hickox
✧ Chandos CHAN 0548 [D] **F**

    Ino (cantata) Alexander (sop), Hampson (bar), VCM,
Harnoncourt
(+ Handel: *Apollo e Dafne*)
✧ Teldec 2292-44633-2 [D] **F**

    Die Tageszeiten (cantata) Bach (sop), Georg (mez), Blochwitz
(ten), Mannov (bs), Freiburg Collegium Musicum,
Hengelbrock
✧ DHM RD 77092 [D] **F**

THOMSON, Virgil (1896–1989) USA

O   *Film Music: Louisiana Story (Suite); The Plow that Broke the
Plains (Suite); Power Among Men (Fugues & Cantilenas)* New
London O, Corp
Hyperion CDA 66576 [D] **F**

    *Portraits Nos. 1, 17 & 21; Sea Piece with Birds; The Seine at Night;
Wheat Field at Noon; *5 Blake Songs* Philadelphia O, Thomson;
*Harrell, Philadelphia, Ormandy
(+ Bloch: *3 Jewish Poems*)
Bay Cities BCD-1006 [A] **F**

TIOMKIN, Dmitri (1894–1979) RUSSIA/USA

O   Film music excerpts: *The Fall of the Roman Empire; The Guns of
Navarone; A President's Country; Rhapsody of Steel; Wild is the
Wind* Royal College of Music O, Willcocks
Unicorn-Kanchana DKPCD 9047 [D] **F**

TIPPETT, Michael (born 1905) ENGLAND

O   **Piano Concerto; Triple Concerto* *Tirimo (pno), Kovacic (vln),
Caussé (vla), Baillie (vcl), BBC PO, Tippett
Nimbus NI 5301 [D] **F**

    Symphony No. 3; Praeludium Robinson (sop), Bournemouth
SO, Hickox
Chandos CHAN 9276 [D] **F**

    *Symphony No. 4; *Fantasia on a Theme of Handel; Fantasia
Concertante on a Theme of Corelli* *Shelley (pno), Bournemouth
SO, Hickox
Chandos CHAN 9233 [D] **F**

C   *String Quartets Nos. 1–4* Britten Quartet
Collins 70062, 2CDs [D] **F**

    String Quartet No. 4 Lindsay Quartet
(+ Britten: *String Quartet No. 3*)
ASV CDDCA 608 [D] **F**

C   *String Quartet No. 5* Lindsay Quartet
(+ Wood: *String Quartet in A min., etc.*)
ASV CDDCA 879 [D] **F**

S   *Piano Sonatas Nos. 1–4* Crossley (pno)
CRD 3430/1, 2CDs [D] **F**

V   *Bonny at Morn; Crown of the Year; Dance, Clarion Air; Music; 5
Negro Spirituals from 'A Child of our Time'; The Weeping Babe*
Christ Church Cathedral Ch, Darlington
Nimbus NI 5266 [D] **F**

     A Child of our Time (oratorio) Robinson (sop), Walker (mez),
Garrison (ten), Cheek (bs), CBSO & Ch, Tippett
Collins 13392 [D] **F**

     A Mask of Time Robinson (sop), Walker (mez), Tear (ten),
Cheek (bs), BBC Singers, BBC SO, A. Davis
EMI CMS7 64711-2, 2CDs [D] **F**

TISHCHENKO, Boris (born 1939) RUSSIA

O   *Violin Concerto No. 2* Stadler (vln), Leningrad PO, Sinaisky
Olympia OCD 123 [A] **F**

     Symphony No. 5 USSR Ministry of Culture SO,
Rozhdestvensky
Olympia OCD 213 [A] **F**

TOMKINS, Thomas (1572–1656) WALES

V   *Above the Stars; Almighty God; Behold, the hour cometh; Glory be to
God; My beloved spake; My Shepherd is the living Lord; O God, the
proud; O sing unto the Lord; Sing unto God; Then David mourned;
Third Service; When David heard* St. George's Chapel Ch,
Robinson
Hyperion CDA 66345 [D] **F**

TORELLI, Giuseppe (1658–1709) ITALY

O   *Concerti grossi, Op. 8: Nos. 2, 3, 6, 8, 9 & 12* I Musici
Philips 432 118-2 [D] **F**

TORKE, Michael (born 1961) USA

O   *Adjustable Wrench; *Rust; Slate; Vanada; *The Yellow Pages*
Torke (pno), London Sinfonietta, Nagano, *Miller
Argo 430 209-2 [D] **F**

     Ash; Bright Blue Music; Ecstatic Orange; Green; Purple Baltimore
SO, Zinman
Argo 433 071-2 [D] **F**

TOURNEMIRE, Charles (1870–1939) FRANCE

S   *Suite évocatrice, Op. 74* Filsell (org)
(+ Vierne: *Organ Symphony No. 3;* Widor: *Organ Symphony No. 9*)
Herald HAVPCD 145 [D] **F**

TUBIN, Eduard (1905–1982) ESTONIA

O   *Ballade for Violin and Orchestra; Double-bass Concerto; Violin
Concerto No. 2; Estonian Dance Suite; Valse triste* Garcia (vln),
Ehren (db), Gothenburg SO, Järvi
BIS BIS-CD 337 [D] **F**

     Balalaika Concerto; Music for Strings; Symphony No. 1
Sheynkman (balalaika), Gothenburg SO, Järvi
BIS BIS-CD 351 [D] **F**

O *Piano Concerto; Sinfonietta on Estonian Motifs; Symphony No. 7
*Pöntinen (pno), Gothenburg SO, Järvi
BIS BIS-CD 401 [D] **F**

*Violin Concerto No. 1; Prelude solennel; Suite on Estonian Dances
*Lubotsky (vln), Gothenburg SO, Järvi
BIS BIS-CD 286 [D] **F**

Symphonies Nos. 2 & 6 Swedish RSO, Järvi
BIS BIS-CD 304 [D] **F**

Symphonies Nos. 3 & 8 Swedish RSO, Järvi
BIS BIS-CD 342 [D] **F**

Symphonies Nos. *4 & 9; Toccata *Bergen SO, Gothenberg SO,
Järvi
BIS BIS-CD 227 [D] **F**

Symphony No. 5; Kratt Bamberg SNO, Järvi
BIS BIS-CD 306 [D] **F**

*Symphony No. 10; Requiem for Fallen Soldiers *Gothenberg
SO, Lundin (cont), Rydell (bar), Hardenberger (tpt), Lund
Choral Society, Järvi
BIS BIS-CD 297 [D] **F**

S Piano Sonatas Nos. 1 & 2; Album Leaf; Ballad on a Theme by Mart
Saar; Estonian Folkdances; 4 Folksongs; A Little March; Lullaby; 3
Pieces for Children; Prelude; 6 Preludes; 7 Preludes; Sonatina in D
min.; Suite on Estonian Shepherd Melodies; Variations on an
Estonian Folktune Rumessen (pno)
BIS BIS-CD 414/6, 3CDs [D] **F**

TURINA, Joaquín (1882–1949) SPAIN

O Danzas fantásticas, Op. 22; La Procesión del Rocío, Op. 9; Ritmos
(fantasía coreográfica), Op. 43; Sinfonía Sevillana, Op. 23
Bamberg SO, Almeida
RCA RD 60895 [D] **F**

Piano Trio No. 1, Op. 35 Borodin Trio
(+ Debussy: Piano Trio; Martin: Piano Trio)
Chandos CHAN 9016 [D] **F**

TURNAGE, Mark Anthony (born 1960) ENGLAND

O 3 Screaming Popes CBSO, Rattle
EMI TSP2 04681-2 [D] **M**

TYE, Christopher (c.1505–c.1572) ENGLAND

C Amavit; Christus resurgens; 4 Dum transissets; In nomine a 4; In
nomine a 6; 19 In nomines; Laudes deo; O lux; Rubem quem; Sit fast
Hesperion XX, Savall
Astrée Auvidis E8708 [D] **F**

V Mass 'Euge bone' Clerkes of Oxenford, Wulstan
(+ Sheppard: Gaude vir Christophera; In manus tuas II; Libera
nos, salva nos I & II; Regis Tharsis)
Proudsound PROUDCD 126 [D] **F**

Christ rising again; Deliver us; From the depth; Give alms; Gloria
laus; I lift my heart; In pace; Kyrie; Mass Euge Bone; Nunc dimittis;
Omnes gentes; Quaesumus; To Father Cambridge University
Chamber Ch, Brown
Gamut GAMCD 519 [D] **F**

v *Mass: Western Wynde; Christ rising again; My trust, O Lord; Omnes gentes, plaudite; Peccavimus cum patribus* New College Ch, Higginbottom
CRD 3405 [A] **F**

VAČKÁŘ, Dalibor (1906–1984) BOHEMIA

o *Trumpet, Piano and Percussion Concerto* Wallace (tpt/dir), Kvapil (pno), Glennie (perc), Wallace Collection
(+ Janáček: *Capriccio;* Hindemith: *Concert Music, Op. 49*)
Nimbus NI 5103 [D] **F**

VARÈSE, Edgar (1883–1965) FRANCE/USA

o *Ameriques; Arcana; Ionisation; Intégrales; *Density 21.5; Offrandes* Yakar (sop), NYPO, Ensemble InterContemporain, Boulez; *Beauregard (fl)
Sony CD45844 [A/D] **M**

Ameriques; Arcana; Hyperprism; Octandre; Offrandes Bryn-Julson (sop), French National O, Nagano
Erato 4509 92137-2 [D] **F**

c *Ionisation* Kocsis (pno), Amadinda Percussion Group
(+ Cage: *Amores; Double Music; Third Construction; 4'33";* Chavez: *Toccata*)
Hungaroton HCD 12991 [D] **F**

VAUGHAN WILLIAMS, Ralph (1872–1958) ENGLAND

o *Oboe Concerto; Fantasia on a Theme by Thomas Tallis; Fantasia on Greensleeves; The Lark Ascending; 5 Variants of Dives and Lazarus; The Wasps: Overture* Maurice Bourgue (ob), English String O, Boughton
Nimbus NI 7013 [D] **F**

Piano Concerto in C Shelley (pno), RPO, Handley
(+ Foulds: *Dynamic Triptych*)
Lyrita SRCD 211 [A] **F**

*Double Piano Concerto; Symphony No. 5 in D *Markham (pno), *Broadway (pno), RPO, Menuhin
Virgin VJ5 61105-2 [D] **M**

English Folksong Suite; Fantasia on Greensleeves; In the Fen Country; The Lark Ascending; Norfolk Rhapsody No. 1; Serenade to Music NPO, LPO, LSO, Boult
EMI CDM7 64022-2 [A] **M**

*Fantasia on a Theme by Thomas Tallis; Fantasia on Greensleeves *Allegri Quartet, Sinfonia of London, Barbirolli
(+ Elgar: *Introduction and Allegro; Serenade in E min.*)
EMI CDC7 47537-2 [A] **M**

Job (a masque for dancing) Nolan (vln), LPO, Handley
Classics for Pleasure CD-CFP 4603 [D] **B**

*The Lark Ascending; 5 Variants on 'Dives and Lazarus'; The Wasps (Aristophanic Suite) *Nolan (vln), LPO, Handley
EMI Eminence CD-EMX 9508 [D] **M**

Romance in D♭ Reilly (harmonica), ASMF, Marriner
(+ Jacob: *5 pieces;* Moody: *Little Suite;* Tausky: *Concertino*)
Chandos CHAN 8617 [D] **F**

Symphony No. 1 (A Sea Symphony) Harper (sop), Shirley-Quirk (bar), LSO & Chorus, Previn
RCA GD90500 [A] **M**

O   *Symphony No. 2 (A London Symphony); *Concerto accademico in D min.; The Wasps (Aristophanic Suite): Overture* *Buswell (vln), LSO, Previn
RCA GD90501 [A] **M**

Symphonies: No. 2 (A London Symphony); No. 8 in G min. Hallé O, Barbirolli
EMI CDM7 64197-2 [A] **M**

Symphonies: No. 3 (A Pastoral Symphony); No. 4 in F min. LSO, Previn
RCA GD90503 [A] **M**

Symphonies: No. 4 in F min.; No. 5 in D BBC PO, A. Davis
Teldec 4509 90844-2 [D] **F**

Symphony No. 5 in D; Elizabeth of England (film music): Suite LSO, Previn
RCA GD90506 [A] **M**

Symphonies: No. 5 in D; No. 6 in E min. Philharmonia O, Slatkin
RCA RD 60556 [D] **F**

Symphony No. 6 in E min.; Fantasia on a Theme by Thomas Tallis; *The Lark Ascending *Little (vln), BBC SO, A. Davis
Teldec 9031-73127-2 [D] **F**

Symphonies: No. 6 in E min.; No. 9 in E min. LSO, Previn
RCA GD90508 [A] **M**

Symphony No. 7 (Sinfonia Antartica) Armstrong (sop), LPO & Ch, Haitink
EMI CDC7 47516-2 [D] **F**

Symphonies: No. 7 (Sinfonia Antartica); No. 8 in D min. Richardson (narr), Harper (sop), LSO & Ch, Previn
RCA GD90510 [A] **M**

Symphonies: No. 8 in D min.; No. 9 in E min. LPO, Boult
EMI CDM7 64021-2 [A] **M**

The Wasps (Aristophanic Suite): Overture LSO, Previn
(+ Walton: *Symphony No. 1*)
RCA GD87830 [A] **M**

C   **Phantasy Quintet; String Quartets Nos. 1 & 2* *Blume (vla), English Quartet
Unicorn-Kanchana DKPCD 9076 [D] **F**

String Quartet No. 1; *On Wenlock Edge *Langridge (ten), *Shelley (pno), Britten Quartet
(+ Ravel: *String Quartet*)
EMI CDC7 54346-2 [D] **F**

6 Studies in English Folksong Hilton (cl), Swallow (pno)
(+ Bax: *Clarinet Sonata*; Bliss: *Clarinet Quintet*)
Chandos CHAN 8683 [D] **F**

V   **10 Blake Songs; **Songs of Travel; Songs: Linden Lea; Orpheus with his Lute; Silent Noon; The Water Mill* Tear (ten), *Black (ob), **Ledger (pno)
(+ Butterworth: *A Shropshire Lad*)
Decca 430 368-2 [A] **M**

3 Choral Hymns; The Hundredth Psalm; Magnificat; The Shepherds of the Delectable Mountains; A Song of Thanksgiving Gielgud (spkr), Dawson (sop), Wyn-Rogers (cont), Bowen (ten),

J. Best (bs), Corydon Singers, City of London Sinfonia, Best
Hyperion CDA 66569 [D] **F**

V   *Dona nobis pacem; 4 Hymns; O Clap your Hands; Lord, Thou hast been our refuge; Toward the Unknown Region* Howarth (sop), Ainsley (ten), Allen (bar), Corydon Singers & O, Best
Hyperion CDA 66655 [D] **F**

Hodie (A Christmas Cantata); Fantasia on Christmas Carols Gale (sop), Tear (ten), Roberts (bs), LSO & Ch, Hickox
EMI CDC7 54128-2 [D] **F**

Lord, Thou hast been our refuge; Prayer to the Father of Heaven; A Vision of Aeroplanes Finzi Singers, Spicer
(+ Howells: *Requiem, etc.*)
Chandos CHAN 9019 [D] **F**

Mass in G min.; Te Deum in G Corydon Singers, Best
(+ Howells: *Requiem*)
Hyperion CDA 66076 [A] **F**

On Wenlock Edge Thompson (ten), Delmé Quartet, Burnside (pno)
(+ Gurney: *Ludlow and Teme; Western Playland*)
Hyperion CDA 66385 [D] **F**

*Serenade to Music; *Flos campi; Fantasia on Christmas Carols; 5 Mystical Songs* *Imai (vla), Allen (bar), Corydon Singers, Soloists, ECO, Best
Hyperion CDA 66420 [D] **F**

*5 Tudor Portraits; *Benedicite; **5 Variants of 'Dives and Lazarus'* Bainbridge (sop), Carol Case (bar), *Harper (sop), Bach Ch, NPO, *LSO, Willcocks; **Jacques O, Willcocks
EMI CDM7 64722-2 [A] **M**

VERDI, Giuseppe (1813–1901) ITALY

O   Opera Overtures and Preludes: *Un ballo in maschera; La Battaglia di Legnano; Il Corsaro; Ernani; La forza del destino; Luisa Miller; Macbeth; I Masnadieri; Nabucco; Rigoletto; La Traviata; I Vespri Siciliani* BPO, Karajan
DG 419 622-2 [A] **F**

C   *String Quartet in E min.* Delmé Quartet
(+ R. Strauss: *String Quartet in A*)
Hyperion CDA 66317 [D] **F**

V   *Messa da Requiem; 4 Sacred Pieces* Studer (sop), Lipovšek (cont), Carreras (ten), Raimondi (bs), Vienna State Opera Ch, VPO, Abbado
DG 435 884-2, 2CDs [D] **F**

VICTORIA, Tomás Luis de (1548–1611) SPAIN

V   *Ascendens Christus; Missa Ascendens Christus; Missa O magnum mysterium; O magnum mysterium* (motet) Westminster Cathedral Ch, Hill
Hyperion CDA 66190 [D] **F**

Ave Maria; Ave maris stella; Missa Vidi speciosam; Ne timeas; Sancta Maria; Vidi speciosam Westminster Cathedral Ch, Hill
Hyperion CDA 66129 [D] **F**

Missa Ave maris stella; Missa O Quam gloriosum; O Quam gloriosum (motet) Westminster Cathedral Ch, Hill
Hyperion CDA 66114 [D] **F**

V   *Nigra sum* Tallis Scholars, Phillips
(+ De Silva: *Nigra sum;* Lhéritier: *Nigra sum;* Palestrina: *Missa Nigra sum*)
Gimell CDGIM 003 [D] **F**

Officium defunctorum Westminster Cathedral Ch, Hill
Hyperion CDA 66250 [D] **F**

Officium Hebdomadae Sanctae (Tenebrae responses)
Tallis Scholars, Philips
Gimell CDGIM 022 [D] **F**
Westminster Cathedral Ch, Hill
Hyperion CDA 66304 [D] **F**

VIERNE, Louis (1870–1937) FRANCE

C   *Piano Quintet in C min., Op. 42; Violin Sonata, Op. 23* Charlier
(vln), Hubeau (pno), Viotti Quartet
Erato 2292-45524-2 [D] **F**

S   *24 Pièces de fantaisie, Opp. 51 & 53–55* Latry (org)
BNL 112742, 2CDs [D] **F**

Organ Symphonies: No. 1 in D min., Op. 14; No. 2 in E min., Op. 20 Sanger (org)
Meridian CDE 84192 [A] **F**

Organ Symphonies: No. 3 in F♯ min., Op. 28; No. 4 in G min., Op. 32 Sanger (org)
Meridian CDE 84176 [A] **F**

Organ Symphony No. 3 in F♯ min., Op. 28 Filsell (org)
(+ Tournemire: *Suite Evocatrice;* Widor: *Organ Symphony No. 9*)
Herald HAVPCD 145 [D] **F**

Organ Symphonies: No. 5 in A min., Op. 47; No. 6 in B min., Op. 59 Sanger (org)
Meridian CDE 84171 [A] **F**

VIEUXTEMPS, Henry (1820–1881) BELGIUM

O   *Cello Concertos: No. 1 in A min., Op. 46; No. 2 in B min., Op. 50*
Schiff (vcl), Stuttgart RSO, Marriner
EMI CDC7 47761-2 [D] **F**

Fantasia apassionata, Op. 35 Kremer (vln), LSO, Chailly
(+ Chausson: *Poème;* Milhaud: *Le Boeuf sur le toit: Le printemps;* Satie: *Choses vues à droite et à gauche*)
Philips 432 513-2 [A] **F**

VILLA-LOBOS, Heitor (1887–1959) BRAZIL

O   **Guitar Concerto; 12 Études; 5 Preludes* Bream (gtr), LSO, Previn
RCA 09026 61604-2 [A] **M**

Piano Concertos Nos. 1–5 Ortiz (pno), RPO, Gómez-Martínez
Decca 430 628-2, 2CDs [D] **F**

C   *Assobio a jato; Bachianas Brasileiras No. 6; Canção do amor; Chôros No. 2; Distribuição de flores; Modinha; Wind Quintet; Wind Trio* Bennett (fl), Tunnell (vcl), O'Neill (bsn), Wynberg (gtr), King (cl), Black (ob), Knight (cor ang)
Hyperion CDA 66295 [D] **F**

Bachianas Brasileiras Nos. 1 & *5; Preludes and Fugues from Bach's 48; Suite for Voice and Violin *Gomez (sop), Manning (vln), Pleeth Cello Octet
Hyperion CDA 66257 [D] **F**

C *Bachianas Brasileiras Nos. 1, *5 & 7* *Hendricks (sop), RPO, Bátiz
EMI CDC7 47433-2 [D] **F**

*Violin Sonatas Nos. 1–3; Danças características africanas; Suite floral *Yao (vln), Heller (pno)
Etcetera KTC 1101 [D] **F**

String Quartets Nos. 1–3 Bessler-Reis Quartet
Chant du Monde LDC 278 1052 [D] **F**

String Quartets Nos. 4–6 Bessler-Reis Quartet
Chant du Monde LDC 278 901 [D] **F**

String Quartets Nos. 15–17 Bessler-Reis Quartet
Chant du Monde LDC 278 948 [D] **F**

S *Bachianas Brasileiras No. 4; Chôros No. 5; Cicio brasileiro; Valsa da dor* Petchersky (pno)
ASV CDDCA 607 [D] **F**

V *Alleluia; Ave Maria; Bendita sabedoria; Cor dulce, cor amabile; Magnificat; Missa São Sebastião; Panis angelicus; Pater noster; Praesepe; Sub tuum* Corydon Singers, Best
Hyperion CDA 66638 [D] **F**

VIVALDI, Antonio (1678–1741) ITALY

O *The Complete Vivaldi Edition* Various artists
Philips 426 925-2, 19CDs [A] **M**

12 Concerti, Op. 3 (L'Estro armonico)
ASMF, Marriner
Decca 430 557-2, 2CDs [A] **M**
English Concert, Pinnock
✧ DG Archiv 423 094-2, 2CDs [D] **F**

12 Concerti, Op. 4 (La Stravaganza)
ASMF, Marriner
Decca 430 566-2, 2CDs [A] **M**
AAM, Hogwood
✧ L'Oiseau-Lyre 417 502-2, 2CDs [D] **F**

6 Violin Concerti, Op. 6 Carmirelli (vln), I Musici
Philips 426 939-2 [A] **M**

12 Concerti, Op. 7 Schellenberger (ob), I Solisti Italiani
Denon CO-75498/9, 2 CDs [D] **F**

12 Concerti, Op. 8 Accardo (vln), Holliger (ob), I Musici
Philips 426 940-2, 2CDs [A] **M**

4 Concerti, Op. 8 Nos. 1–4 (Four Seasons) Loveday (vln), ASMF, Marriner
Decca 414 486-2 [A] **F**

12 Concerti, Op. 9 (La Cetra) Standage (vln), AAM, Hogwood
✧ L'Oiseau-Lyre 421 366-2, 2 CDs [D] **F**

6 Flute Concerti, Op. 10 Beznosiuk (fl), English Concert, Pinnock
✧ DG Archiv 423 702-2 [D] **F**

6 Concerti, Op. 11 Ritchie (vln), de Bruine (ob), AAM, Hogwood
✧ L'Oiseau-Lyre 436 172-2 [D] **F**

6 Violin Concerti, Op. 12 Accardo (vln), I Musici
Philips 426 951-2 [A] **M**

○ *Complete Bassoon Concerti, RV466–504* Smith (bsn), ECO,
Ledger; Zagreb Soloists, Ninic
ASV CDDCX 615, 6CDs [D] **M**

*Cello Concerti: in C, RV399; in C min., RV401; in D min., RV405;
in B♭, RV423; in F, RV538: Largo; *Concerto for Cello and
Bassoon in E min., RV409* Harnoy (vcl), *McKay (bsn),
Toronto CO, Robinson
RCA RD 87774 [D] **F**

*Cello Concerti: in C min., RV402; in D, RV403; in D min., RV406;
in F, RV412; in G, RV414; in A min., RV422; in B min., RV424*
Harnoy (vcl), Toronto CO, Robinson
RCA RD 60155 [D] **F**

*Cello Concerti: in C min., RV401; in F, RV412; in G, RV413; in G
min., RV416; in A min., RV418; in B min., RV424* Coin (vcl),
AAM, Hogwood
✧ L'Oiseau-Lyre 421 732-2 [D] **F**

*Flute Concerti: in D, RV427; in D, RV429; in E min., RV431; in E
min., RV432; in G, RV436; in G, RV438a; in G, RV438; in A min.,
RV440; in C min., RV441* Rampal (fl), I Solisti Veneti, Scimone
Sony/CBS CD 45623, 2CDs [D] **M**

*Mandolin Concerto in C, RV425; Double Mandolin Concerto in G,
RV532; Viola d'amore and Lute Concerto in D min., RV540;
Chamber Concertos in D, RV93; Trio Sonatas in C, RV82; in G
min., RV85* Jeffrey (mandolin), O'Dette (mandolin), Parley of
Instruments, Goodman, Holman
✧ Hyperion CDA 66160 [D] **F**

*Oboe Concerti: in C, RV446; in C, RV447; in C, RV452; in A min.,
RV461* Holliger (ob), I Musici
Philips 411 480-2 [D] **F**

*Recorder Concerti: in C min., RV441; in F, RV442; in C, RV443;
in C, RV444; in A min., RV445; Chamber Concerto, RV108*
Holstag (rec), Parley of Instruments, Holman
✧ Hyperion CDA 66328 [D] **F**

String Concerti: RV117, 134, 143, 159, 413, 418, 547, 549 & 575
Tafelmusik, Lamon
✧ Sony CD 48044 [D] **F**

*Viola d'amore Concerti: in D, RV392; in D min., RV393; in D min.,
RV394; in D min., RV395; in A, RV396; in A min., RV397* Paris
(gmba), I Musici
Philips 422 051-2 [D] **F**

*Violin Concerti: in C min. (Il sospetto), RV199; in D
(L'inquietudine), RV234; in E (Il riposo), RV270; in E
(L'amoroso), RV271; in E min. (Il favorito), RV277* Vicari (vln),
Gallozi (vln), Cotogni (vln), Ayo (vln), Michelucci (vln),
I Musici
Philips 422 493-2 [A] **M**

*Double Concerti for: 2 Cellos in G min., RV531; 2 Flutes in C,
RV533; 2 Oboes in D min., RV535; 2 Mandolins in G, RV532; 2
Trumpets in C, RV537; 2 Violins in A min., RV523* Various
artists, I Musici
Philips 426 086-2 [A] **M**

*Double Concerti for: 2 Violins, RV505; 2 Oboes, RV535; 2 Violins,
RV511; 2 Cellos, RV531; 2 Violins, RV523; Oboe & 2 Violins,
RV554* Comberti (vln), Coe (vcl), Watkin (vcl), Robson (ob),

Lartham (ob), Collegium Musicum 90, Standage (vln/dir)
✧ Chandos CHAN 0528 [D] **F**

Lute and Viola d'amore Concerto in D min., RV540; Chamber Concerto for Lute and 2 Violins, RV93; Trio Sonata for Violin, Lute and Continuo, RV82 Fernández (gtr), ECO, Malcolm
(+ Giuliani: *Guitar Concerto in A*)
Decca 417 617-2 [D] **F**

Chamber Concerti: in C, RV88; in D, RV90 (Il Gardellino); in D, RV94; in F, RV99; in G min., RV106; in G min., RV107 London Harpsichord Ensemble, Francis
Unicorn-Kanchana DKPCD 9071 [D] **F**

Cello Sonatas: in A min., RV43; A min., RV44; in B♭, RV46; in B♭, RV47; in E min., RV40; in F, RV41 Coin (vcl), Hogwood
✧ L'Oiseau-Lyre 421 060-2 [D] **F**

Cello Sonatas: in B♭, RV45; in E♭, RV39; in G min., RV42; *Cello Concertos: in G min., RV402; in D min., RV406; in G, RV414 Coin (vcl), Ferre (baroque gtr), Hogwood (hpd); *Coin (vcl), AAM, Hogwood
✧ L'Oiseau-Lyre 433 052-2 [D] **F**

12 Trio Sonatas, Op. 1 Accardo (vln), Gulli (vln), Canino (hpd), de Saram (vcl)
Philips 426 926-2 [A] **M**

12 Trio Sonatas, Op. 1 Nos. 8 in D min., 9 in A♭ & 11 in B min.; Trio Sonatas: in F, RV68; in B♭, RV77; Violin Sonatas: in C, RV2; in C min., RV6 Purcell Quartet
✧ Chandos CHAN 0511 [D] **F**

Trio Sonatas: in E♭, RV65; in F, RV70; in G, RV71; in G min., RV72; in B♭, RV76; in B♭, RV78; Violin Sonata in A, RV29 Purcell Quartet
✧ Chandos CHAN 0502 [D] **F**

12 Violin Sonatas, Op. 2 Accardo (vln), Canino (hpd), de Saram (vcl)
Philips 426 929-2 [A] **M**

6 Violin Sonatas, Op. 5 Accardo (vln), Gazeau (vla), Canino (hpd), de Saram (vcl)
Philips 426 938-2 [A] **M**

12 'Manchester' Violin Sonatas Manze (vln), Toll (hpd), North (lte)
✧ HM HMU 907089/90, 2 CDs [D] **F**

Beatus vir, RV597; Credo, RV592; Magnificat, RV610 Soloists, John Alldis Ch, ECO, Negri
Philips 420 651-2 [A] **M**

Beatus Vir, RV598; Dixit Dominus, RV594; Introduzione al Dixit: Canta in prato in G, RV636; Magnificat in G min. (ed. Negri) Soloists, John Alldis Choir, ECO, Negri
Philips 420 649-2 [A] **M**

Crediti propter quod, RV105; Credo, RV591; Introduction to Gloria, RV639; Gloria, RV588; Kyrie, RV587; Laetatus sum, RV607 Soloists, John Alldis Ch, ECO, Negri
Philips 420 650-2 [A] **M**

Gloria in D, RV642; Introduction to Gloria, RV642; Lauda Jerusalem, RV609; Laudate Dominum in D min., RV606; Laudate pueri Dominum in A, RV602 Soloists, John Alldis Ch, ECO, Negri
Philips 420 648-2 [A] **M**

v *Gloria in D, RV589* Argenta (sop), Attrot (sop), Denley (mez), English Concert O & Ch, Pinnock
(+ A. Scarlatti: *Dixit Dominus*)
◇ DG Archiv 423 386-2 [D] **F**

*Gloria in D, RV589; Magnificat in G min., RV611 *Vaughan (sop), *Baker (mez), King's College Ch, ASMF, *Willcocks, Ledger
(+ Pergolesi: *Magnificat*)
Decca 425 724-2 [A] **M**

Gloria in D, RV589; Ostro picta, RV642 Kirkby (sop), Bonner (sop), Chance (alt), Collegium Musicum '90 O & Ch, Hickox
(+ J.S. Bach: *Magnificat*)
◇ Chandos CHAN 0518 [D] **F**

Juditha Triumphans (oratorio) Finnilä (mez), Springer (mez), Hamari (cont), Ameling (sop), Berlin CO, Negri
Philips 426 955-2, 2CDs [A] **M**

VOŘÍŠEK, Jan Vaclav (1791–1825)

s *Piano Sonata in B♭ min., Op. 20; Fantasia, Op. 12; 6 Impromptus Op. 7; Variations in B♭, Op. 20* Kvapil (pno)
Unicorn-Kanchana DKPCD 9145 [D] **F**

WAGNER, Richard (1813–1883) GERMANY

o Opera excerpts: *Rienzi; Der fliegende Holländer; Lohengrin; Tannhäuser; Tristan und Isolde* Philharmonia O, Klemperer
CDM7 63617-2 [A] **M**

Opera excerpts: *Götterdämmerung; Die Meistersinger; Parsifal; Das Rheingold; Siegfried; Die Walküre* Philharmonia O, Klemperer
CDM7 63618-2 [A] **M**

Opera excerpts: *Die Meistersinger; Tannhäuser; Tristan und Isolde* BPO, Karajan
DG 413 754-2 [D] **F**

WALTON, William (1902–1983) ENGLAND

o Film scores: *As You Like it; Hamlet* Bott (sop), Gielgud (narr), ASMF, Marriner
Chandos CHAN 8842 [D] **F**

Film score excerpts: *Battle of Britain; Escape me never; The First of the Few; Three Sisters; A Wartime Sketchbook* ASMF, Marriner
Chandos CHAN 8870 [D] **F**

Capriccio Burlesco; Music for Children; Portsmouth Point Overture; The Quest: Suite; Scapino Overture; Siesta; *Sinfonia Concertante *Katin (pno), LSO, LPO, Walton
Lyrita SRCD 224 [A] **F**

Capriccio burlesco; The First Shoot; Galop Final; Granada Prelude; Johannesburg Festival Overture; Music for Children; Portsmouth Point Overture; Prologo e fantasia; Scapino Overture LPO, Thomson
Chandos CHAN 8968 [D] **F**

*Cello Concerto; Improvisations on an Impromptu of Benjamin Britten; Partita; *Passacaglia for Solo Cello *R. Wallfisch (vcl), LPO, Thomson
Chandos CHAN 8959 [D] **F**

O *Viola Concerto in A min.; Violin Concerto in B min.* Kennedy
(vla/vln), RPO, Previn
EMI CDC7 49628-2 [D] **F**

Façade (An Entertainment) Scales, West (speakers) LMP,
Glover
(+ Sitwell: *Poems*)
ASV CDDCA 679 [D] **F**

Façade (An Entertainment): Suites Nos. 1 & 2 English Northern
PO, Lloyd-Jones
(+ Bliss: *Checkmate;* Lambert: *Horoscope*)
Hyperion CDA 66436 [D] **F**

Henry V (film score); *A Shakespeare Scenario* (arr. Palmer)
Plummer (narr), Westminster Cathedral Ch, ASMF,
Marriner
Chandos CHAN 8892 [D] **F**

Film score excerpts: *Macbeth; Major Barbara; Richard III
(Shakespeare scenario)* Gielgud (narr), ASMF, Marriner
Chandos CHAN 8841 [D] **F**

The Quest (ballet); *The Wise Virgins* (ballet): Suite LPO,
Thomson
Chandos CHAN 8871 [D] **F**

Sinfonia concertante Stott (pno), RPO, Handley
(+ Bridge: *Phantasm;* Ireland: *Piano Concerto*)
Conifer CDCF 175 [D] **F**

*Symphonies: No. 1 in Bb minor; *No. 2* LPO; *LSO, Mackerras
EMI Eminence CD-EMX 2206 [D] **M**

Symphony No. 1 in Bb min. LSO, Previn
(+ Vaughan Williams: *Wasps Overture*)
RCA GD 87830 [A] **M**

Symphony No. 2; Partita; Variations on a Theme of Hindemith
Cleveland O, Szell
Sony/CBS CD46732 [A] **M**

C *Piano Quartet; Violin Sonata* Sillito (vln), Smissen (vla), Otton
(vcl), Milne (pno)
Chandos CHAN 8999 [D] **F**

String Quartet (1919–22); String Quartet in A min. Gabrieli
Quartet
Chandos CHAN 8944 [D] **F**

S *Passacaglia for Solo Cello* R. Wallfisch (vcl)
(+ Bax: *Rhapsodic Ballad;* Bridge: *Cello Sonata;* Delius: *Cello
Sonata*)
Chandos CHAN 8499 [D] **F**

V *All this time; Cantico del Sole; Jubilate Deo; King Herod and the
Cock; A Litany; Magnificat and Nunc dimittis; Make we joy now in
this feast; Missa brevis; Set me as a seal* (antiphon); *The Twelve;
What cheer? Where does the uttered music go?* Trinity College Ch,
Marlow
Conifer CDCF 164 [D] **F**

*Anon in love; Christopher Columbus: Suite; Daphne; Long steel
grass; Old Sir Faulk; A song for the Lord Mayer's table; Through
gilded trellises; The Twelve* Finnie (mez), Davies (ten), Hill
(ten), Gomez (sop), Westminster Singers, City of London
Sinfonia, Hickox
Chandos CHAN 8824 [D] **F**

V *Belshazzar's Feast* (cantata); *Improvisations on an Impromptu of Benjamin Britten; Portsmouth Point Overture; Scapino Overture*
*Shirley-Quirk (bar), LSO & Ch, Previn
EMI CDM7 64723-2 [A] **M**

Belshazzar's Feast (cantata); *In Honour of the City of London*
Wilson-Johnson (bar), LSO & Ch, Hickox
EMI Eminence CD-EMX 2225 [D] **F**

Gloria; Te Deum; Façade Suites Nos. 1 & 2; Crown Imperial; Orb and Sceptre CBSO & Ch, Frémaux
EMI CDM7 64201-2 [A] **M**

WARLOCK, Peter (1894–1930) ENGLAND

O *Capriol Suite; Serenade for Frederick Delius's 60th Birthday*
Ulster O, Handley
(+ Moeran: *Serenade in G; Nocturne*)
Chandos CHAN 8808 [D] **F**

V *29 Songs* Luxon (bar), Willison (pno)
Chandos CHAN 8643 [D] **F**

WAXMAN, Franz (1906–1967) GERMANY/USA

O Film score excerpts: *The Bride of Frankenstein; MGM Fanfare; Old Aquaintance; The Philadelphia Story; A Place in the Sun; Prince Valiant; Rebecca; Sunset Boulevard; Taras Bulba* National PO, Gerhardt
RCA GD 80708 [A] **M**

Mr. Skeffington (film score): *Forsaken* National PO, Gerhardt
(+ film scores by Korngold, Steiner)
RCA GD 80183 [A] **M**

WEBER, Carl Maria von (1786–1826) GERMANY

O *Andante e Rondo ungarese in C min.; Bassoon Concerto in F*
Thunemann (bsn), ASMF, Marriner
(+ Hummel: *Bassoon Concerto*)
Philips 432 081-2 [D] **F**

The Complete Concertos Klöcker (cl), Wandel (cl), Hartmann (bsn), Buschmann (bsn), Schmalfuss (ob), Dunschede (fl), Schroeder (hn), Slovak RSO, Tamayo
Novalis 150 104-2, 3CDs [D] **F**

Clarinet Concertino; Clarinet Concertos: No. 1 in F min.; No. 2 in E♭
Pay (cl), Age of Enlightenment O
✧ Virgin VC7 59002-2 [D] **F**
Neidich (cl), Orpheus CO
(+ Rossini: *Introduction, Theme and Variations*)
DG 435 875-2 [D] **F**

Horn Concertino in E min. Baumann (hn), LGO, Masur
(+ R. Strauss: *Horn Concertos Nos. 1 & 2*)
Philips 412 237-2 [D] **F**

Invitation to the Dance (orch. Berlioz); Opera overtures: *Abu Hassan; Euryanthe; Der Freischütz; Oberon; Peter Schmoll; Ruler of the Spirits* BPO, Karajan
DG 419-070-2 [A] **M**

Overtures: *Abu Hassan; Euryanthe; Der Freischutz; Oberon; Peter Schmoll; Ruler of the Spirits; Invitation to the Dance* (orch. Berlioz)
Hanover Band, Goodman
✧ Nimbus NI 5154 [D] **F**

⟩ *Symphonies: No. 1 in C; No. 2 in C* Hanover Band, Goodman
◇ Nimbus NI 5180 [D] **F**

⟩ *Clarinet Quintet in B♭; Flute Trio* Nash Ensemble
CRD 3398 [A] **F**

⟩ *Piano Sonatas: No. 1 in C; No. 2 in A♭; Rondo brillante in E♭ (La gaieté); Invitation to the Dance* Milne (pno)
CRD 3485 [D] **F**

Piano Sonatas: No. 3 in D min.; No. 4 in E min.; Polacca brillante
Milne (pno)
(+ Liszt: *Polonaise brillante: Introduction*)
CRD 3486 [D] **F**

WEBERN, Anton (1883–1945) AUSTRIA

⟩ *Passacaglia, Op. 1; 5 Pieces, Op. 5; 6 Pieces, Op. 6; 5 Pieces, Op. 10; Symphony, Op. 21; Variations, Op. 40; 6 Bagatelles, Op. 9; Concerto for 9 Instruments, Op. 24; 3 Little Pieces, Op. 11; 5 Movements, Op. 5; 4 Pieces, Op. 7; Quartet, Op. 22; String Quartet, Op. 28; String Trio, Op. 20; Variations, Op. 27; Das Augenlicht, Op. 26; 5 Canons, Op. 16; Cantatas Nos. 1 & 2; Entflieht auf leichten; 5 Sacred Songs; 5 Songs, Op. 4; 2 Songs, Op. 8; 4 Songs, Op. 12; 4 Songs, Op. 13; 6 Songs, Op. 14; 3 Songs, Op. 18; 2 Songs, Op. 19; 3 Songs, Op. 25; 5 Songs, Op. 3; 3 Songs from 'Viae invaie'; 3 Traditional Rhymes, Op. 17* Various artists, Boulez
Sony CD 45845, 3CDs [A] **M**

5 Movements, Op. 5; Passacaglia, Op. 1; 6 Pieces, Op. 6; Symphony, Op. 21 BPO, Karajan
(+ Berg: *Lyric Suite, etc.*; Schoenberg: *Pelleas und Melisande, etc.*)
DG 427 424-2, 3CDs [A] **M**

5 Pieces, Op. 10 LSO, Dorati
(+ Berg: *3 Orchestral Pieces; Lulu: Symphonic Suite;* Schoenberg: *5 Orchestral Pieces*)
Philips Mercury 432 006-2 [A] **M**

6 Bagatelles, Op. 9; 5 Movements, Op. 5; String Quartet (1905); String Quartet, Op. 28 LaSalle Quartet
(+ Berg: *Lyric Suite; String Quartet, Op. 3;* Schoenberg: *String Quartet in D; String Quartets Nos. 1–4*)
DG 419 994-2, 4CDs [A] **M**

Langsamer Satz Carmina Quartet
(+ Szymanowski: *String Quartets Nos. 1 & 2*)
Denon CO-79462 [D] **F**

String Trio, Op. 20; Movement for String Trio; Piano Quintet (1907); Rondo for String Quartet (1906) Litwin (pno), LaSalle Quartet
(+ Schoenberg: *Ode to Napoleon Bonaparte*)
DG 437 036-2 [A] **M**

Variations, Op. 27 Pollini (pno)
(+ Boulez: *Piano Sonata No. 2;* Prokofiev: *Piano Sonata No. 7;* Stravinsky: *3 Movements from Petrushka*)
DG 419 202-2 [A] **F**

8 Lieder Fischer-Dieskau (bar), Reimann (pno)
(+ Berg: *4 Lieder, Op. 2;* Schoenberg: *Gurrelieder, 8 Lieder*)
DG 431 744-2, 2 CDs [A] **M**

WEELKES, Thomas (1576–1623) ENGLAND

V   *Alleluia; Evening Service a 5; Evening Service No. 9; Give ear; Give
the king; Gloria in excelsis; Hosanna; O Lord, arise; When David
heard* Christ Church Cathedral Ch, Darlington
Nimbus NI 5125 [D] **F**

WEILL, Kurt (1900–1950) GERMANY/USA

O   **Violin Concerto; Kleine Dreigroschenmusik* *Lidell (vln),
London Sinfonietta, Atherton
DG 423 255-2 [A] **M**

Symphonies Nos. 1 & 2 Lisbon Gulbenkian O, Swierczewski
Nimbus NI 5283 [A] **F**

C   *Cello Sonata* Goritzki (vcl), Levine (pno)
(+ Schoeck: *Cello Sonata*)
Claves CD50-8908 [D] **F**

V   *Songs* Lemper (sop), Berlin Radio Ensemble, Mauceri
Volume 1
Decca 425 204-2 [D] **F**
Volume 2
Decca 436 417-2 [D] **F**

WEISS, Sylvius (1686–1750) GERMANY

S   *Lute works (Volumes Nos. 1 & 2)* Kirchof (lte/theorbo)
Sony CD 48391, 2CDs [D] **F**

WESLEY, Samuel (1766–1837) ENGLAND

O   *Symphonies: in B♭; in D; in E♭; in A* Milton Keynes CO,
Wetton
Unicorn-Kanchana DKPCD 9098 [D] **F**

WESLEY, Samuel Sebastian (1810–1876) ENGLAND

V   *Ascribe unto the Lord; Blessed be the God; Cast me not away; Let us
Lift; Thou wilt keep him; The Wilderness* Worcester Cathedral
Ch, Partington (org), Hunt
Hyperion CDA 66446 [D] **F**

*The face of the Lord; Man that is born; O give thanks; O Lord, thou
art my God; Praise the Lord; Wash me thoroughly* Worcester
Cathedral Ch, Partington (org), Hunt
Hyperion CDA 664469 [D] **F**

WIDOR, Charles-Marie (1844–1937) FRANCE

C   *Piano Quartet in A min., Op. 66* Ames Piano Quartet
(+ R. Strauss: *Piano Quartet*)
Dorian DOR 90176 [D] **F**

Piano Quintet No. 1 in D min., Op. 7; Piano Trio in B♭, Op. 19
Prunyi (pno), New Budapest Quartet
Marco Polo 8.223193 [D] **F**

S   *Organ Sonatas Nos: 1–10* (complete) Kaunzinger (org)
Novalis 150 105-2, 5CDs [D] **F**

Organ Symphonies: No. 1 in C min., Op. 13/1; No. 2, Op. 13/2
Kaunzinger (org)
Novalis 150 073-2 [D] **F**

*Organ Symphonies: No. 5 in F min., Op. 42/1; No. 6 in C min., Op.
42/2; No. 8, Op. 42/4; No. 9 in C min. (Gothic), Op. 70; 3 Nouvelles
pièces, Op. 87* Trotter (org)
Argo 433 152-2 [D] **F**

S *Organ Symphonies: No. 5 in F min., Op. 42/1; No. 6 in C min., Op. 42/2* Kaunzinger (org)
Novalis 150 015-2 [D] **F**

Organ Symphonies: No. 9 in C min. (Gothic), Op. 70; No. 10 (Roman), Op. 73 Kaunzinger (org)
Novalis 150 038-2 [D] **F**

Organ Symphony No. 9 in C min. (Gothic), Op. 70 Filsell (org)
(+ Tournemire: *Suite évocatrice;* Vierne: *Organ Symphony No. 3*)
Herald HAVPCD 145 [D] **F**

WIENIAWSKI, Henryk (1835–1880) POLAND

O *Violin Concertos: No. 1 in F# min., Op. 14; No. 2 in D min., Op. 22; Légende, Op. 17* Shaham (vln), LSO, Foster
(+ Sarasate: *Zigeunerweisen*)
DG 431 815-2 [D] **F**

Violin Concerto No. 2 in D min., Op. 22 Perlman (vln), Paris O, Barenboim
(+ Saint-Saëns: *Violin Concerto No. 3*)
DG 410 526-2 [D] **F**

WIKMANSON, Johan (1753–1800) SWEDEN

C *String Quartet No. 2 in E min., Op. 1/2* Chilingirian Quartet
(+ Arriaga: *String Quartets Nos. 1–3*)
CRD 3312/3, 2CDs [A] **F**

WILSON, Thomas (born 1927) SCOTLAND

O **Piano Concerto; Introit (Towards the Light...)* *Wilde (pno), SNO, Thomson
Chandos CHAN 8626 [D] **F**

WIRÉN, Dag (1905–1986) SWEDEN

O *Violin Concerto; *String Quartet No. 5, Op. 41; **Triptych, Op. 33; ***Wind Quintet, Op. 42* Sparf (vln), Stockholm PO, Comissiona; *Saulesco Quartet; **Stockholm Sinfonia, Wedin; ***Stockholm Wind Quintet
Caprice CAP 21326 [A/D] **F**

WOLF, Hugo (1860–1903) AUSTRIA

O *Italian Serenade; Penthesilia; Scherzo and Finale; Der Corregidor* (opera): *Prelude; Intermezzo* Paris O, Barenboim
Erato 2292-45416-2 [D] **F**

V *9 Lieder* von Otter (mez), Gothoni (pno)
(+ Mahler: *Lieder selection*)
DG 423 666-2 [D] **F**

27 Goethe & Morike Lieder Auger (sop), Gage (pno)
Hyperion CDA 66590 [D] **F**

Italienisches Liederbuch Schwarzkopf (sop), Fischer-Dieskau (bar), Moore (pno)
EMI CDM7 63732-2 [A] **M**

Morike Lieder (selection) Fassbaender (cont), Thibaudet (pno)
Decca 440 208-2 [D] **F**

Spanisches Liederbuch Schwarzkopf (sop), Fischer-Dieskau (bar), Moore (pno)
DG 423 934-2, 2CDs [A] **M**

WOLF-FERRARI, Ermanno (1876–1948) ITALY

O Overtures: *L'amore medico; La Dama Boba; Il Campiello; I Gioielli della Madonna; I quattro Rusteghi; Il Segreto di Susanna* ASMF, Marriner
EMI CDC7 54585-2 [D] **F**

WOOD, Charles (1866–1926) ENGLAND

C *String Quartet in A min.* Lindsay Quartet
(+ Tippett: *String Quartet No. 5, etc.*)
ASV CDDCA 879 [D] **F**

V *St. Mark Passion* Kendall (ten), Harvey (bs), Gonville & Caius College Ch, Webber
(+ Holloway: *Since I Believe*)
ASV CDDCA 854 [D] **F**

WOOD, Hugh (born 1932) ENGLAND

O *Cello Concerto, Op. 12; Violin Concerto, Op. 17* Welsh (vcl), Parikian (vln), RLPO, Atherton
Unicorn-Kanchana UKCD 2043 [A] **M**

WORDSWORTH, William (1908–1988) ENGLAND

O *Symphonies: No. 2 in D, Op. 34; No. 3 in D, Op. 48* LPO, Braithwaite
Lyrita SRCD 207 [D] **F**

WRIGHT, Maurice (born 1949) USA

S *Piano Sonata* Hamelin (pno)
(+ Ives: *Piano Sonata No. 2 'Concord Mass'*)
New World NW378-2 [D] **F**

XENAKIS, Iannis (born 1922) ROMANIA/FRANCE

O *A l'île de Gorée; Komboï; Khoai; Naama* Chojnacka (hpd), Xenakis Ensemble, Kertens
Erato 2292-45030-2 [D] **F**

S *Palimpsest; Dikhthas; Epeï; Akanthos* Various artists
Wergo WER 6178-2 [D] **F**

YSAYE, Eugène (1858–1931) BELGIUM

S *6 Sonatas for Solo Violin, Op. 27* Shumsky (vln)
Nimbus NI 5039 [D] **F**

ZELENKA, Jan (1679–1745) BOHEMIA

O *Capriccios Nos. 1–5; Concerto in G; Hipocondrie in A; Overture in F; Sinfonia No. 8 in A min.* Berne Camarata, Wijnkoop
DG Archiv 423 703-2, 3CDs [A] **M**

C *6 Trio Sonatas* Holliger (ob), Bourgue (ob), Thunemann (bsn), Gawriloff (vln), Buccarella (db), van der Meer (bs)
DG Archiv 423 937-2, 2CDs [A] **M**

V *The Lamentations of Jeremiah* Chance (alt), Ainsley (ten), George (bs), Chandos Baroque Players
◇ Hyperion CDA 66426 [D] **F**

Litanae Lauretanae; Missa dei fili Argenta (sop), Chance (alt), Prégardien (ten), Jones (bs), Stuttgart Chamber Ch, Tafelmusik, Bernius
◇ DHM RD 77922 [D] **F**

ZELINSKI, Wladyslaw (1837–1921) POLAND

C *Piano quartet in C min., Op. 61* Polish Piano Quartet
(+ Noskowski: *Piano Quartet*)
Olympia OCD 381 [D] **F**

ZEMLINSKY, Alexander von (1871–1942) AUSTRIA

O *Ein Lyrische Symphonie, Op. 18* Varady (sop), Fischer-Dieskau
(bar), BPO, Maazel
DG 419 261-2 [D] **F**

Symphony No. 2 in B♭; Psalm 23, Op. 14 Ernst-Senff Chamber
Ch, Berlin RSO, Chailly
Decca 421 644-2 [D] **F**

C *Piano Trio in D min., Op. 3* Beaux Arts Trio
(+ Korngold: *Piano Trio*)
Philips 434 072-2 [D] **F**

String Quartets Nos. 1–4 LaSalle Quartet
(+ Apostel: *String Quartet No. 1*)
DG 427 421-2, 2CDs [A] **M**

*Lieder: Gesänge, Op. 5 Books 1 & 2; 6 Gesänge, Op. 6; 5 Gesänge,
Op. 7; 4 Gesänge, Op. 8; 6 Gesänge, Op. 10; 6 Gesänge, Op. 13;
Lieder, Op. 2 Books 1 & 2; 6 Lieder, Op. 22; 12 Lieder, Op. 27;
Schummerlied* Blochwitz (ten), Bonney (sop), von Otter (mez),
Schmidt (bar), Garben (pno)
DG 427 348-2, 2CDs [D] **F**

Collections

○ *American Orchestral Music* Barber, Piston, Griffes, etc.
Eastman-Rochester O, Hanson
Philips Mercury 434 307-2 [A] **M**

Ernest Ansermet Edition Various composers
OSR, Ansermet
Decca 433 803-2 , 12 CDs [A] **M**

Armchair Concerts 1 Beethoven, R. Strauss
LPO, Tennstedt
EMI CDM7 64439-2 [D] **M**

Armchair Concerts 3 Dukas, Gershwin, Holst
LSO, Previn
EMI CDM7 64441-2 [A] **M**

The Art of Itzhak Perlman Brahms, Sibelius, Bach, etc.
Perlman (vln), Various artists
EMI CMS7 64617-2, 4 CDs [A/D] **F**

Baroque Recorder Concertos Telemann, Vivaldi, etc.
Petri (rec), ASMF, Sillito
Philips 412 630-2 [D] **F**

Baroque Trumpet Music Vivaldi, Albinoni, Corelli, etc.
Wallace (tpt/dir), Wallace Collection
Nimbus NI 7012 [D] **F**

Brass music Britten, Carter, Tippett, etc.
Wallace Collection, Wallace
Collins 12292 [D] **F**

A Chance Operation...A John Cage Tribute
Various artists
Koch 3-7238-2, 2 CDs [D] **F**

Contemporary Orchestral Music Boulez, Ligeti, Nono, etc.
VPO, Abbado
DG 429 260-2 [D] **F**

Early Romantic Overtures Berlioz, Mendelssohn, etc.
LCP, Norrington
◇ EMI CDC7 49889-2 [D] **F**

English Music for Strings Elgar, Holst, Warlock, etc.
Bournemouth Sinfonietta, Hurst
Chandos CHAN 8375 [D] **F**

Estonian Music Eller, Lemba, Pärt, Tormis, etc.
SNO, Järvi
Chandos CHAN 8656 [D] **F**

L'Eventaille de Jeanne (ballet by 10 French composers)*; Les
Maries de la Tour Eiffel* (ballet by five of Les Six)
Philharmonia O, Simon
Chandos CHAN 8356 [D] **F**

Favourite Cello Concertos Dvořák, Elgar, Haydn, etc.
Du Pre (vcl), Various Os & conductors
EMI CMS7 63283-2, 3 CDs [A] **M**

Fête à la française Bizet, Chabrier, Dukas, etc.
Montreal SO, Dutoit
Decca 421 527-2 [D] **F**

○ *Flute Concerto Collection* Honegger, Ibert, Mozart, etc.
Stinton (fl), Browne (hp), Brewer (pno), Scottish CO, ECO,
Philharmonia O, Bedford, Vasáry
Collins 7005-2, 2CDs [D] **M**

The Four Seasons Milhaud, Rodrigo, Chaminade, Serebrier
Guttman (vln), RPO, Serebrier
ASV CDDCA 855 [D] **F**

French Orchestral Works Fauré, Bizet, Delibes, etc.
RPO, Beecham
EMI CDM7 63379-2 [A] **M**

The Great Guitar Concertos Giuliani, Rodrigo, etc.
Williams (gtr), ECO, Philharmonia O, LSO, Barenboim,
Previn, Frémaux
Sony/CBS CD 44791, 2CDs [A/D] **F**

EDITORS' CHOICE (see page 15): *The Bernard Haitink Symphony
Edition:* Beethoven, Brahms, Bruckner, Mahler, etc.
Royal Concertgebouw O, Haitink
Philips 442 355-2, 35 CDs [D/A] **F**

Harp Music Beethoven, Boieldieu, Handel, etc.
Robles (hp), ASMF, Marriner
Decca 425 723-2 [A] **M**

EDITORS' CHOICE (see page 15): *The Jascha Heifetz Complete
Edition*
Heifetz (vln), Various Os, conductors & accompanists
RCA 09026-61778-2, 65 CDs [A] Mono/Stereo **F**

The Vladimir Horowitz Edition
Horowitz (pno), Various artists
RCA 09026-61655-2, 22 CDs [A] Mono/Stereo **F**

One Hundred Years of Dutch Orchestral Music
Het Residentie Orchestra, Various conductors
Volume 1: Schuyt, Sweelinck, Rosier, etc.
Olympia OCD 500 [A] **F**
Volume 2: Hellendaal, Lentz, Graaf, etc.
Olympia OCD 501 [A] **F**
Volume 3: Wilms, vam Bree, Verhulst
Olympia OCD 502 [A] **F**
Volume 4: Verhey, Zweers
Olympia OCD 503 [A] **F**
Volume 5: Wagenaar, Pijper, Andriessen, etc.
Olympia OCD 504 [A] **F**
Volume 6: Vermeulen, Ketting, De Leeuw, etc.
Olympia OCD 505 [A] **F**
Volume 7: Escher, Janssen, Laman, etc.
Olympia OCD 5006 [A] **F**
Volume 8: Diepenbrock, Badings, Andriessen, etc.
Olympia OCD 507 [D] **F**

Lollipops Berlioz, Chabrier, Debussy, Delius, etc.
RPO, Beecham
EMI CDM7 63412-2 [A] **M**

The Pierre Monteux Edition Beethoven, Debussy, etc.
SFSO, CSO, Boston SO, Monteux
RCA 09026 61893, 15CDs [A] **M**

Music for Cello and Orchestra Cui, Glazunov, Tchaikovsky, etc.
Isserlis (vcl), COE, Gardiner
Virgin VC7 59595-2 [D] **F**

o *Music for String Orchestra* Respighi, Wiren, Walton, etc.
English String O, Boughton
Nimbus NI 5347 [D] **F**

Musica Mexicana: Volume 1 Chavez, Ponce, Revueltas
RPO, Batiz
ASV CDDCA 738 [D] **F**

Musica Mexicana: Volume 2 Chavez, *Ponce, Revueltas
*Szeryng (vln), Mexico PO, RPO, Batiz
ASV CDDCA 866 [D] **F**

Musica Mexicana: Volume 3 *Halffter, Moncayo, Ponce,
Revueltas
*Szeryng (vln), Mexico PO, Batiz
ASV CDDCA 871 [D] **F**

Overtures Berlioz, Mendelssohn, Rossini, Suppé, etc.
RPO, Beecham
EMI CDM7 63407-2 [A] **M**

Popular Baroque Albinoni, Bach, Corelli, Pachelbel, etc.
Orpheus CO
DG 429 390-2 [D] **F**

Popular Baroque Pachelbel, Handel, Vivaldi, etc.
AAM, Hogwood
◇ L'Oiseau-Lyre 410 553-2 [D] **F**

The Complete Recordings Michael Rabin
Rabin (vln), Various accompanists, Os & conductors
EMI CMS7 64123-2, 6CDs [A] Stereo/Mono **M**

Romantic Overtures Humperdinck, Schumann, Weber, etc.
NPO, Philharmonia O, Klemperer
EMI CDM7 63917-2 [A] **M**

Scandinavian Suite Grieg, Nielsen, Wiren, etc.
Guildhall String Ensemble
RCA RD 60439 [D] **F**

The Spirit of England Delius, Elgar, Holst, etc.
English String O, Boughton
Nimbus NI 5210/3, 4CDs [D] **F**

The Stokowski Sound Bach, Debussy, Albéniz, etc.
Cincinnati Pops O, Kunzel
Telarc CD 80129 [D] **F**

The Ultimate Guitar Collection The Julian Bream Edition
Bream (gtr), Various artists
RCA 09026-61583-2, 28 CDs [D/A] **M**

A Venetian Coronation A. & G. Gabrieli
Gabrieli Consort & Players, McCreesh
◇ Virgin VC7 59006-2 [D] **F**

Victorian Concert Overtures Macfarren, Sullivan, etc.
English Northern Philharmonia, Lloyd-Jones
Hyperion CDA 66515 [D] **F**

Viola music Hindemith, Reger, Schnittke, etc.
Bashmet (vla/dir), Moscow Soloists
RCA RD 60464 [D] **F**

Works for Cello and Orchestra Fauré, Lalo, etc.
Rose (vcl), Philadelphia, Ormandy
Sony CD 48278 [A] **F**

Works for Flute and Orchestra Godard, Ibert, Saint-Saëns, etc.
Milan (fl), City of London Sinfonia, Hickox
Chandos CHAN 8840 [D] **F**

Works for Horn and Orchestra Dukas, Glière, etc.
Baumann (hn), LGO, Masur
Philips 416 380-2 [D] **F**

An American Recital Barber, Copland, Hanson, etc.
Stinton (fl), Martineau (pno)
Collins 13852 [D] **F**

Bream and Williams Live Albéniz, Granados, Sor, etc.
Bream (gtr), Williams (gtr)
RCA RD 89645 [A] **F**

British Cello Music Arnold, Britten, Ireland, etc.
Lloyd Webber (vcl), McCabe (pno)
CDDCA 592 [D] **F**

British Works for Flute Arnold, Delius, Elgar, etc.
Smith (fl), Rhodes (pno)
Volume 1: *Summer Music*
ASV CDDCA 739 [D] **F**
Volume 2: *Folk & Fantasy*
ASV CDDCA 768 [D] **F**

La Clarinette française Poulenc, Ravel, etc.
Johnson (cl), Back (pno)
ASV CDDCA 621 [D] **F**

A Contemporary Flute Collection Alwyn, Demase, Jolivet, etc.
Stinton (fl), Brewer (pno)
Collins 12972 [D] **F**

Elizabethan and Jacobean Consort Music
Julian Bream Consort
RCA RD 87801 [D] **F**

Encore Beethoven, Ravel, etc.
Midori (vln), McDonald (pno)
Sony SK 52568 [D] **F**

English Clarinet Music Arnold, Finzi, Ireland, etc.
de Peyer (cl), Pryor (pno)
Chandos CHAN 8549 [D] **F**

Flute Fantasie Fauré, Gaubert, etc.
Milan (fl), Brown (pno)
Chandos CHAN 8609 [D] **F**

French Clarinet Music Debussy, Poulenc, Saint-Saëns, etc.
de Peyer (cl), Pryor (pno)
Chandos CHAN 8526 [D] **F**

French Violin Music Fauré, Poulenc, Ravel, etc.
Heifetz (vn), Smith (pno)
RCA GD 87707 [A] **M**

Glyndebourne Wind Serenades Harvey, Osborne, Saxton, etc.
LPO members, Age of Enlightenment O members, Dove,
Pay, Parrott
EMI CDC7 54424-2 [D] **F**

Heart's Ease Viol Consort Music by Byrd, Gibbons, etc.
Fretwork
✧ Virgin VC7 59667-2 [D] **F**

C *Italian Recorder Music* Cima, Frescobaldi, Merula, etc.
Amsterdam Loeki Stardust Quartet (recs)
✧ L'Oiseau-Lyre 430 246-2 [D] **F**

The Lindsays: 25 Years Barber, Wiren, Wood, etc.
Lindsay Quartet
ASV CDDCA 825 [A] **F**

Lollipops for Piano Duet Goldstone, Clemmow (pno duo)
Meridian CDE 84238 [D] **F**

Midori Live at Carnegie Hall Beethoven, Ravel, etc.
Midori (vln), McDonald (pno)
Sony CD 46742 [D] **F**

Piano Circus Volans, Reich, etc.
Piano Circus
Argo 440 294-2 [D] **F**

Piano Music for Four Hands Dvořák, Rachmaninov, etc.
Duo Tal & Groethuysen
Sony CD 47199 [D] **F**

Romantic works Debussy, Fauré, Tournier, etc.
Stinton (fl), Brewer (hp)
Collins 10082 [D] **F**

Three Parts Upon a Ground: Sonatas and other works for 3 violins
Hollaway, Ritcie, Manze (vlns), Toll (hpd), North (lte)
HM HMU 907091 [D] **F**

Together Albéniz, Lawes, Sor, etc.
Bream (gtr), Williams (gtr)
RCA 09026 61450-2 [A] **M**

Together Again Albéniz, Carulli, Giuliani, etc.
Bream (gtr), Williams (gtr)
RCA 09026 61452-2 [A] **M**

Violin Recital Bartók, Brahms, Falla, etc.
Takezawa (vln), Moll (pno)
RCA 09026 60704-2 [D] **F**

The Virtuoso Violin Brahms, Ravel, Shostakovich, etc.
Little (vln), Lane (pno)
EMI Eminence CD-EMX 2196 [D] **M**

Wind music Barber, Berio, Françaix, etc.
Ensemble Wien-Berlin
Sony CD 48052 [D] **F**

S *American Piano Classics* Garner, Ives, Nancarrow, etc.
MacGregor (pno)
Collins 12992 [D] **F**

Arabesque Romantic harp music of the 19th century Volume 2
Drake (hp)
Hyperion CDA 66116 [D] **F**

Baroque Guitar Bach, Scarlatti, Weiss, etc.
Bream (gtr)
RCA 09026 61592-2 [A] **M**

Jorge Bolet Live Liszt, Franck, etc.
Bolet (pno)
Decca 436 648-2 [D] **F**

S *Caprices and Fantasies* Romantic harp music of the 19th
century Volume 3
Drake (hp)
Hyperion CDA 66340 [D] **F**

Carnegie Hall Debut Liszt, Schumann, etc.
Kissin (pno)
RCA 09026 61202-2 [D]**F**

Classic Guitar Diabelli, Giuliani, Sor, etc.
Bream (gtr)
RCA 09026 61593-2 [A] **M**

The Complete Masterworks Recordings (1962–73)
Horowitz (pno)
Sony CD 53456, 13 CDs [A] **M**

Echoes of a Waterfall Alvars, Glinka, Spohr, etc.
Drake (hp)
Hyperion CDA 66038 [D] **F**

The Essential Harpsichord Arne, Rameau, Scarlatti, etc.
Black (hpd)
Collins 50242 [D] **F**

Fandango Virtuoso Sonatas from 18th Century Spain
Puyana (hpd)
L'Oiseau-Lyre 417 341-2 [D] **F**

Guitarra Granados, Mudarra, Narvaez, Sanz, Sor, etc.
Bream (gtr)
RCA 09026-61610-2 [D] **M**

The Harmonious Blacksmith Bach, Handel, Rameau, etc.
Pinnock (hpd)
DG Archiv 413 591-2 [D] **F**

Hommage à la France Transcriptions by Allcoat
Allcoat (org)
Herald VLRCD 1571 [D] **F**

Horowitz in Moscow Mozart, Rachmaninov, Scarlatti, etc.
Horowitz (pno)
DG 419 499-2 [D] **F**

Horowitz at the Met Chopin, Liszt, Rachmaninov, etc.
Horowitz (pno)
RCA 09026 61416-2 [D] **M**

The Last Romantic Bach, Mozart, Schubert, Rachmaninov, etc.
Horowitz (pno)
DG 419 045-2 [D] **F**

Late Russian Romantics Rachmaninov, Scriabin, etc.
Horowitz (pno)
Sony CD 53472 [A] **F**

Live at the Wigmore Hall Haydn, Scarlatti, Berg, etc.
Demidenko (pno)
Hyperion CDA 66781/2, 2 CDs [D] **F**

Live in London Chopin, Schumann, Scriabin
Horowitz (pno)
RCA 09026 61414-2 [D] **M**

Netherlands Harpsichord music Bustijn, Sweelinck, etc.
van Asperen (hpd)
Sony CD 46349 [D] **F**

S *The Nimbus Recordings* Mussorgsky, Rachmaninov, etc.
Cherkassky (pno)
Nimbus NI 1793 [D] **F**

North German Organ Music Lorentz, Bohm, Ritter, etc.
Leonhardt (org)
Sony CD 53371 [D] **F**

Organ Fireworks Herrick (org)
Volume 1
Hyperion CDA 66121 [D] **F**
Volume 2
Hyperion CDA 66258 [D] **F**
Volume 3
Hyperion CDA 66457 [D] **F**
Volume 4
Hyperion CDA 66605 [D] **F**
Volume 5
Hyperion CDA 66676 [D] **F**

Organ Spectacular Franck, Karg-Elert, Widor, etc.
Hurford (org)
Decca 430 710-2 [D] **F**

A Paganini Ernst, Milstein, Rochberg, Schnittke
Kremer (vln)
DG 415 484-2 [D] **F**

The Piano Album 1 Godowsky, Paderewski, etc.
Hough (pno)
Virgin VC7 59509-2 [D] **F**

The Piano Album 2 Tausig, Levitzki, etc.
Hough (pno)
Virgin VC7 59304-2 [D] **F**

Popular French Romantics Franck, Gigout, Widor, etc.
Parker-Smith (org)
Volume 1
ASV CDDCA 539 [D] **F**
Volume 2
ASV CDDCA 610 [D] **F**

Rare Piano Encores Bizet, Gershwin, Rossini, etc.
Howard (pno)
Hyperion CDA 66090 [D] **F**

Rêverie Brahms, Debussy, Godowsky, etc.
Fergus-Thompson (pno)
ASV CDWHL 2066 [D] **M**

The Sviatoslav Richter Edition
Richter (pno)
Philips 442 464-2, 21CDs [A] **M**

Rosa Elizabethan Lute Music
Wilson (lte)
Virgin VC7 59034-2 [D] **F**

Russian Piano Music Balakirev, Borodin, Mussorgsky, etc.
Fingerhut (pno)
Chandos CHAN 8439 [D] **F**

Spanish Guitar Music Albéniz, de Falla, Granados, etc.
Williams (gtr)
Sony CD 46347 [A] **B**

s *Spanish Piano Music* Albéniz, de Falla, Granados, Halffter, Monmpou, Soler, Turina, etc.
de Larrocha (pno)
Volume 1
Decca 433 920-2, 2CDs [A/D] **M**
Volume 2
Decca 433 923-2, 2CDs [A/D] **M**
Volume 3
Decca 433 926-2, 2CDs [A] **M**
Volume 4
Decca 433 929-2, 2CDs [A/D] **M**

The Studio Recordings (1962–3) Chopin, Liszt, etc.
Horowitz (pno)
Sony CD 53457, 2 CDs [A] **F**

Tchaikovsky and his Friends Arensky, Lyadov, Glazunov, etc.
Fingerhut (pno)
Chandos CHAN 9218 [D] **F**

Theme & Variations I Brahms, Mendelssohn, Mozart etc.
Brendel (pno)
Philips 426 272-2 [D] **F**

Virtuoso Guitar Transcriptions
Hall (gtr)
Decca 430 839-2 [D] **F**

Virtuoso Piano Showpieces Godowsky, Moszkowski, etc.
Jones (pno)
Nimbus NI 5326 [D] **F**

Virtuoso Transcriptions Tausig, Balakirev, etc.
Fowke (pno)
CRD 3396 [A] **F**

Virtuoso Victoriana
Schiller (pno)
ASV CDWHL 2051 [D] **M**

Works for Solo Cello Britten, Crumb, Ligeti, Reger
Haimowitz (vcl)
DG 431 813-2 [D] **F**

Airs de Cour French Court Music of the 17th Century
Vallin (sop), van Egmond (bar), Kirchof (lte)
✧ Sony CD 48250 [D] **F**

American Collection Barber, Fine, Reich, etc.
The Sixteen, Christophers
Collins 12872 [D] **F**

An Evening with Victoria de los Angeles
de los Angeles (sop), Parsons (pno)
Collins 12472 [D] **F**

Anglo-Saxon Christmas
Schola Gregoriana of Cambridge, Berry
Herald HAVPCD 151 [D] **F**

Anthology of Gregorian Chant
Various choirs & directors
DG Archiv 435 032-2, 4CDs [A] **M**

Avis Maris Stella: Life of the Virgin Mary in Plainsong
Niederaltaicher Scholaren, Ruhland
Sony CD 45861 [D] **F**

V *Awake, Sweet Love* Campion, Dowland, Ford, etc.
Bowman (alt), Miller (lte), Kings Consort
Hyperion CDA 66447 [D] F

EDITORS' CHOICE (see page 12): *Cantus Selecti: Gregorian Chant*
Choralschola of the Niederaltaicher Scholaren, Ruhland
Sony CD 53372 [D] F

Carmina Burana
New London Consort
Volume 1
L'Oiseau-Lyre 417 373-2 [D] F
Volume 2
L'Oiseau-Lyre 421 062-2 [D] F
Volumes 3 & 4
L'Oiseau-Lyre 425 117-2, 2 CDs [D] F

Codex Las Huelgas (Music from 13th Century Spain)
Huelgas Ensemble, van Nevel
Sony CD 53341 [D] F

Christmas Music from Mediaeval and Renaissance Europe
The Sixteen, Christophers
Hyperion CDA 66263 [D] F

Collectio Argentea: An Anthology of Early Music
Various artists
DG 437 070-2, 20CDs [A] B

Courtly Love Songs from Northern France (c.1175–1300)
Sequentia
DHM RD 77155, 2CDs [D] F

Crown of Thorns Browne, Davy, Sheryngham, etc.
The Sixteen, Christophers
Collins 13162 [D] F

The Dante Troubadours Daniel, Faidit, Vidal, etc.
Martin Best Medieval Ensemble
Nimbus NI 5002 [D] F

La Dissection d'un Homme armé Six Masses
Huelgas Ensemble, van Nevel
Sony CD 45860 [D] F

Elizabethan Lute Songs
Pears (ten), Bream (gtr)
RCA 09026 61602-2 [A] M

Elizabethan Songs 'The Lady Musick'
Kirkby (sop), Rooley (lte)
L'Oiseau-Lyre 425 892-2 [D] F

The English Anthem Volume 1 Gardiner, Stainer, Wood, etc.
St. Paul's Cathedral Ch, Lucas (org), Scott
Hyperion CDA 66374 [D] F

The English Anthem Volume 2 Bainton, Finzi, Stanford, etc.
St. Paul's Cathedral Ch, Scott
Hyperion CDA 66519 [D] F

English Ayres and Duets
Camerata of London
Hyperion CDA 66003 [D] F

Febus Avant! (Music at the Court of Gaston Febus)
Huelgas Ensemble, van Nevel
Sony CD 48195 [D] F

∨ *From Tallis to Byrd* Tallis, Sheppard, Mundy, Dering, etc.
Clare College Chapel Ch, Brown
Gamut IMCD 701 [D] **F**

The Garden of Zephirus Briquet, Dufay, Reyneau, etc.
Gothic Voices, Page
Hyperion CDA 66144 [D] **F**

The Girl with the Orange Lips Falla, Ravel, etc.
Upshaw (sop)
Elektra-Nonesuch 7559-79262-2 [D] **F**

In Morte di Modanna Laura Madrigal cycle on Petrarca
Huelgas Ensemble, van Nevel
Sony CD 45942 [D] **F**

Italian Songs
Bartoli (mez), Schiff (pno)
Decca 440 297-2 [D] **F**

Lieder Recital Berg, Korngold, R. Strauss
Von Otter (mez), Forsberg (pno)
DG 437 515-2 [D] **F**

Madrigals and Wedding Songs for Diana Weelkes, etc.
Kirkby (sop), Thomas (bs), Consort of Musicke, Rooley
Hyperion CDA 66019 [D] **F**

The Medieval Romantics
Gothic Voices, Page
Hyperion CDA 66463 [D] **F**

Miserere Allegri, Parry, Schubert, etc.
Trinity College Ch, Marlow
Conifer CDCF 219 [D] **F**

Music for the Lion-Hearted King
Gothic Voices, Page
Hyperion CDA 66336 [D] **F**

Music from Renaissance Portugal Lobo, Carreira, Fernandez, etc.
Cambridge Taverner Ch, Rees
Herald HAVPCD 155 [D] **F**

Music from the Court of King Janus at Nicosia (1374–1432)
Huelgas Ensemble, Van Nevel
Sony 53976 [D] **F**

Music from the Time of the Crusades
Early Music Consort, Munrow
Decca 430 264-2 [A] **M**

Music of the Gothic Era
Early Music Consort, Munrow
DG Archiv 415 292-2 [A] **F**

Music of the Italian Renaissance Alberti, de Roré, etc.
Huelgas Ensemble, van Nevel
Sony CD 48065 [D] **F**

Music of the Portuguese Renaissance Morago, Melgas
Pro Antiqua Musica, Brown
Hyperion CDA 66715 [D] **F**

Nights Black Bird Consort Music by Byrd & Dowland
Fretwork, Wilson
Virgin VC7 59539-2 [D] **F**

V *La Procession – 80 Years of French Song* Chausson, etc.
Varcoe (bar), Johnson (pno)
Hyperion CDA 66248 [D] F

The Rose and the Ostrich Feather Browne, Cornyshe, etc.
The Sixteen, Christophers
Collins 13142 [D] F

The Sea Borodin, Debussy, Ireland, etc.
Walker (mez), Allen (bar), Vignoles (pno)
Hyperion CDA 66165 [D] F

Shakespeare's Kingdom Brahms, Schubert, Schumann, etc.
Walker (mez), Johnson (pno)
Hyperion CDA 66136 [D] F

Song Collection Borodin, Glinka, Mussorgsky, etc.
Vishnevskaya (sop), Rostropovich (pno)
Erato 2292-45643-2, 2CDs [D] F

Songs and Dances of Death Rimsky-Korsakov, Mussorgsky,
Rubinstein, etc.
Hvorstovsky (bar), Kirov O, Gergiev
Philips 438 872-2 [D] F

Songs by Finzi and his Friends Finzi, Gill, Milford, etc.
Partridge (ten), Roberts (bar), Benson (pno)
Hyperion CDA 66015 [A] F

Songs to Shakespeare Addisdon, Ireland, Tippett, etc.
Rolfe Johnson (ten), Johnson (pno)
Hyperion CDA 66480 [D] F

Sweet Power of Song Brahms, Chausson, Fauré, etc.
Lott (sop), Murray (mez), Johnson (pno)
EMI CDC7 49930-2 [D] F

War's Embers Butterworth, Finzi, Gurney, etc.
George (bs), Hill (ten), Varcoe (bar), Benson (pno)
Hyperion CDA 66261/2, 2CDs [D] F

50 Historical Recordings

For the purposes of this Guide we have labelled any recording in monaural sound (in the great majority of cases pre-1956) as 'historical'. Although a certain degree of tolerance is often called for in terms of the recorded quality, and a number of CD transfers of this material have proved less than entirely successful in the past, the artistic endeavour enshrined therein is often of a uniquely compelling quality. Listed below is a selection of fifty recommended 'historical' CDs, chosen not so much for the actual repertoire but for the outstanding quality of musicianship displayed by the artists involved. This is not intended as a 'league' table, nor have we been able to include a number of distinguished artists whom we both greatly admire; however, we feel that it provides an excellent starting point for any collector, and hope that it will encourage further exploration of this musical treasure trove. Opera recordings and recitals will be found in our companion guide, *Opera on CD*.

BACH, Johann Sebastian (1685–1750) GERMANY

> *Goldberg Variations*
> Gould (pno)
> Sony CD 52594 [A] **M**

> *The Well-Tempered Clavier* (complete)
> Fischer (pno)
> EMI CHS7 63188-2, 3 CDs [A] **M**

> *Landowska plays Bach*
> Landowska (hpd)
> Pearl GEMMCD 9489 [A] **M**

BARTÓK, Bela (1881–1945) HUNGARY/USA

> *Bartók Performs Bartók – *Contrasts, Mikrokosmos*
> Bartók (pno), *Goodman (cl), *Szigeti (vln)
> CBS/SC CD 47676 [A] **M**

BAX, Arnold (1883–1953) ENGLAND

> *Symphony No. 3*
> Halle O, Barbirolli
> (+ Ireland: *These Things Shall Be; Forgotten Rite; April*)
> EMI CDH7 63910-2 [A] **M**

BEETHOVEN, Ludwig van (1770–1827) GERMANY

> *Piano Concertos Nos. 1-5; Rondos, Op. 51*
> Kempff (pno), BPO, van Kempen
> DG 435 744-2, 3 CDs [A] **M**

> *Symphony No. 3 in E♭ (Eroica), Op. 55*
> Concertgebouw O, E. Kleiber
> Decca 433 406-2 [A] **M**

> *Symphonies: No. 5 in C min., Op. 67; No. 7 in A, Op. 92*
> BPO, Furtwängler
> DG 427 775-2 [A] **M**

> *String Quartets: No. 7 in F (Razumovsky), Op. 59/1; No. 13 in B♭, Op. 130*
> Busch Quartet
> CBS/Sony CD 47687 [A] **M**

> *The Complete Piano Sonatas*
> Schnabel (pno)
> EMI CHS7 63765-2, 8 CDs [A] **M**

BRAHMS, Johannes (1833–1897) GERMANY

Violin Concerto in D, Op. 77
Neveu (vln), Philharmonia O, Dobrowen
(+ Sibelius: *Violin Concerto*)
EMI CDH7 61011-2 [A] **M**

Wilhelm Backhaus Plays Brahms – Ballades, Rhapsodies, Scherzo, etc.
Backhaus (pno)
Pearl GEMMCD 9385 [A] **M**

CHOPIN, Frédéric (1810–1849) POLAND

Cortot plays Chopin
Cortot (pno)
Biddulph LHW 001 [A] **M**

Artur Rubinstein plays Chopin, Volume 2
Rubinstein (pno)
EMI CHS7 64697-2, 2 CDs [A] **M**

DEBUSSY, Claude (1862–1918) FRANCE

Préludes (complete)
Gieseking (pno)
EMI CDH7 61004-2 [A] **M**

DELIUS, Frederick (1862–1934) ENGLAND

*Brigg Fair; In a Summer Garden; On Hearing the First Cuckoo in Spring; Summer Night on the River; *Sea Drift; Koanga: La Calinda*
*Brownlee (bar), RPO, Beecham
Sir Thomas Beecham Trust BEECHAM 3 [A] **M**

ELGAR, Edward (1857–1934) ENGLAND

*Violin Concerto in B min., Op. 61; *Cello Concerto in E min., Op. 85*
Menuhin (vln), LSO, Elgar; *Harrison (vcl), New SO, Elgar
EMI CDH7 69786-2 [A] **M**

Symphonies Nos. 1 & 2; Falstaff; Dream of Gerontius (excerpts); *Music Makers* (excerpts); *Civic Fanfare; National Anthem* (arr.)
LSO, Royal Albert Hall O, Elgar
CDS7 54560-2, 3 CDs [A] **M**

IRELAND, John (1879–1962) ENGLAND

These Things Shall Be; Forgotten Rite; April
Jones (ten), Halle Ch & O, Barbirolli
(+ Bax: *Symphony No. 3*)
EMI CDH7 63910-2 [A] **M**

KORNGOLD, Erich (1897–1957) AUSTRIA-HUNGARY/USA

Violin Concerto
Heifetz (vln), LAPO, Wallenstein
(+ Rozsa: *Violin Concerto;* Waxman: *Carmen Fantasy*)
RCA GD 87963 [A] **M**

KREISLER, Fritz (1875–1962) AUSTRIA

Kreisler plays Kreisler
Kreisler (vln), Various accompaniments
EMI CDH7 64701-2 [A] **M**

MAHLER, Gustav (1860–1911) AUSTRIA

Das Lied von der Erde
Ferrier (cont), Patzak (ten), VPO, Walter
Decca 414 194-2 [A] **F**

MOZART, Wolfgang Amadeus (1756–1791) AUSTRIA

Horn Concertos Nos. 1–4
Brain (hn), Philharmonia O, Karajan
EMI CDH7 61013-2 [A] **M**

MUSSORGSKY, Modest (1839–1881) RUSSIA

Complete Songs
Christoff (bs), Labinsky (pno), FRNO, Tzipine
EMI CHS7 63025-2, 3 CDs [A] **M**

PAGANINI, Nicolo (1782–1840) ITALY

24 Caprices, Op. 1
Rabin (vln)
EMI CDM7 64560-2 [A] **M**

RESPIGHI, Ottorino (1879–1936) ITALY

Fountains of Rome; Pines of Rome; Roman Festivals
NBC SO, Toscanini
RCA GD 60262 [A] **M**

SCHUMANN, Robert (1810–1856) GERMANY

Dichterliebe, Op. 48; Frauenliebe und Leben, Op. 42
Lehmann (sop), Walter (pno)
CBS/Sony CD 44840 [A] **M**

SIBELIUS, Jean (1865–1957) FINLAND

Violin Concerto in D min., Op. 47
Neveu (vln), Philharmonia O, Susskind
(+ Brahms: *Violin Concerto*)
EMI CDH7 61011-2 [A] **M**

TCHAIKOVSKY, Pyotr (1843–1893) RUSSIA

Piano Concerto No. 1 in B♭ min., Op. 23
Horowitz (pno), NBC SO, Toscanini
(+ Beethoven: *Piano Concerto No. 5*)
RCA GD 87992 [A] **M**

COLLECTIONS

The Young Claudio Arrau Liszt, Schumann, Debussy, Chopin
Arrau (pno)
Pearl GEMMCD 9928 [A] **M**

Simon Barere At Carnegie Hall, Volume 2 Balakirev, Bach,
Schumann, etc.
Barere (pno)
APR CDAPR 7008, 2 CDs [A] **M**

Caruso in Song Di Capua, Rossini, Pergolesi, etc.
Caruoso (ten), Various accompaniments
Nimbus NI 7809 [A] **M**

Cziffra – The Hungaraton Recordings 1954–56 Liszt, Schumann,
Grieg, etc.
Cziffra (pno), Various Os and conductors
APR CDAPR 7021, 2 CDs [A] **M**

Mischa Elman – Solo Recordings 1921–24 Brahms, Schubert, Lalo, etc.
Elman (vln), various accompaniments
Biddulph LAB 038 [A] **M**

Feuermann – The Columbia Recordings – Volume 1 Haydn, Chopin, Schubert, etc.
Feuermann (vcl), various accompaniments
Pearl GEMMCD 9442 [A] **M**

Godowsky – UK Columbia Recordings 1928–30 Beethoven, Schumann, Grieg, Chopin
Godowsky (pno)
APR CDAPR 7010, 2 CDs [A] **M**

Josef Hassid and Ginette Neveu – Selected Recordings Kreisler, Dvořák, Sarasate, etc.
Hassid (vln), Neveu (vln), various accompaniments
Testament SBT 1010 [A] **M**

Klemperer in Amsterdam Schoenberg, Mendelssohn, Mozart, etc.
Concertgebouw O, Klemperer
Memories HR 4248/9, 2 CDs [A] **M**

Dinu Lipatti – Piano Recital Bach, Scarlatti, Mozart, etc.
Lipatti (pno)
EMI CDH7 69800-2 [A] **M**

A. B. Michelangeli – Early Recordings Bach, Scarlatti, Grieg, etc.
Michelangeli (pno)
EMI CDH 64490-2 [A] **M**

Nathan Milstein – American Columbia Recordings Tchaikovsky, Beethoven, etc.
Milstein (vln), Chicago SO, Stock; Balsam (pno)
Biddulph LAB 063 [A] **M**

Benno Moseiwitsch – Solo Piano Recordings 1938–50 Liszt, Mussorgsky, Debussy, etc.
Moseiwitsch (pno)
APR CDAPR 7005, 2 CDs [A] **M**

The Art of Gregor Piatigorsky Brahms, Shostakovich, Weber, etc.
Piatigorsky (vcl), Stewart (pno), Newton (pno)
Music & Arts MACD-644 [A] **M**

Sergei Rachmaninov – The Complete RCA Recordings
Rachmaninov, Chopin, Mendelssohn, etc.
Rachmaninov (pno/cond), Kreisler (vln) Philadelphia O, Ormandy, Stokowski
RCA 09026 61265-2, 10 CDs [A] **M**

The Art of Segovia – The HMV Recordings 1927–1939 Bach, Albéniz, Ponce, etc.
Segovia (gtr)
EMI CHS7 61047-2, 2 CDs [A] **M**

A Stokowski Fantasia Mussorgsky, Tchaikovsky, Dukas, etc.
Philadelphia O, Stokowski
Pearl GEMMCD 9488 [A] **M**

The Art of Joseph Szigeti, Volume I Bach, Paganini, Dvořák, etc.
Szigeti (vln), Ruhrseits (pno)
Biddulph LAB 005/6, 2 CDs [A] **M**

Index of Selected Works